D1527701

BISHOP'S UNIVERSITY
LIBRARY
LENNOXVILLE

Land, Man, and the Law

LAND, MAN, AND THE LAW

The Disposal of Crown Lands in British Columbia, 1871-1913

Robert E. Cail

University of British Columbia Press
Vancouver

LAND, MAN, AND THE LAW

THE DISPOSAL OF CROWN LANDS IN BRITISH COLUMBIA, 1871-1913

© The University of British Columbia 1974
All Rights Reserved

This book has been published with the help of a grant from the Humanities Research Council of Canada using funds provided by the Canada Council and a grant from the Real Estate Council of British Columbia.

Cataloguing in Publication Data

Cail, Robert Edgar, 1920-58
Land, man, and the law

Originally presented as the author's thesis (M.A.), University of British Columbia, under title: Disposal of crown lands in British Columbia, 1871-1913.

1. Crown lands-British Columbia. 2. British Columbia-History. I. Title.

(Moys : KN 82.C334) 346.046'711

International Standard Book 0-7748-0029-1
Library of Congress Catalog Number 74-77497

Printed in Canada

CONTENTS

LIST OF ILLUSTRATIONS AND MAPS

ILLUSTRATIONS

MAPS

PHOTOGRAPHIC CREDITS

Photographs appear through the courtesy of the Vancouver City Archives, the Provincial Archives of British Columbia, the Victoria City Archives, the New Westminster Public Library Photography Collection, the Vernon Museum and Archives, and Mrs. Louis Marchand.

FOREWORD

Of the four western provinces, only British Columbia entered Confederation having control of its public lands. This patrimony had been managed by Sir James Douglas in such a manner as to encourage an orderly settlement process and curb speculation in lands, forests, and mines. Douglas's successors, however, lacked his vision and his practicality and, yielding to the pressures of the moment, often squandered the province's valuable natural resources.

In this study, the late Robert Cail examines the essence of the policies which Douglas forged at the height of the gold rush and recounts the compromises made by those political successors who yielded to the insistent demands of their contemporaries for the opportunity to exploit the province's natural wealth. The vastness of the area contained within provincial boundaries encouraged their feeling that the province's resources were inexhaustible. In the course of time, however, it became apparent that the amount of arable land is severely limited and that other natural resources are widely dispersed over a mountainous terrain.

The myopic vision of early legislators led to a bitter dispute with the Dominion of Canada over the location and boundaries of the railway lands. More tragically, it strained the harmonious relations with the native peoples, a relationship which Douglas had fostered.

Robert Cail was a graduate student in History at the University of British Columbia when he completed this study in 1955. The subject remains highly relevant to discussions of public policy which are taking place today. After taking his M.A. degree, the author proceeded to the University of Minnesota to continue his graduate work. He was engaged in writing his Ph.D. dissertation when he died on July 18, 1958 in an automobile collision. Had Robert Cail lived he would have returned to his native province, and undoubtedly his work would have further enriched our historical literature.

MARGARET A. ORMSBY

INTRODUCTION

Throughout the last century the most complex and comprehensive legislation in British Columbia was that concerned with public lands. There was no precedent readily available to the colony prior to entering Confederation, and Governor James Douglas, upon whose shoulders rested the responsibility for devising land policy, had to formulate that policy before the example of the American Homestead Act of 1862 was available for guidance. Instructions from the Colonial Office and his own common sense were his only guides. Even had the American example been at hand, it is unlikely that Douglas would have considered granting 160 acres free to bona fide settlers.[1] Nor was any advice forthcoming from Canada. There had been practically no interchange of ideas between Canada and the two Pacific colonies, and not until after the union of the two colonies of Vancouver Island and British Columbia in 1866 was there any appreciable Canadian element on the West Coast. Hudson's Bay Company employees had never greatly concerned themselves with the formulation of a land policy providing for the organized settlement of the country, and on his appointment as governor of "Vancouver's Island" in 1851, James Douglas had to work out his own procedures. In doing so he devised a policy that was a surprisingly good one.

Creating a policy for the disposal of public lands in British Columbia where ownership had to be reconciled with water, timber, and grazing rights, with mining claims, and the urgent need for agricultural development, was both complicated and difficult. Until after British Columbia entered Confederation, it was gold, not land, that brought men to the Pacific colony (but of those who came,

[1] Section 1 of the American Homestead Act, 1862, provided for the preemption of a quarter-section, or less, of unappropriated public lands provided that "any person owning and residing on land may, under the provisions of this act, enter other lands lying contiguous to his or her said land, which shall not, with the land so already owned and occupied, exceed in the aggregate one hundred and sixty acres." United States, *Statutes at Large*, vol. 12, p. 392.

many remained to settle). It is significant that Douglas's chief concern from 1858, when he severed his connection with the Hudson's Bay Company, until 1864, when he retired from public life, was to draw up regulations governing miners' rights and claims. Second to this was his concern with the disposal of land for settlement. Because placer mining could locate only the surface gold, hydraulic developments soon appeared, and for these, water was necessary. Very early then, land legislation had to recognize the miners' water requirements, and, in so doing, had to abandon the English common law relating to riparian rights in water.[2] The fact that much of British Columbia was heavily timbered also influenced land legislation. Although the economic significance of timber was not recognized until after 1900, legal provision for the disposal of timbered lands had to be made much earlier. After the union with Canada in 1871, both American and Canadian land legislation were taken into account — often with the inevitable confusion arising from the application of half-understood principles — but, on the whole, the land acts of British Columbia were in answer to the province's specific and peculiar needs.

Complications in administering the land laws, as in framing them, were many. The first difficulty was a result of the vastness of the colony. However well-devised the law, it was worse than useless if it could not be administered with some degree of efficiency and uniformity. The miners returning from the Cariboo gold fields after 1860 were not greatly concerned with niceties of phraseology in a land act which they had never read and for which there was no administrative agency close at hand. Communication was slow and difficult; small wonder that unauthorized homesteads were

[2] The civil and criminal laws of England, as the same existed on November 19, 1858, were declared to have force of law in British Columbia on that date. "Proclamation . . . to declare that English law is in force in British Columbia," in British Columbia, [*Proclamations and Ordinances, 1858-1864* (Victoria, New Westminster, 1858-64)].

This proclamation was repealed in 1867, but at the same time it was confirmed that the laws of England, as of November 19, 1858, were applicable in British Columbia so far as they were not "from local circumstances inapplicable" and as "modified and altered by all past Legislation" of the two colonies before union. British Columbia, *The Laws . . . Consisting of the Acts, Ordinances & Proclamations of the Formerly Separated Colonies, Vancouver Island and British Columbia, and of the United Colony of British Columbia*, by authority compiled and published under the "Revised Statutes Act, 1871" (Victoria: Printed at the Government Printing Office, 1871), p. 214, 1867, 30 Vict., no. 70, s. 2.

taken up throughout the Fraser Valley and on Vancouver Island.[3] Such homesteads had to be legalized later in revisions and amendments.

It was also difficult to ensure that lands were taken by genuine settlers and not by speculators. For fifty years the official documents, correspondence, and reports dealing with land were filled with innumerable references to the existence of speculators, or to the fear of their existence. Starting with Douglas and continuing to the present, the land acts have tried to make it impossible for land to be taken except for beneficial purposes. For many years, provided that the land was to be used in all good faith, unlimited quantities might be had for practically nothing. For this reason, every act stipulated that occupation must begin within a specified period and certain improvements be made by a definite date after the pre-emption was recorded. Failure to comply resulted in forfeiture.

Because no effective administrative machinery was provided until after 1900, earlier regulatory clauses were often disregarded. Governor Douglas made every effort to see that his proclamations were rigidly enforced, but hampered as he was by a meagre and uncertain revenue, he could do little.[4] Even when money became available after 1871, only desultory attempts were made to enforce the regulations. For thirty years the prevalent attitude was to be that land was plentiful but most of it useless, and should anyone have enough initiative to pay a nominal price, no hindrance ought to be placed in his way.

Indians did not qualify as settlers, nor, for the first few years, were they considered to be speculators. So long as Douglas remained governor, little difficulty arose over Indian lands. Douglas left the tribes entirely unmolested on any lands already settled or used by them, and he had begun to buy out their beneficial interest in all

[3] Pioneers intending to raise foodstuffs to feed the miners took up isolated, unauthorized homesteads wherever they considered the conditions suitable. This led to the Crown granting isolated blocks of land of which the geographic position was not definitely known. British Columbia, Department of Lands, "Surveyor-General's Report [1911]," British Columbia, Legislative Assembly, *Sessional Papers*, 12th Parl., 3d sess., 1912, p. G9.

[4] As early as November 14, 1861, Douglas was borrowing money to finance road construction and maintenance. "Proclamation, no. 13, A.D. 1861," in B.C., [*Proclamations and Ordinances, 1858-1864*]. After 1861, such loans became annual events.

lands on Vancouver Island. After Douglas retired in 1864, however, Indian reserves became an increasingly troublesome issue in British Columbia and, along with the complications stemming from the existence of the Railway Belt within the province, gave rise to the strained relations between Victoria and Ottawa that culminated in the Secession Resolution of 1878.[5]

The most troublesome of administrative problems, however, arose as a result of the Terms of Union under which the colony entered Confederation in 1871. Article 11 specified that in return for railway connection with Canada, British Columbia should convey to the Dominion a strip of land forty miles wide along the line of rail wherever it was to be located. Five years were spent in surveying and locating the route which, as then planned, was to come through the Rockies by the Yellowhead Pass, through the gap in the Cascades provided by the Thompson River Valley, and through the Coast Range by means of the lower Fraser Valley. Then as now, this route was through the most heavily settled portion of the province. The transfer to the Dominion of a forty-mile strip of land through this heartland created a dual administration in British Columbia: one set of regulations administered by the Dominion for what came to be known as the Railway Belt, and another, administered by the province, for the rest of British Columbia. The resulting complications required sixty years to disentangle.[6] In the process, British Columbia came close to withdrawing from Confederation; and the dominion government was badgered almost beyond endurance. The wonder is not that British Columbia did not withdraw from Confederation, but rather that Canada did not

5 On August 30, 1878, the Secession Resolution proposed by Premier George A. Walkem passed the assembly by a vote of fourteen to nine. The motion said, in part, "that British Columbia shall thereafter have the right to exclusively collect and retain her Customs and Excise duties and to withdraw from the Union." In the confusion attendant upon the general election in Canada that September, the resolution was "mislaid" in Ottawa and did not reach London until January 24, 1879. In the meantime, a much more conciliatory attitude had replaced the former hostility and the resolution was forgotten both by the Walkem ministry and the newly elected John A. Macdonald government in Ottawa. British Columbia, Legislative Assembly, *Journals*, 3d Parl., 1st sess., 1878, pp. 110, 107; Frederic W. Howay, "Political History, 1871-1913," in *Canada and Its Provinces*, Adam Shortt and Arthur Doughty, general eds., 23 vols. (Toronto: Brook, 1914-17), 21:202-204.

6 For the genesis and first fifteen years of this problem, see Margaret A. Ormsby, "The Relations between British Columbia and the Dominion of Canada, 1871-1885" (Ph.D. diss., Bryn Mawr, 1937).

try to rid herself of what became the most involved and unpleasant problem in domestic politics for fifty years.

But all this was to come in the future. To follow the story of the disposal of public lands in British Columbia from 1871 to 1913, it is essential to return to colonial days. Governor Douglas's regulations formed a firm basis for the new province's land legislation framed subsequently to 1871.

CHAPTER 1

Colonial Land Settlement Policy

With the revocation of the Hudson's Bay Company licence of exclusive trade west of the Rocky Mountains in 1858, Douglas, as governor of both Vancouver Island and British Columbia, faced the problem of framing legislation for the disposal of public lands. There was no thought then of railroads and conflicting jurisdictions, nor was there any intimation of the value crown lands were later to acquire. It is all the more remarkable, therefore, that Douglas's proclamations covered every major contingency that has yet arisen in the land policy of the province. Close study of Douglas's ordinances and a comparison of them with later land acts lead to the conclusion that had Douglas continued the role of leadership in British Columbia until after union with Canada, few of the land problems which did plague the province for so many years would have arisen.

Douglas would no doubt have been a leader in any society, or at any period; not necessarily popular, but certainly respected, and deferred to, for his qualities of mind. His capacity for clear and concise thinking is constantly evident in his despatches to the Colonial Office asking for instructions on land policy, or giving analytical and informed reasons for actions he had already taken. The problem Douglas faced was the need to provide for the systematic alienation of public land in an uncharted wilderness of unknown area and unsuspected resources, inhabited by many thousands of Indians and a few thousand transient miners. Douglas had to devise a land system for not only most unaccommodating, but also widely scattered, areas of arable land. He had three sources upon which he could draw; the provisions under which the

Hudson's Bay Company had allotted lands, the Colonial Office, and his own experience.

Under the grant made by the Royal Proclamation of January 13, 1849, the Hudson's Bay Company had been given absolute lordship over, and proprietorship of, Vancouver Island, its land and its minerals, in perpetuum, subject only to the domination of the British Crown, an annual rent of seven shillings, and agreement to settle a colony of British subjects on the island within five years. It was solely to gain this last condition that the home government had acceded to the Company's request when it was before Parliament in 1849. The stipulation to which Douglas had first to direct his attention required the Company to dispose of land at reasonable prices for purposes of colonization, retaining as a service charge 10 per cent of all money received from the sale of land and coal, or other minerals. The remaining 90 per cent was to be applied to public improvements and, in particular, to building roads. The Company was empowered to reserve such lands as were necessary for improvements, but every two years an accounting was to be made to the Colonial Office of these reservations, the number of colonists settled on the island, and of the lands sold. The Crown reserved the right to recall the grant at the end of five years should the Company fail to effect colonization, and to repossess after ten years on reimbursing the Company for all expenses, civil or military, incurred in its administration of the island. Repossession was effected in 1858.

The articles of the proclamation that must have interested Douglas particularly were those specifying price, size of holdings, provisions for surveying, and rights reserved to the Company. No grant was to contain less than twenty acres; the price was to be fixed at one pound per acre; after payment the land was to be held in "free and common socage"; the island was to be divided into districts of from five to ten square miles; and all minerals, wherever found, were to belong to the Company and might be mined upon payment of adequate compensation for any surface damage.[1]

So long as the colony was held *imperium in imperio*, Douglas had no quarrel with the terms under which the land had been granted to the Company, although he recognized that these terms

[1] The complete text of the grant may be found in British Columbia, Provincial Archives Department, "Report . . . 1913," B.C., *Sessional Papers*, 13th Parl., 2d sess., 1914, p. V73-74.

were inimical to colonization. Notwithstanding the high price of one pound per acre, he himself purchased land, but he stated that other Company men were "scared at the high price charged."[2] He knew that Vancouver Island from 1849 to 1858 would have been a favourable field for settlement under other auspices, and that the Company had had sufficient capital to successfully carry out any scheme of colonization had it been so inclined. The Company had been familiar with the country and its resources; its officials had understood the natives thoroughly and could have conducted trade and developed the country in a way not possible to individual effort. But Douglas also knew that what had happened had been just the reverse. Bancroft, an historian of the Pacific Northwest never too charitable toward the Hudson's Bay Company, remarked that:

> Not alone must the pound per acre for wild, and thus far worthless, land, stolen from the savages, be paid the imperial government, but to the representative of the government as the representative of a crushing monopoly must the settler go for every necessity, every article of comfort or form of requirement, paying therefor often two or three hundred per cent on London cost; to this same hydra-head he must carry his produce, and receive for it whatever the company might please to pay. Who among nineteenth-century Englishmen would leave his happy English home with all its hallowed memories, and take up his residence in this far-away north-west wilderness only to breathe so stifling an atmosphere as this? Nobody.[3]

An American himself, Bancroft overlooked the fact that had it not been for the presence of this "hydra-head" the territory might well have fallen into American hands by default, but it was true that settlers were conspicuously absent. In 1849 there were no more than twenty and these had been obliged to retire at least ten miles from Victoria, since the Company had reserved for its own use a ten-mile radius around the fort — an area which contained the

[2] Douglas to A. C. Anderson, March 18, 1850, in Frederic W. Howay, "The Raison d'Etre of Forts Yale and Hope," *Proceedings and Transactions of the Royal Society of Canada*, 3d ser., 16 (1922), sec. 2, p. 63.

[3] Hubert Howe Bancroft, *History of British Columbia, 1792-1887*, Works of Hubert Howe Bancroft, vol. 32 (San Francisco: History Company, 1887), p. 311. For reasons why the grant should not have been made to the Company if colonization were the primary aim, *see* R. E. Gosnell, "Colonial History, 1849-1871," in *Canada and Its Provinces*, Shortt and Doughty, eds., 21:83-84.

best and most easily cleared farm land.[4] Douglas was aware of the frustrations experienced by the settlers because the lands at the periphery of the company's reserve were heavily timbered and devoid of adequate communication with the fort. By the end of 1853, applications had been made for about twenty thousand acres and approximately nine thousand pounds had been paid. Between July 12, 1855 and October 10, 1856, public lands amounting to 2,137 acres were sold to settlers at one pound per acre.

Douglas, then, could find little help in the terms under which the Company he had served for thirty-seven years had held the land. All that had really been accomplished between 1849 and 1859 was to demonstrate that under more favourable conditions the country might have had possibilities for greater settlement. Even before his investiture as governor of the mainland colony on November 19, 1858, Douglas had transmitted his views on a land policy to the Colonial Office. To this body he now turned for guidance. He very well knew that he was without any legal authority to make regulations designed to protect British interests on the mainland, but as the only official in the region, he felt constrained to do all in his power to reduce to some order the chaotic conditions resulting from the influx of the hordes of miners and adventurers going up "Fraser's River" to the gold fields.[5] Because he felt that "the country will be filled with lawless crowds, the public lands unlawfully occupied by squatters of every description, and the authority of the Government will ultimately be set at naught," he recommended that as "a measure of obvious necessity" the whole country should immediately be thrown open for settlement, and that "the land be surveyed, and sold at a fixed rate, not to exceed twenty shillings an acre."[6] From these measures

4 The Company did release some of its reserved land to encourage its retired servants to become settlers, but this was a special concession and was confined to its employees. Bancroft, *History of British Columbia*, p. 313.

5 On November 19, 1858, the day that he was invested as governor of the mainland colony of British Columbia, Douglas's previous administrative acts were announced "to have been valid in Law." "Proclamation . . . to indemnify the Governor . . . for Acts done before the Establishment of any Legitimate Authority in British Columbia," in B.C., [*Proclamations and Ordinances, 1858-1864*].

6 Douglas to Edward Henry Stanley, 15th earl of Derby, secretary of state for the colonies, June 10, 1858, no. 2, Great Britain, Colonial Office, *Papers Relative to the Affairs of British Columbia*, presented to both Houses of Parliament by command of Her Majesty, 1859-1862, 4 pts. (London: Printed by George Edward Eyre and William Spottiswoode . . . for Her Majesty's Stationery Office, 1859-62), 1:14.

he hoped both to secure order and to acquire a large revenue for the service of the government.

Before this despatch of June 10 had reached the Colonial Office, Sir Edward Bulwer Lytton, colonial secretary, had written cautioning Douglas to make the colony self-supporting as soon as possible and suggesting that this could be done by the disposal of public lands, especially of town lots, "for which I am led to believe there will be a great demand." Lytton wrote that "many of our early Colonial Settlements" possessed lands which had "afforded" them "safe though not very immediate sources of prosperity," but he believed British Columbia possessed "in a remarkable degree, the advantage of fertile lands, fine timber, adjacent harbours, rivers, together with rich mineral products." These would "furnish the Government with the means of raising a Revenue which will at once defray the necessary expenses of an establishment."[7]

When Lytton received Douglas's despatch of June 10, he again warned him that he must manage the colony without any financial assistance from the home government. He spoke of the colony's "immense resources" which gave him confidence that the mother country would be freed "from those expenses which are adverse to the policy of all healthful colonization."[8]

In a second despatch of August 14, 1858, Lytton laid down five principles regarding public lands which, had they been followed, would have prevented much speculation and the consequent retardation of settlement and dissatisfaction of the settlers. But a lack of a sufficient revenue from those "immense resources" rendered his and Douglas's efforts fruitless.

In his despatch, Lytton authorized Douglas to sell land solely for agricultural purposes whenever the demand for it arose. It was to be many years before the wisdom of this principle was appreciated in British Columbia. Secondly, he advised that the land be sold at an upset price determined by Douglas after taking into consideration the price charged in neighbouring American territories. An upset price of at least one pound per acre was considered by Lytton to be necessary if the government were to profit from sales and "mere land jobbing . . . be in some degree checked." With regard to land for "town purposes (to which speculation is almost certain to direct itself in the first instance), I cannot caution

[7] Lytton to Douglas, July 31, 1858, no. 6, ibid., p. 45.

[8] Lytton to Douglas, August 14, 1858, no. 8, ibid., p. 48.

you too strongly against allowing it to be disposed of at too low a sum."

Thirdly, Douglas was directed to open lands for settlement gradually, to sell only what was surveyed or ready for immediate survey, and to prevent, "as far as in you lies," squatting on unsold land. Next, he was to keep a separate account of all revenue from land sales. These revenues were to be used for the time being for the dual purposes of survey and communication, the first charges on all land revenue.

Finally, recognizing the presence in the colony of a great many aliens, Lytton directed that while foreigners as such were not entitled to grants of waste crown lands, "it is the strong desire of Her Majesty's Government to attract to this territory all peaceful settlers, without regard to nation. For this reason, naturalization should first be granted to all who asked for it, and then the right to acquire public land be accorded."[9] This precedent established by Lytton and incorporated by Douglas into the land ordinances, has been followed ever since.

These were most statesmanlike proposals and Douglas did his utmost to follow them. Immediately upon receipt of the despatch, Douglas sent Surveyor General Joseph D. Pemberton to lay out townsites at Fort Langley, Fort Hope, and Fort Yale. On October 11, 1858, he was able to tell Lytton that a public sale of lots at Fort Langley would be held in the near future, such lots to be 64 by 120 feet and to be sold at an upset price of "100 dollars." (There is no explanation as to why Douglas quoted the price in dollars other than that the Americans in Victoria dealt in dollars. British Columbia used the British system of pounds, shillings, and pence until 1866.) Douglas permitted himself to hope that the disposal of these lots and the sale of public lands would, besides opening the country for settlement, "prove a prolific source of revenue." He took the opportunity to remind the Colonial Office that he had been called upon to act without legal authority while at Yale and Hope, although he had doubtless at the time hoped that such actions would be subsequently legalized. He said that the

[9] Lytton to Douglas, August 14, 1858, no. 9, ibid., p. 50. Naturalization was granted by Proclamation, May 14, 1859. B.C., *Revised Statutes, Appendix . . . 1871, Containing Certain Repealed Colonial Laws Useful for Reference, Imperial Statutes Affecting British Columbia, Proclamations, Etc.* (Victoria, B.C.: Printed by Richard Wolfenden . . . at the Government Printing Office, n.d.), pp. 57-59, 1859, 22 Vict., no. 14.

most urgent appeals had been made to him by potential settlers for the purchase of town lots and that, because of the approaching winter, he had granted continuation of monthly leases with preemption rights until the lands could be legally sold.[10] He had evidently taken Lytton's advice to charge a high enough price for his losses. He granted them at forty-one shillings a month. At that rental, speculators would have been taking a dangerous chance.

Following the first public auction of lands held in British Columbia on November 25, 1858, Douglas could report that the result had been "highly satisfactory." It showed public confidence in the resources of the colony and, more important, provided a needed supply of money for defraying current heavy expenses. From the sale of a portion of the 3,294 lots at Fort Langley which had been carved from 900 surveyed acres at the townsite, over £13,000 had been realized. Although the upset price had been £20.16.8 sterling, or $100, the keen competition from the large gathering had resulted in prices going as high as $725. Ten per cent of the price had to be paid down, while the remainder was to be paid within one month. Failing this, the lots were to be forfeit and resold.[11]

Two precedents were set here which were to affect land policy after 1871; the first was sale by public auction and the second, deferred payment. These became the subject of Lytton's next despatch. Referring to sale by public auction as opposed to a fixed price, Lytton found two advantages; namely, it formed the best available precaution against disposing of lands at an inadequate price, and secondly, it prevented "both the occurrence and even the suspicion or imputation of any favouritism or irregularity in the disposal of the public property." Lytton need not have concerned himself on that score; throughout all the correspondence and official records there is not the slightest evidence that Douglas ever displayed any favouritism towards the Hudson's Bay Company although there are numerous references to the opportunities that he had to do so. The only objections Lytton could find to the sale

[10] Douglas to Lytton, October 11, 1858, no. 14, Gt. Brit., *Papers Relative to British Columbia,* 1:38. After receiving authorization for his actions, Douglas issued a proclamation on December 2, 1858, stating that henceforth the governor could "grant to any person or persons any Land belonging to the Crown" and that such grants were valid. B.C., *Revised Statutes, Appendix, 1871,* p. 53, 1858, 22 Vict., no. 11.

[11] Douglas to Lytton, November 29, 1858, no. 28, Gt. Brit., *Papers Relative to British Columbia,* 2:37; Joseph D. Pemberton, acting colonial surveyor, to Douglas, November 30, 1858, "Enclosure 1 in No. 28," ibid., p. 38.

by auction were that it might have served to "discourage enterprise by exposing the discoverer of eligible lands to be outbid at their sale," and that such a method might have caused some delay in effecting transfer of title. In summary, however, Lytton found the advantages outweighed the drawbacks by far, particularly as auctions afforded "the inestimable advantage of perfect confidence in the purity of the land administration." Any objections to auctioning lands could be met by adopting the system common to other colonies and permitting an applicant to purchase country lands at the upset price once the land had been unsuccessfully offered for sale. Thus, there would always be an adequate "common land ready for appropriation by any settler ... unwilling to wait for a periodical auction."[12]

Had such a policy been followed after 1871, thousands of acres bought for speculative purposes at the very low prices established by statute, might have been retained by the government for purposes of bona fide settlement. Like many governments which came after, Douglas's administration suffered from chronic poverty, and not even he could refrain from letting large acreages go at nominal prices in order to secure revenue. Having assumed the responsibility for administering the country from the proceeds of its own resources, and having been refused financial aid from England to supplement the very meagre colonial revenue, Douglas had no alternative but to abandon the auction system before it was well started. To supply the pressing needs of government, land — the readiest asset upon which to draw — was sold on terms that were the most likely to prove attractive to investors. Had the home government seen fit to lend its credit to the colony, the land might have been more wisely conserved, and settlement more systematically directed, to ensure compact and gradual expansion. In this way, provision might have been made for improvements that would have been a boon to the settler and a manageable burden to the government. Although Lytton had a remarkably clear grasp of the numerous problems involved in developing and settling a new colony, he seems to have been unduly influenced by reports reaching him of British Columbia's wealth, overlooking the fact that very little of that wealth had found its way into the colonial government's treasury.

In the matter of payments, Lytton also gave sound advice, but again he did not recognize the exigencies of colonial life in British

12 Lytton to Douglas, February 7, 1859, no. 9, ibid., p. 78.

Columbia. He wrote that for three reasons he had "not a doubt ... that prompt payment is the proper rule." It would serve as the best indication of a purchaser's having adequate means to cultivate his land; it would avoid harassing the government with the existence of a whole population of small debtors from whom it would be next to impossible to collect; and, finally, it would maintain "a sounder state of society by not encouraging the premature conversion into petty and impoverished landowners of those who ought to be labourers."

When he read that two partial payments had been permitted at the auction of the Fort Langley lots, and saw Douglas's Land Proclamation of February 14, 1859, Lytton again drew Douglas's attention to the difficulties which might arise:

> Under the present rules, if payment of the second moiety should be resisted, it would be extremely difficult to eject persons who by the very conditions of the case would have been in occupation of their lands for a period of two years. And again, if some of the landowners do pay their obligation, whilst others do not, a grievance arises out of the distinction.

For these reasons, Douglas was asked to give further consideration to the matter of prompt payments.[13]

On February 19, 1859, Douglas had forwarded to Lytton a copy of this first proclamation concerning public lands. The preamble, issued five days before, stated that "it is expedient to publish for general information, the method to be pursued with respect to the alienation and possession of agricultural lands, and of lands proposed for the sites of towns in British Columbia." The first nine of the provisions were as follows:

1. All the lands of British Columbia, and all the mines and minerals therein, belong to the Crown in fee.
2. The price of lands, not being intended for the sites of towns, and not reputed to be mineral lands, shall be ten shillings per acre, payable one-half in cash at the time of sale, and the other half at the end of two years from such sale. Provided, that under special circumstances, some other price, or some other terms of payment, may from time to time be specially announced for particular localities.
3. It shall be competent to the Executive, at any time, to reserve such portions of the unoccupied Crown Lands, and for such purposes as the Executive shall deem advisable.

[13] Lytton to Douglas, May 7, 1859, no. 24, ibid., p. 86.

4. Except as aforesaid, all the lands in British Columbia will be exposed in lots for sale, by public competition, at the upset price above mentioned, as soon as the same shall have been surveyed and made ready for sale. Due notice will be given of all such sales. Notice, at the same time, will be given of the upset price and terms of payment when they vary from those above stated, and also of the rights reserved (if any) for public convenience.
5. All lands which shall remain unsold at any such auction may be sold by private contract, at the upset price, and on the terms and conditions herein mentioned, on application to the Chief Commissioner of Lands and Works.
6. Unless otherwise specially notified at the time of sale, all such sales of Crown Land shall be subject to such public rights of way as may at any time after such sale, and to such private rights of way, and of leading or using water for animals, and for mining and engineering purposes, as may at the time of such sale be specified by the Chief Commissioner of Lands and Works.
7. Unless otherwise specially announced at the time of sale, the conveyance of the land shall include all trees and all mines and minerals within and under the same, except mines of gold and silver.
8. When any "Ditch Privilege" shall be granted, there shall be included (unless excluded by express words) the right to lop, dress, or fell any trees standing on unoccupied Crown Lands which, in the opinion of the proprietors of the ditch, might by their accidental fall, or otherwise, endanger the safety of the ditch or any part thereof.
9. Until further notice, gold claims and mines shall continue to be worked subject to the existing regulations.

No words were wasted in the proclamation; the principles were clearly defined. The constitutional right of the Crown to all lands and all mines and minerals was stated; lands were to be divided into town, general country, and special settlement, and offered for sale by public auction subject to a previously announced upset price. In his covering despatch, Douglas drew Lytton's attention to the fact that all known mineral lands, as well as those reputed to contain minerals, would be reserved. He expressed his intention of also reserving large tracts for roads, churches, schools, and other public purposes, as well as for towns and villages, but not to the point of retarding the progress, improvement, or settlement of the colony. He said that, as a general rule, no land was to be offered for sale without first having been surveyed and mapped under government authority. To calm any fears the Colonial Office may have had about the low upset price established in the proclamation, Douglas said that there were many reasons for departing from Lytton's advice. The first reason (expressed in an oblique manner) was Douglas's distrust of the many Americans within British territory.

> We think it a matter of the greatest importance to encourage emigration from England, in order to supply the want now so much felt of an English element in the population, a want which, in fact, lies at the root of all the difficulties which now so much embarrass all attempts at legislation for the country. We are, therefore, especially desirous of placing before the English public the attraction of cheap land.

He also feared that the establishment of a higher price for land would drive "the sturdy yeomen expected this year from Canada, Australia, and other British Colonies" across the frontier "in hundreds" to seek homes on American territory where it was the custom to grant free land. Finally, however, Douglas hoped that a low upset price would "guard the land operations of the Colony, as much as in the nature of things is practicable, from the designs of speculators who make purchases of land not for actual settlement but merely for profitable resale."

To amplify the "special circumstances" mentioned in his proclamation (item 2), Douglas explained his plan for a special settlement along the American border. There he proposed to create a military reserve on behalf of the Royal Engineers, "and if possible also otherwise to settle it with a population composed exclusively of English subjects."[14] Douglas had lived through the 1840's in Oregon, and he would have still remembered the spirit that had been abroad in a land where the president-elect had chanted with conviction: "Fifty-four forty or fight!"

The last two clauses of the proclamation dealt with laying out and selling lands in the colony's capital, New Westminster, the name bestowed on the city by the Queen. Three-quarters of the lots were to be sold at public auction, but the remaining quarter was to be reserved for purchasers in the United Kingdom and in the British colonies. So objectionable did Lytton find this reservation that no government in British Columbia was to have the

[14] "Proclamation, Enclosure in No. 51," ibid., p. 65; Douglas to Lytton, February 19, 1859, no. 51, ibid., pp. 64-65.

temerity to embark on a similar scheme until 1896. Lytton could hardly find words strong enough to condemn the measure. Besides being "decidedly objectionable," it could serve no purpose but to "stimulate the acquisition of property by non-residents." Pointing to this as one of the worst evils to which any new community could be subjected, he continued, "the lots [would be] bought by speculators who [would] hold them on a chance of a rise in value, with the effect in the meanwhile of obstructing the progress of the town, interrupting its communications, and creating a nuisance to the holders of adjoining lots." This objectionable measure was ordered to be rescinded at once.[15]

Douglas had no alternative in the face of this order but to abandon the plan, but he held out temporarily on other points. He accepted Lytton's advice of one general upset price and of all sales by auction, but he did not give in at once to the requirement of all-cash sales. He wished to make it easier for settlers with little capital — the bulk of the population of that time — to acquire land. He might have abandoned this plan also had he not been in dire need of the money which such sales could provide. In order to assure a sufficient quantity of surveyed lands for immediate requirements, Pemberton had been sent to "Fraser's River" with instructions to survey as quickly as possible all open districts "so that the Country may be laid out for immediate settlement and occupation."[16]

The Colonial Office persisted, however, and by the end of the year Douglas agreed to require prompt payment for land.[17] But the attempt was unsuccessful. On January 4, 1860, the Land Ordinance for the mainland made provision for payment by instalments, and this practice continued for twenty-five years. The new ordinance incorporated all Douglas had learned from experience in the past year, his first in land operations. Among other things he had discovered that the Royal Engineers, sent out by Lytton in 1858 and charged with surveying among other tasks, could not keep pace with the demand for land. In addition, the cost of transporting the Engineers to localities where surveys were required would have exceeded the price of the land. Lytton's recommendation that

15 Lytton to Douglas, May 7, 1859, no. 24, ibid., pp. 86-87.

16 Douglas to Lytton, May 23, 1859, no. 11, ibid., 3: 12.

17 Douglas to Henry Pelham Clinton, 5th duke of Newcastle, colonial secretary, November 10, 1859, no. 27, ibid., p. 69.

the cost of the actual survey be added to the price of the land did not solve the problem of insufficient surveyors.

In order to remove "so pregnant a cause of complaint," and to hasten settlement by promoting the acquisition of unsurveyed agricultural land, the new ordinance authorized the occupation of such land to the extent of 160 acres, with a pre-emptive right, by any person immediately occupying and improving the land, provided the settler paid the price of ten shillings an acre when the survey was completed and when the title was granted. Thus, for the first time in either colony, provision was made for the pre-emption of crown land. At the same time, Douglas provided for the purchase "of larger tracts of unsurveyed country land ... as [might] be desired by persons of larger means, [but] in order to guard against the speculative holding of land ... 5s an acre [was] to be paid down, and the residue at the time of survey." As the object of the new ordinance was "solely to encourage and induce the settlement of the country," occupation of the land was "made the test of title, and no pre-emption title [could] be perfected without compliance with that imperative condition."[18]

Douglas discussed the land problem with his council in March, 1860. It was recorded in the minutes that " 'the council are unanimously of the opinion that a low price ... combined with occupation and improvement, would conduce to the general settlement of the country.' " From this sound observation it is apparent that Douglas and his advisers, although constantly short of money for administrative purposes, had already abandoned the idea of enriching the treasury from the sale of public lands. Instead, the real problem — that of encouraging settlement — was squarely met. The council went on record to say that if the price were to be reduced, then conditions should be imposed to prevent any large-scale alienation of land for speculative purposes prejudicial to those settlers of more limited means who wished to cultivate it; that further provisions should be made for the pre-emption of unsurveyed land; that pre-emptions must be limited to 160 acres; and, finally, that all waste land should not be tied up in pre-emptions. Some waste land should be available to the capitalist wishing " 'extensive quantities of land ... for laudable ... purposes,' " at a higher price and such a grant should be circumscribed

[18] Douglas to Newcastle, January 12, 1860, no. 35, ibid., p. 90; "Proclamation, Enclosure in no. 35," ibid., pp. 91-92.

by "'conditions that would prevent abuse.'"[19] In devising this last clause, the council surely must have realized it was trying to do the impossible. Not one of Douglas's later ordinances was to contain any such provision, although every other suggestion was to be enacted by February, 1861.

Particularly important was a provision giving pre-emptors of 160 acres the right to acquire further land at the price of ten shillings per acre.[20] This principle was to be embodied in future land ordinances and proclamations, but neither then, nor at any future date, did such additional purchase exempt the settler from the necessity of improving his pre-emption. He was under no obligation to improve his more recently purchased land and might do as he wished with it, but, as of January, 1860, he had to either better his first claim or forfeit it to another who would put the land to beneficial use. It should be noted in passing that this principle of "beneficial use" came to be applied to any type of claim — land, mineral, or timber — and to water rights and coal leases. It was designed not only to prevent speculation in public lands, but also to offer every possible encouragement to the settler, prospector, free miner, or farmer, whose intentions were honest. By holding out such inducements, successive governments hoped to settle the country with people who would develop the natural resources to benefit themselves and to contribute indirectly to the government's income through duties, taxes, and royalties. Had Douglas achieved nothing else by 1864, he would still deserve a place of honour in British Columbia's history for implementing this principle.

As will become evident, not all later governments were to insist upon strict conformity with the statutory provisions respecting improvements, but the principle had been established and was never to be questioned officially. It would appear, however, that fortunes both great and small were made, in defiance of the statute. From the 1860's until at least 1910 there was scarcely a public figure in British Columbia who did not acquire large holdings of agricultural, pastoral, or mineral lands. As far as it is possible to trace transactions through official sources, these acquisitions appear legal, but, undoubtedly, information acquired as a member of the government, or as a confidant of such a member, would have had potential value.

19 Quoted in Gosnell, "Colonial History, 1849-1871," pp. 109, 110.

20 B.C. *Revised Statutes, Appendix, 1871*, p. 63, 1860, 23 Vict., no. 15, s. 7.

In February, 1861, conditions on Vancouver Island necessitated a new ordinance to lower the upset price of country lands to four shillings and twopence per acre, and to legislate other conditions for the acquiring of land. Douglas had been so preoccupied in guiding the development of the mainland colony that he had found little time to consider the state of affairs closer to home. The 1861 Ordinance was the first to give detailed regulations in either colony for pre-empting crown land. It stipulated that all British male subjects (and aliens who had taken the oath of allegiance) over eighteen years of age could pre-empt waste crown land, excepting Indian reserves or settlements, to the extent of 150 acres for a single man, 200 acres for a married man whose wife was resident in the colony, and 10 acres for each child under eighteen years. Having selected his land the settler had to record his claim with the surveyor general in Victoria and pay the required fee. If the land were unsurveyed, as it usually was, his application had to be accompanied by the "best possible description thereof in writing," and a map. As soon as the land was surveyed, he had to pay the required four shillings and twopence per acre. Should the pre-emption be on land already surveyed, however, three years were allowed in which to make full payment. Two years after securing his certificate of record, and upon the satisfactory evidence of third parties that he had continued in permanent occupation for the two years and had effected improvement amounting to two shillings per acre, the settler was entitled to a certificate of improvement. The land could not be transferred until this certificate had been issued. When all requirements had been fulfilled and all payments made, a crown grant was issued, but the right to repossess any part of the land for roads or other public purposes and the right to work any precious minerals were reserved to the Crown. Once the settler received a crown grant to his pre-emption, he could buy any additional amount of land at the current price. This land had to be, of course, surveyed land. The settler was allowed to be absent from his claim for only two months; longer than that and the claim was forfeit to the surveyor general.[21]

Following the report of the Select Committee set up in 1863 by the House of Assembly to investigate the condition of crown

[21] Ibid., pp. 25-28, 1861, 24 Vict., no. 4.

lands,[22] it was ruled that the most land a pre-emptor could purchase in addition to his pre-emption was 480 acres at four shillings and twopence an acre. Any quantity of land could be leased, however, for agricultural purposes and water could be diverted for the same purpose.[23]

Douglas probably appointed the Select Committee of 1863 as a result of a memorial presented to him in April, 1861, by J. A. R. Homer and other citizens of New Westminster. Homer criticized the absence of a land tax, the careless administration of public lands, and the failure to establish a Land Registry Office.[24] What perhaps the memorialists overlooked and what the Colonial Office never seemed to have understood was that Douglas was hampered constantly in his plans for the two colonies by a lack of revenue. His only sources of income on the mainland were land sales, a customs import of 10 per cent, and liquor and miners' licences. To levy miners' fees and to collect them were two quite different matters. Although millions of dollars in gold were taken from the Cariboo gold fields, the royalty owed the colonial administration was generally evaded. Thus, rich as some miners became, their wealth added little to the colonial treasury other than indirectly through the volume of general business. To open the country and to meet the requirements of the population meant large annual expenditures for public works. Douglas had to ask the Colonial Office for financial relief and cut down drastically on public spending in the two colonies in order to avoid bankruptcy. He referred the complaint that public lands had been wrongly administered to Colonel Richard Moody, commander of the Royal Engineers and chief commissioner of lands and works. Douglas forwarded both his own and Moody's reports on the matter to the Colonial Office on April 22, 1861.[25] No action was taken by the Colonial Office,

22 Vancouver Island, House of Assembly, Committee on Crown Lands, Vancouver Island, *Report, June 14th, 1864*, 3d Parl., 1st sess., 1863-64, [committee print]; later published with the evidence of witnesses, idem, *Minutes of Proceedings of a Select Committee of the House of Assembly Appointed to Inquire into the Present Condition of the Crown Lands of the Colony, with Reference to the Proposal of Her Majesty's Secretary of State for the Colonies Dated 15th June, 1863, to Hand Over the Crown Lands to the Legislature* (Victoria: Printed by Harries ... for Her Majesty's Government, 1864).

23 B.C. *Revised Statutes, Appendix, 1871*, pp. 85-93, 1865, 28 Vict., no. 23.

24 "A Memorial from the British Columbian Convention to the Imperial Government," *British Columbian* (New Westminster), February 28, 1861.

25 Douglas to Newcastle, April 22, 1861, Great Britain, Colonial Office, "CO 60, British Columbia Original Correspondence, 1858-1871: Despatches from

but Douglas did take steps to establish a Registry Office in New Westminster.

Just before his retirement Douglas was forced to confess to the commencing session of the first Legislative Council at Sapperton that the results of his land policy had been disappointing. His policy, he said, had been to advance public works as quickly as possible in order to give the waste lands of the colony a value they had not until then possessed. With a view solely to increasing population by encouraging settlement, he had thrown open the public lands to settlers on the most liberal terms, but the results had not fulfilled his expectations. No doubt Douglas was disappointed at the slow pace development had taken, but he could hardly be held responsible. With Lytton's despatches to guide him and his own keen sense of what was needed, he had met realistically the requirements of the two colonies, and in so doing he had displayed an advanced and liberal conception of the philosophy necessary to a public land policy in a new country. With 254 pre-emptions recorded between 1858 and 1862 on the mainland and encompassing 50,000 acres, Douglas need not have been so pessimistic.[26]

Essentially, it was the legislation formulated by Douglas that was still in effect when the province joined Confederation in 1871. The Land Ordinance of 1870, effective in 1871, closely resembled those written by Douglas before his retirement in 1864. Certain details, however, were changed. Pre-emptions of unsurveyed land were restricted to 320 acres east of the Cascades and 160 acres west; pre-emptors were forbidden to hold two claims simultaneously; and improvements were to be made to the value of two dollars and fifty cents an acre. Under section 16 there was to be "continuous *bona fide* personal residence of the pre-emptor," a restriction added to prevent the practice of constructing a shanty on the claim and running cattle on the land, but living elsewhere. This personal residence clause, however, was to become inoperative after four years of "continuous occupation," presumably on the assumption that within that time the government would have sur-

the Governors of British Columbia, Draft Replies, Interdepartmental and Miscellaneous," microfilmed (London: microfilm made on behalf of the Public Archives of Canada from the Public Record Office, London, n.d.), pp. 168-89, 5166 British Columbia.

26 D. Borthwick, "Settlement in British Columbia," *Transactions of the Eighth British Columbia Natural Resources Conference ... 1955* (British Columbia Natural Resources Conference, 1955), p. 100.

veyed the claim. After being surveyed, the land might be bought at one dollar an acre, payable in four equal annual instalments. A crown grant conveying the land in fee simple was obtainable once all payments were made.

No restriction was placed on the quantity of surveyed land that might be purchased at the upset price of one dollar an acre. Lands reputed to contain minerals, townsites and their suburbs, were reserved from sale. Provision was made for the governor to set the upset price of town lots as circumstances dictated, a wise stipulation which secured to the government any advance in current land prices. The Crown reserved the right to enter any land for the purpose of obtaining road-building materials, but, save for this provision or unless otherwise specially announced, all trees, mines, and minerals except gold and silver were to be conveyed by the terms of sale. The only other reservations made were rights-of-way for leading animals to water, for mining, or for engineering purposes, but only if these reservations were already in existence at the time of sale.

For the purpose of pasturing cattle or horses, section 26 permitted the leasing of any amount of un-pre-empted and unsurveyed waste crown land, but only to genuine pre-emptors or buyers in the immediate vicinity and at such rent as the Governor in Council might specify. The only restriction placed on such leases was that within six months the lessee was required to stock his land with the number of animals per 100 acres required by the land commissioner. Leased land was subject at any time to pre-emption, government reserve, or purchase. As a benefit to the cattlemen who were unlikely to sit idly by while their range land was pre-empted, only 500 acres of waste land could be leased for cutting hay and, then, only for five years.[27]

[27] Because this ordinance will be used extensively as the standard by which to gauge subsequent progress, it is included as Appendix A.

CHAPTER 2

Provincial Land Policy to 1880

The land legislation prevailing at the time the united colony of Vancouver Island and British Columbia entered Confederation in 1871 has been briefly presented. Since the history of land laws during the next forty years was to be the history of the expansion of the 1870 Ordinance, the principles of this law merit study. Those sections pertaining to timber leases, mining claims, free miners' privileges, and water rights are treated in later chapters.

By 1871 the first and most important principle underlying land legislation was that of beneficial use. The fact is inescapable that the 1870 Ordinance was unwise legislation despite its restrictions because it did not recognize that good agricultural land was severely limited. To this day, only 1,600,000 acres in the province have been developed as agricultural land, although 6,500,000 acres are classified as arable or potentially so. It would have been in the better interests of both the province and conservation had the agricultural land been surveyed and divided into smaller holdings to benefit a greater number. Douglas had done his utmost to retain the land for the Crown until it had been surveyed, but lack of money, resulting in the recall of the Royal Engineers in 1863, frustrated his plans. Further, it was to be forty years before systematic surveys of the province were undertaken to determine precisely the extent of cultivable land. Until the results of these surveys were known, the land had appeared to be limitless; to have restricted sales to 160 acres would have seemed miserly indeed.

The second principle to be found in the Ordinance of 1870 was sale by public auction with a previously established upset price. This principle was based on the premise that arable land would be eagerly sought by a confidently expected annual flood of immigrants. When the flood turned out to be a mere trickle, and when buyers realized that it would be foolish to bid one another up at auction, it became the practice to wait until after the sale in order to obtain the land at the upset price. The provision for sale by auction became a dead issue.

More realistic was the third principle, that of payment by instalments. Under section 21 pre-emptors were given four years after their claims had been surveyed within which to make payment. Before 1870, full payment had been required upon survey. Since government surveys were frequently delayed, the pre-emptor often paid for his own private survey and bought the land in the usual way. Only one pre-emption claim could be held at any one time, and the residence requirement called for continuous bona fide personal occupation of four-years' duration. Both these last stipulations were designed to prevent speculation.

Fourthly, it was firmly established that no crown grant to any land could be secured until the land had been surveyed. This requirement was rigidly enforced, as indeed it had to be, lest Land Office records become hopelessly confused. Finally, the Crown reserved to itself certain rights and privileges: namely, the right to repossess a portion of granted lands for public purposes, and the rights to gold and silver wherever found, unless these were specifically exempted in the conveyance.

These were the principles formulated by Douglas and they have been altered only slightly by subsequent land acts. On occasion one or more of these principles was to be dropped, only to be shortly reinserted and, today, they still form an integral part of the provincial land legislation.

But what of agriculture itself in 1871? It was estimated that 13,384 acres were being cultivated, almost entirely in the New Westminster and Victoria districts. In that year 125,000 bushels of potatoes, 140,000 bushels of turnips, and 215,000 bushels of grain, were grown. On pastoral land 28,737 head of cattle were run, and 2,373 tons of hay were cut. The faith of the settlers in the future of their province was high although they realized that until the railway connecting them with Canada was built, development must be slow. Until that railway link became a reality in 1885, the major market for the province's exports had to be found in San Francisco. Exports in 1872, confined almost entirely to gold, coal, and furs, amounted to $1,792,347; "miscellaneous" items, including agricultural produce, amounted to only $59,231. These figures show how extensive was the market within the province itself for farm produce.

And what of population in the year of union? The population of 9,092 whites, 459 coloureds and 1,319 Chinese, was found chiefly in the Victoria and New Westminster areas, with only scattered settlements throughout the interior.[1] The future of these settlers — closely dependent on the land laws — looked secure and prosperous.

Beyond the 13,000 acres under cultivation, the fort property, town lots, and several thousand acres of farming lands retained by the Hudson's Bay Company around Victoria, there was still a vast area to be settled, mining resources to be developed, timber lands to be exploited. Consequently, a more specific legal code had to be established. Although by 1871 Hudson's Bay officials, and prospectors, miners, hunters, trappers, and travellers, had explored much of the province, no one had any idea of the total area of the land surface, much less what proportion was arable. It has since been determined that the province contains a total land area of 359,279 square miles and a fresh water area of 6,976 square miles, or a total of approximately 230,000,000 acres of land, of which about 3 per cent is now considered to be arable agricultural land.

In his speech from the throne to the second session of the first provincial Legislative Assembly on December 17, 1872, Lieutenant-Governor Joseph Trutch stated:

> A bill will be submitted to you substituting for the existing Land Laws a measure on a sounder and more liberal basis, which it is believed will be more satisfactory to the Public and more conducive to the speedy settlement of the Province. Provision will also be made for accurate and extensive Surveys of those Districts in the Province most available for settlement.[2]

As chief commissioner of lands and works in the colony from 1864 to 1871, Trutch must have found it bitter to read the speech written for him on this occasion. Amor De Cosmos no doubt had had a hand in this as it was he who had successfully proposed a motion

1 E.O.S. Scholefield and R. E. Gosnell, *A History of British Columbia*, 2 pts. in 1 vol. (Vancouver: British Columbia Historical Association, 1913), 2:1, 3.

2 B.C., Legislative Assembly, *Journals*, 1st Parl., 2d sess., 1872-73, p. 2.

at the Yale Convention in 1868 condemning the Land and Works Department and its land policy. His resolution asking for "free grants of at least 320 acres to actual settlers upon public lands" was not to receive consideration, but, doubtless, he had many remarks to make in the assembly amplifying his condemnatory motion.

> That the Office of Lands and Works is maintained at a great annual expense, amounting in 1868, for a Chief Commissioner and three clerks, to 8,490 dollars, and in former years to a far larger sum. That the greatest ignorance prevails in the department as to the lands in Vancouver Island and on the mainland, although a land office has been kept open in the former place 17 years, and in the latter for 10 years. That nothing is done by the department to assist in the sale and settlement of the public lands, except recording a few pre-emptions on Vancouver Island, and on the mainland the pre-emptions are recorded by the magistrates. That a few parcels of public lands are leased for the purpose of trade, agriculture, lumbering, and mining, and the rents collected for the same. That instalments on lands sold or pre-empted are collected. That a few maps are made or extended occasionally. That the above includes the total services performed by this department pertaining to land, and could all be transacted by one clerk. That the public works carried on by the department are confined to repairing roads, constructing some small bridges, cutting out or keeping open a trail, or repairing or enlarging a public building, and are either performed by contract or by temporary service. That the entire public works, including map-making, could be well attended to by one competent civil engineer.[3]

Such a forthright denunciation of the department which he had headed must have incensed Trutch, and the aspersions cast on his ability as an engineer must have caused him to regard De Cosmos and his associates with active hostility. Since De Cosmos headed the second provincial ministry as premier after John Foster McCreight's defeat on December 23, 1872, this personal animosity was to have serious consequences for the province.

[3] [Confederation League], "Minutes of a Preliminary Meeting of the Delegates, Elected by the Various Districts of British Columbia, Convened at Yale [September 14-16, 1868], Pursuant to the Following Call: Yale Convention," Enclosure 1 in no. 6, Frederick Seymour to Richard Chandos Grenville, 3d duke of Buckingham and Chandos, colonial secretary, November 30, 1868, no. 6, in *Papers on the Union of British Columbia with the Dominion of Canada* ... ordered by the House of Commons to be printed, 3 August 1869 (n.p.,n.d.), p. 22, in [Great Britain, Colonial Office], *Miscellaneous Papers Relating to British Columbia, 1859-1869*, 5 papers in 1 vol. ([London, 1859-69]).

Leaving aside temporarily the consideration of free lands as proposed by De Cosmos, the assembly gave its attention to other changes which might be made in the 1870 Ordinance. To accomplish these changes, a select committee was appointed in 1872. Chief among its recommendations were simplification of the process of granting pre-emption records, and the easing of the occupation requirement so that it might be met by either the pre-emptor or his agent "provided no such agent shall be an Indian or a Chinaman." Instead of having to wait until after the land had been surveyed, a pre-emptor could now secure a certificate of improvement which entitled him to a crown grant after four-years' continuous occupation. To protect pre-emptors of lands located among pastoral leases from the wrath of the cattlemen, pre-emptors were granted "the right of passing and re-passing over such leased lands without being deemed trespassers," and the pre-emptor who cultivated at least ten acres of his pre-emption was allowed to run up to fifty head of his stock on a lessee's range during the winter months and subject to an annual payment. Finally, under section 16 dealing with the sale of land, no mention of a required survey was made, a complete reversal of former policy. The provision for the sale of lands at public auction was set aside, in a clause reading that land would be auctioned only "whenever so ordered by the Lieutenant-Governor in Council . . . as may be deemed by him expedient."[4]

In the same speech from the throne Trutch intimated that some provision would be made for free grants of land. The select committee recommended in 1873, the following year, that limited free grants of land be made, at the governor's discretion, to any settler who made the requisite improvements, and the grant be issued at any time after the improvements had been made.[5] Clauses 21 to 31, inclusive, of the Amendment of February 21, 1873 dealt with such free grants. Any land suitable for cultivation and settlement,

[4] B.C., Legislative Assembly, Select Committee On Land Ordinance, 1870, "Report," B.C., *Journals*, 1st Parl., 2d sess., 1872-73, appendix, *Sessional Papers*; B.C., *Statutes*, 1873, 36 Vict., no. 1.

[5] The Select Committee had, undoubtedly, been greatly influenced by the dominion statute which had thrown the prairies open to settlement at one dollar an acre with a 640-acre limit, or, for homesteaders, 160 acres free on the sole condition of three-years' occupancy and cultivation, Canada, *Statutes*, 1872, 35 Vict., c. 23. In 1874, the pre-emption of a further quarter-section was allowed. The dominion statutes closely followed the American example and, by this indirect route, British Columbia's land laws were influenced by the American precedent. O. D. Skelton, "General Economic History," in *Canada and Its Provinces*, Shortt and Doughty, eds., 21: 112.

whether surveyed or not, could be used for these free grants to a maximum of 250 acres. This was 90 acres in excess of what the Dominion was granting in the Northwest under its Homestead Act of 1872. No one could receive a free grant who had already obtained land by any other means. To prevent speculation, any applicant for a free grant had to sign an affidavit declaring that the land sought was solely for his personal use for settlement and cultivation and not for any other purpose. Provided that twenty acres were brought under cultivation within three years of the application, and a habitable house built, a crown grant could be secured. An indication of how anxious the government was to obtain settlers and of how willing it was to relax previous attitudes, was the new regulation that the "locatee" of such a free grant, who was supposed to reside on his "location," could still be absent more than six months a year "provided such land be cultivated as aforesaid." This provision enabled settlers to work elsewhere part of the year for the cash to finance their land venture. Under section 29 these favoured "locatees" were guarded against attachment of the land for any debt or liability before the initial three-year period had expired. After the crown grant was issued, provided the original settler and his family still occupied the land and excepting "any debt secured by a valid mortgage . . . subsequently to the issuing," the guarantee was extended for another twenty years.[6]

Such was British Columbia's first tentative venture into the competitive race to attract immigrants by offering free land. During the session of 1873, a land return was tabled by Robert Beaven, then chief commissioner of land and works, later to be premier, showing that only 8,284 acres of land had been sold by auction at an average price of $1.21 49/100 an acre, 20 per cent higher than the upset price of $1.00, for a total of $10,064.50.[7] This acreage, in a province the size of British Columbia, was negligible. Hence the De Cosmos ministry, dissatisfied with the land policy, decided to offer free land to all comers. The United States had been offering free land since 1862 and Canada had followed suit ten years later. Now that the railway reserve imposed on all provin-

6 B.C., *Statutes*, 1873, 36 Vict., no. 1.

7 B.C., Department of Lands and Works, "Return Showing Results of Land Sales by Auction," in "Report of the Chief Commissioner of Lands and Works . . . 1873," B.C., *Journals*, 1st Parl., 3d sess., 1873-74, appendix, *Sessional Papers*, p. 64. The reports of the chief commissioner were also separately published during the years covered by this study.

cial lands under article 11 of the Terms of Union was about to lapse because of the Dominion's failure to begin railway construction, British Columbia was free for the first time to compete with Canada and with the United States for Europe's land-hungry immigrants.

An illustration of how completely another of Lytton's principles — that of prompt and full payment — had been abandoned, is shown in a further return tabled by Beaven, giving both the number of acres sold and the price received for lands on the mainland for the years 1870, 1871, and 1872. This return showed that 75 per cent of the land was bought by deferred payment. Of 27,880 acres sold, only 6,955 were paid for in full; of the $16,919.82 received, only $1,224.01 or 14 per cent, represented full payment.

A third conclusion can be drawn from Beaven's returns. Figures tabled by him show 11,134 acres sold in the last six months of 1870, 13,512 acres in 1871, but only 3,234 acres in 1872. Obviously the delay of the railway was beginning to have its effect in demoralizing public business in the province.

Still another return indicated that the government had placed under reserve 190,857.8 acres throughout the province for purposes of Indian settlements, and for schools, parks, military and naval establishments, and townsites; 78,520 acres of coal lands, and 39,100 acres of timber. Pre-emption claims had been recorded for 44,827.5 acres, at an average of 210 acres per claim.[8]

Finally, Beaven included in his report a list of all the holders of pastoral leases, showing name of lessee, the district, acreage, rental, and a comment indicating that certain leases had not as yet been issued. At the rate of 3¢ to 6¢ an acre charged for the 80,342.9 acres under lease, the government was to receive $3,393.68 a year in rent. Because it reveals the cattle-raising regions of the province, and because it gives the names of several men who later became figures of some importance in the province, the complete return is reproduced below.

On March 2, 1874, the provincial legislature passed the first land act since union with Canada, a complete revision of the 1870 Ordinance and its amendments. Fortunately, the last section provided that the new act should not come into force until published

[8] "... Return of Government Reserves," B.C. *Journals*, 1st. Parl., 2d sess., 1872-73, appendix, *Sessional Papers*; "Return ... of Pre-emptions in ... British Columbia, from 1st January to 30th November, 1872," ibid.

Return of Pastoral Leases[9]

Name of Lessee	*District*	*Acreage*	*Rate*	*Remarks*
Maxwell & Lummey	Salt Spring Island	852	3 cents per acre per annum.	
John Tod, Junior	Pender Island	2330	6 do. do.	
Do. do.	Do.	2000	6 do. do.	Lease not yet issued.
Buckley & Hope	Do.	4100	6 do. do.	Do. do.
Do.	Do.	1400	6 do. do.	Do. do.
Samuel Trueworthy	Saturna Island	940	6 do. do.	Do. do.
O. W. Browne	New Westminster	382	$10 per annum.	
Samuel Herring	Do.	....	$150 do.	
D. W. Miller	Do.	303	4 cents per acre per annum.	
A. Smith & J. D. Evans	Do.	400	10 do. do.	
E. G. Perry	Yale	6200	4 do. do.	
Whitfield Chase	Do.	1085	4 do. do.	
Cornwall Bros.	Do.	10000	3⅓ do. do.	
W. H. Sandford	Do.	3430	3⅓ do. do.	
H. Ingram	Do.	1711	4 do. do.	
Jas. Uren	Do.	$1154\frac{90}{100}$	4 do. do.	
Nicholas Hare	Do.	2425	4 do. do.	
C. A. Vernon	Do.	3252	4 do. do.	
A. G. Pemberton	Do.	3505	4 do. do.	
Jacob Duck	Do.	1710	4 do. do.	
Charles Heuling	Do.	400	4 do. do.	
Gannon, McKinlay & Manson	Do.	4000	4 do. do.	Lease not yet issued.
James Stuart	Do.	1400	4 do. do.	
J. B. Greaves	Do.	4940	4 do. do.	
Charles A. Semlin	Do.	2880	4 do. do.	
John Wilson	Do.	10980	4 do. do.	
Henry Morton	Do.	1710	4 do. do.	Lease not yet issued.
F. Peranet	Do.	1147	4 do. do.	Do. do.
William Fortune	Do.	2055	4 do. do.	Do. do.
P. Gotin	Do.	1151	4 do. do.	Do. do.
Haynes & Lowe	Kootenay	2500	4 do. do.	Do. do.
		$80342\frac{90}{100}$		

[9] "Report of the Chief Commissioner of Lands . . . 1873," p. 65.

in the *British Columbia Gazette*. The second, or interpretation clause, defined crown lands as "all lands of this Province held by the Crown in fee and common socage."[10] When the act reached Ottawa, Telesphore Fournier, minister of justice, drew attention to this definition as one which applied only to lands of the Crown acquired from some previous owner. Were this definition intentional, he said, it could only mean that the province was recognizing the original Indian sovereignty over its lands and thus the Crown as tenant by freehold. Although the province had no intention of giving such recognition, the minister of justice had no quarrel with the definition on constitutional grounds. He did find it objectionable that the act made no provision for Indian reservations, and that Indians were not accorded any rights or privileges in respect to lands, reserves, or settlements. On the contrary, he found sections 3 and 24 specifically exempted the Indians from any rights of recording unsurveyed land or of pre-empting surveyed land if they had not previously obtained written permission from the Lieutenant-Governor in Council. Fournier also pointed out that there was no provision in the act for reserving land for railway purposes as required under article 11 of the Terms of Union. He noted that the dominion government had not lived up to those terms which required construction to begin by 1873, and he drew to the cabinet's attention the great embarrassment which might result later should it be found that the provincial government had unknowingly granted pre-emptions in the forty-mile strip yet to be definitely located. He recommended disallowance.[11] The act was disallowed by an Order in Council, March 16, 1875.

After communication with the British Columbia government, it was agreed that the act should not be proclaimed and that a new bill should be introduced at the next provincial legislative session. Trutch assented to this new land act on April 22, 1875. There were only two important changes from the 1874 version. The definition of crown lands now read, "all lands of this Province held by the Crown in fee simple," and section 60, dealing with reserves, was added:

10 B.C., *Statutes*, 1874, 37 Vict., no. 2.

11 William Egerton Hodgins, comp., *Correspondence, Reports of the Ministers of Justice and Orders in Council upon the Subject of Dominion and Provincial Legislation, 1867-[1920]*, compiled under the direction of the ... minister of justice, 2 vols. (Ottawa: Government Printing Bureau, 1896-1922), 1:1024, 1028, 1029.

> The Lieutenant-Governor shall, at any time, by notice, signed by the Chief Commissioner of Lands and Works, and published in the British Columbia *Gazette*, reserve any lands not lawfully held by record, pre-emption, purchase, lease, or Crown Grant, for the purpose of conveying the same to the Dominion Government, in trust, for the use and benefit of the Indians, or for railway purposes, as mentioned in Article 11 of the Terms of Union, or for such other purposes as may be deemed advisable.

While these two were the most significant additions to the provincial land laws, there were others of a less radical nature. Although pre-emptions on surveyed land still could not exceed the 320-acre limit east of the Cascades and 160 acres west, the new act did provide for claims of 40, 80, and 120 acres, thereby permitting pre-emptions where the topography precluded a larger acreage. Still only one claim could be held under pre-emption, but in order to legalize the existing conditions within the province, section 15 provided that any settler could have his claim surveyed at his own expense. Under section 24 settlers, designated now as "homestead settlers," might pre-empt surveyed lands as defined in section 23. This definition of surveyed lands was a departure from past procedure. Since the only surveyed lands in the province were near Victoria and New Westminster, surveyed ten years before by the Royal Engineers and long since settled, the provision was largely meaningless. After two years' continuous occupation and permanent improvements of $2.50 an acre, a certificate of improvement could be obtained. Then, upon payment of the five dollar fee, the homestead settler was entitled to a crown grant. Under section 66, such land was free. Steps in this direction had been previously taken by the amendments of 1873, and now, with no restrictions, all land under pre-emption was granted free of charge. For this reason, the act of 1875 was known as the "Free Grant Act."

The rules governing unlimited pastoral leases and 500-acre hay leases were retained. Anyone wishing to buy surveyed land could do so for one dollar an acre, but unsurveyed land could only be bought after the land had been surveyed at the buyer's expense. Lytton's concern that deferred payment would lead to default was proving legitimate and section 79 authorized the chief commissioner to give notice in the *British Columbia Gazette* to those from whom the balance of purchase money was overdue that, unless the money was paid, their records or agreements would be cancelled.[12]

[12] B.C., *Statutes*, 1875, 38 Vict., no. 5.

A return tabled on April 25, 1876, showed that in the six land divisions established in the province, $56,596.38 was owing. Twenty-two persons in New Westminster alone owed $7,906.46.

As there were still no specific reservations for Indian lands, Edward Blake, now minister of justice in Ottawa, was no more satisfied with this act than his predecessor had been with the act of 1874, but because the Indian land problem had been temporarily solved by the agreement to appoint a Joint Reserve Commission, and because "great inconvenience and confusion might result from its disallowance," he decided to leave the act in operation.[13]

In the session of 1875, returns were tabled listing all lands taken up in the New Westminster district between 1872 and April 14, 1875. These informative records list the name, the location of land, the acreage, the type of land, the price, and the section of the land act under which the land was acquired. For instance, there were 380 pre-emption records, all of which were for 160 acres, plus 3,860 acres of irregular size, including a claim by Charley Brew, an Indian of Langley. Purchased outright were 22,761.5 acres — nearly all in 160-acre blocks — at one dollar an acre, and, purchased by deferred payment, were a further 15,884 acres at fifty cents an acre at a public auction on September 30, 1873.[14]

In his report for the year, Beaven assessed the worth of the "free grant system" introduced two years before:

> The liberality of the Province in dealing with its lands far exceeds that of any other Province or State on this continent, as settlers now coming in can record 160 acres West of the Cascades and 320 acres East of the same mountain range, in any part of the Mainland portion of the Province, and can eventually obtain the land as a "Free Grant" simply by residence and improvement. The question, therefore, as to whether indiscriminate "Free Grants" have a tendency to quickly settle up the Province has had, for the last two years, a practical test. Many settlers, and others who have given the subject consideration, are strongly of the opinion that it would eventually be more beneficial to the Province if the "Free Grant" system was confined to certain surveyed Townships, instead of virtually giving away the Crown Lands throughout the Province, and having subsequently, in all probability, to resort to a direct tax to make up the loss

13 Hodgins, *Dominion and Provincial Legislation*, 1:1039.

14 ". . . Return of Lands Taken Up by Purchase, by Pre-emption, by Timber Lease . . . with the Names of Parties Holding or Applying for the Same, in the New Westminster District . . . 1872, Inclusive, to the Present Time," B.C., *Journals*, 1st Parl., 4th sess., 1875, appendix, *Sessional Papers*, pp. 705-23.

> to the Provincial revenue. The machinery of the present Land Act, in reference to the adjustment and "proving up" of claims, has worked admirably, and saved the Province a considerable expenditure in ascertaining the exact locality of the different claimants, who, in many instances, are absent, and the improvements under which they have obtained their certificates, years ago, having become obliterated.[15]

Since the act granting free land had been Beaven's creation, his enthusiasm over what he chose to consider its success is pardonable. It is highly doubtful, however, that he had any real conception of the country to which he expected settlers to flock to take up 320-acre pre-emptions under the act's inducements. Only in regard to the size of the free pre-emptions did the act differ from either the dominion or the American homestead acts.

Despite free pre-emptions, some settlers continued to buy land outright in order to circumvent the residence and improvement requirements for free grants. In 1877, a return gave details of all lands sold in the province from July 31, 1871 to December 31, 1876. A comparison of the following figures with the ones given earlier for New Westminster will show that at this time — as for thirty-five years to come — government statistics were at least two years in arrears, but they are revealing nevertheless. Of the 195 individual sales totalling 33,507.49 acres, 78 were on Vancouver Island (7,701.38 acres at a total price of $7,395.38); 71 in New Westminster (9,900 acres; $8,465.86); 3 in the Cariboo District (acreage not given; $162.00); 11 in Yale (3,087.41 acres; $2,897.41); and 32 in Lillooet (12,818.90 acres; $12,875.50).

These statistics show that land sales had not been large — a mere 6,700 acres a year, mostly sold at the statutory price of one dollar an acre. They indicate that lands on Vancouver Island were still being sold in 100-acre blocks, following the practice established twenty-five years before by the Hudson's Bay Company. In the New Westminster district the average size of each purchase was 140 acres, suggesting that there was still a good supply of farming land available along the Fraser River flats. In the Cariboo, however, assuming the standard price of one dollar per acre, the three sales made were more than likely for mineral claims as fifty acres was the size later allowed for such claims, and the law generally

[15] B.C., Department of Lands and Works, "Report of the Chief Commissioner of Lands and Works ... 1875," B.C., *Sessional Papers*, 2d Parl., 1st sess., 1876, p. 531.

followed the precedent of established practice. The Yale average of 280 acres and the Lillooet of 400 reflect the predominant occupation of the settlers in cattle raising. In Yale District Cornelius O'Keefe was able to buy 480 acres at Okanagan Lake in October 1871 and 162 more the following March, all at one dollar an acre.[16]

By the time the next land returns had been tabled in the Legislature, covering the period from April, 1875, to February, 1878, there were 279 applicants to purchase 86,942.5 acres of unsurveyed land. Five of these applications were refused with no reason stated. During 1877 there were 31,282 acres of every other classification sold, and town lots, nearly all in Hastings and Granville,[17] were sold to 41 buyers. For the same year there were only 127 preemptions recorded for free grants under the 1875 Free Grant Act, indicating either that British Columbia's pioneers were an independent breed, or that the lands available to them as free grants were so far removed from the settled districts that few settlers wanted them.

An 1878 return showing the arrears in rent on pastoral leases since 1870 indicated that few lessees were paying their rent and that the government was not taking action. Twenty-one lessees, including the Cornwalls and C. A. Semlin, were in arrears to the extent of $7,114.63 on land of which the annual rental amounted to $2,300.06. A note at the bottom of the return said that "the apparently large amounts of rent due are caused by the difficulty of collection, on account of the additional charge of Road Tax; disputes respecting boundaries, and pre-emptions, etc.; many of the above Leases, though not formally cancelled, being regarded by

16 "Approximate Statement of Land Sold in British Columbia from 31st July, 1871, to 31st December, 1876 . . . ," B.C., *Sessional Papers,* 2d Parl., 2d sess., 1877, pp. 481-87.

See Appendix B, Table 3, "Certificates of Purchase, 1873-1913, Inclusive," for further statistics on land sales in British Columbia. The discrepancy between the figures given in Table 3 and those given in the text above demonstrates the troublesome fact that statistics taken from different sources published during the province's early years, seldom agree. The 400-acre average purchase in the Lillooet district given in the text is calculated on the basis of the thirty-five individual sales listed for the years 1871-76 ("Land Sold 1871-1876," pp. 486-87), but the figure for individual sales during the same years based on statistics given in the annual reports of officials of the Land Department and compiled in Table 3, is only twenty-three.

17 ". . . Return Showing . . . All Applications to Purchase Unsurveyed Lands since 1st April, 1875; All Lands Sold since 31st December, 1876; and All Town Lots Sold since 31st December, 1872," B.C., *Sessional Papers,* 2nd Parl., 3d sess., and 3d Parl., 1st sess., 1878, pp. 581-93.

the Lessees as surrendered."[18] Probably this explanation meant simply that the lessees had no intention of paying their rent and the government chose to do very little about it. Here is evidence that lack of supervision was already rendering many clauses of the land act inoperative.

By this year, 1878, the Land Office had brought its records slightly more up to date. The returns for lands sold since July 31, 1871, now showed in Vancouver Island Districts, 17,601.38 acres; Cariboo District, 3,087.41 acres; and Lillooet District, 12,818.70 acres. At the 1878 session of the legislature there was a renewed determination to collect rental or purchase money from those in arrears. Lytton had warned Douglas about instalment purchases, saying that just such a contingency as that now confronting the province could arise. An amendment to the act was passed imposing no less than 24 per cent interest per annum on all unpaid purchase money for surveyed crown land, and on all arrears in rentals for leases. If these payments were not made after a notice had appeared in the *British Columbia Gazette*, any records or agreements were to be cancelled at once.

When the act reached Ottawa, there was a mild flurry in the Justice Department. In reporting to the minister of justice, then Sir John A. Macdonald, Z. A. Lash, deputy minister, opened with the comment that "the provisions of this statute are of a startling nature." After outlining the provisions, he said the amendment cast upon persons who had purchased or leased crown lands, "a liability never contemplated by them when the purchases or leases were made." He added that had the subject matter of the act been entirely within the competence of the province to enact, he would feel some difficulty in recommending disallowance "merely because its provisions did not accord with my views of justice." But because it dealt with interest, a subject assigned exclusively to the Dominion, and because of the difficulty any individual would experience in testing the validity of the act in court, he had no hesitation in recommending its disallowance.[19] This was done by Order in Council, August 15, 1879.

After this disallowance, a further amendment in the following year insisted on immediate payment for land bought outright;

18 ". . . . Return of All Rents Due on Pastoral Leases since 1870," B.C., *Sessional Papers*, 2d Parl., 3d sess., and 3d Parl., 1st sess., 1878, p. 628.

19 Hodgins, *Dominion and Provincial Legislation*, 1: 1066.

wiped out the provision for free grant pre-emptions, but extended the time for payment of the dollar an acre now once again to be charged pre-emptors. Prior to the Free Grant Act of 1875, two years had been allowed for these pre-emption payments, but now four years were given to complete payment in equal annual instalments, although the last instalment was not payable on unsurveyed land until it had been surveyed. Default on any one of those instalments might result in forfeiture. Section 5 again required public auction of all surveyed lands "which are not the sites of towns or the suburbs thereof, and not Indian settlements" at the upset price of one dollar.[20] These provisions clearly indicate that the government hoped to end the former laxity in administration of public lands. R. E. Gosnell, an historian of the province's history of this period, sweepingly denounces the public lands policy both before and after union with Canada:

> Without any system of surveys except those made by the owners of land and without practically any conditions attaching to the sale, vast areas could be alienated. As a matter of fact, wide tracts of the best and most available land were parted with in large blocks, to the detriment of bona fide settlement, and, consequently, of the development of agriculture.... This unwise legislation appears all the more deplorable when it is considered that arable land was extremely limited, and that it was obviously in the best interests of the province that it should be carefully conserved and surveyed into small holdings for the benefit of the greatest number.[21]

The reforms of 1879 showed swift results. The number of pre-emption records dropped from 245 in 1878 to 100 in 1879, while, in the same year, the certificates of purchase reached the highest point they were to reach between 1870 and 1884. Victoria residents seem to have been the worst offenders in letting payments lapse. In 1879 the certificates of purchase in Victoria jumped 290 per cent, whereas in New Westminster there was an increase of one purchase only from the previous year's total of 198, a mere .5 per cent.[22] Cash received for the year's land transactions doubled, going from $21,100 in 1878 to $40,100 in 1879, so there was little doubt the

20 B.C., *Statutes*, 1879, 42 Vict., c. 21.

21 R. E. Gosnell, "History of Farming," in *Canada and Its Provinces*, Shortt and Doughty, eds., 22: 544.

22 Appendix B, Table 3. Four hundred and four purchases were recorded in 1879 as compared to 317 in 1878 and 236 in 1880. Ibid.

legislature was getting results. Having spent two years in the Opposition ranks, George A. Walkem was once again premier and was making his strength felt.

As part of the general tightening-up process, section 6 of the 1879 Amendment required every intending purchaser to give two months' notice of his intention in both the *British Columbia Gazette* and in a local newspaper at his own expense. He was to list his name, locality, the boundaries, and the extent of the land applied for, as well as its distance from any mining or mineral claims. The notice was to be dated and a copy of it posted in a conspicuous spot on the land itself and in the neighbouring local government office, should there be one. This provision was to prevent the many conflicting claims which rendered the work of the local assistant commissioners, as well as that of the head office, exceedingly difficult. In the same section it was specified that land could be neither surveyed nor sold in such a manner as to dispose of less than 160 acres. Moreover, any application for land still pending could not be given complete title under the statute relevant at the time it was entered. "Every applicant for land . . . to whom a Crown Grant has not been issued, shall comply with the provisions of Section 6 of this Act." Nor could any applicant hope to remain anonymous so far as the public was concerned. Any notice of survey inserted in the *Gazette* on any purchaser's behalf was to contain the applicant's name.[23]

It is interesting to speculate why the free grant system was abandoned so unceremoniously. During the years 1874 to 1879 while the Free Grant Act was in effect, only 437 grants were made under its provisions and only 349 certificates of improvement were issued. It was undoubtedly the correspondingly high number of certificates of purchase, 1498, that moved the government to cancel free grants. Four out of five persons acquiring land for any purpose, were paying for it outright, and the government reasoned that if four could pay, the fifth could do so also. Walkem was convinced that the free grant system had outlived its usefulness in British Columbia although it was still retained both in the Northwest Territories to the east and in Washington Territory to the south. Free grants of land to the settlers in British Columbia, except under unusual circumstances, were never heard of again.

The totals for 1879 indicate that the usefulness of the free home-

[23] B.C. *Statutes*, 1879, 42 Vict., c. 21.

stead legislation had, apparently, passed; those for New Westminster indicate it to be the area profiting most from the legislation.[24] It should be remembered, however, that New Westminster district then included the entire lower Fraser Valley from Hope to what is now the city of Vancouver.

Homestead Pre-emptions under the 1874 and 1875 Land Acts

Year	*Victoria*	*Cowichan and Salt Spring*	*Nanaimo and Comox*	*New Westminster*	*Yale*	*Kamloops*	*Osoyoos*	*Lillooet*	*Kootenay*	*Cariboo*	*Cassiar*	*Total*
1874				5								5
1875				69								69
1876				49								48
1877	1	5	11	110								127
1878		11	21	98	1		3					134
1879	6	2	15	12	1	13		3		1		53
Total	7	18	47	343	2	13	3	3		1		437

24 Appendix B, Table 3.

CHAPTER 3

Provincial Land Policy 1880-1913

A possible reason that the free grant system was abandoned is that the districts in which land was most sought after by settlers had by then been placed under reserve for railway purposes. By Order in Council of August 3, 1878, a forty-mile belt of land from the Yellowhead Pass to tidewater on Burrard Inlet had been reserved, as had a similar belt from Esquimalt to Seymour Narrows. Since extensive areas had also been withdrawn from settlement for use as Indian reserve lands, it seems obvious that insufficient land was available to make the free grant system practicable.

The Chinese problem which was causing so much public agitation in the province found its way into a special act concerning crown lands in 1884. The act made it unlawful for any commissioner of lands or any other person "to issue a pre-emption record of any Crown land, or sell any portion thereof, to any Chinese, [or] grant authority ... to any Chinese to record or divert any water from the natural channel of any stream, lake or river in this Province."[1] The secretary of state for Canada, J. A. Chapleau, wrote to John Robson, provincial secretary, to say that although the act was within the competence of the local legislature, he wondered if perhaps such an act, applying as it did to only one segment of the population, was constitutional, but he was willing to let the courts decide the issue should a case arise.[2]

[1] B.C., *Statutes*, 1884, 47 Vict., c. 2, s.1.

[2] Chapleau to Robson, April 8, 1885, "Correspondence Respecting the Acts Passed by the Legislature ... British Columbia ... 1884," B.C., *Sessional Papers*, 4th Parl., 3d sess., 1885, p. 464.

This same year — 1884 — saw a new land act. Its major provision raised the price of both surveyed and unsurveyed agricultural land from $1.00 to $2.50 an acre. The provision for pastoral leases was removed, but the act provided that "mountainous tracts of land, which are unfit for cultivation and valueless for lumbering purposes, may be purchased at the rate of $1 an acre." To ensure that it was truly waste land, the applicant had to make a statutory declaration to that effect. The chief commissioner of lands and works reserved the right to refuse any such application should he have any reason to doubt the declaration. One dollar remained the price of pre-empted land, and the provision for four equal annual instalments also stood, but the first payment was not due for two years from the date of recording. As formerly, the last payment was not due until the land had been surveyed. Of much greater significance was the provision stating that no more than 640 acres of unsurveyed land might be bought.

Fortunately for those whose applications were already being processed, section 76 of the 1884 Act provided that titles to land applied for under any previous act, although now repealed, could be acquired as if the present act were not passed.[3] A return tabled March 5, 1885, shows that title to 109,959.25 acres was acquired under that clause by 101 applicants. Among these were Thomas Greenhow who secured 3,460 acres, F. G. Vernon who obtained 4,739 acres, T. Harper who profited the most with 12,146 acres, and G. B. Wright who acquired 1,800 acres.[4] Instead of receiving from these four, the $55,362 to which the government would have been entitled under the new rate of $2.50, the treasury was enriched only to the extent of $22,145 at the former rate of $1.00 an acre.

The provisions raising the price of good land and limiting the amount of unsurveyed land that might be purchased show the government's realization that agricultural land was not abundant and was therefore to be conserved. Land transactions had doubled in 1883, largely as a result of the influx of population attendant upon the building of the Canadian Pacific and the Esquimalt and Nanaimo railways. Since the figures issued by the Land Office for 1884 show that land transactions had again doubled in spite of the

3 B.C., *Statutes*, 1884, 47 Vict., c.16.

4 "Return . . . Showing . . . All persons Who . . . Applied . . . to Purchase Lands . . . Prior to the Passing of the Land Act, 1884, . . . Section 76 of the Last-Named Act, and the Number of Acres Obtained by Each Person," B.C., *Sessional Papers*, 4th Parl., 3d sess., 1885, pp. 573-74.

increased price per acre, the wisdom of the new statute becomes obvious. Total land transactions for the two years had increased from 436 in 1882, to 1,847 in 1884, and the total amount deeded increased from 23,609 to 146,197 acres.

The established statutory price of $2.50 an acre was, of course, the minimum price of good land. Desirable lands were still being sold by auction at many times the upset price. For example, a return in 1885 lists all those persons who had bought town lots at auction that November at English Bay. None of the lots was more than one mile from the water; and a total of ninety-eight acres was sold at a net price of $145.84 per acre. Sale expenses amounted to $805.96, and the cost of the survey was estimated at $3,000.[5] This sale was held on the eve of the completion of the Canadian Pacific Railway and this, no doubt, contributed to the advanced price of the lots. Even so, the buyers must have considered a price of $145 an acre extravagant for heavily timbered lots at least fifteen miles from the terminus of the railway at Port Moody.

Two incidents occurred in 1886 and 1887 which well illustrate the great difficulty involved in satisfying everyone claiming favourably situated lands. In the first case, four different settlers wanted to buy the same eighty acres on Lulu Island. Each of these — Hugh Youdall, D. S. Milligan, Hugh Boyd, and James G. Jaques — thought he had a prior claim to the land. Numerous situations of this kind undoubtedly arose each year, but because this involved the integrity of John Robson, provincial secretary and minister of finance and agriculture, questions were asked in the House which resulted in the tabling of an interesting correspondence. Boyd based his claim on a previous conversation ("the Lot I was talking to you about") with his friend, John Robson, in a letter to Robson on July 8, 1886, in which he also wrote, "I would ask you as a great favour to try and get it for me." Youdall based his claim on prior notice given to the local government agent, C. Warwick, of his intention to buy the land as soon as the government reserve on it was removed. His intention, which he had previously discussed with William Smithe, both premier and chief commissioner of lands and works, was to settle on the land five or six families of Newfoundland fisherfolk. Milligan contended that the land should be his by virtue

5 "Return . . . of all Orders in Council and Correspondence Respecting the Land at English Bay and Vicinity, Recently Offered for Sale at Auction by the Government . . . ," B.C., *Sessional Papers*, 4th Parl., 4th sess., 1886, pp. 449-54.

of the letter he had written to Smithe in September making application for the land, adding that "I am prepared to pay for same at once." Jaques, who had been quietly waiting until December 1 when the government reserve was cancelled, appeared, money in hand, at the government office when it opened at nine that morning. His money was refused. He sent a telegram to Smithe at once. "He [Warwick] refused ... saying land already disposed of, and declines to say how. Instruct at once, as I am first purchaser, and I consider I am alone entitled to Crown Grant of such land."

On September 1, however, W. S. Gore, the surveyor general, had notified Warwick that the next issue of the *British Columbia Gazette* would contain a notice cancelling the reserve on the land, subject to the three months' notice required by law, and that after December 1 the land would be open to purchase. "You will, however," he added, "please make a note that a sale is not to be made before you are more particularly instructed from this office." There was no legal basis for Gore's instructions, as Jaques, Youdall, and Boyd well know and which led them to the conclusion that here was nepotism at its worst. W. Norman Bole, solicitor for Jaques, arrived at the same conclusion. It was Bole, elected in 1886 as one of the members from New Westminster district, who asked that all the pertinent correspondence be tabled.

Smithe telegraphed back the same day that he received Jaques's wire to say that the land would be sold at public auction in conformity with the statutory requirement. But this was not to be the easy way out that Robson and Smithe had hoped. Within a week Youdall wrote to Smithe that he could not believe the land was to be auctioned as he was quite prepared to fulfil all the conditions previously agreed upon with regard to his colonization scheme. He said that he had several Newfoundland fishermen already making preparations to come to British Columbia in the spring. With commendable caution he added that "I have been told — what truth there is in it I do not know — that Mr. Robson has been working tooth and nail to get this lot put up at auction, so as to fill some obligations to a Mr. Milligan, who owns 900 acres adjoining, and who dyked in some 30 acres of the lot and used it for a number of years."

A week later Smithe assured Youdall that if indeed he had not dropped his plan for bringing out the fishermen, the government would certainly honour its agreement, but warned Youdall that he would have to pay Milligan $500 for his improvements.[6] Should the Robson papers ever be located, it will be interesting to see if there is not a letter from Robson to Milligan sometime in the week of December 7 to 13, 1886, asking Milligan to set a price on his improvements and to withdraw his claim to the land.

Not to be outmanoeuvered, Bole drew up and presented to Lieutenant Governor Cornwall on December 28 a petition headed "Let right be done," outlining his client's case. But the appeal to the foot of the throne was made in vain. As it was a cash transaction, no further record of the land is found in the *Gazette*. On March 8, 1887, Youdall acquired the land. His certificate of purchase was endorsed as follows:

> This Certificate of Purchase issued pursuant of Mr. Youdall's Agreement to settle five or six families of Newfoundland fishermen upon the land (Sec. 4, B 4 N, R 7 W) and upon the express condition that a Crown Grant will not be issued until Mr. Youdall's said obligation is fulfilled.

That obligation, written into the endorsation on the certificate of purchase, was fulfilled. On January 21, 1890, the five fishermen — James Millis, Joshua Parsons, Thomas William Horne, Robert Gordon, and George Waugh — as well as Youdall himself, wrote to the chief commissioner as follows:

> We the undersigned residents of "Terra Nova" being anxious to secure a Title to our respective homes. The same being parts of Sec. 4, Block 4 North Range Seven West are desirous that a Crown grant of the said Section be issued to Mr. Hugh Youdall.

Less than one month later, the crown grant was issued from the Land Office.[7]

The following letter, concerning a similar case shortly afterward, illustrates not only the complications which arose continually with

[6] Boyd to Robson, July 8, 1886, "Return . . . for Copies of All Correspondence . . . Respecting Section 4, Block 4 North, Range 7 West, New Westminster District . . . ," B.C., *Sessional Papers*, 5th Parl., 1st sess., 1887, p. 339; Warwick to Smithe, August 31, 1886, and enclosure, Youdall to Warwick, August 31, 1886, ibid., pp. 339, 340; Milligan to Smithe, September 24, 1886, ibid., p. 340; Jacques, per Bole, to Smithe, December 1, 1886, ibid., p. 341; Gore to Warwick, September 1, 1886, ibid., p. 340; Smithe to Bole, December 1, 1886, ibid., p. 341; Youdall to Smithe, December 7, 1886, ibid., p. 342; Smithe to Youdall, December 13, 1886, ibid.

[7] The information and quotations pursuant to the certificate of purchase and the crown grant (no. 849, dated February 24, 1890) were supplied by the provincial Lands Department, Victoria, to the author.

regard to lands, but also something of the spirit in which public business was occasionally carried on. Neither of the protagonists in the dispute warrants any sympathy, nor does the client; it must be reserved for Warwick, the same government agent from New Westminster whose task it was to administer the land laws in an impartial manner. An error on his part might have led to serious political difficulties, and it is quite likely that errors both of execution and of judgment were made throughout the province in those early years. Neither nepotism nor patronage was unknown, as Bole's letter to Smithe suggests:

> I beg to call your attention to a most extraordinary circumstance which occurred, as I am informed by Mr. Kelly, in the Land Office here, today. Mr. Philip Kelly, a client of mine, who has pre-empted a piece of land on Burrard Inlet, north of Lot 204, Group 1, New Westminster District, inadvertently placed on the counter of the office a document, referring to said land, signed by one Stalker, and which Mr. Kelly had no intention of parting with, or using. Mr. Warwick's name appeared in the document, and that gentleman seeing the document took it up, and insisted on keeping it, notwithstanding Mr. Kelly's formal demand for the return thereof; Mr. Warwick further remarking "that" (referring to the document in question) "will be sufficient to prove Henderson's claim." Mr. Kelly is, as you are already aware, the *bona fide* pre-emptor of the land in question, while Mr. Henderson is but a speculative purchaser, representing, probably, much bigger individuals in a convenient background. May I trust that you, officially entertain as strong a repugnance to speculative land purchasers as Mr. Robson, on behalf of himself and his colleagues from his place in the House, when discussing the Jaques' claim, as if that gentleman, which I doubt, honestly meant what he said, his Government now has an opportunity of proving their sincerity, and preferring the claim of the *bona fide* settler to the speculative purchaser. I am, therefore, to request that you will direct Mr. Warwick forthwith to return to me, on behalf of Mr. Kelly, the document above referred to. Your refusal to do so I must deem conclusive evidence that your Government are siding with Mr. Henderson against Mr. Kelly, who is determined, however, to exhaust every legal remedy before he surrenders his just rights. May I venture the hope that in expecting an answer of some kind to this letter, that I am not imposing too severe a strain on your official courtesy.

No, Bole could not be counted among Smithe's supporters, nor had he forgiven Robson for having bested him in the Lulu Island land affair. If this was the tenor of official correspondence between one member of the legislature and another, it may well be imagined that in the House there were verbal altercations which, had they been, and were they still, preserved verbatim, would indeed make interesting reading now.

Three days later Surveyor General Gore wrote to Warwick asking for details of the complaint, and Warwick replied the same day, explaining that he had received three separate applications for the land all within a week. On Monday, February 14, J. B. Henderson had applied for the 160 acres in question; by the afternoon mail of the same day Hugh Stalker of Moodyville had applied; and on Friday, February 18, Kelly had applied in person. "I, as a matter of course, informed Mr. Kelly that there were already two applications in for the land in question, and that his application could not be granted." Warwick then explained how at that point Kelly had become "quite hostile," insisting that as he had been occupying and improving the land for the last six months, he was going to have it at whatever cost. At this point Kelly drew from his pocket a letter from Stalker, dated February 7, and addressed to Warwick, in which Stalker had abandoned all claim to the land, saying that he had had no idea Kelly had made permanent improvements on the land. (Warwick did not explain how Kelly had come by the letter, but the logical answer would seem to be that Kelly had gone to Stalker, explained the situation, and received the letter from Stalker for transmission to the government agent.) As Kelly was about to leave the Land Office with the letter, Warwick said that he asked for it on the grounds that it belonged, not to Kelly, but to the office files. After an argument, Kelly agreed to leave it, and Warwick then offered to see Henderson when he returned to town in a few days' time and to ask him to withdraw his application in favour of Kelly. At this, Kelly had seemed satisfied, but in a few minutes he returned to the office accompanied by one of Bole's clerks and made an unsuccessful attempt to retrieve the letter. Warwick did, however, permit the clerk to make a copy. Finally, Warwick could report to Gore than on the next day he had seen Henderson, who had agreed to withdraw, and that a record for the land had then been issued to Kelly. This had cleared up the entire difficulty to everyone's satisfaction.

Apparently this long and diplomatic letter from Warwick containing all the details had been intended to be the official answer, and for that reason confirmed itself to a bare recital of the facts. In a separate letter of the same date, Warwick briefly outlined what had led to the difficulty:

> The whole trouble in connection with the land ... originated in Mr. Bole's office.
>
> It appears Kelly left instructions with Mr. Bole some months ago to file his application when the land in question came into market, that is, on the expiration of the timber lease within which the land was situated.
>
> Previous to the land coming into market Mr. Kelly had occasion to go up the coast, and on his return, about the 17th inst., found that his instructions had not received any attention. Hence the trouble.

Armed with the facts as reported by his official in New Westminster, Smithe answered Bole's letter.

> Having received the report ... I find that the occurrence to which you are pleased to allude as a "most extraordinary circumstance" consisted simply in Mr. Warwick's most commendable determination to retain possession of a letter which, though addressed to himself, was not his personal property, but belonged to the archives of the office of which he is in charge.
>
> I also find that Mr. Warwick showed very proper courtesy in allowing your clerk to take a copy ... in the interest of your client, Mr. Kelly; but it seems to have been convenient to you to omit mention of that circumstance when preferring your complaint.
>
> In view of the fact that Mr. Warwick did nothing more than his duty in retaining possession of the letter in question, that he went beyond the requirements of official duty and succceeded in arranging the matter in the interest of your client, I can only characterize the charge brought by you against that officer as frivolous, if not something worse.
>
> It is more difficult to find words in which to convey adequate censure of the tone of discourtesy — perhaps insolence would be the more appropriate expression — which pervades your letter; and this appears all the more inexcusable in the light of Mr. Warwick's explanatory note, to the effect that Mr. Kelly's troubles were the result of your own professional lackes [*sic*] in not having attended to his instructions at the proper time.
>
> This is not the first time I have received a letter from you of a character undeserving of a reply; and I have to request that in any future correspondence with this Department you will endeavour, as far as may be in your power, to observe those rules of politeness common among gentlemen.[8]

[8] Bole to Smithe, February 18, 1887, "Return ... for ... All Correspondence ... Having Reference to a Piece of Land on the North Side of Burrard Inlet and ... North of Lot 204, Group 1, New Westminister District," B.C. *Sessional Papers*, 5th Parl., 1st sess., 1887, p. 423; Gore to Warwick, February 21, 1887, ibid.; Warwick to Gore, February 23, 1887, ibid., p.

A discreet silence should now have fallen over the entire affair, but an election was in the offing. Without awaiting a reply, Smithe published his own letter. This action was later characterized by Bole as a "mean and spiteful way by which Mr. Robson, through you, is trying to get even on me for my part in the debate of the 10th March, 1887, when, in the discharge of my public duty, I had occasion to make some severe remarks on the conduct of the Provincial Secretary." Bole denied the charge that he had been neglecting his professional duties, and told Smithe that he, as neither a slave nor follower of the government, intended to exercise his own judgment as to the best method by which official correspondence should be conducted, "even with so high and mighty an individual as the Chief Commissioner of Lands and Works," because "whatever other claims you may have to distinction, I was unaware that you claimed to be considered the Government Chesterfield."[9]

When the public accounts were submitted to the legislature late in the fall of 1887, Bole voted in favour of James Orr's motion of censure against Robson for having dispensed patronage with a lavish hand in the New Westminster riding the previous summer. The contention was that, while travelling through the district soliciting votes, Robson had given orders for the expenditure of large sums on public works, and that while he was provincial secretary, and minister of mines, agriculture, and finance, he had acted as if he were also the chief commissioner of lands and works, and that the accounts showed his orders had been honoured by the Lands Department. Robson's accusers appear to have put together

---

424; the letter produced by Kelly, Stalker to Warwick, February 7, 1887, ibid.; Warwick to Gore, February 23, 1887, ibid., p. 425; Smithe to Bole, March 5, 1887, ibid.

Robson presented this correspondence to the House, March 15, 1887. B.C., *Journals*, 5th Parl., 1st sess., 1887, p. 46.

9 Bole to Smithe, March 24, 1887, "Return to an Order ... Directing the Chief Commissioner of Lands and Works to Send Down ... a Copy of a Letter ... Respecting Philip Kelly's Claim to Certain Land ...," B.C., *Sessional Papers*, 5th Parl., 1st sess., 1887, p. 489. (This order was granted on a motion by W. M. D. Ladner, senior MLA for New Westminster, April 6, 1887, and Robson complied by presenting the letter to the House that same day. B.C., *Journals*, 5th Parl., 1st sess., 1887, p. 89.)

In this same letter, Bole made the charge that Robson was the real writer of the letter of March 5, 1887 (see note 8, Smithe to Bole), although the signature was Smithe's. This may well be the truth as Smithe, re-elected in July, 1886, was too ill to take his seat during the 1887 session and, indeed, died in March of that year.

a good case but when the vote was taken, the motion was defeated fifteen to eight.[10]

However much indignation Bole could show at patronage, he was quite willing to avail himself of the liberal land law in order to acquire extensive tracts of public land. In 1889 he made application to purchase one block of 8,400 and another of 1,600 acres of pastoral land in the Osoyoos district.[11] Land of this type, providing it were "mountainous" and unfit either for cultivation or lumbering, could still be had in unlimited quantities for one dollar an acre, and there was no requirement other than that it should be surveyed. As chairman of a select committee in 1887 on the sale of timber lands, Bole had introduced some sweeping changes with regard to limiting the size of timber leases, but the assembly did not consider it necessary to alter the requirements under which surveyed agricultural or pastoral land could be obtained.

No further significant changes were made in the land act until 1888 when a further amendment was enacted and an extensive consolidation made. Land was now classified as first or second class. The former was land suitable for cultivation, lumbering, or hay meadows and was priced as formerly at $2.50 an acre; the latter, land unsuitable for any of these purposes and also priced as previously at $1.00 an acre.

The second important change concerned hay leases and indicated the growing importance of the cattle industry. Whereas animals and and their produce had not merited inclusion in the export statistics of 1872, by 1891 the value of such produce had increased to $346,159, third only to mines and fisheries, and ahead of timber products by $20,000. By 1891 there were 251,367 head of livestock in the province for which 102,146 tons of hay were cut. Cattle raising in the interior had become big business. The change in the land act in 1888 with regard to hay leases was made in order to reflect the actual situation. It provided that if there were two or more applicants for the same hay lease, then bids must be tendered and the bidder who submitted the highest cash bonus was to receive the lease.[12] As amendments to the act were not added until after circumstances had made them necessary, this change reveals clearly

10 B.C., *Journals*, 5th Parl., 1st sess., 1887, p. 43.

11 *British Columbia Gazette*, January 3, 1887, p. 4.

12 B.C., *Statutes*, 1888, 51 Vict., c. 16, s. 9.

that cattle raising was one of the major industries of the province by this time.

A glance at the application for land in the *British Columbia Gazette* for the years 1888 to 1891 shows that it was during this period that many of the "landed" families of the province acquired most of their holdings. Although at the time some of the land was good only for pasturage, subsequent irrigation developments have increased the value of the land many times over. In the 1889 *Gazette* the name of Judge Bole is not the only one to appear more than once as acquiring surveyed acreages. Cornelius O'Keefe was applying for a further 808 acres at the head of Okanagan Lake; Samuel L. Robins of the Vancouver Coal Company at Nanaimo was applying for 30,000 acres on the west coast of Vancouver Island, as was also Judge M. W. Tyrwhitt Drake; and J. S. Chase and others were asking for 20,480 acres in the Kootenay district. The application for the greatest acreage came from John Irving, R. P. Rithet, James A. Laidlaw, and James Carrall, all of Victoria, who together applied for 65,920 acres in Rupert district, in northern British Columbia. The pages listing these names throughout the year read like a *Who's Who* for the province. Among others, D. M. Eberts, J. C. MacLure, Thomas Earle, and John Bryden were, or were to become, prominent in provincial affairs. Certificates of purchase for 1889 increased 63 per cent from the year before, and the total acreage deeded increased 42 per cent, but both the number of pre-emption records and certificates of improvement decreased.[13] These figures suggest that in the alienation of public lands, new settlers were running a poor second to established residents bent on acquiring more land, possibly for personal use but more probably, for speculative purposes. No doubt many of these shrewd men, influential in the affairs of the province, foresaw the imminent end to unrestricted buying of large acreages at cheap prices.

Restrictions and price increases came into effect, in fact, in the Land Act of 1891. To reduce the amount of speculation, a limit was placed on the amount of surveyed land that might be purchased. Henceforth 640 acres was to be the limit of land that might be bought, *whether surveyed or unsurveyed*. As was true since 1884, no land was to be bought before it had been surveyed and the survey had been approved. From now on, however, the provincial land surveyor was to classify land as first, second, or third class. Agricul-

[13] See Appendix B, Table 5.

tural, hay, and timber lands, as before, were to be designated first-class land, but now they were worth five dollars an acre. Agricultural lands requiring irrigation or drainage were to be sold as second-class land at $2.50 an acre. "Mountainous and rocky tracts wholly unfit for agricultural purposes" which could not "under any reasonable conditions" be brought under cultivation were now classed as third-class land and still priced at one dollar an acre. Neither second- nor third-class land was to contain more than 5,000 feet of timber per acre. Only when the chief commissioner of lands and works was satisfied that the land had been correctly classified and the applicant had paid the cost of surveying plus the full purchase price, was the sale to be allowed. Even then, the proceedings were to be cancelled if the applicant had not completed all requirements within six months after making his original application accompanied by 10 per cent of the purchase price. To make doubly sure that speculation was halted, this section specified that no person might secure any other land until he had been in occupation of his first purchase for two years and had effected permanent improvements thereon of $5.00, $2.50, or $1.00 an acre for first-, second-, and third-class land, respectively. Land which was actually cultivated was to be considered as improved, and it came to be generally accepted that the running of a specified number of cattle per acre on the land constituted improvement.[14] Although the increase in deeded acreage appeared to have reached a high point in 1892 — 309,878 acres — and was not to be so high again until 1897, this figure was actually a reflection of the fact that many applications made the previous fall under the former act were only then being processed in Victoria. Not until 1894 did the drastic reductions effected in deeded acreage under the Amendment of 1891 show up in official records. In 1894 only 47,167 acres were alienated, but this decrease was, in part, also a reflection of the severe depression then prevailing throughout America and Europe. Land sales in 1894 accounted for only $33,917 of the provincial income, whereas in 1890, $244,529 had been received from this source. It seems clear from this sharp drop in revenue that the 1891 Amendment did satisfactorily achieve its purpose of reducing speculation.

By a further amendment in 1892 pre-emptions of forty- and eighty-acre lots were once again authorized. This figure was reduced again in 1894 to permit the leasing of twenty-acre lots on land

[14] B.C., *Statutes*, 1891, 54 Vict., c. 15, s. 4.

surveyed and subdivided for the sole purpose of personal occupation and cultivation. The lease was good for five years, but if the annual rental of the value of the land as determined by the chief commissioner were paid regularly for those five years, and if a house were built on the lot the first year and all other residence and improvement qualifications fulfilled, the lessee was then to receive a crown grant to the lot.[15]

In January of 1895 an accounting of all crown grants issued in the province, for whatever reason, from January 1, 1880, to the end of 1894, was called for by the Legislative Assembly. It was to show the name of the grantee, the acreage, the method by which the land had been obtained, and the district in which the grant was situated. The reply tabled on February 5 by G. B. Martin, chief commissioner, is interesting:

> The Return called for covers a period of 15 years, during which time some 5,400 Crown grants have been issued.
>
> To prepare such a Return will necessitate repeated reference to all the numerous Land Registers in the office of Lands and Works, and will involve considerable expense.
>
> The Return will cover over 350 pages of foolscap and will form a volume nearly as large as the Sessional Papers.
>
> It is not apparent that such a Return is a matter of public interest or value. Any Member wishing for particular information as to the issue of Crown grants can always ascertain what he desires by applying at the Land Office.[16]

Getting down to more manageable business, Beaven introduced an amendment to the land act in the 1895 session which reduced the size of pre-emptions east of the Cascades from 320 to 160 acres. Hoping to capitalize on the rapidly increasing activities apparent in the Kootenays, the government now permitted settlers east of the Cascades to buy 320 acres of waste crown land adjoining their locations at one dollar an acre.[17]

In view of the numerous changes which had been made in the land act since its consolidation in 1888, another consolidation was made in 1896, but there was only one important change having to do with agricultural land. As land subsidies were being granted to many of the railway companies who applied for them, the prov-

15 B.C., *Statutes*, 1892, 55 Vict., c. 25, s. 2; B.C., *Statutes*, 1894, 57 Vict., c. 24, s. 2.

16 "Memorandum," B.C., *Sessional Papers*, 7th Parl., 1st sess., 1894-95, p. 667.

17 B.C., *Statutes*, 1895, 58 Vict., c. 27, s. 9.

ince determined to reap some benefit from this development by returning to the principle of reserving one-quarter of the lots in any crown-granted land subdivided into town lots. When Douglas had reported a similar procedure to Lytton in connection with lots in New Westminster, he had been ordered to rescind the provision immediately. Now, however, the province was to reap a rich harvest from its share of these town lots. At the same time, the deposit accompanying applications to purchase lands was increased to 25 per cent, and prospective pre-emptors were warned that no pre-emptions would be granted for other than agricultural purposes and that neither certificates of improvement, nor crown grants, would be issued until ten acres, at least, had been brought under cultivation.[18]

From 1896 until the end of the century all types of land transactions showed a marked increase as a result, particularly, of railway construction and mining activity in the Kootenays. Throughout the entire decade preceding 1900, however, the Okanagan Valley regularly accounted for from 25 to 50 per cent of all pre-emption records in the province, and — an indication of the serious intentions of the residents of the Okanagan — more certificates of improvement were issued for that area than for any other district in the province. In 1900, of the 113 certificates issued, 58 went to Osoyoos land district which embraced the whole of the Okanagan Valley from the border to Enderby. But in the entire province for any one of the years during the 1890's, five or six times as many certificates of purchase were issued as were certificates of improvement. The Kootenays showed by far the greatest number both of certificates of purchase and of crown grants. Six hundred and twenty of the 1,101 certificates of purchase issued in 1900 were for lands in the Kootenays.

Although an extensive consolidation of the land act was made in 1897, no significant changes were made until 1908, when a completely new act was written, designed to incorporate changes in the industrial pattern of the province. One such change, for instance, is reflected in a return for 1903 which shows that of the 10,032,700 acres under government reserve, every tenth acre was being reserved for applicants for pulp leases.[19] Since the 1908 Act

18 B.C., *Statutes*, 1896, 59 Vict., c. 28, s. 13.

19 "Return ... for ... Every Reserve ... of Provincial Lands Now in Force, Stating the Purpose for Which Each Reserve is Made ...," B.C., *Sessional Papers*, 9th Parl., 4th sess., 1903, p. J23.

found its way with very few changes into the revised edition of the statutes in 1911, the edition in effect in 1913, its major provisions are significant.

First of all, since the work of the chief commissioner of lands and works had become exceedingly onerous, a separation of his duties was effected. Since 1871, the work of the chief commissioner had increased to the point where he found himself responsible for such diverse matters as roads, bridges, government buildings, water rights, drainage and irrigation works, maps and surveys, and government lands — agricultural, timber, mineral, and coal. On all of these he was required to make a yearly report. From 1908 on there were to be both a minister of lands and a minister of public works. Thomas Taylor became the first minister of public works and Price Ellison became the first minister of lands.

Under the 1908 Act an innovation to permit the pre-emption of surveyed and subdivided lots not exceeding forty acres for bona fide personal occupation and cultivation was introduced.[20] This provision was made as a result of repeated complaints from J. H. Turner, agent general for British Columbia in London, that he had had to discourage a good many of those intending to emigrate who wanted a smaller allotment than was allowed under the existing pre-emption regulations. In his 1904 report to Premier McBride he had said that:

> A large proportion of the inquirers from the agricultural parts of Britain are very desirous for information as to the possibility of obtaining small holdings in British Columbia on easy terms, and if there was any provision of that nature hundreds would emigrate and take advantage of it.[21]

Apparently the 1894 arrangement for five-year leases of twenty-acre lots did not satisfy these would-be immigrants.

Pre-emptions of surveyed or unsurveyed crown land were still not to exceed 160 acres, and were to be obtained at one dollar an acre. After two years of continuous personal occupation and after making improvements of $2.50 an acre, the pre-emptor was to receive his crown grant. The restriction to one claim at one time was still to hold good. In this year, 1908, the category "third-class

[20] B.C., *Statutes*, 1908, 8 Edw. 7, c. 30, s. 10.

[21] British Columbia, Office of the Agent General for British Columbia, London, Eng., "First and Second Reports ... 1902-03," B.C., *Sessional Papers*, 10th Parl., 1st sess., 1903-1904, p. G45.

land" was abolished, but the other two classifications were retained. First-class land, suitable for agricultural purposes, now cost ten dollars an acre — a doubling of land prices since 1891 — and second-class land, five. In addition, the minister reserved the right to increase the price on either class should he so decide.

Timber lands were now defined as lands containing 5,000 feet of milling timber per acre east of the Cascades and 8,000 feet west, and they were no longer for sale for agricultural purposes. No purchase of any land might exceed 640 acres nor be below 40 acres. No second purchase was to be permitted until the previous one had been completed and improvements to the extent of three dollars an acre made. Cultivation constituted improvement. Hay leases were still available, and Chinese were still not allowed to pre-empt or buy land.[22]

In 1908, the year this act was passed, 1,535 pre-emptions were filed, and the surveys amounted to 66,788 acres. The 2,438 certificates of purchase accounted for another 147,980 acres, an average of 60 acres per purchase. Only 1,667 crown grants were issued, and, as usual, the number of certificates of improvement lagged far behind at 256. Cash received for purchased land, due to go up 400 per cent in the next two years, amounted to $548,036.[23]

A radical departure from established practice was made in 1911 when all unsurveyed lands along the rights of way of the Canadian Northern and Grand Trunk Pacific railroads were reserved but with the requirement that any land taken out of these reserves after it had been surveyed by the government must be disposed of by public auction. In this way the government secured to itself some of the increase in price caused by the inflation resulting from railway construction and escaped having to sell the land at the minimum prices provided for in the act. The second reason for the reserving of these lands was to make some belated attempt to regulate settlement throughout the districts served by the railways. By forcing settlement into those areas already surveyed, it was felt that the new settler could establish himself more easily. For many years the scattered settlements had constituted a grave communications problem for the government. In placing the reservation on

22 B.C., *Statutes*, 1908, 8 Edw. 7, c. 30.

23 B.C., Department of Lands and Works, "Report of the Chief Commissioner ... 1907-08," B.C., *Sessional Papers*, 11th Parl., 3d sess., 1909, p. H58. The figures relating to acreage surveyed may be found in Appendix B, Table 7.

these lands, the government realized that temporarily its revenue would drop, but hoped to be able to recoup its losses within a very short time as land within the reserve was surveyed and released for sale by auction. It was anticipated that within two years at most, 1,500,000 acres of reasonably good land would be available for sale.

In the same report, hope was derived from the fact that 624 certificates of improvement had been issued for 1911, as against 439 for 1910. The remark that "these figures are interesting in that they disclose the *bona fides* of the pre-emptor rather than the issuance of the certificate of pre-emption record"[24] pin-points the weakness of the entire pre-emption system. Without government inspectors it was easy to exploit the land for the two, three, or four years allowed and then to acquire it by purchase at the lower pre-emption price without making the required improvements. For the period 1871 to 1913 there were 34,216 pre-emption records, but only 7,811 certificates of improvement were issued.[25] Part of the discrepancy can be accounted for by the fact that a good many pre-emptors chose to pay for their survey and for the land without waiting the full period allowed under the statute and, in this case they would have received a certificate of purchase, not one of improvement. No doubt a large number of pre-emptions were simply abandoned and many others were never "proved-up."

To provide some check on claims, authority was provided at the next legislative session to appoint pre-emption inspectors whose job it was to examine, and report on, the compliance of the pre-emptors with residence and improvement requirements under the land act.[26] By 1913 Robert A. Renwick, deputy minister, was able to report to William R. Ross, minister of lands, that:

> The Department has taken up the closer supervision of pre-emptors and pre-emptions with a view to securing due performance, on the part of the pre-emptor, of the requirements of the

[24] B.C., Department of Lands, "Report of the Minister of Lands ... 1911," B.C., *Sessional Papers*, 12th Parl., 3d sess., 1912, pp. G5-6. Land sales had fallen from 2,000,000 acres in 1910 to 900,000 in 1911 (ibid., p. G5) but this drop is not reflected in Tables 5 and 6, Appendix B, because it is not possible to determine what mineral, railway, or coal sales are included in the minister's total figure.

[25] See Appendix B, Tables 1 and 2. Note that statistics for 1871 and 1872 are not given in the tables because they were not presented in sufficient detail to tabulate with the more detailed figures of later years, but they are included in the totals in the text above.

[26] B.C., *Statutes*, 1912, 2 Geo. 5, c. 16, s. 12.

"Land Act" as to residence. On this work, one Inspector of Pre-emptions was in the field for several months, effecting a fairly complete examination of the pre-emptions throughout two agencies. His reports justify his employment, as in a great number of instances it was found pre-emptors were availing themselves of the privileges conferred by this part of the "Land Act" for the sole purpose of securing title by cash payment at the rate of $1. per acre with scant regard to the Statute requirement as to occupation. It is the intention to have a number of Pre-emption Inspectors in the field during the present year.[27]

As was to be expected, the innovation was welcomed by those who were honestly trying to comply with the requirements of the law and whole-heartedly resented by those whose efforts were directed toward holding the land under pre-emption record with complete disregard for the residence and improvement requirements. H. Cathcart, superintendent of the inspection branch, and his five inspectors visited 1,497 pre-emptions during 1913, of which 819 were found occupied and in the course of improvement; 660 pre-emptors were notified that they must conform more closely to the statutory provisions, and 222 pre-emptions were cancelled and reopened to settlement. The inspections undoubtedly encouraged the genuine settlers and served to convince the delinquents that they must either conform or make way for settlers who were prepared to do so. In his first report, Cathcart expressed the hope that by the end of 1914 his branch would have covered the entire province. He was furnishing the department with a formal report on every pre-emption claim in the province in which the details of occupation, of improvement or improvements, and the value of these, were to be listed. As each report was to be attached to each individual file, the long-standing confusion over the exact status of such pre-emption claims would be terminated. Where inspection indicated that the settler was delinquent, he was to be given sixty days in which to show cause why his record should not be cancelled. Failure to do so would result in immediate cancellation of the claim. Whenever it was apparent that the settlers were making a genuine attempt to live up to the spirit of the law even though seeking employment off their claims in order to earn a living, Cathcart instructed his men to be as lenient as possible by confining

[27] B.C., Department of Lands, "Report of the Deputy Minister of Lands [1912]," B.C., *Sessional Papers*, 13th Parl., 1st sess., 1913, p. D8.

their admonitions to a reminder to live up more closely to the contracted obligations.[28]

As a special condition written into the agreement with the railway company gave the province a half interest in many of the townsites being developed along the Grand Trunk Pacific, these inspectors were called upon to select the government lots in them. Squatters presented their greatest difficulty. In addition to these tasks, it also fell to them to clear and dispose of government lots by public auction in Point Grey, Kitsilano, and Hastings. After paying $380 an acre to have the 9.6 acres in Kitsilano cleared, the inspectors sold the 96 lots at an average price of $914. In Hastings, 59.4 acres were cleared at $225 an acre; for the 128 lots sold, the average price obtained was $1,162. These lots were sold by auction on May 20, 1913. During the summer, the 122 acres in Point Grey bounded by English Bay, Alma Road, Tenth Avenue and Crown Street were cleared, but only 10 blocks of 16 lots each were sold at the auction held November 3. Although the returns were not then all in, Cathcart reported that thus far $240,000 had been received from the sale, indicating that even then a house in Point Grey was likely to prove expensive.

The previous year the second sale of government townsite lots along the Grand Trunk Pacific had been held at Prince Rupert. A most successful sale it had been, completely vindicating the 1896 decision to incorporate in the Land Act provision for the reservation of one-quarter of all such lots to the government. In 1909 at the first sale, 1,346 lots had sold for $765,191, an average of $570 a lot; but at the 1912 sale, at which only 282 lots were sold, $1,192,475 was realized, an average price per lot of $4,228.

With three railroads being built — the Grand Trunk Pacific to Prince Rupert, the Canadian Northern down from the Yellowhead Pass to Vancouver, and the Pacific Great Eastern northward to Quesnel — the government might well have taken some comfort in contemplation of its holdings of town lots and might have looked for a material increase in the provincial revenue. Unfortunately, a depression intervened in 1913, and the war began the next year. Land purchases fell off from a total of over 1,000,000 acres in 1912 to less than half that amount in 1913, with a decrease in revenue for the same two years of over $1,500,000. But having embarked

[28] B.C., Department of Lands, "Report of the Inspection Branch [1912]," B.C., *Sessional Papers*, 13th Parl., 2d sess., 1914, pp. D15-16.

on an ambitious plan for assisting and directing settlement, the government was pleased that, despite falling sales, pre-emptions had increased over 50 per cent for the year. The outstanding increase from 2,383 pre-emptions in 1911 to 3,655 in 1912 was largely accounted for by settlers having been enticed into the areas served by the two new transcontinental railroads, but the government was now fully prepared for these settlers.

Having kept abreast of the requirements in the way of adequate surveys of lands previously set aside for pre-emption entry, the government was securing data on the adaptability of various sections of the province to different agricultural pursuits. By means of pamphlets and adequate maps the Department of Lands could inform any settler of the type of land to be found where he proposed to locate. For those who wanted to buy land, its average selling price, including the cost of survey, was now $6.00 an acre, which compared very favourably with the average price of $12.68 an acre being charged by the Canadian Pacific and by large land-holding companies throughout the rest of Canada.[29]

For the final year before the war there was a marked falling off in land revenues. Much of the drop was accounted for by the transference of $1,000,000 to the newly established Forestry Department in 1912. Because of the "financial stringency prevailing," there was a noticeable decrease in land activities. Sales fell off rapidly because of the department's decision to hold no further auctions during the period of depression. It was expected that the deficit would be overcome when the Grand Trunk Pacific was completed later in the year. In the spring lots had been sold in Prince George for about $1,000 cash.[30]

Thus at the end of 1913 provincial land legislation was such that it had the effect Lytton had envisaged for it in 1858. Town lots were being sold by public auction in order to capitalize on local land booms, and at such prices that even if the lots were being bought for speculation, the government had no cause for complaint. Land for settlement by pre-emptors was being surveyed before it was made available to settlers. Immediate cash payment in full was being required from purchasers. Speculation in country lands was being forestalled by the upper limit of 640 acres placed on sale

[29] "Report of the Deputy Minister of Lands [1912]," pp. D7-8.

[30] B.C., Department of Lands, "Report of the Deputy Minister of Lands [1913]," B.C., *Sessional Papers*, 13th Parl., 2d sess., 1914, p. D7.

of crown lands. No unreasonable impediment to pre-emption was placed in the way of settlers whose desire to fulfil their pre-emption obligations was sincere. Better still, although no systematic classification for agricultural purposes was being made during the survey of land held under government reserves, the Department of Lands was now fairly launched on a program of directing settlement into areas where the settler would at least have the benefit of railway outlets for what produce he might grow.

For its programme to have been of maximum benefit, however, the Department of Lands should have insisted that its surveyors carefully classify the land surveyed with a view to its agricultural potential. Paid as they were on an acreage basis, and in all probability not too well qualified to make such classifications in any event, the surveyors were not inclined to differentiate between good and bad farm land. In British Columbia, where soil conditions are so variable, a much more detailed examination of the land should have been required by surveyors than was given in any field notes sent to the Land Office. The result was that in many instances settlers took up lands totally unsuited for agriculture. Because pre-emptors were usually men of limited financial means and frequently of equally limited experience in the selection of lands, it should have been manifest that it was the government's responsibility to safeguard them from wasting their time, money, and energy on marginal land. The sincere settler who was willing to spend his life in turning the wilderness into a productive farm might reasonably have felt entitled at least to good land. Rather than leave the choice of location to the settler himself, with his limited knowledge of the country, the government should have accepted the responsibility. But since it did not, anyone who cares to look may find the ruins of hundreds of abandoned homesteads in any one of a number of valleys in British Columbia, some perched on mountainsides, others on benches, and still others beside small creeks, all deserted because the cost of clearing was excessive, the soil was unproductive, or no market was available.

Between 1859 and 1913 then, the wheel had gone full circle in certain aspects of land legislation. The pre-emption price of four shillings twopence established on Vancouver Island in 1861 by Douglas was not far removed from the one dollar per acre charged pre-emptors from 1870 to 1913. Deferred payments, allowed by Douglas, were still allowed in 1913. Douglas, too, had restricted pre-emptions to 160 acres, a provision to which the provincial government returned in 1908. Thus it can be seen that though changes in the act from 1860 to 1913 in regard to pre-emptions were numerous, comparatively few had any significance.

Changes in the act with respect to purchasing government land outright were perhaps more significant. From 1871 an almost steady increase in price per acre is apparent. By 1871 the original price of ten shillings had been reduced to four shillings twopence and then to one dollar an acre. But in 1884 it was raised to $2.50 for all except "mountainous tracts," which still cost only $1.00. In 1891 price of first class land became $5.00, with second class at $2.50, and third class at $1.00 an acre. Finally in 1908 the best land was selling at $10.00, second class at $5.00, and the category of third class was abandoned altogether. At this time it was specified that the minister of lands could increase the price of any land if he so wished. The many changes in the act from year to year chiefly regulated whether payments were to be cash or deferred, and whether land must be surveyed or not before payment was made. If the settler had the money, the amount of Crown land that could be bought outright in 1871 was unlimited. In 1884 the first limits were imposed when the amount of unsurveyed government land that could be bought was limited to 640 acres. In 1891 came the one big restriction on outright purchase — no more than 640 acres could be purchased, whether surveyed or not, nor could a second purchase be made until the first had been occupied for two years and improvements made equal to the original cost of the land. These limits were still in effect in 1913.

Certain motives become clear at each stage of provincial policy in the disposal of agricultural lands. When Douglas realized in 1860 that his ordinance of the previous year dealing only with the sale of land could not meet the requirements of miners who had been unsuccessful in their search for gold, he instituted the pre-emption system. With minor alterations, the privilege of pre-emption remained permanently in effect, its purpose being to make land readily available at a nominal charge to bona fide settlers. The charge of one dollar an acre was levied in an attempt to forestall speculation only, never as a means of raising revenue.

By 1875, when government morale was at its lowest point owing to the non-fulfilment of article 11 of the Terms of Union, and when the province was competing for immigrants with eastern Canada and the United States, free grants were instituted, only to be abandoned in 1879 when the actual construction of the Canadian Pacific was well under way. The year before its completion in 1885, when immigrants became more numerous, and there was a sharp increase in the demand for land, the upset price was raised to $2.50, although no change was made in the pre-emption price. In 1891 the further rise in price to five dollars and the 640-acre limitation placed on any type of land that could be bought showed the continuing trend. After the turn of the century, as a result of the promotional activities of the agent general in London, the provincial Bureau of Information in Victoria, and the numerous land companies, the demand for public lands rose to its highest point,[31] and the price of land was raised again, this time to ten dollars for good farming land, and more severe limitations were placed on the quantity that could either be bought or pre-empted.

By 1913 the government had realized finally that good farm land in British Columbia was not inexhaustible and that it had an obligation to settlers to direct them away from isolated areas and onto land which would be served at least by railway communication. Thus the problem confronting the government by the end of 1913 was not the increased alienation of agricultural land, but the development of the lands already granted.

31 Some indication of the increasing interest in lands in the province can be gained from the fact that in 1890 the Department of Lands received 4,168 letters; by 1900, the figure was 12,943, and in 1910, a total of 37,188 queries was received — an average of 100 letters a day for every day of the year. Appendix B, Table 5.

CHAPTER 4

Land Surveys

Many of the problems of land disposal in British Columbia before 1913 arose from the ever-present difficulty of having the land surveyed before pre-emption or settlement. Although Douglas's intentions with regard to surveying the vacant lands of the colony were of the best, he was unsuccessful in practice. It was his intention — indicated in a letter to Lord Stanley of the Colonial Office — to survey the land before opening it for settlement. This survey he considered to be a "measure of obvious necessity."[1] To facilitate this operation, Lytton informed Douglas on July 31, 1858, that he was sending out a detachment of the Royal Engineers, whose most important task was "to survey those parts of the country which may be considered most suitable for settlement." At the same time, Lytton said that it would only be "reasonable and proper" to expect private individuals buying land to pay for the cost of survey.[2] This practice differed from that in other Canadian provinces. In discussing the most urgent demands upon the public revenue of the colony, Lytton listed police, absolutely necessary officials, public works to facilitate landing and travelling, and, above all, surveying. In citing for Douglas what he considered to be the guiding principles for the disposal of public lands, Lytton emphasized the value of not selling land "beyond the limits of what is either surveyed or ready for immediate survey."[3] Douglas acted upon this principle

[1] Douglas to Stanley, June 10, 1858, no. 2, Gt. Brit., *Papers Relative to British Columbia*, 1:14.

[2] Lytton to Douglas, July 31, 1858, no. 6, ibid., p. 45.

[3] Lytton to Douglas, August 14, 1858, no. 8, ibid., p. 48; Lytton to Douglas, August 14, 1858, no. 9, ibid., p. 49.

without delay by sending the Royal Engineers to the mainland to survey "all the open districts of land on Fraser's River, so that the country may be laid out for immediate settlement and occupation."[4]

The theory of requiring lands to be surveyed before sale was excellent. In practice, Douglas soon discovered that it would not work, for development of the colony would have been seriously impeded and squatting on government lands would have become widespread. On January 12, 1860, Douglas was compelled to confess to the Colonial Office that since the surveys could not begin to keep pace with the demand for land, he had authorized the preemption of 160 acres of unsurveyed crown land intended for agricultural purposes, subject to a charge of ten shillings an acre at the time of survey.[5] The same regulation with regard to surveying was in effect in 1913:

> Any pre-emptor of unsurveyed land shall have the land recorded by him surveyed at his own expense (subject, however, to a rectification of boundaries) within five years from the date of the pre-emption recorded by a surveyor approved of and acting under instructions from the Minister.[6]

By the end of 1858 "a few thousand acres" in the immediate neighbourhood of Victoria had been surveyed. By the end of 1860, 175,000 acres had been completed and divided into 100-acre lots on Vancouver Island, and 41,000 acres of valuable delta lands at the mouth of the Fraser River had been laid out in 160-acre blocks in conformity with the system adopted in the United States.[7] The surveys on Vancouver Island were not done by the Royal Engineers, and were subsequently found to be very incomplete; checks on those made by the Engineers on the mainland revealed that their work required no corrections of any kind.

Between 1860 and 1871 only insignificant sums were appropriated by the colonial government for surveys; most of the work that was completed was done on Indian reserves and a few preemption claims. Large tracts of land for timber cutting and pastoral purposes were surveyed, but the cost of these surveys was borne entirely by the lessees. The colonial government, with an empty treasury, was confronted with the task of surveying an area

[4] Douglas to Lytton, May 23, 1859, no. 11, ibid., 3:12.

[5] Douglas to Newcastle, January 12, 1860, no. 35, ibid., p. 90.

[6] B.C., *Revised Statutes*, 1911, 1 Geo. 5, c. 129, s. 25.

[7] "Report of the Chief Commissioner of Lands and Works . . . 1873," pp. 54-55.

considerably larger than any one of the prairie provinces. Moreover, the land was so rugged as to make a systematic survey of the whole practically impossible, particularly as much of it was covered with a growth of timber which rendered the country absolutely inaccessible, even to packhorses. Members of survey parties had to pack their own supplies. After the arrival of the Royal Engineers, provision was made for the office of surveyor general. Colonel Moody was the first of a succession of surveyors general who tried to do what they could with the meagre resources at their disposal, but found that the annual appropriation for the purpose was grossly inadequate to meet the demands of the developing province.

After 1871, the importance of surveying the public lands in some uniform way was recognized by every government, but, even in 1873, Beaven, then chief commissioner of lands and works, was complaining that the $10,000 voted in 1872 was "totally inadequate." In addition to a lack of funds, the department was seriously hampered in its work by the acute shortage of properly trained surveyors. The provision contained in section 10 of the 1870 Land Ordinance permitting the surveyor to survey lands "by such motes and bounds [as] he may think proper" and the absence of a trained corps of surveyors resulted in the Crown granting isolated blocks of land of which the position was only roughly known to the Land Office.

The confusion became even greater after 1875 when surveyors hired by private individuals were permitted, if necessary, to depart from the official polyconic, or township, system adopted in 1873 "as nearly as circumstances [would] permit" and even to omit connecting the survey by a tie line with some known point established in a previous survey if it were found impracticable to do so.

A further difficulty arose after 1871 from the confusion surrounding the location of the land to be granted to the dominion government for railway purposes. The appropriation for provincial surveys fell from a peak of $40,000 in 1874 to a low of $500 in 1879. Beaven said in his report for 1873 that the early beginning on a systematic survey was delayed "from the same causes which existed last year, viz., the restriction placed upon our lands by the Terms of Union, and the uncertainty which existed as to what lands would be claimed by the Dominion Government for railway purposes." He even made an attempt to get the Dominion to agree to reimburse the province for the cost of any surveys made on lands subsequently found to be included within the Railway Belt, but "this, however, was unsuccessful."[8]

On July 21, 1873, the day on which the time limit set for the Dominion to commence construction of the railroad expired, Beaven sent two surveyors into the New Westminster district to subdivide townships into sections of one square mile each. Under this system, which had already been adopted by the dominion government and used in Manitoba, and was currently employed in the United States, each township contained thirty-six sections, each section containing one square mile or 640 acres. By placing a post in the centre of each section, four quarter-sections of 160 acres each could be obtained. It was a simple system which had the advantage of conforming with surveys elsewhere on the continent, of making it easy for settlers to locate their lands, and of reducing, by its simplicity, the cost of surveying and the possibility of mistakes. Since many of the townships surveyed in the New Westminster area under this plan were done on contract, the price varied, but, in 1873, Township no. 7 was surveyed by W. D. Patterson at a cost of nineteen dollars per mile. At this rate, it would have cost $1,596 to survey the entire township. It was the custom in eastern Canada to adopt a fixed survey price per mile for all the different classes and grades of survey, but such a plan was to be found impracticable in British Columbia. There were not enough surveyors; there were too many conflicting claims which the surveyor had to check; there were too many old lines of previous surveys that had to be discovered, taken up correctly, and traced through dense timber and underbrush. Such factors rendered a fixed price out of the question for British Columbia. Surveyors would not accept it.

It was with much pleasure that Beaven could inform the Assembly in 1875 not only that the pre-emption claims taken up by settlers fifteen years before in the main settlement centres had now been surveyed, but also, that the government had at its disposal, for new settlers, a large area of surveyed land of which "the nature and character . . . are minutely described upon the maps in the Land Office, thus enabling intending settlers to obtain as much reliable information in reference to the lands as it is possible to gain without personal inspection." And indeed, the survey of 160,729 acres throughout the Fraser, Thompson, and Nicola

[8] Ibid.

valleys was a creditable performance.[9] But as the gloom deepened over the failure of the railway from eastern Canada to materialize, the Walkem government decided in 1876 to reduce the expense of surveying "until the influx of population and the financial circumstances of the Province warrant the expenditure."[10] Accordingly, the appropriation was reduced from $8,000 in 1877 to $5,000 in 1878, and the next year it went down to a mere token allotment of $500. Not until 1907 did the amount of money expended on surveys again begin to reflect the urgent need for extensive government surveys.

Codification of the survey system to be employed throughout the province found its way into the land act in 1879 for the first time. It was the township, or polyconic, system, the details of which were exactly the same as those found in the dominion Homestead Act of 1872. At the same time, instructions were given by which surveyors were to be guided in keeping their field notes, certified copies of which had to be sent to the Land Office in Victoria for approval. Approval was to be given only after the notes had been checked in detail to see that they agreed with previous surveys and field notes made in the same district. Seventeen different instructions were included for the surveyor's guidance, each of which was to be followed in detail and in sequence. Beginning with the instructions as to the manner in which the pages of his book were to be ruled, the act went on to tell him to place the date as the first entry each morning; to make full notes as to the character of the country and its soils, lakes, and timber; to make all entries in pencil and to make no additional entries therein; to keep duplicate copies in ink; to construct a plan on the scale of four inches to the mile; to chain correctly; and to note the direction, width, and volume of all rivers or streams crossed; to make a general description of each township as it was completed; to note carefully the location of all bearing trees; to make an especially careful record of the kinds of timber, and the sizes of trees; to locate accurately all Indian villages, cabins, and fields; to describe all settlers' cabins and improvements and to give the names of the settlers; to locate all roads and trails

9 "Report of the Chief Commissioner of Lands and Works ... 1875," p. 531.

10 B.C., Department of Lands and Works, "Report of the Chief Commissioner of Lands and Works ... 1876," B.C., *Sessional Papers*, 2d Parl., 2d sess., 1877, p. 350.

"with their direction whence and whither"; and then to proceed with the survey.[11]

Reports submitted by all surveyors were included in the annual report of the Lands and Works Department each year up to 1898, but thereafter they were deleted. Not until G. H. Dawson was appointed surveyor general to replace E. B. McKay in 1911 were the reports published again. Under statutes which had been passed in 1886 and 1891 to protect surveyors from action for trespassing and to regulate the qualifications for admission to practice, the government surveyors had been doing what they could within their severely restricted budget to survey timber, mineral, agricultural, and coal lands, as well as to make valuable exploratory surveys throughout the province. But not until Dawson took over the surveyor general's office were the reports submitted to the Land Office considered to be of sufficient interest to the public to warrant their inclusion in the *Sessional Papers* where the public could have access to them. Upon assuming office, Dawson thoroughly overhauled the entire division by increasing the staff, obtaining new and increased office space, and establishing new branches within the department.

Dawson soon discovered that the system of surveys in the province, regardless of what the statutory provisions had been, or were, was quite unlike anything he had previously encountered. To begin with, he found that government surveys of crown lands were lagging far behind the other western provinces. But it is to be noted that the Dominion had been responsible for the surveying of Manitoba and the Northwest Territory lands, and the surveys carried out there are generally considered to be among the best in the world. Dawson recognized these facts. The lack of funds had, of course, seriously retarded surveys, but so had the terrain with which surveyors had had to contend. In addition, British Columbia had a far greater variety of natural resources than the other three western provinces, all of which had to be surveyed before development could proceed. Obviously Dawson had at hand extenuating circumstances for the conditions he found in his department. He did not complain of what he found; indeed, in explaining why British Columbia could not be compared with any of the other western regions, he said that "it is seldom that a country is so wonderfully endowed by nature that portions of its Crown lands

[11] B.C., *Statutes*, 1879, 42 Vict., c. 21, s. 8.

can be sold several times, and made a more or less permanent source of revenue by taxation, under a variety of Statutes, without serious inconvenience by the holders of any of the rights covered by the grants in question."[12]

The work of the Survey Branch involved, among other duties, making surveys under the Mineral Act and the Coal and Petroleum Act in addition to the Land Act, for no claim could be crown-granted until it had been surveyed. By the Land Act, the Survey Branch was called upon to survey pre-emptions, purchases, and leases, and, until the establishment in 1911 of the Forest Branch, it was also called upon to survey all timber leases and limits. The Survey Branch was to regulate surveys made under all these acts; the overseeing and regulating were not always done, but provision had been made. Surveys made under the Land Act were by far the most numerous; titles given under that act reserved to the Crown all the coal and minerals to which crown grants might be obtained separately under the appropriate acts. As the surveyor general pointed out, it was possible, therefore, to have on the maps of the department a piece of land to which a crown grant to the surface had been given under the Land Act, another crown grant under the Coal and Petroleum Act, and a third crown grant issued under the Mineral Act. At the same time, the whole area embraced within these three crown grants might have been included in a timber leasehold granted before 1892. And then, to add to the existing confusion, a fifth record might have been, or still might be, given to another to partly divert the water contained in any stream running by or through the property. Such a piece of land would have required surveying at least four separate times, and would have four official designations, all of which would appear on the department map. Until 1912, the Survey Branch had little actual control over the work of private surveyors who did much of the provincial surveying; any or each of these might have submitted notes that did not agree with those of the others.

The annual expenditures on surveys listed in the public accounts for each year show how little was spent on this essential service before 1909. From 1871 to 1900 inclusive, a total of $466,970 was expended on surveys, an average of $16,102 a year, hardly enough to pay for the surveying of the pre-emption claims for which certi-

12 B.C., Department of Lands, "Report of the Surveyor-General [1912]," B.C., *Sessional Papers*, 13th Parl., 1st sess., 1913, p. D230.

ficates of improvement had been issued. As late as 1906, only $6,987 was being spent on this vital service, but with the general reorganization that took place within the Department of Lands and Works in 1909, and with the establishment of a separate Ministry of Lands, this sum rose to $190,188 that year, and to $448,885 in 1911. Expenditures in 1909, 1910, and 1911 were largely to survey the reserved lands along the Grand Trunk Pacific Railway.[13] By the end of 1912 the entire portion of the province extending from the Alberta border to Prince Rupert was completed, making it the first such carefully planned and completely executed survey of its kind in British Columbia.

When Dawson took over his new duties in 1911, he found that the plotting and gazetting of lands from the books of field notes sent to Victoria had fallen seven months in arrears. So great was the increased land activity throughout the province — reports of which had to be funnelled through the Land Department — that the entire attention of the staff was being devoted to the handling of field notes to the exclusion of other work such as plotting the tie lines necessary for the compilation of connected plans of surveyed lands which the public was demanding. He was able to state in his annual report for 1911 that because of the increased staff, field notes which required no amending were being dealt with three weeks after their receipt and that the Geographic Branch was utilizing the information thus obtained to prepare new maps as quickly as possible.[14]

To convey some idea of the magnitude of the task assigned the Survey Branch, the following table will be helpful:

Work of the Survey Branch, 1907-1913[15]

Year	*Books received*	*Lots surveyed*	*Lots gazetted*
1907	1,622	1,830	1,762
1908	1,862	2,161	2,145
1909	2,204	3,365	2,942

13 Ibid., p. D227.

14 "Surveyor-General's Report [1911]," pp. G8, G9.

15 Compiled from B.C., "Report of the Surveyor-General [1912]," p. D231, and B.C., Department of Lands, "Report of the Surveyor-General [1913]," B.C., *Sessional Papers*, 13th Parl., 2d sess., 1914, p. D313.

1910	2,893	5,098	3,072
1911	5,259	7,312	6,737
1912	4,791	6,345	7,950
1913	4,750	7,378	6,770

When a government survey of a district was made, all pre-emption records, applications to purchase, and leases were assigned to district lots, or portions of lots, which had been surveyed on a regular system, a procedure which meant that the work to be done in Victoria was comparatively light. When an isolated pre-emption had to be dealt with, however, the procedure was not always so simple. Upon receipt of a pre-emption record, the settler had his land surveyed at his own expense and the surveyor's field notes were sent to Victoria. If the description contained in the original certificate of record was clear, if the boundaries as determined by the private survey agreed with that description, and if the pre-emption was so situated as to leave no possibility of its conflicting with other pre-emptions or applications, the field notes were then checked and plotted on the official plan and on the master reference map. Then a notice was published in the *British Columbia Gazette* indicating that the claim had been surveyed and the survey found to be satisfactory, and the local government agent was supplied with a copy of the official plan of the survey. If a crown grant was applied for within the time specified in the act, two more copies of the plan had to be made. But if the pre-emption was located in the vicinity of an old crown grant, or of an unsurveyed timber or coal licence, or of any application which predated the pre-emption record, the department had to be satisfied that there was no interference. To do this meant protracted correspondence with the surveyor, and the process of checking a single set of field notes might drag on for a year. Fortunately for the department and for the settler, it would seem that there were not too many negotiations of this kind, as the number of books of field notes and the number of lots gazetted in each year in the chart given above coincide reasonably well.

By 1913 the full effect of the reorganization begun in 1911 was being felt, not only in the office work, but also in surveying throughout the province. There were now seventy-five surveyors working in the field, and they were no longer confined to the vicinity of the transcontinental railway lines. One million acres of crown land had been surveyed for the government, most of which was subdivided into lots varying in size from 40 to 160 acres; 400 miles of district boundaries were run; explorations of the Cassiar and Peace River districts were carried out and, in conjunction with the governments of Alberta and the Dominion, a beginning was made on the survey of the Alberta-British Columbia boundary.[16]

Private surveys for the year covered 1,500,000 acres of land held under special timber licence, an acreage which represented only about 30 per cent of all land held under such licences but still unsurveyed at the beginning of the year. In addition, 500,000 acres of land held under application to purchase were surveyed privately.

In spite of a late beginning, government surveys accounted for a quarter of all surveys made in the province since the turn of the century. Altogether, 13,980,360 acres had been surveyed since 1900, distributed fairly evenly among agricultural, mineral, and timber lands.[17] Much of this surveying had been greatly facilitated by the "Canadian Pacific traverse," a base line established through the Railway Belt to Port Moody by the Canadian Pacific Company. Lines were run from either side of this established base throughout the province. Including the area surveyed in the Railway Belt, 26,299,689 acres of provincial territory had been surveyed at the end of 1913, roughly a ninth of the total land area.

As predicted by Tom Kains, surveyor general in 1891, Dawson found that to survey British Columbia in a way that would conform to the survey system uniformly adopted elsewhere in Canada was a task "attended with enormous expense."[18] Because of its rugged terrain, British Columbia was not at all suited to the township system of surveying. Dawson himself admitted that were the surveying of the province to be started again, it was unlikely that the township system would be used. Of the $1,557,515 spent on government surveys to the end of 1911, as listed in the annual public accounts, half had been expended in 1910 and 1911. The great amount of work involved in connecting all the isolated and

16 "Report of the Surveyor-General [1913]," p. D297; Arthur O. Wheeler, "Boundary Survey between the Provinces of British Columbia and Alberta," ibid., pp. 317-22.

17 Appendix B, Table 7.

18 "Report of the Surveyor-General [1912]," pp. 228-29. In 1891 the system of triangulation was being used in the Railway Belt. Two surveyors covered 60 miles a year at a cost of $2.50 per square mile, or 2¢ an acre, "certainly a very cheap rate considering the character of the country surveyed." B.C., *Sessional Papers*, 6th Parl., 2d sess., 1892, pp. 352-53.

scattered surveys which had been made in the previous fifty years, and in making these surveys conform to the township plan, required all the money Dawson could persuade the legislature to grant.

The main reason, however, why British Columbia's policy deviated from that adopted in the rest of Canada lay in the statutory authority accorded by Douglas's Land Proclamation of 1860 to the practice of alienating crown lands before they were surveyed; a usage which was to be continued through subsequent years. The principle, so well understood by Douglas, that lands should be surveyed before being sold, had had to give way in the face of the realities of British Columbia's topography.

Total Area Surveyed by 1913 Including Land Transferred to the Dominion in Connection with the Canadian Pacific, and Esquimalt and Nanaimo, Railways[19]

	In Area under Provincial jurisdiction	*In Railway Belts, Dom. Govt. & E. & N.*	*Total*
AREA OF:	*Acres*	*Acres*	*Acres*
land surveyed	16,635,000	2,967,659	19,602,659
timber surveyed	4,182,000	1,581,863	5,763,863
coal lands surveyed	....	....	546,000
mineral claims surveyed	....	....	387,167
			26,299,689

19 Taken from "Report of the Surveyor-General [1913]," p. D300.

CHAPTER 5

Mining Legislation

It is sometimes maintained that the people of British Columbia have been "robbed" of their heritage of natural wealth. Were the natural resources recklessly exploited? A detailed examination of past government policy in handling mineral lands, timber lands, and water rights reveals how painstaking were the efforts made to encourage enterprising individuals willing to face the hazards of a new country; to discourage those bent only on speculation; and, at the same time, obtain sufficient revenue to maintain and develop such a remote and sparsely populated part of the world. By 1913 perhaps 500,000 acres of land had been alienated for mining activities and about 8,500,000 acres for timber purposes. Out of British Columbia's 230,000,000 acres, this amount does not seem excessive. It is true that once the minerals were extracted they could not be restored and that once the timber was cut it could not be replaced for many years. But the revenue from these activities sustained and developed the province during its struggling years so that British Columbians, today, are reaping the increasing benefits of its growth.

A great amount of legislation was enacted to regulate the use of these resources of mine, forest, and water course. Precious mineral resources were the first to engage the attention of the early legislators. Much later, base metals and coal were to come in for their share of legislation, but the regulating of gold mining was the major problem confronting the first governor of the colony of British Columbia.

One hundred years ago when millions of acres of easily cultivated land were available for settlement on the central plains of North America, settlers would not have been attracted to British

Columbia for its agricultural lands alone. Until 1858 the Hudson's Bay Company, interested only in furs, was left in sole possession of New Caledonia and "Vancouver's Island," its activities undisturbed by landseekers. As yet the treeless acres of the interior dry belt were unsettled, and the fur-trade era might have continued undisturbed for another generation had not the purser of the Hudson's Bay steamer *Otter* taken some gold dust to the mint at San Francisco in 1858. Within a year, word had spread among the California mining camps that a rich strike had been made in British territory to the north. The rush to the new gold fields which began in 1858 marked the end of one era and the beginning of another in British Columbia. Men searching for gold, not land, pushed the fur traders from their last stronghold.

Knowing of the presence of gold on the mainland at least as early as 1856, Governor Douglas took steps in 1857 to protect the interests of the Crown. As in the case of California, the mining-frontier preceded the settlement-frontier in British Columbia. Laws relating to mining were enacted even before provision was made for the disposal of agricultural lands.

To regulate the conditions under which gold might be mined by the first swarm of immigrants, Douglas's Proclamation of December 28, 1857, declared that "by law all mines of gold," whether on lands "of the Queen or any of Her Majesty's subjects," belonged to the Crown. Anyone disturbing the soil in search of gold without authorization was to be prosecuted. Authorization was granted by a mining licence, obtainable in Victoria at a cost of ten shillings a month (later raised to twenty-one shillings). Conveyance of land carried no right to the gold (later, silver was added) under the land. Rights to gold had to be obtained by the formal staking of a claim in accordance with the regulations issued with Douglas's proclamation.[1] The principle, so early established, that precious metals should remain in the possession of the Crown unless formally claimed under the relevant mining act has not yet been rescinded.

1 "Proclamation [December 28, 1857]," [Great Britain, Colonial Office], *Copies or Extracts of Correspondence Relative to the Discovery of Gold in the Fraser's River District in British North America*, presented to both Houses of Parliament by command of Her Majesty, July 2, 1858 (London: Printed by George Edward Eyre and William Spottiswoode ... for Her Majesty's Stationery Office, 1858), p. 9. As was his custom, Douglas enclosed a copy of this proclamation in a despatch to the Colonial Office. Douglas to Henry Labouchere, Baron Taunton, secretary of state for the colonies, December 29, 1857, ibid., p. 8.

Subsequent legislation was to define how claims were to be recorded and the size and shape they might be. As placer mining gave way to more expensive and elaborate hydraulic operations, provisions had to be made to enable the Crown to lease or grant mineral lands, but Douglas's omission of such provision was not an oversight. The only type of gold mining known to Douglas was confined to the banks of creeks and sandbars of rivers, where the gold content was soon exhausted, and, hence, owning the land was unnecessary. Even the longer-term hydraulic operations required comparatively small tracts of land.

To clarify the situation regarding leases of mineral lands, Lytton told Douglas that surface rights were to be secured to those holding leases for base metals and coal, but should gold and silver be involved, the surface rights were to remain with the Crown.[2] Upon issuing his first Land Proclamation of February 14, 1859, Douglas pointed out that all the lands in British Columbia "and all the mines and minerals therein," belonged to the Crown. No lands reputed to be mineral lands might be bought, but purchase of agricultural lands not known to contain minerals would include rights to all minerals discovered later, except gold and silver. Until further notice, gold claims and mines were to be worked under the 1857 regulations.[3]

On August 31, 1859, Douglas proclaimed the Gold Fields Act. In this important document, miners' rights were jealously guarded. As a class, miners were free from the levy of any direct tax beyond the annual charge of one pound for a miner's certificate, but without this certificate they had no rights whatsoever. Mining leases might be secured to cover ten acres for as many years on payment of twenty-five pounds. Bar diggings, that part of the creek or river bank covered at high water, were to be 25 feet wide; dry diggings, never covered by water, were to be 25 by 30 feet, and quartz claims might extend 100 feet along the seam. Only one claim by preemption might be held by any one miner, although he might purchase any number of claims. The discoverer of a mine, however, was entitled to two pre-emption claims, or if the mine had been discovered by a party of men, each might hold one and a half claims. Having seen for himself some of the rich claims along the

2 Lytton to Douglas, February 7, 1859, Gt. Britain, *Papers Relative to British Columbia*, 2:76-79.

3 "Proclamation of February 14, 1859," s. 1, 2, 7, 9, ibid., 2:65.

creeks in the Cariboo, Douglas considered that 25 feet was an adequate width for such claims. Since all claims had to be recorded, any dispute concerning the ownership of a claim was to be settled by the gold commissioner on the basis of prior registration, not prior discovery.[4]

Between the time the Gold Fields Act was issued in 1859 and his retirement in 1864, Douglas issued seven further mining proclamations, all designed either to regulate gold mining in order to prevent troublesome litigation, or to define further the privileges of free miners.[5] In each land ordinance, the right of free miners to enter any waste crown land, or any private land held under pre-emption or purchase, was upheld, providing that reasonable compensation for any damage done to the surface was paid.

When British Columbia entered Confederation in 1871, mining was regulated by the extensive Gold Mining Ordinance of 1867 which consolidated all the enactments of the previous years. Bench claims to the land located behind the dry diggings which, in turn, backed the bar diggings, were added to the variety of claims that might be staked. These bench claims might be as much as 100 feet square; bar diggings, extending from high water mark into the bed of the stream, 100 feet wide; and dry diggings, 100 feet square. In recognition of the fact that the richer bar and dry diggings were being exhausted, hill claims were also added to provide for those areas where no benches existed above the creeks or rivers. These hill claims were to have a base line of 100 feet, and to extend to the tops of the hills on which they were located.

Free miners' certificates were issued to either men or women over the age of sixteen, at a cost of five dollars a year. The record to each claim held under these certificates had to be renewed each year. A free miner was allowed to hold any number of claims by purchase as formerly, but now he was also permitted to hold two pre-emption claims in the same locality provided one were a quartz

4 Douglas to Newcastle, September 13, 1859, no. 1, ibid., 3:58-65.

5 A listing of these may be found in B.C., *Consolidated Statutes* [1877], pp. v-xxxviii, nos. 152, 188, 191, 197, 200. "Rules and Regulations for the Working of Gold Mines," January 6, 1860; "Ditches. Rules and Regulations . . . ," September 29, 1862; "Rules and Regulations . . . ," February 24, 1863, "Proclamation, no. 4, A.D. 1863," March 25, 1863; "Proclamation, no. 7, A.D. 1863," May 27, 1863; "An Ordinance to promote the Drainage of Mines," February 1, 1864; "An Ordinance to extend and improve the Laws relating to Gold Mining," February 26, 1864, are found in [*Proclamations and Ordinances, 1858-1864*]. They were superseded March 28, 1865, by "An Ordinance to amend and consolidate the Gold Mining Laws," ibid.

claim. This provision meant that he might have one claim near the water and another, 1,500 by 400 feet, along a lode or vein. In addition, he might hold two further claims, provided that one was near the water and the other along a lode, and neither of them on the same hill, creek, ravine, or bench as his first claims. The interest in each claim was held to be a chattel interest, equivalent to a lease, but valid only as long as he worked each claim regularly and renewed his certificate of record annually.

The 1867 Ordinance made the first provisions for the operation of mining companies. As placer mining along the creek beds was no longer yielding the sizable returns secured ten years before, it became necessary to dig down to bedrock. Lying on top of the bedrock was a rich layer of gold, but the labour and expense involved in washing away the surface soil was beyond the resources of the individual miner. As a means to overcome these obstacles, the ordinance provided for the formation of bedrock flume companies by any three or more miners.

On payment of $125, such a company was entitled to construct a flume to convey the water necessary to wash away the surface soil. Permission was granted not only to divert into the flume water from any nearby stream, but also to build the flume over any free miner's claim. The water record, however, was subject to the limitations imposed by any previous water record, and the free miner's rights were safeguarded by granting him the right to use as much water from the flume as he needed, provided he returned the water to the flume after it had served his purpose.

Subject to the governor's approval, leases might be secured for ten acres of dry diggings, half a mile of new bar diggings, and a mile and a half of abandoned bar diggings and quartz reefs. These leases might not be obtained where such land was either being, or likely to be, worked by free miners, and in any case, might only be secured "for the miner-like working thereof." Operations had to begin within a specified time and all rights were to be cancelled should these operations cease for more than seventy-two hours. In this way, beneficial use of the lease was assured, and the holding of mineral lands for speculative purposes was thwarted.[6]

The temporary and transient nature of the mining operations in

[6] *Ordinances Passed by the Legislative Council of British Columbia . . . 1867* (New Westminster: Government Printing Office, n.d.), 1867, 30 Vict., No. 34.

the two colonies up to 1866 is indicated by the omission from the 1867 Ordinance of any mention of crown grants to free miners for the lands held by them as mining claims. Leases were provided and the miners were secured in all rights to their claims other than surface rights, but there was no authority by which a miner could obtain a crown grant to his pre-emption. By 1869, however, mining operations had altered from easy panning in creek beds to more tedious prospecting in the hills. Recognition of this change prompted the Mineral Ordinance of 1869. The new regulations introduced a prospector's licence for coal and base metals, provided for purchase of coal lands, and arranged for crown grants to mineral claims.

The prospecting licence, an innovation designed to encourage the search for silver and base metals, entitled a free miner to seek for and mine all minerals, except coal, on all lands, but coal on vacant crown lands only. Should the prospector discover a mine of silver, copper, lead, iron, or cinnabar, he was authorized to work it regardless of location. The free miner with a gold claim had a secure right to all the gold in the claim, but from now on the prospector might pursue his search for any mineral other than gold on or under the free miner's claim. Occasionally the latter had uncovered less valuable mineral deposits in his search for gold and disregarded them. When such a deposit was uncovered by the prospector, he might work it for two years under the authority provided by the newly created licence and at the end of the two years, he might select half an acre of land for purchase. The price was high at $50 the half acre plus the cost of surveying, but this was waived if $1,000, at least, had been expended on the mine within the time covered by the prospecting licence.

The prospector's licence entitled the holder to seek and mine coal on all waste crown lands. Thus coal mining, which gave the earliest impetus to permanent mining development under the aegis of the Hudson's Bay Company at Fort Rupert, received legislative attention in the 1869 Mineral Ordinance. For the first time, coal lands could be purchased. A crown grant conveying outright ownership to 1,000 acres could be secured by a company of at least ten persons at the rate of five dollars an acre. Again, the purchase price was waived if at least $10,000 had been expended on the development of the property prior to the expiry of the company's licence. Before the grant could be secured, conclusive proof was required by the gold commissioner that the mine had been worked continuously for the preceding two years.[7]

When British Columbia entered Confederation in 1871, placer mining for gold was the only mining of any consequence in the province. According to the mining returns for 1879 there were 505 companies authorized to work mining claims, 31 of which were bar claims, 236 creek claims, 42 bench claims, 109 hill claims, and 3 quartz claims.[8] If the same proportion held true for individuals' claims, the creeks of the province were obviously still the scene of the most mining activity. Although it is true that mining laws regulated lode and coal mining as well as placer mining, no annual returns on lode mining appeared until 1887, and coal output was slight until the 1880's. By 1871, the Fraser and Cariboo diggings had been followed by discoveries at Granite and Rock Creeks, at Wild Horse Creek in the East Kootenay, and at the Big Bend on the Columbia River. The Cariboo fields remained the most important and permanent, but the other discoveries created minor rushes. In 1871 the Omineca mines were discovered and following this rush, came the Cassiar discoveries. After these, a comparative lull in placer mining followed until the Atlin strike of 1898.

Only spasmodic returns concerning the number of free miners' certificates were available during the early years of the province, but in 1872 Peter O'Reilly, the local gold commissioner, reported that he had issued such certificates to the value of $4,672.50 for the Omineca district alone. At the fee of five dollars per certificate, it can be assumed that approximately 900 such certificates were issued in Omineca in the peak year. Lost certificates could be replaced for $2.50, which would account for the uneven multiple in O'Reilly's returns. Mining licences required by prospectors accounted for $2,645 of the total revenue of $14,707.32 collected by O'Reilly for the same year.[9] Again, at five dollars each, that would have meant that 529 prospectors were searching for minerals in his district alone.

[7] *Ordinances Passed by the Legislative Council of British Columbia ... 1868-9* (Victoria: Government Printing Office, n.d.), 1869, 32 Vict., no. 22.

[8] B.C., Department of Mines, "Report of the Minister ... 1879," B.C., *Sessional Papers*, 3d Parl., 3d sess., 1880, chart preceding p. 235. These claims, 100 feet long, were to extend from base to base of the hill, or bench, on each side of the creek. B.C., *Statutes*, 1872, 35 Vict., no. 4, s. 2.

[9] "... Report from the Gold Commissioner on the Omineca District ... 1872," B.C., *Journals*, 1st Parl., 1st sess., 1872, appendix, *Sessional Papers*, p. 86.

By the end of 1873, mining exports at $1,224,362 accounted for 70 per cent of the total exports of the province.[10] To take charge of the expanding mining activities, the office of minister of mines was added to the Executive Council in 1874, but its duties were assigned to one of the existing ministers at no additional salary. John Ash, provincial secretary, assumed the new portfolio. In his first report as minister of mines he indicated that the income for the first year from free miners' licences, including renewals and 1,841 new licences, amounted to $11,232.50; that 470 claims had been staked and recorded, and that 67 water records had been issued. Sometime between the issuing of this report and the preparation of the next, Ash must have realized the discrepancy between the number of claims recorded and those actually worked. Hence the second report made clear that although 1,117 claims had been recorded, only 293 were being worked.[11] The prospector was a gambling man who staked to the limit of the law, but in most areas found that little more than a quarter of what he had staked was worth working.

Owing to its ephemeral nature, placer mining did not result in any appreciable alienation of crown lands. Although diggings abandoned after the initial strikes were often reworked by Chinese miners and other prospectors content with a small return for their labour, there was little reason for acquiring permanent title to the land on which the claims were located. Because of the remoteness of the placer camps, the anticipated boom in the Cariboo and Omineca diggings failed to materialize even when hydraulic methods were introduced.

In fact, until the completion of the Canadian Pacific Railway in 1885, mining activities were relatively slow. The speculation consequent to the rich strikes of the 1860's did not indicate real prosperity, even though the excitement did bring a population which sought new employment as the original incentive was lost. Many of the thousands who went to the Cariboo took up land and formed a nucleus of an agricultural settlement. Others who had been lured into British territory by the stories of fabulous strikes

10 "Returns of Imports and Exports for the Year Ending June 30, 1873," p. 14, B.C., *Journals*, 1st Parl., 3d sess., 1873-74, appendix, *Sessional Papers*.

11 B.C., Department of Mines, ". . . Report of the Minister of Mines . . . 1874," B.C., *Journals*, 1st Parl., 4th sess., 1875, appendix, *Sessional Papers*, chart preceding p. 545; idem, "Mining Statistics for the Year 1875," B.C., *Sessional Papers*, 2d Parl., 1st sess., 1876, chart following p. 596.

turned to trading, lumbering, fishing, transportation, and shipping. The population of the interior in 1871 was scattered and sparse, but the origins of the present commercial and industrial pursuits of the province were laid as a result of the gold strikes.

Placer mining for gold, then, contributed indirectly to the disposal of large tracts of crown land for agricultural and industrial purposes, particularly before Confederation, but its activities required no permanent acreage. Lode mining and coal mining, on the other hand, required holdings of a more permanent nature, but the total acreage alienated, either directly as mining property or indirectly for settlement, formed a negligible amount of British Columbia's vast area.

Although the output from placer mines was decreasing in the 1870's and that from lode mines and collieries was comparatively slight until the 1890's when the Kootenay and Nanaimo developments came into serious production, the government still continued to regulate mining procedures conscientiously with frequent amendments and revisions of the mining laws.

In the years after 1871, regulations for obtaining a crown grant to mining pre-emptions were often changed. In 1873, in conformity with the free grant policy initiated that year by the legislature, the land in which the mineral claim was situated was given to the miner. The dollar an acre charged was looked upon merely as the fee for recording the claim. If the miner improved his holding within the next two years to the extent of ten dollars an acre, the land was his. In 1877, under the Walkem administration, the size of a mining claim was enlarged to 1,500 by 660 feet, or 20.6 acres. A crown grant to it could be obtained by paying five dollars an acre and the cost of surveying. This arrangement which did not require "proving up" must have been popular since the number of crown grants doubled in 1878.[12] The next year, however, requirements were raised, with $5,000 expenditure in money or labour required before the crown grant was issued. At this time a company was required to pay a tax of five cents an acre on a claim that was being worked, and fifty cents a lineal foot on an unworked claim, amounting to $750 a year on a regulation 1,500-foot claim.

Perhaps these regulations were found to be too rigorous, or perhaps the initial stages of the Canadian Pacific Railway's con-

[12] B.C., *Statutes*, 1873, 36 Vict., no. 4, s. 2, 5; ibid., 1877, 40 Vict., no. 14, s. 2, 8. See Appendix B, Table 4.

struction were luring miners elsewhere. At any rate, in 1879 the revenue derived from free miners' certificates dropped from nearly $12,000 to $4,600, and general mining receipts from $8,500 to $2,600.[13] Four years later, in 1883, requirements for obtaining the crown grant were made easier through another amendment to the mineral act. Now only $1,000 had to be expended in money or labour in "proving up" the mining pre-emption. Also under this same amendment a miner could be absent from his claim for six months instead of for the seventy-two hour limit previously in effect.

In 1884, still another amendment, designed no doubt to close the ever-present gap between the number of mineral claims recorded and those being worked, provided that the miner applying for a crown grant had to swear that a vein or lode had actually been found, that he was in undisputed possession, that the survey had been accurate, and that $500 had been expended in money or labour. In 1892 the size of the claim was again increased, making it 1,500 feet square, or nearly 52 acres, as it is still. By 1898 the expenditure on a mining claim had only to be $100 a year, but this amount had to be maintained for five years before obtaining the crown grant. This regulation was still in effect in 1913.

As was the case with agricultural lands, ownership of mineral claims through outright purchase of the crown land was always possible for anyone having the money and wishing to bypass the "proving up" process of the pre-emption system. In 1869 a half acre had cost $50 plus the cost of survey; in 1883 a full acre could be bought for the same amount. In 1886 the price was lowered to $25 an acre, but in the 1898 peak of mining activity the cost of one acre rose to $500.[14]

As with placer mining, no figures are available on the total amount of crown land alienated for mineral claims up to 1913, but a table of government surveys of the years 1900 to 1913 gives some basis for an opinion. During these years, a total of 265,871 acres were surveyed for mining claims, excluding coal claims. In comparison with over 10,000,000 acres surveyed during the same period for disposal in other ways this acreage is small and suggests, in the

[13] Appendix B, Table 6.

[14] B.C., *Statutes*, 1883, 46 Vict., c. 19, s. 4; ibid., 1884, 47 Vict., c. 10, s. 68; ibid., 1892, 55 Vict., c. 32, s. 5; ibid., 1886, 49 Vict., c. 14, s. 10; ibid., 1898, 61 Vict., c. 33, s. 6.

absence of more exact figures, that the amount of land permanently alienated for mineral purposes was not great.[15]

Because coal deposits usually cover a much larger area than do other mineral deposits, special regulations were enacted as early as 1869. These were changed through the years as circumstances dictated. The 1,000 acres which a company could obtain at five dollars an acre in 1869 was reduced in 1873 to 640 acres at one dollar an acre. In 1883, the Act to Encourage Coal Mining provided for the sale of coal land at ten dollars an acre east of the Cascades and five dollars west of the Cascades. In 1892 an amendment to the Coal Mines Act provided for the right to purchase up to 640 acres of coal lands at five dollars an acre, but the prospective buyer had first to lease the land for five years at ten cents an acre, pay for the surveying, and pay a royalty of five cents per ton on all coal and one cent per barrel on all petroleum that was taken out.[16]

By 1913, coal-prospecting licences still allowed holders to buy 640 acres, and the compulsory five-year lease remained in effect. The price was now fifteen cents an acre annually for the lease, and the purchase price had risen to fifteen dollars an acre. Before leasing, the miner had to pay the survey charges as formerly, spend a fixed sum on development, and prove that coal existed. After 1899, all the provisions with respect to coal also applied to petroleum, but petroleum reserves to the Crown were not to provide any revenue to the provincial government for another half century.

By 1913, 546,000 acres of coal-bearing land had been surveyed, but this did not mean, necessarily, that the land had been alienated. It meant only that it might now be leased at the current price.[17] Unless a coal mine was proving lucrative, the lessee was better advised to work his mine on a lease as long as he could, and pay the annual rental rather than apply for a crown grant. Between 1884 and 1900, coal-prospecting licences were taken out at the rate of 15 a year; between 1900 and 1913, an average number of 859 were issued annually, reaching a peak of 2,223 in 1911.[18] No

15 Appendix B, Table 7.

16 B.C., *Statutes*, 1873, 36 Vict., no. 3, s. 3; ibid., 1883, 46 Vict., c. 3, s. 13; ibid., 1892, 55 Vict., c. 31, s. 5.

17 B.C., *Statutes*, 1913, 3 Geo. 5, c. 44, s. 9.

18 Averaged from figures given in the annual reports of officials of the Lands Department, 1886 to 1911, and in those of the Minister of Mines, 1912 and 1913. B.C., *Sessional Papers*, 1885-1914.

licence was given until the prospector swore under oath that his land contained coal or petroleum, and the lease was not granted until the land had been surveyed and coal proven to exist by actual production.

Predictions were being made that coal mining would become one of the major activities of the province, but just as progress in the Cariboo, Cassiar, and Atlin gold fields needed the development of hydraulic mining, the real advance in coal mining had to await adequate and cheaper transportation facilities. By 1910 only 32 million of the 40-billion-ton provincial coal reserves had been mined. The comment in 1912 of R. A. Renwick, deputy minister of lands, that a "remarkable stimulus" had been given to prospecting for coal by the completion of the railway lines of the southern interior is supported by the peak issue of 2,223 coal-prospecting licences in 1911.[19] Speaking of coal lands along the Grand Trunk Pacific Railway, Renwick predicted that coal mining would "doubtless contribute greatly [to] providing a market for the farmers . . . and tonnage for the railway."[20]

Although Renwick's prediction that coal mining would become a major mining activity of the province was not fulfilled, in 1913 there were 697,000 acres of coal lands held under 1,090 coal licences and 114,307 acres held under leases. Since 864,640 acres of coal lands were known to exist, this leaves about 53,000 acres of coal lands that must have been alienated by 1913.[21]

The matter of overlapping mineral rights in crown grants is an interesting and often tortuous subject. Under the laws in force by 1873, it was possible for one piece of land to be crown-granted three separate times for mining purposes — once for gold only, again for minerals other than coal, and, yet a third time, for coal. Further, there was nothing to prevent any free miner or prospector from entering coal lands to seek for gold or other minerals; in fact, every encouragement was given him to do so.

In 1878, one source of confusion was removed when rights to precious metals and to base metals were included in the same mineral claim. Henceforth, whatever minerals with the exception

19 "Report of the Minister of Lands, 1911," p. G6.

20 Ibid.

21 B.C., Department of Lands, "Report of Office Statistics," B.C., *Sessional Papers*, 13th Parl., 2d sess., 1914, p. D10. The dominion coal reserve in the Crow's Nest Pass amounted to 50,000 acres, and the Dunsmuir acreage at Nanaimo accounted for most of the remainder.

of coal that a miner encountered in his diggings were lawfully and solely his. But farmers and holders of coal lands had no right to any precious metals found on their crown-granted property, and a free miner could still prospect there at will. Gold and silver continued to be reserved whenever crown land was granted, sold, or leased for purposes other than mining.

Coal rights followed a less straightforward pattern, although it was recognized generally that coal lands carried rights to coal only and that other lands carried no coal rights unless it was specified otherwise. In the mineral acts of 1878 and 1882, coal was reserved to the Crown when a mineral claim was granted, and in the Land Act of 1882 coal was added to gold and silver as a mineral reserved to the Crown on the disposal of agricultural lands. In the Coal Prospecting Act of 1883, however, it was specified that an owner of agricultural land who found coal on his property could purchase the coal rights at nine dollars an acre. In the land act of the next year, it was decided to include coal rights in future crown grants to non-mineral lands, and, retroactively, in all such grants already issued, provided that the owner paid a royalty of five cents a ton if he mined the coal. By 1891 this policy was reversed and coal was once more reserved to the Crown. Again in 1899 coal and petroleum were expressly reserved from all crown-granted land, and in 1913 natural gas was similarly reserved.[22]

As the judges' bench books in the Provincial Archives attest, these shifting mining laws were a prolific source of litigation. And as if sufficient ground for dispute were not provided by the mining laws, a further complication was added in 1871, with the introduction of provision for the Railway Belt.

The confusion arising from the defeat of Sir John A. Macdonald's government in 1873 and from the many delays in deciding the actual route of the railway through the mountains, prevented the setting up of the expected dominion administrative machinery. Crown lands in British Columbia were placed under reserve in accordance with the Terms of Union, but when construction of the railway failed to begin within the prescribed two years, the provincial government proceeded to administer these lands in all matters, but especially with regard to minerals, as if they

[22] B.C., *Statutes*, 1878, 41 Vict., c. 13; ibid., 1882, 45 Vict., c. 8; ibid., 1882, 45 Vict., c. 6, s. 5, 6; ibid., 1883, 46 Vict., c. 3, s. 14; ibid., 1884, 47 Vict., c. 16, s. 72, 73; ibid., 1891, 54 Vict., c. 15, s. 11; B.C., *Revised Statutes*, 1924, 15 Geo. 5, c. 131, s. 119, 120.

were, once again, the province's. Thirteen years later, the formal transfer of the land to dominion control was completed by the provincial Settlement Act, ratified by the Dominion on April 19, 1884. The Dominion provided for the disposition of the land in these words:

> The lands granted ... shall be placed upon the market at the earliest date possible, and shall be offered for sale on liberal terms to actual settlers....
>
> The Governor in Council may, from time to time, regulate the manner in which and terms and conditions on which the said lands shall be surveyed, laid out, administered, dealt with and disposed of.[23]

This was sparse and cryptic language in which to legislate for the transfer of so large and vital a strip through the heartland of the province. Misunderstanding and litigation between the two governments resulted from the ambiguity of the administrative jurisdiction within the belt. One of the questions to be answered was whether the grant carried only surface rights or, also, included rights to the minerals beneath the surface.

The years immediately following the Settlement Act were the worst possible ones for the dominion government to be taking issue. British Columbia was in no mood for temporizing, for these were also the years in which endless difficulties were arising between Victoria and Ottawa over Indian lands. When A. W. Vowell, the provincial gold commissioner in the Kootenays, reported in the summer of 1884 to the provincial Executive Council through the Minister of Mines, John Robson, that he had been accused by A. M. Burgess, deputy minister of the interior, of issuing gold miners' licences illegally, the Executive Council issued a minute which was transmitted at once to Ottawa. The minute minced no words in laying claim to the right to the precious metals within the Railway Belt.

> The Committee ... desire to call [to] the attention of the Dominion ... that the right to the precious metals within the twenty-mile belt is not in the Dominion but in the Province, and that the Province has the right, under the "Mineral Act, 1884" ... to grant free mining licences and to authorize the entry by free miners upon lands within the belt, for the purpose of mining for the precious metals — subject to the provisions of section 23 of such statute, and section 64 of the "Land Act, 1884."

[23] Canada, *Statutes*, 1884, 47 Vict., c. 6, s. 11.

> There is nothing to indicate that in the granting of these lands it was intended to part with the sovereignty of the Crown, as represented by the Province, or that any greater right to the Dominion was conferred than the right of sale for railway purposes, or that the province intended to part with those rights of the Crown which, without being expressly mentioned, would not pass. If these lands had been separated from the Province, if they had become part of the territory of the Dominion, then, it is conceded, the right to the precious metals would not have remained in the Province. But as there has been no such separation, and as the Crown as represented by the Dominion is not possessed of the sovereignty of these lands, all prerogative rights remain in the Crown as represented by the Province.
>
> An opposite conclusion would go far towards withdrawing the lands from the operation of the Provincial Statutes relative to the acquisition of rights of way and water, and the like for public and private purposes.[24]

The dominion government's failure to issue any regulations governing mining affairs within the Railway Belt lent weight to the province's argument. The province contended that had the Dominion really believed it had such rights under the Settlement Act, it would have issued regulations immediately. The Dominion's Land Act of 1883 did include sections dealing with "mining and mining lands," but section 42 said that "Lands containing coal or other minerals . . . shall be disposed of in such manner and on such terms and conditions as may, from time to time, be fixed by the Governor in Council by regulations to be made in that behalf."[25] These regulations had not as yet been issued for British Columbia.

On February 17, 1885, the Dominion requested British Columbia to provide a test case for the courts. Having given the matter study, A. E. B. Davie recommended to the Executive Council that, as a test case would undoubtedly be appealed from the Exchequer Court to the Supreme Court, and from there to the Privy Council, no arguments should be presented to the first two courts in order to save time. In addition, he advised the council to seek permission from the Dominion to continue the administration of mineral

[24] "Papers Relating to the Ownership of the Precious Metals within the Railway Belt," B.C., *Sessional Papers*, 4th Parl., 4th sess., 1886, p. 361. Section 23 of the 1884 Mineral Act provided for compensation to be paid by a free miner to the occupant or owner for any loss or damages, provided the occupant or owner were in lawful possession of the land. Section 64 of the 1884 Land Act gave free miners the right to enter any lands in the province to search for and work mineral lands, provided security were given any previous lawful occupant. B.C., *Statutes*, 1884, 47 Vict., c. 10 and c. 16.

[25] Canada, *Statutes*, 1883, 46 Vict., c. 17.

lands under provincial statutes. On April 27, 1885, Davie's recommendations were incorporated in a Minute in Council and forwarded to Ottawa.[26]

Meanwhile, a week earlier, on April 20, 1885, the Dominion had belatedly issued a series of regulations for the disposal of dominion lands within the railway belt in the province of British Columbia. To these regulations the province took immediate and violent exception:

> The committee regret to observe that these "Regulations" by reason of cumbersome and vexatious provisions and excessive imposts, are altogether unsuited to the wants and conditions of this Province; ... and it is believed that any attempt to enforce them would be prejudicial to the best interests, if not dangerous to the peace, of the community.

The Executive Council felt that section 27 which reserved all minerals, in particular, could not be carried out. Since British Columbia reserved only gold and silver, the committee desired "respectfully but most emphatically, to protest against any innovation so inconsistent with the principles of justice and common law." It was also felt that the charge of $100 for a crown grant to a mining claim within the Railway Belt, as laid down by the dominion regulations, was excessive. At this time the province was charging nothing, although it was requiring expenditure on the claim of at least $500. After roundly declaring each of the remaining regulations to be also detrimental to the best interests of the province, the minute concluded:

> It is respectfully submitted that the people of British Columbia are the best judges of what is calculated to promote internal prosperity and well-being, and the simple circumstance of their own Legislature in dealing with the Provincial Lands, imposing regulations immeasurably less onerous and charges less than one-fourth of those under review may fairly be accepted as a very conclusive argument in support of the contention that the Dominion Land Regulations are illiberal and burdensome....
>
> The Committee most respectfully submit that the true interests of the country, both Dominion and Provincial, would be best promoted by having the lands within the railway belt administered on terms similar or approximating to those governing contiguous Provincial lands.[27]

[26] "Precious Metals within the Railway Belt," p. 363.

[27] "Papers Relating to Dominion Lands within the Province," B.C., *Sessional Papers*, 4th Parl., 4th sess., 1886, p. 368.

After considering these emphatic communications, the Dominion undertook to clear the way for appeal to the Privy Council, and at the same time permitted mineral lands in the belt to continue to be under provincial jurisdiction. This permission was in no way to be considered as waiving dominion claims. Should the case be decided in favour of the Dominion, British Columbia was to be held to a strict accounting of all money collected.[28]

In 1887 while the case to decide the ownership of the precious metals within the Railway Belt was still before the courts, the Dominion issued a new set of regulations governing the disposal of mineral lands within the belt, but excepting gold and silver in British Columbia, until the case should be settled. These regulations conformed exactly to those in effect in British Columbia.

Among other clauses, these regulations provided that a free miner could explore vacant unreserved dominion lands with a view to obtaining a mining location, but no location or mining claim was to be granted until the actual discovery of a mine had been made. Having discovered a mineral deposit, the miner could secure his mining location by suitably marking it, by filing an affidavit with the dominion land agent within sixty days of having uncovered mineral, and by paying the five dollar fee. The receipt issued to the miner entitled him to entry to his location for five years, provided he renewed it annually during that period. These renewals would only be granted if he expended $100 each year on his location. Having fulfilled these requirements, he was permitted to remove and sell any minerals. Once he had expended a total of $500 on his location, he was permitted to buy it for cash at five dollars an acre. First, however, he had to deposit fifty dollars with the land agent to cover the cost of survey. Not until the survey was complete might a patent be issued.

As in the provincial mining law, priority of right was determined not by priority of discovery, but by fulfillment of all obligations entailed in securing a receipt. The miner was restricted to one location — not to exceed 1,500 by 600 feet — on any one vein or lode. No surface rights were conveyed, but the right was granted to use any water flowing through or upon the claim. With the consent of the minister of the interior the right to divert any other water from streams or lakes was granted for five years. The water so diverted had to be put to beneficial use and might be neither

[28] Ibid., p. 362.

wasted nor sold.[29] Precisely the same regulations were enacted on October 1, 1887 — expanded in May of the following year — to be applied to obtaining mining locations on abandoned and surrendered Indian lands. A forty-acre location could now be secured.[30]

On April 3, 1889, the Judicial Committee of the Privy Council rendered its decision in what has subsequently become known as the *Precious Metals Case*. The Judicial Committee supported the view of the province that the jurisdiction over precious metals within the Railway Belt lay with the provincial government. In delivering the judgment, Lord Watson passed some general remarks on the nature of the transfer of the belt which were later to cause a great deal of discussion:

> Leaving the previous metals out of view for the present, it seems clear that the only "conveyance" contemplated was a transfer to the Dominion of the provincial right to manage and settle the lands, and to appropriate their revenues. It was neither intended that the lands should be taken out of the Province, nor that the Dominion Government should occupy the position of a freeholder within the Province. The object of the Dominion Government was to recoup the cost of constructing the railway by selling the lands to settlers. Whenever land is so disposed of, the interest of the Dominion comes to an end. The land then ceases to be public land, and reverts to the same position as if it had been settled by the Provincial Government in the ordinary course of its administration. That was apparently the consideration which led to the insertion, in the agreement of 1883, of the condition that the Government of Canada should offer the land for sale, on liberal terms, with all convenient speed.[31]

With the province's claim maintained, the dominion government passed an Order in Council agreeing to make no further leases or other dispositions of any minerals in the Railway Belt, excepting coal, other than by outright sale of the lands wherein

[29] "Regulations Governing the Disposal of Dominion Lands Containing Minerals," in *The Consolidated Orders in Council of Canada under the Authority and Direction of His Excellency the Governor-General in Council*, compiled by Harris H. Bligh (Ottawa: Printed by Brown Chamberlain, Printer to the Queen . . . , 1889), pp. 871-901.

[30] "Indian Lands, Mining Regulations," in Bligh, *Consolidated Orders in Council*, pp. 182-209.

[31] *Attorney-General of B.C.* v. *Attorney-General of Canada* (1889) 14 App. Cas. 295 at 301. The case is also reported in R. A. Olmstead, *Decisions of the Judicial Committee of the Privy Council Relating to the British North America Act, 1867 and the Canadian Constitution 1867-1954*, 3 vols. (Ottawa: Queen's Printer, 1954), 1: 251-63.

such minerals lay. This agreement was all that was necessary. There never had been any dispute concerning the province's right to administer lands in the belt once they had been permanently alienated by crown grant from the Dominion. The Order in Council added that thereafter all minerals in the belt (again, excepting coal) should be administered under the local government's regulations and that any dominion lands which might be for sale from time to time within the belt containing minerals within the meaning of the provincial Mineral Act, "not being Indian reserves or settlements or portions thereof, and not being under licence or lease from the Dominion Government," should be open to purchase by the province at the price of five dollars an acre.[32] Lieutenant-Governor Nelson conveyed to Ottawa the province's acceptance of the Dominion's conciliatory Order in Council, on March 13, 1890.[33]

Now that the *Precious Metals Case* was decided, the government in British Columbia enacted legislation in 1890 stating that no railway chartered locally was to have any rights in any mines of iron, slate, or other minerals on lands purchased by it unless such rights were expressly stated and the minerals named in the conveyance. Any miner who wanted to continue working his mine at a distance of forty yards or less from the line of the railway was entitled to do so. Should the railway company consider the mining operations detrimental, it might buy out the owner of the mine, at a price to be determined by arbitration if this were necessary.[34]

So that the dominion regulations would conform with the provincial laws governing the mining of coal, a dominion Order in Council of 1895 authorized the minister of the interior to permit settlers in the Railway Belt to mine a certain quality of coal for domestic purposes only upon payment of the royalty in advance. The royalty was nominal, consisting of twenty cents a ton for anthracite, fifteen cents for bituminous, and ten cents for lignite. In 1899 the price to the provincial government of all lands within the belt containing minerals was reduced to one dollar an acre. However, when Premier Dunsmuir, on his mission to secure better terms in 1901, asked the Dominion that the province be permitted to administer

32 *Canada Gazette*, February 11, 1890, p. 353.

33 "Administration of Mineral Lands in the Railway Belt," B.C., *Sessional Papers*, 5th Parl., 4th sess., p. 461.

34 B.C., *Statutes*, 1890, 53 Vict., c. 39, ss. 21 and 22.

the base minerals under Indian reserves — half the royalties going as payment to the province for administrative costs — his request was not granted. At the same time Dunsmuir stated that gold and silver on Indian lands were "clearly within the right of the Province."[35] On this score the Dominion remained discreetly silent. The Department of the Interior had no intention of admitting any such claim, but, rather than begin another dispute, it kept silent on the whole matter of mineral rights under Indian lands. Minerals so located had until this time been administered for the benefit of the Indians, and they continued to be so administered.

Throughout the whole period from 1871 to 1913, the large mineral resources of the province were developed under laws adapted to the circumstances of the province. These laws seem to have been both wise and liberal. During the decade after 1903 the government gave a great deal of care and attention to the framing of laws regulating the mining of coal, both in regard to the nature of the claims and to the manner in which it should be mined. The Coal Mining Act of 1913 seems to have met with the approval of both the owners and the miners. Since mineral claims other than coal had been restricted to 51.6 acres since 1891, and as much of the coal mining (apart from the Dunsmuir operations at Nanaimo and the Crow's Nest Pass Company in the East Kootenay) had been done on leases, only a small acreage of provincial crown lands had been alienated for mining purposes. By nature the placer mines were of temporary value, and, as a rule, only those miners engaged in lode or hydraulic operations were interested in crown grants.

By 1913, a total of 387,167 acres of mineral claims exclusive of coal had been surveyed. This figure indicates the highest possible acreage that could have been alienated from the Crown for mineral purposes, since no patent was allowed until the survey had been made. The true figure, however, must have been considerably less. For the majority of miners, there was little advantage in buying the land when they might hold it from year to year simply by rerecording the claim and renewing their free miners' certificates. Claims were undoubtedly, and intentionally, allowed to revert to the Crown once the mineral had been exhausted.

But even if 387,167 acres had, indeed, been permanently alien-

[35] James Dunsmuir to Clifford Sifton, minister of the interior, February 2, 1901, B.C., *Sessional Papers*, 9th Parl., 2d sess., 1901, p. 582.

ated for mining purposes by 1913, it would still have been a negligible acreage in contrast with British Columbia's 230,000,000 acres. The revenue derived from mining was equally insignificant. Total government revenue from all sources in the forty-three years from 1871 to 1913 amounted to $93,560,441. Of this amount, only $7,642,678, roughly 8 per cent, was derived from mining sources.[36] This seems to be small revenue from British Columbia's rich deposits of gold, base minerals, and coal, but it must be remembered that the risks to the individual miner were great and the rewards often small. If the frequent changes in the mineral acts are considered, it becomes apparent that British Columbia's legislators did their best not only to provide for maximum revenue but also to render mining sufficiently profitable to attract the adventurous spirits who pioneered the development of this remote and rugged province.

36 See Appendix B, Table 6. Free miners' certificates, mineral tax, general mining receipts, and royalty and tax on coal account for this figure. In Table 6, revenue from the sale of mineral land is included under the general heading of land sales.

CHAPTER 6

Timber Legislation

As in the case of the alienation of agricultural and mineral lands, British Columbia evolved unique legislation to deal with its forests. In spite of the failure of provincial governments for years to recognize the value of timber resources, a surprisingly small area of forested land was permanently alienated by 1913. The outstanding principle incorporated into the timber legislation by 1913 was to separate the disposal of timber and land. In addition, the government retained the right to vary from year to year its royalty and rental of the timber granted under the differing forms of tenure. Thus, by 1913 the government had become a "sleeping partner" in forest exploitation and a sharer in the profits of the lumber industry.

Although British Columbia was spared the wholesale alienation of forest land which took place in the United States where four-fifths of the public forests were acquired by speculators and "timber-barons" under the Timber and Stone Act,[1] the earliest forest legislation cannot be given the credit. Only the lack of interest in British Columbia's timber during the years when forest lands were being alienated in huge acreages in the United States saved the province's forests from falling into private hands. Not until the economic life of the province had surged forward as a result of the railway link with Canada did the provincial government become aware of its potential forest wealth. In the 1880's this realization resulted in

[1] A. C. Flumerfelt, "Forest Resources," in *Canada and Its Provinces*, Shortt and Doughty, eds., 22:491.

the first systematic legislation, and by 1900 the basis of a sound forest policy had be laid.

From the colonial period to the First World War, timber lands were disposed of in four ways. The first method, inaugurated by Douglas as early as 1859, was outright sale of the land on which the timber stood. The second method, initiated in 1870, was a lease on the land; the third, introduced in 1884 and found the most satisfactory of the first three, was a system of timber licenses. In 1912 the best method yet devised was introduced, the sale of the timber by auction with the land being retained for the Crown. By 1913 approximately 1,000,000 acres of forests had been alienated under the first two methods, while licensing had alienated 7,500,-000 acres, more or less in perpetuity.

Throughout the colonial period in British Columbia timber lands could be acquired by purchase and crown grant in the same way as any other land and at the same price. Douglas's Land Proclamation of February 14, 1859, laid the basis for this policy by declaring that "unless otherwise specially announced at the time of sale, the conveyance of the land shall include all trees."[2] Thus, crown grants to land carried all timber rights without any reservation or royalty. Valuable although not extensive tracts were acquired under this proclamation at the nominal charge of ten shillings per acre, lowered on Vancouver Island in 1861 to four shillings twopence. The magnificent timber stands of the coast were looked upon by the early settlers more as a nuisance and an obstacle to progress than as an economic asset. Of so little worth did Douglas consider timber lands that he did not even mention them in the proclamation issued in 1851 dealing with country lands on Vancouver Island. It is ironic that the same proclamation did reserve the precious metals to the Crown, for the forests of Vancouver Island have produced far greater wealth than have all the precious metals yet found there.

At Confederation in 1871 timber lands were still available for purchase at the current rate of one dollar an acre. Section 47 of the 1870 Land Ordinance retained the earlier clause stating that the conveyance of land included all trees, and there was no limit on the acreage that could be bought. As early as 1884, however, the law did forbid the sale of timber lands. In the absence of any

[2] "Proclamation, Enclosure in no. 51," Douglas to Lytton, February 19, 1859, no. 51, Gt. Brit., *Papers Relative to British Columbia*, 2:65-66.

administrative staff to enforce compliance and in the face of the public's attitude that standing timber was of no value, the law became a dead letter for twenty years. Indeed, until 1906 timber lands were sold like any other lands. Throughout these twenty years a legend persisted that the provincial timber lands amounted to at least 182,000,000 acres, and they were consequently regarded as inexhaustible.[3]

The Land Act of 1884 clearly intended only the lease of timber land.[4] Its provisions were reinforced in the Act of 1887 where it was stated that "none of such of the public lands of the Province as are chiefly valuable for timber shall be disposed of by public or private sale." An applicant for the purchase of land, by the 1887 Act called "patented land," was required to make a declaration before a Justice of the Peace that the land for which he sought a crown grant was not chiefly valuable for its timber.[5]

The language of the 1884 and 1887 Acts seems to have been clear enough. But the comprehensive Land Act of 1888 reveals either the existence of pressure applied to members of the government to leave a loop-hole in the law, or some very muddled thinking in regard to the legislation. It was still stated that timber lands were not for sale, and for the first time provision was made to collect revenues on lands containing timber but not classified primarily as timber land. The royalty, amounting to fifty cents per thousand board feet on "all timber suitable for spars, piles, saw logs, or railroad ties,"[6] was to be levied on all timber cut on any subsequently granted lands. In effect, the provision meant that timber was no longer to be given away, but was henceforth to be sold. Yet, under the land classification system begun by the same act, no restrictions of any kind were imposed on the purchase of crown land by the ordinary methods.

This Land Act of 1888, curiously described as the first "coherent

3 "Final Report of the Royal Commission of Inquiry on Timber and Forestry, 1909-1910," B.C., *Sessional Papers*, 12th Parl., 2d sess., 1911, pp. D14-15.

4 B.C., *Statutes*, 1884, 47 Vict., c. 16, s. 35.

5 B.C., *Statutes*, 1887, 50 Vict., c. 17, ss. 1 and 2. The owners of these patented lands, as well as pre-emptors who had not proved up, were required by this act to obtain licences to cut timber on their land if the timber were for other than domestic or farm use or for clearing and improving. These licences permitted owners to cut timber for manufacture of lumber. The licences cost 25 cents per thousand board feet for the amount of timber applied for in the application.

6 B.C., *Statutes*, 1888, 51 Vict., c. 16, s. 21.

legislation"[7] dealing with timber, dwelt at length with the classification and sale of crown lands. All unsurveyed land could be bought for $2.50 an acre, and surveyed lands were divided into two classes. First class lands included those suitable not only for cultivation but also for lumbering and sold at $2.50 an acre. Second class lands, priced at one dollar an acre, were the marginal lands valuable neither for cultivation nor for lumbering. How this statute could be called "coherent" in the face of the two contradictory clauses dealing with the sale of timber lands is difficult to understand. On the one hand, no lands chiefly valuable for timber were to be sold; on the other, first class lands suitable for lumbering could be purchased in the usual manner. Whatever the intent of the act may have been, timber lands continued to be sold.

The difficulty probably lay in the failure of the act to define timber lands. But even after this omission was rectified by section 4 of the 1891 Act,[8] timber lands continued to be sold as usual. By the 1891 Act, lands fit for lumbering, still first class lands but now worth five dollars an acre, were loosely defined as those containing 5,000 board feet per acre on each 160 acres. This was the first attempt to define timber lands, and it was the first time an upward limit of 640 acres had been placed on purchases. By placing the square mile limit and by requiring improvements to the original value of the land, an attempt was being made to limit the sale of timber and to encourage agricultural development.

Not until 1896 was timber land more carefully defined as land having 8,000 board feet per acre west of the Cascades and 5,000 feet per acre east of the summit.[9] This was still the statutory description of timber lands in the province in 1913. By the 1896 Act, such lands were removed from the classification of first class lands and reserved from sale. In spite of the repeated attempts made to reserve timber lands from sale, lack of inspection forestalled the clear intent of the various acts. It would be reasonable enough to assume, too, that the definition of timber lands could in many cases have been liberally interpreted by such government timber cruisers as were available from the Lands Department. Difficult as it was to enforce, the 1896 Act did, however, establish the principle of the public ownership of all timber lands and pro-

7 Flumerfelt, "Forest Resources," p. 492.

8 B.C., *Statutes*, 1891, 54 Vict., c. 15, s. 4(2).

9 B.C., *Statutes*, 1896, 59 Vict., c. 28, s. 12(2a).

vide a form of licensing tenure by which only the timber could be disposed of. In 1905 the modifications to the licensing system made that method of holding timber land so desirable that purchase was no longer attractive. It is generally agreed that by 1906 there was no longer any outright sale of timber lands.

The government also showed concern over timber resources in its taxation policy in 1905. A tax of four per cent was levied on all wild land. All unimproved land, including timber land, was classified as wild land for taxation purposes. But the act permitted all private holdings of timber lands to be taxed at half the wild land rate. Had the higher tax been retained on private holdings, the holders of these crown-granted lands would have resorted to wasteful logging methods in their haste to get the timber off and let the land revert to the Crown.[10]

The low value attached to crown-granted timber lands is indicated by the lowering of the assessed value of certain stands on Vancouver Island known to contain 50,000 board feet measure per acre from six to four dollars an acre in 1901. Although the assessed value of timber lands in private ownership was to rise measurably before 1913, their value was set at only $1,907,546 in 1906, and the revenue to the Crown derived from the two per cent tax was only $38,150.[11] By 1913, there were 922,949 acres of privately held timber land, all acquired by outright sale.[12]

Leasing, the second method adopted for disposing of timber land, ran concurrently for thirty five years with the outright sale of the land and the timber on it. The issuing of timber leases goes back to the Land Ordinance of 1870. Section 28 permitted the leasing of unlimited areas of crown land "for the purpose of cutting spars, timber, or lumber." The only stipulation was that before a lease was granted the lessee had to be in the lumber business. Once again, as in the case of agricultural and mineral lands, the principle of beneficial use was re-affirmed. So well had Lytton in 1859 impressed upon the administrators of the colony the need to prevent speculation in its public lands that, however little attention may have been paid to the regulations at times, the actual use of the land for its stated purpose was always incorporated into the regula-

10 Flumerfelt, "Forest Resources," p. 504.

11 "Royal Commission on Timber and Forestry," pp. D16 and D22.

12 See Appendix B, Table 8, "Timber Statistics," Part 2. (Compiled from forestry inspectors' reports in the reports of the chief commissioners of lands and works, 1883-1911, inclusive.)

tions governing its disposal. Equally important, however, could have been the recognition of the need for some form of tenure "distinct from the ownership of the land." As a result of the introduction of this principle, British Columbia "has retained an interest in and control over by far the greater part of its forest resources,"[13] a unique situation in North America.

The timber lease clause enacted in 1870 was re-enacted in the Land Acts of 1875 and 1884 and remained unchanged until 1888. The yearly rent was from one to ten cents per acre, and the royalty was set at twenty to twenty-five cents per thousand feet.

Timber-cutting Leases, 1873

Lessee	*District*	*Acreage*	*Date*	*Rate*
W. P. Sayward	Chemainus	1,370	June 23, 1868	2¢ per acre per annum
Michael and John Muir	Sooke	3,316	Jan. 13, 1872	1¢ per acre per annum
George Askew	Chemainus	519	Dec. 8, 1870	2¢ per acre per annum
R. P. Rithet	Coast District	15,000	Feb. 22, 1873	1¢ per acre per annum
Hastings Saw Mill Co.	New Westminster	18,559	Nov. 30, 1865	1¢ per acre per annum
Moody, Dietz and Nelson	New Westminster	2,634	Jan. 31, 1866	1¢ per acre per annum
Moody, Dietz and Nelson	New Westminster	11,110.58	Jan. 1, 1870	1¢ per acre per annum
W. T. Collinson	New Westminster	365	Feb. 25, 1870	$15 per annum
Jeremiah Rogers	New Westminster	780	Nov. 30, 1868	$40 per annum
Walker, Bowes, and Robertson	Omineca	425	March 5, 1872	1¢ per acre per annum
		54,078.58		$603.23

[13] Canada, Commission of Conservation, Committee on Forests, *Forests of British Columbia,* by H. N. Whitford and R. D. Craig (Ottawa, 1918).

The first indication of the area of timber lands taken up under lease was contained in the 1873 report of Robert Beaven, chief commissioner of lands and works. Beaven's report listed the names of ten lessees who had been granted a total of 54,078.58 acres.[14]

As most of these leases had been granted for a period of twenty-one years, the annual charge can only be regarded as a holding charge and not as a source of revenue. To the lumberman of today, the rental of one cent an acre charged the Moody Sawmill owners in the 1870's on their seventeen square miles of virgin coastal timber at the head of Burrard Inlet must seem incredible. In the early 1870's, however, the provincial government was only too glad to grant timber leases to individuals or companies actually engaged in sawmill operations in order to ensure a supply of lumber for purely local needs. Until this time much of the lumber used in the colony had been imported from San Francisco. One proof that speculators were discouraged was the refusal of the applications of William Sutton and W. A. Robertson in 1875 for leases of 27,000 acres in the Cowichan district because they did not operate sawmills in the neighbourhood of the lands specified.[15] The second list of leases tabled in 1876 includes an application for a lease at Quatsino for 15,769 acres.[16] A comparison with the first list makes it obvious that the major attack on the forests had begun in the most accessible and most heavily timbered areas of the province. The timber lands secured by lease in the early years were in the regions of New Westminster, Chemainus, and northern Vancouver Island.

The first of many such Select Committees was appointed in the 1875-76 session of the legislature to study the efficacy of the timber lease clause within the Land Act. The brief report of the Committee is interesting because it reflects the casual attitude of the government towards its timber resources. The single recommendation in the report called for the easing of the regulations to permit the granting of more extensive leases.[17] It is difficult to see how the regulations could have been eased except by permitting speculators who did not operate sawmills to acquire leases. As it was, leases

14 "Report of the Chief Commissioner of Lands and Works ... 1873," p. 66.

15 "Return ... of timber cutting leases," B.C., *Sessional Papers*, 2d Parl., 1st sess., 1876, p. 707.

16 Ibid., p. 706.

17 "Report of the Select Committee upon the Method of Granting Leases," ibid., p. 739.

were being granted for "any extent" of unalienated crown land at a nominal rental and for twenty-one years.

That timber leases were not an important source of revenue is evident from the fact that in 1876, the year the Select Committee recommended easing restrictions, rental of $52.27 on 4,686 acres held in two leases was the sole income received from this source. The four holders of the remaining 24,727 acres of leased timber land paid no rental that year, and there is no indication that the government felt any concern about the situation. Lumbermen took their cue from official laxity, and by 1878 there was not a single holder of a large lease paying rent. William Sutton, who had finally secured a 187-acre lease, was the only one to pay rent, the sum of $175.83.[18]

By 1888 the provincial government had begun to realize that some revenue might be derived from leases, and the 1888 Land Act levied a rental of five cents an acre on all leases granted between 1879 and 1888. Future leases were to be granted for a term not to exceed thirty years at an annual rent of ten cents per acre and a royalty of fifty cents per thousand. The royalty was also applied to the leases granted since 1879. The annual charge of ten cents an acre gave owners of sawmills, or those who would undertake to build a mill with a capacity of 1,000 board feet per day for each 400 acres leased, exclusive cutting rights over an unlimited forest area. By establishing a reasonably low rental, the government demonstrated its desire to encourage the lumber industry, but low though the rental was, it served as a brake on the indiscriminate alienation of the province's best timber lands.

In 1891, leases good for thirty years were authorized for cutting hemlock bark for tanning purposes,[19] but this section of the Land Act was not used until 1905-06, "when 32,252 acres were leased at a rental of two cents per acre for the first five years and five cents per acre thereafter."[20] Before one of these hemlock leases was granted, the applicant had to prove that he operated a tannery. All the leases of this type granted in 1905 and 1906 were still being held in 1913.

18 ". . . Return of all moneys received from leases of Timber Lands," B.C., *Sessional Papers*, 2d Parl., 3d sess. and 3d Parl., 1st sess., 1878, p. 627; and B.C., *Sessional Papers*, 3d Parl., 2d sess., 1879, p. 393.

19 B.C., *Statutes*, 1891, 54 Vict., c. 15, s. 13.

20 *Forests of B.C.*, p. 86.

In 1901, ten years after hemlock leases were granted, the government authorized the granting of still another form of lease — a lease for cutting pulp-wood. These leases were granted for twenty-one years, a term decided upon in 1895, at an annual rental of two cents an acre and a royalty of twenty-five cents per cord on all pulp-wood cut. Again to forestall speculators, leaseholders were required to build a pulp-mill in the province with a capacity of one ton of pulp or a half-ton of paper per day for every square mile of land leased. Before such leases were abolished in 1903, four of them comprising 354,399 acres of choice merchantable timber had been granted, and a further 1,300,480 acres had been placed under reserve for similar pulp leases.[21]

In 1901, as a means of securing greater revenue from leases, the government tried offering perpetual renewal of their leases in consecutive periods of twenty-one years at new and increased rentals to all leaseholders who would surrender their leases within one year. Not only would the government be able to impose the new rates set in 1898 of fifteen cents per acre per annum plus a royalty of fifty cents per thousand, but also the leaseholder would know that by surrendering the lease and taking it up again under the new rates he would be assured the right to the timber as long as he wished. By promising to renew these leases at the end of twenty-one years at the then existing rates, the government hoped to secure to itself a fairer share of the appreciation in timber value.

Even so, it had become obvious by 1905 that leases were no longer in the best interests of the province. Too often leases had been granted to speculators, particularly since the operation of a sawmill ceased to be required in 1897. When a return tabled in that year showed that between July 1, 1903, and February 21, 1905, eleven leases totalling 109,228 acres of first-rate timber land had been granted for twenty-one year periods,[22] the government became convinced that to leave the rental and stumpage fixed on these acreages, in addition to all the older leases, for twenty-one years, was shortsighted. Because so little was definitely known concerning the extent of British Columbia's timber and because there

21 "... Return showing the agreements ... for the manufacture of pulp ...," B.C., *Sessional Papers*, 9th Parl., 3d sess., 1902, pp. 791-92; and "... Return ... of every reserve (of not less than 25,000 acres) of Provincial lands ...," B.C., *Sessional Papers*, 9th Parl., 4th sess., 1903, p. J23.

22 "... Return showing the number of timber leases ...," B.C., *Sessional Papers*, 10th Parl., 2d sess., 1905, p. F35.

was the probability of a sharp increase in the demand for that timber with the immense new market opening on the prairies, the McBride government felt that to tie up extensive acreages for twenty-one years at a nominal holding charge was a poor way of drawing immediate profit from a substantial portion of the best timber areas. Therefore, all granting of timber leases was abolished.

And although the low revenue derived from the leasehold system was the final reason for its abolition, the fact that it was such a wasteful system weighed heavily against it. No provision required that a single lease be in one large block. It could contain ten or more lots scattered over a wide area within the same forest district. Some of these lots were as small as 150 acres. As the Royal Commission on Timber and Forestry pointed out in its report in 1910, the system resulted in the culling of the finest stands. The intervening, less valuable, stands, irregular in shape, were left as unproductive crown land.[23] Therefore, no new leases were granted after 1905, although those previously granted were still renewable if they contained merchantable timber. By 1913, timber leases, exclusive of those for pulp and hemlock bark, covered 613,000 acres, of which, 386,458 acres were renewable.

The third method by which the Crown disposed of its timber was by licence, a refinement of the policy of disposing of timber apart from the land under it. From 1884 to 1913 the conditions under which licences were granted altered greatly. The original purpose of the licence, in 1884 called a "general" licence, was to make timber available to the small, independent operator who could not afford to own a sawmill, a condition required of all leaseholders. For an annual rental of ten dollars, the holder of the licence obtained cutting rights to 1,000 acres of timber land. The term of tenure was four years; the licence was not transferable; it could be cancelled if the holder did not "continuously proceed to cut and manufacture the timber" within the specified limits.[24] To secure additional revenue from these licences, the holder was required to pay fifteen cents a tree royalty and twenty cents per thousand on the timber cut.

In 1888 the "general" licence became a "special" licence and

[23] "Royal Commission on Timber and Forestry," p. D15.

[24] B.C., *Statutes*, 1884, 47 Vict., c. 32. This act is of interest because it is the first of its kind in the province to deal with the disposal of timber apart from the Land Act.

the term was reduced from four years to one, although the chief commissioner of lands and works could renew it. Each holder was henceforth limited to one licence, and his rental was increased from ten to fifty dollars. Royalty on timber cut under any former tenure — crown lands, patented lands, leaseholds, as well as timber limits or licences — was increased to fifty cents per thousand. Indicative of an awakening interest in an export market was the provision in section 22 of the act for rebating half the royalty if the lumber were exported from the province.[25] In the first six months of its operation, 25 per cent of the royalty collected by the government on all timber handled by the twenty-five sawmills in operation in 1888 was rebated. Of the total royalty of $12,675.59 paid on the 31,868,384 board feet of timber going through the mills, $3,051.40 was rebated.[26]

The licensing system was soon to become popular. At the end of 1888 there were seventy-eight general licences still in force, and thirty-six of the new special licences had been issued. R. J. Skinner, the first forestry inspector, predicted a rapid expansion in the provincial timber business, but at the same time he sounded a note of warning on the need for much closer supervision of the growing industry:

> It is satisfactory to note that as far as can be judged from present appearances and circumstances, there is a prospect of a very considerable increase in the timber business of this Province taking place in the immediate future. Eastern as well as local capital is now being directed to and invested in that industry. . . .
>
> The revenue which will accrue . . . from the Crown Lands and Timber Limits of the Province, judging from the increased number of General and Special Licenses now, and soon to be, issued promises to be much greater than it has been in former years. The increase in the number of licenses and the more extended operations carried on by them will render it necessary that a close and careful supervision should be kept, and will at the same time considerably increase the difficulties (now sufficiently apparent) there are in making such a supervision thoroughly effective over the very large scope of country in which the lumbering industries of the Province are distributed.[27]

25 B.C., *Statutes*, 1888, 51 Vict., c. 16.

26 B.C., *Sessional Papers*, 5th Parl., 3d sess., 1889, p. 151. These statistics are from the first "Forestry Inspector's Report" to be issued by the chief commissioner of lands and works.

27 Ibid., p. 152.

Before the licence system was completely abandoned, a total of 65,180 special licences had been issued.[28] Skinner's warning was none too soon. Even though the area of timber which could be held under licence was reduced from 1,000 acres to 640 in 1901, and the fees increased to $100 in 1901 and then to $140 west and $115 east of the Cascades in 1903,[29] these areas comprised by far the largest timber holdings in the province by 1913. Licensees held 8,600 square miles (5,504,000 acres) west of the Cascades and 6,400 square miles (4,096,000 acres) in the interior of the province.[30]

Although the licences were renewable, their holders were placed at a distinct disadvantage to lease holders who had their acreages at the original rental and royalty for a twenty-one- or thirty-year period. In 1903, therefore, the period for which a licence was valid was raised from one year to five. As a result, the number of licences issued jumped from 129 in 1901 to 1,307 in 1903.[31] Even so, the growth of the lumber industry required a more stable supply of timber than a five-year licence provided so that the licence holder could secure financial support for his enterprise. His chief asset, an assured supply of timber, he did not have under his licence.

When the McBride government wiped out the leasing system entirely in 1905, it also stopped issue of limited, non-transferable licences. A completely new principle of disposing of timber was adopted. First, transferable licences good for twenty-one years on a specified square mile of forest were issued, and existing licences were extended for sixteen years.[32] What made British Columbia's timber policy unique on the continent, however, was the reservation of the government's share in the increasing value of standing timber as it should accrue. It was left entirely to the government to fix the payments, both rental and royalty, that would be charged for renewal of the option each year. The method was attractive as well as unique, since the operator, for a small outlay, was able to stake

28 Compiled from forestry inspectors' reports for the years 1888-1910, inclusive, in the *Sessional Papers* for those years. Appendix B, Table 8, Part 1, lists 81,132 licences up to 1911 but that total contains all the older general as as well as the newer special licences.

29 B.C., *Statutes*, 1901, 1 Ed. 7, c. 30, s. 8, and B.C., *Statutes*, 1903-4, 3 & 4 Edw. 7, c. 30, s. 8.

30 Flumerfelt, "Forest Resources," pp. 505-06.

31 See Appendix B, Table 8, Part 1.

32 *Forests of B.C.*, p. 89.

a timber claim without waiting for survey. The claim was his for twenty-one years so long as he renewed his licence each year.

The effect of the new legislation was immediate and startling. Writing about it thirteen years later, the Committee on Forests of the Dominion Commission of Conservation said:

> Coming at a time when speculation was rife in land and timber, and when the conservation propaganda in the United States was calling attention to the failing timber supplies in that country, this legislation, permitting the acquiring of timber with such small initial expense, resulted in a real timber boom, and the number of licenses increased from 1,451 in 1904 to over 15,000 in 1907. Including the cost of locating, which probably averaged $50 per license, and advertising, about $15, the average claim cost the stakers about $205 on the coast and $180 in the interior. This gave them the right to cut anywhere from 5,000,000 to 40,000,000 feet, depending on the timber staked. By the end of 1907, there was little accessible timber not staked and much, with slight prospect of ever being exploited by means then known, had been taken up. As surveys were not required, except as the land was to be logged, much confusion has resulted from the overlapping of claims, and considerable additional revenue has accrued to the Government as a result. As one example of what has happened, the case may be cited of six different licensees who, for several years, paid fees on the same block of 400 acres of timber. The failure of many licensees to locate their limits accurately also resulted in the unnecessary inclusion of non-timbered lands, such as burns, areas above timber-line, etc., with consequent loss to themselves.[33]

In 1908, the peak year, the fees alone from the 17,700 licences issued accounted for $2,301.449.47, or 90 per cent of the total revenue from forests.[34] The major objective of the new policy had been to increase revenue from forests materially. In accomplishing its objective, the policy was an immediate success. By the end of 1907 when more than 9,000,000 acres were held under licence, some uneasiness was being felt at the "insatiable nature of the continental demand for standing timber."[35] The new policy pleased the timber interests, many of whom were American, and resulted in an astonishing increase in revenue, but it also jeopardized the future welfare of the province.

33 Ibid., p. 90.

34 "Timber Inspector's Report [1908]," B.C., *Sessional Papers,* 11th Parl., 3d sess., 1909, p. H49.

35 "Royal Commission on Timber and Forestry," p. D16.

Having given the matter serious consideration, the government issued an Order in Council on December 27, 1907, withdrawing all unalienated timber lands from all forms of alienation.[36] The 15,000 licences then held by operators were still valid, as were the rights to 792,295 acres held under lease,[37] but the market then in sight could not absorb in twenty-one years all the timber held under lease or licences.

Between 1905 and 1908, the holders of licences made a concerted effort to persuade the government to grant them the same privilege of unlimited tenure as was enjoyed by lease holders. All they had under the present regulations were cutting rights for twenty-one years. To settle the complicated matter of timber land tenure, the government appointed a Timber and Forestry Commission in July, 1909. As a result of its recommendations, in 1910 the government permitted licensees to convert their licences. The new regulations required licence holders to surrender the twenty-one year licence within two years in return for a new, transferable licence, renewable annually so long as merchantable timber remained on the land. The new licence thereby became to all intents and purposes perpetual.[38] The result has been the more or less permanent alienation of some 7,500,000 acres of valuable timber stands under the 12,850 licences converted by their holders. The Timber and Forestry Commission's final report estimated the acreage held under licence to represent 60 per cent of the merchantable timber acreage in the province. The report also stated that the largest number of licences known to be in the possession of a single holder was 375 and that there were a number of licensees who held between one and two hundred.[39]

The following table shows how the lumber industry had spread through the province by 1915.

Location of Licences

East of Cascades:	7,046
West of Cascades:	6,701[40]

[36] Ibid.

[37] "Timber Inspector's Report [1907]," B.C., *Sessional Papers,* 11th Parl., 2d sess., 1908, p. H46.

[38] *Forests of B.C.*, pp. 90-91.

[39] "Royal Commission on Timber and Forestry," p. D27.

[40] *Forests of B.C.*, p. 93.

Forest District	*Number of Licences*
Cranbrook	908
Hazelton	560
Kamloops	1,672
Lillooet	53
Nelson	1,306
Prince Rupert	1,248
Fort George	962
Tete Jaune	1,001
Vernon	328
Vancouver	3,352
Vancouver Island	2,357
Total	13,747

Although all unalienated timber land had been summarily placed under reserve in 1907 by an alarmed government, it was impossible to arrive at even a rough estimate of the acreage under reserve until every timber limit had been surveyed. By August, 1910, only 1,466 of the 15,000 licences had been surveyed and located on a map,[41] a total of 869,585 acres. An informed guess set the reserve at 3,750,000 acres, one-quarter of the merchantable timber, estimated to be 15,000,000 acres.[42]

Whatever the exact acreage may have been, it remained under reserve until the passage of the Forest Act in 1912. This major item of legislation provided for a fourth method of timber disposal, that of timber sales, the only method by which Crown timber was disposed of from 1912 until the introduction of tree farm licences and public sustained yield units. The Forest Branch examined, cruised, and surveyed the area, and set an upset stumpage price. If it were considered in the public interest to do so, the standing timber was then sold to the highest bidder. The highest bidder was

41 "Royal Commission on Timber and Forestry," p. D28.

42 Ibid., p. D17.

the operator who submitted the highest cash bonus per thousand feet of merchantable timber. Rentals and royalty were paid as the timber was cut on the same scale as that charged holders of licences. The distinguishing feature of the sale system was that the fair market value of the timber, or more if the bidding exceeds the upset price, went into the public treasury. The timber was sold for a much higher price than the land would bring, and the land still belonged to the Crown. As the land was logged, it was released for settlement.

The introduction of the sale system marked an end to the former exploitation and the beginning of a modern, enlightened forest policy in British Columbia. The early systems of granting leases and licences to cut timber while retaining the land underneath and the later method of reserving all unalienated timber lands and selling only the timber crop left the province in control of all but 4 per cent of its forested area.

From 1871 to 1913, then, British Columbia disposed of its timber in four ways — by outright sale of the timber along with the land, by leasing timber land, by issuing a licence to cut timber, and by sale of the timber apart from the land. In addition, the government disposed of some of its timber lands indirectly as part of subsidies to railway companies. In 1883 the dominion government was granted the forty-mile Railway Belt through the centre of the province and a 2,000,000-acre block on Vancouver Island. Later, provincially incorporated railway companies were granted more than 6,000,000 acres in southeastern British Columbia, also as subsidy lands. By 1913 some of this land had been sold by the companies into private hands and permanently alienated. However 4,065,076 acres were repurchased by the government from the Columbia and Western and the British Columbia Southern. Reports from the companies stated in 1910 that practically none of the remaining land could be classified as timber land.[43] No statistics concerning timber in the Canadian Pacific Railway Belt were available other than the estimate of a dominion forester who said that 1,280,000 acres in the Belt were under licence and permit in 1910.[44]

[43] Ibid., p. D23.

[44] Ibid., p. D17, n. 6.

In the case of the Esquimalt and Nanaimo Railway lands, however, there was no doubt as to the existence of valuable timber stands. The subsidy lands for this railway had been given by the province to the Dominion in 1883; the Dominion in turn gave the lands to the Esquimalt and Nanaimo Railway Company to construct the Island portion of the Canadian Pacific.

An interesting court case developed in 1948 over the taxing of some of the timber on these lands. For three decades, the 375,000 acres of valuable unsold timber stands still in the possession of the Esquimalt and Nanaimo Railway Company had caused provincial governments concern because they yielded neither royalty nor tax.[45] In 1945, while conducting an enquiry into the provincial forest resources, Chief Justice Sloan, acting as a commissioner under the Public Inquiries Act of British Columbia, was struck by the fact that these timber lands were yielding no revenue to the province. In his report, Sloan suggested that the province should be collecting a tax on this timber and, in addition, might also assess the Island Railway Belt lands for the fire protection tax levied on all timber lands since 1912.[46]

The Lieutenant-Governor in Council, acting under the Constitutional Questions Determination Act,[47] referred a number of questions to the British Columbia Court of Appeal for hearing and consideration. The Esquimalt and Nanaimo Railway Company argued that the imposition of a tax on the company's timber lands in the Island Railway Belt would be contrary to the contract entered into between the Dominion and the railway company on August 20, 1883, subject to the provisions of section 22 of the Settlement Act of 1883:

> The lands to be acquired by the company from the Dominion Government for the construction of the Railway shall not be subject to taxation unless and until the same are used by the company for other than railroad purposes, or leased, occupied, sold, or alienated.[48]

The Province contended that there was no existing contract between the Province and the company, regardless of any contractual relationship between the Dominion and the company. The

45 *Forests of B.C.*, pp. 85-86.
46 B.C., *Statutes*, 1912, 2 Geo. 5, c. 17, ss. 125-133.
47 B.C., *Revised Statutes*, 1936, c. 50.
48 B.C., *Statutes*, 1883, 46 Vict., c. 14, s. 22.

company also argued that the imposition of a tax, being a fixed sum per thousand feet board measure of the timber cut, would be *ultra-vires* the Province. The Court of Appeal held that there was no contract between the Province and the company but that the imposition of the tax would be *ultra-vires.*

On appeal to the Supreme Court of Canada[49] it was held that there was a contract between the Province and the company and also that the imposition of the tax would be *ultra-vires*. On further appeal to the Privy Council,[50] the Judicial Committee held that there was no contract and did not consider the constitutional validity of a provincial tax based on the quantity of timber cut. However, the Committee agreed with the decision of the Supreme Court of Canada in regard to the imposition of the six cents an acre charge levied on unalienated timber land held by the company under the clauses of the act authorizing a forest protection charge. Authority for this tax, it was stated, was derived directly from section 22 of the Settlement Act which exempted the unalienated lands of the company from taxation, and therefore it could not be imposed.[51] Thus the company was forced to pay the provincial government the timber taxes but not the forest protection tax.

Mr. H. R. MacMillan, British Columbia's first chief forester, estimated in 1913 that over 100,000,000 acres of provincial land were timbered, of which about 65,000,000 acres held merchantable timber. According to one tabulation made in that year, only 16,000,000 acres of first class timber, a small fraction of the total potential, had been accounted for, under the following forms of tenure:

Timber Land Acreage

	Acreage	*Average Stand per acre ft.*
Vancouver Island crown grant timber	344,000	35,000

[49] *Esquimalt and Nanaimo Rly. Co.* v. *Attorney-General of British Columbia* (1948) S.C.R. 403.

[50] *Attorney-General of British Columbia* v. *Esquimalt and Nanaimo Rly. Co.* (1950) A.C. 87.

[51] Ibid., p. 88.

Mainland crown grant timber	484,000	10,000
Esquimalt & Nanaimo Railway Co.	350,000	14,500
Canadian Pacific Railway (unpublished conjecture)	822,000	....
Timber leaseholds	613,000	26,000
Special licence timber	9,000,000	12,000
Mill timber on pulp leaseholds	387,000	13,000
	12,000,000	
Reserve timber land (conjecture)	4,000,000[52]	
	16,000,000	

In the final report of the 1909-1910 Commission, the commissioners predicted that "the value of standing timber in British Columbia is destined to rise to heights that general opinion would consider incredible today." Evidence before them showed that British Columbia contained half the stand in Canada, that the province faced a rising market east, west, and south, that over 90 per cent of that timber was crown property, and, above all, that government policy had made the province "a sharer in the profits from the lumbering industry." It is not surprising that the commissioners concluded by stating that, as a result of its income from timber, British Columbia should become "that phenomenon of statecraft and good fortune — a country of 'semi-independent means.' "[53]

The policy formulated in 1905 and 1907 has been instrumental in retaining for the public in British Columbia an equity in forests which has become the envy of other countries. That the acreage of

52 Flumerfelt, "Forest Resources," p. 508. Statistics given in "Report of the Minister of Lands," B.C., *Sessional Papers*, 13th Parl., 2d sess., 1914, p. D17, do not correspond exactly with these. The total acreage listed in the *Sessional Papers* as alienated timber land is 11,074,190 acres.

53 "Royal Commission on Timber and Forestry," p. D20. The three commissioners were F. J. Fulton, K.C., chief commissioner of lands and works and acting attorney general; A. S. Goodeve, M.P., Rossland; and A. C. Flumerfelt, J.P., Victoria.

permanently alienated forest land is such a small fraction of the total productive forested area is largely a direct result of the principle of beneficial use applied to the forests, as it was to agricultural and mineral lands and, as will be shown, to water rights.

CHAPTER 7

Water Rights

If lack of interest in forests resulted in casual timber legislation in the early days of the colony, the opposite was true in the case of water courses. Mining, the earliest profitable activity, required the extensive use of water, and early legislation provided detailed instructions for recording water rights. Had these been adhered to, few of the later difficulties would have arisen. But because water in British Columbia was in abundant supply and because water rights produced no revenues for the government, the recording procedure was lax and led inevitably to confusion. As with surveying, the fault lay not with the regulations but with the administration. The division of authority arising from the creation of the Railway Belt added to the chaos. Not until 1913, in fact, was the problem satisfactorily settled.

Under English common law the principle existed that the public and those living on the banks of streams had the right, called "riparian proprietorship," to have the waters of streams flowing through or by their property left undisturbed.[1] Since any diversion of the water was considered damage to the adjoining property, the owner was protected against such diversion. Adherence to this principle in British Columbia would have been impossible in the face of the placer miners' needs, and hence it would have been directly opposed to the best interests of the colony.

In a proclamation in 1859 Governor Douglas recognized the need

[1] H. W. Grunsky, "Water Legislation and Administration in British Columbia," in B.C., Department of Lands, "Report of the Minister of Lands [1912]," B.C., *Sessional Papers*, 13th Parl., 1st sess., 1913, p. D117.

to depart from the principle of riparian ownership. The rules he issued to regulate gold mining provided that:

> Any person desiring any exclusive ditch or water privilege shall make application to the Gold Commissioner . . . stating the name of every applicant, the proposed ditch head and quantity of water, the proposed locality of distribution, and if such water shall be for sale, the price at which it is proposed to sell the same, the general nature of the work to be done, and the time within which such work shall be completed; and the Gold Commissioner shall enter a note of all such matters as of record.[2]

The Land Proclamation of February the same year made provision also for the granting of a "Ditch privilege" to any holder of crown lands.[3] The Land Ordinance of 1870 not only extended the privilege of diverting any water from streams flowing over or adjacent to any land held under pre-emption or purchase, but went so far as to state that no one had any exclusive right to the water in any stream until he had recorded such quantity of water as might be considered necessary. The water so recorded could be diverted across adjoining land, whether held by the Crown, pre-empted, or purchased, upon payment to the lawful owner of reasonable compensation for damage; but the owner of those adjoining lands could not prevent the diversion of the water over his land however extensive the damage or troublesome the ditch. To ensure beneficial use of the water, section 37 required the owner of a ditch or water privilege to "take all reasonable means of utilizing the water taken by him; and if he shall willfully waste any unreasonable quantity of water," the rights to it could be cancelled.

By 1871 it had become firmly established in law that no rights to any water passed with the rights to the land. Water rights had to be secured by means of a water record. As in the case of mining claims, priority of record established priority of right. However disconcerting it may have been to the new settler to discover that the creek or stream on his property was not necessarily his to use as he chose, the exigencies of mining development and of the later irrigation needs dictated the abandonment of the old world principle of riparian ownership. It had already been decided for the

2 "Rules and Regulations for the Working of Gold Mines," s. 7, B.C. [*Proclamations and Ordinances, 1858-1864*].

3 Ibid. Douglas issued this proclamation on February 14, 1859, in order "to publish for general information the method to be pursued with respect to the alienation and possession of lands . . . in British Columbia."

future that there would be no such expansion of the riparian rights doctrine as had taken place in some of the western American states in which "the courts, without the aid of Statutes, had expanded the old common law natural right . . . until it [had] included the right to irrigate large bodies of arid land."[4]

Because the water record was automatically transferred with the transfer of the land or mining claim,[5] it should have been provided that the land on which the water was to be used be specifically designated in all water records. This oversight was later to cause "terrible confusion and endless trouble,"[6] and the benefits to be derived from the transfer of water records were nullified in practice.

Although all water resources were not declared to be in the Crown until 1892,[7] the government proceeded to act as though such were the case. Where some access had been granted to the water for the purposes of watering stock previous to the granting of lands under any form of tenure, such access was preserved in the conveyance of the land. These access rights are explicitly preserved in all land acts.

Until 1892 the only classes of persons mentioned specifically in the sections of the land and mineral acts dealing with water were farmers and miners, and it was further provided that to secure a water privilege the farmer had to be in lawful occupation of his land and actually cultivating it.

> Every person lawfully entitled to hold land under this Act, or under any former Act, Ordinance, or Proclamation, and lawfully occupying and bona fide cultivating lands, may record and divert so much and no more of any unrecorded and unappropriated water from the natural channel of any stream, lake or river adjacent to or passing through such land, for agricultural or other purposes, as may be reasonably necessary for such purposes.[8]

4 Grunsky, "Water Legislation," p. D118.

5 B.C., *Statutes*, 1886, 49 Vict., c. 10, s. 1.

6 P. A. Carson, *Railway Belt Hydrographic Survey for 1911-12*, in Canada, Department of the Interior, Water Power Branch, Water Resources Paper No. 1 (Ottawa: Government Printing Bureau, 1914), p. 29. Also in Canada, Parliament, *Sessional Papers*, 12th Parl., 3d sess., 1914, no. 25f.

7 For full discussion, see Grunsky, "Water Legislation," p. D119. While declarin the Crown's control over all unrecorded water and providing a method by which persons and companies holding water records could gain entry upon land not their own, the act neglected to enumerate the classes of persons entitled to procure water privileges.

8 B.C., *Statutes*, 1884, 47 Vict., c. 16, s. 43. The wording is almost identical with that of section 30 of the 1870 Land Ordinance.

In neither case, however, did any section require that the land or claim on which the water was to be used should be specified.

The Water Clauses Consolidation Act, 1897, rectified the oversight. The land upon which the water was to be used had henceforth to be defined exactly. This was the first act in the province dealing entirely with water, and in it the Crown's right to all unrecorded and unappropriated water was declared, "save in the exercise of any legal right existing at the time . . . or except in the exercise of the general right of all persons to use water for domestic and stock supply." All riparian rights acquired by long usage were denied; every owner of land could secure the right to divert unrecorded water for agricultural, domestic, mechanical, or industrial purposes; every owner of a mine could secure water for milling, concentrating, or any general mining purposes. Section 18 recognized the fact that water records for far more water than could be used had been granted for the past thirty years. Thus it provided that, should existing records of water on his land preclude the obtaining of water by a farmer or miner, he could apply for a record. With his application he was to submit evidence that the previous records had granted excessive quantities of water. The gold or land commissioner was then to adjudicate the needs of the prior record holders and render a decision.[9] The only omission from the act was the listing of the classes of persons entitled to water privileges, and the most serious weakness of the act was it left to the discretion of the already overburdened chief commissioner of lands and works the amount of water to be granted in any record.

As early as 1886 the government was aware of the complications resulting from the inaccurate and incomplete book-keeping. The Land Amendment Act of that year stated that:

> And whereas many records of water rights and privileges have in past times been honestly, but imperfectly, made, and it is desirable that such records should have legal recognition therefore: it is declared and enacted that in all cases where the validity of any water record heretofore made may be called in question, and the Court or Judge before whom the case is pending shall be of the opinion that such record was bona fide made, the same shall be held to be good and valid so far as the making and entry thereof is concerned, and effect shall be given thereto according to the intent thereof.[10]

[9] B.C., *Revised Statutes*, 1898, 61 Vict., c. 190.

[10] B.C., *Statutes*, 1886, 49 Vict., c. 10, s. 3.

But as there were no regular offices established for the purpose of recording these water rights even after 1886, the confusion was compounded rather than clarified.

Each land office in the province performed the duties pertinent to water records after its own fashion. Until 1897 the records were made out in longhand in blank registers at the different government offices, the applicant asking for and receiving without question the right to use any quantity of water from 100 to 1,000 miners' inches with no real consideration of his needs or knowledge of whether the stream could actually supply the quantity of water called for in the record. Regardless of the quantity of water sought, the recording fee of two dollars was the same. If the owner needed 100 inches[11] for the irrigation of his homestead, he almost invariably took out a record for 500 or 1,000 inches. Many pioneers had records for "all the water in the stream."[12] No track was kept of the records from the same water course and many streams were recorded ten times beyond their available supply.

By 1907 clarification of the water rights throughout the province could no longer be neglected. The government appointed a Commission of Investigation and, after receiving its report, passed the Water Act of 1909, the principal feature of which was the creation of a Board of Investigation. Since no system of numbering or registering by districts was carried out, the Board discovered that any record in the interior might be located at Yale, Lytton, Nicola, Ashcroft, Clinton, or Kamloops, depending upon where the original applicant had happened to be when he had made his application.[13] They also discovered that in many cases the original record holder had never received a copy of his record. When all records were called in for examination, the holders of the records had great difficulty in establishing their claims to the use of the water. In some records the quantity of water was not specified; in others, the purpose was not mentioned. Sometimes the land on which the water

11 Under B.C. *Statutes*, 1882, 45 Vict., c. 6, s. 4, a miner's inch was defined as that quantity of water measured at the sluice head in a trough which would go through an opening two inches high and one inch wide with a constant head of seven inches above it.

12 H. W. Grunsky, "Water Rights in the British Columbia Railway Belt," in Canada, Department of the Interior, Dominion Water Power Branch, *Annual Report 1915-16* (Ottawa: n.p., 1917), p. 180.

13 B.C., Department of Lands, "Report of the Water Rights Branch [1912]," B.C., *Sessional Papers*, 13th Parl., 1st sess., 1913, p. D108.

was to be used was not listed. In still other cases the source of supply was either unnamed or impossible to identify.

The basic duties of the Board of Investigation were to hold sittings and to hear claims of all persons holding or claiming to hold water records or other water rights, to determine the priorities of the claimants, to lay down terms upon which new licences should be granted, and to cancel old records.[14] The theory was that every water user in the province should have his right clearly determined and specified. The new licences were to be issued as fast as the Board could determine the validity of existing claims.

Before holding a sitting in any district to adjudicate the claims to water rights on any stream, the Board inserted a notice in the *British Columbia Gazette* and the local paper requiring the filing of all claims before a certain date. As the notice commanded but slight attention, each present record holder was served with individual notification of the date of the sitting. But as holders had not been asked to come supplied with the necessary documents to support their claims, and as many holders did not possess such documents, the Board instituted a search of the books in the Department of Lands to discover what land, if any, the grantee named in the record had occupied lawfully at the time the record had been issued. These findings were placed at the disposal of the claimants.

In this way the problem of dealing with the previous unsatisfactory records was met squarely for the first time. The aim was to erase all past mistakes and to start afresh in water administration. The 1909 Act was an excellent beginning, but after it had been in operation for two years, it was discovered that some of its provisions were unworkable and that there had been serious oversights. For example, there was no mention of irrigation companies whose projects might have saved the individual land owner from embarking upon extensive systems of his own. Nor was there any mention of the inspection of dams or the restraining of waste water. More serious still, the determination of the proper use of water was left in the hands of the local government agent, already too busy with other office duties and quite inexperienced in the management of water resources.

Before these shortcomings could be remedied another and more urgent water rights problem had been thrust upon the province. This problem, like the *Precious Metals Case* of 1889, was a direct

[14] B.C., *Revised Statutes,* 1911, 2 Geo. 5, Parts III, IV, and V.

outcome of Article 11 of the Terms of Union. One of the many questions which arose after the transfer of the Railway Belt lands in 1884 was whether the province was to continue to administer the waters.

Assuming its legal right to do so and noting the absence of any dominion regulations concerning the waters within the Belt, the province continued to administer water rights as it had done since 1871. The Privy Council decision of 1889 which gave the province the right to the precious metals in the Railway Belt strengthened the province's contention that it should also administer the water rights. Since no one within the province realized that the right to the waters might be vested in the Dominion, the settlers on the railway lands after 1884 continued to apply to the provincial authorities for water records. Very few of the settlers were either far-sighted enough or sufficiently versed in law to have applied to the Dominion for their record or for confirmation of provincial ones.

The question of jurisdiction did not become acute until 1906 when several holders of dominion timber licences on Lillooet Lake protested to Ottawa the granting to the Burrard Power Company by the province of a water grant of some 25,000 miners' inches from the lake for water power development. The timber licensees contended that the water grant would render the Lillooet River flowing out of the lake useless for their lumbering operations, and, as holders of dominion licences, not unnaturally asked that the Dominion protect their interests by causing the grant to be withdrawn.

The dominion government decided on a test case to clarify permanently all the water rights problems in the Railway Belt. During the next four years the *Burrard Power Case* proceeded through the Exchequer Court and the Supreme Court of Canada to the Judicial Committtee of the Privy Council, where judgment was rendered on November 1, 1910.[15] The judgment included a concise outline of the entire problem of the divided jurisdiction created by the grant of the Railway Belt in 1884. While the question decided by the Judicial Committee was in itself a most important one for British Columbia, the judgment had an even wider significance. From it undoubtedly arose the province's offer, made by Premier McBride in 1911, to purchase outright the dominion

[15] *Burrard Power* v. *The King* (1911) A.C. 87.

interest in both the Railway Belt and the Peace River Block.[16] For these reasons the judgment delivered by Lord Mersey is quoted in full.

> This is an appeal, by special leave, from the judgment of the Supreme Court of Canada, affirming a judgment of the Exchequer Court of Canada rendered on May 10, 1909.
>
> The only question raised upon the appeal is whether certain water rights in the Railway Belt of British Columbia are vested in the Dominion Government so as to preclude the provincial Legislature from dealing with them. The circumstances in which the dispute has arisen are shortly as follows. The Province of British Columbia was admitted into the Dominion of Canada in the year 1871 under the provisions of the British North America Act, 1867. The admission was subject to the provisions of that Act and also to certain Articles of Union duly sanctioned by the Parliament of Canada and by the Legislature of British Columbia. The 11th of these articles stipulated that the Dominion Government should secure the construction of railway communication between the railway system of Canada and the seaboard of British Columbia, and that the Government of British Columbia should convey to the Dominion Government, "in trust to be appropriated in such manner as the Dominion Government may deem advisable in the furtherance of the construction of the said railway," certain public lands along the line of railway throughout its entire length in British Columbia. In consideration of the land to be so conveyed in aid of the construction of the said railway the Dominion Government agreed to pay to British Columbia from the date of the union the sum of $100,000 per annum. The conveyance contemplated by this part of the 11th article was effected by subsequent statutes of the Legislature of the Province, and the land so conveyed is known as the "Railway Belt." The railway has now been built.
>
> By the Water Clauses Consolidation Act, 1897 (61 Vict. c. 190, Revised Statutes of British Columbia), s. 4, the right to the use of the unrecorded water in any river, lake, or stream was declared to be vested in the Crown in the right of the Province, and it was enacted that save in the exercise of any legal right existing at the time of such diversions or appropriation no person should divert or appropriate any water from any river, watercourse, lake, or stream, excepting under the provisions of the Act. By s. 5 it was provided that no right to the exclusive use of such water should be acquired by any person by length of use or otherwise than as might be acquired or conferred under the provisions of the Act or of some existing or future Act. By

16 McBride to Borden, November 6, 1911. B.C., *Sessional Papers*, 12th Parl., 2d sess., 1911, p. N2.

s. 2 "water" was declared to mean all rivers and water power not being waters under the exclusive jurisdiction of the Parliament of Canada, and "unrecorded water" was declared to mean all water not held under a record under the Act or under certain repealed Acts or under special grant by public or private Act and should include all water for the time being unappropriated or unoccupied or not used for a beneficial purpose.

On April 7, 1906, the Water Commissioners for the district of New Westminster, British Columbia, purporting to act under the provisions of this Act, granted to the appellants, the Burrard Power Company, Limited, at an annual rental of $566, a water record for 25,000 inches of waters out of the Lillooet Lakes and the Lillooet River to be used for generating electricity. These waters are within the Railway Belt.

On December 26, 1906, the Attorney-General for the Dominion of Canada filed an information in the Exchequer Court of Canada against the Power Company, claiming a declaration that the record was invalid and conveyed no interest to the defendant company, and asking that the same should be cancelled. The information alleged that the works of the Power Company if carried out would have the effect of diverting the water of the river, thereby interfering with its navigation, and would otherwise materially diminish the value of the lands of the Dominion Government in the Railway Belt. In support of the claim reliance was placed on the agreement contained in the Terms of Union, and on the provisions of the Acts of the provincial Legislature passed for the purpose of giving effect to that agreement. Reliance was also placed on the provisions of s. 91 of the British North America Act, 1867, which declares that the exclusive legislative authority of the Parliament of Canada shall extend to all matters coming within certain classes of subjects, including the public debt and property and navigation. It was further submitted that, having regard to sub-s. 2 of s. 131 of the Water Clauses Consolidation Act, 1897, the grant of the record by the Commissioners was not authorized by the Water Clauses Act.

After the filing of the information the Attorney-General of British Columbia was added as a party to represent the interests of the Province.

On December 23, 1907, the determination of the issue of fact was referred for inquiry and report to Archer Martin J., who found the facts to be in accordance with the allegations of the Dominion Government, and reported accordingly. Thereupon the Attorney-General of Canada prayed judgment as asked by the information. On April 13, 1909, the case came on for argument before Cassels J., and on May 10, 1909, that learned judge declared that the grant of the record of water in question was invalid and conveyed no interest to the defendant company. The judgment proceeded on three grounds: first, that the grant was an interference with property subject to the exclusive authority of the Dominion of Canada; secondly, that the diversion of water intended to be authorized thereunder would be a very serious interference with the navigability of the river; and thirdly, that the record was not authorized by the provisions of the Water Clauses Act under which it had been granted. From this judgment an appeal was brought to the Supreme Court of Canada. The appeal was dismissed on February 15, 1910.

Their Lordships are of opinion that the judgments of the Courts below are right. The grant by the Province of British Columbia of "public lands" to the Dominion Government undoubtedly passed the water rights incidental to those lands. In the argument addressed to their Lordships this was not really questioned. But it was said that though the proprietary rights of the Province in the land and in the waters belonging thereto were transferred to the Dominion Government, the legislative powers of the Province over the same neither were nor could be parted with, and that therefore it was competent for the provincial Legislature to enact the Water Clauses Act of 1897 under which the record was granted. In support of this contention a passage was cited from the judgment of Lord Watson in *Attorney-General of British Columbia* v. *Attorney-General of Canada*. Their Lordships are of opinion that the contention is wrong, and that the passage in Lord Watson's judgment affords no kind of support for it. The object of article 11 of the Terms of Union was on the one hand to secure the construction of the railway for the benefit of the Province and on the other hand to afford the Dominion a means of recouping itself in respect of the liabilities which it might incur in connection with the construction by sales to settlers of the land transferred. To hold that the Province after the making of such an agreement remained at liberty to legislate in the sense contended for would be to defeat the whole object of the agreement, for if the Province could by legislation take away the water from the land it could also by legislation resume possession of the land itself, and thereby so derogate from its own grant as to utterly destroy it. Lord Watson's reference in the *Precious Metals Case* to the 11th article, so far from supporting the appellants' contention, is against it. He says "the conveyance contemplated was a transfer to the Dominion of the provincial right to manage and settle the lands and to appropriate their revenues." The grant of the water record in the case now under consideration is an attempt on the part of the Province to appropriate the revenues to itself, and would if carried into effect violate the terms of the contract as interpreted by Lord Watson. It is true that Lord Watson adds that the land is not by the transfer taken out of the Province, and that once it is "settled" by the Dominion it ceases to be public land, and "reverts to the same position as if it had been settled by the provincial Government in the ordinary course of its administration." But this also is against the appellants' con-

> tention, for it implies that until settled by the Dominion it remains public land under the Dominion's control.
>
> Their Lordships are of opinion that the lands in question so long as they remain unsettled are "public property" within the meaning of s. 91 of the British North America Act, 1867, and as such are under the exclusive legislative authority of the Parliament of Canada by virtue of the Act of Parliament. Before the transfer they were public lands, the proprietary rights in which were held by the Crown in right of the Province. After the transfer they were still public lands, but the proprietary rights were held by the Crown in right of the Dominion, and for a public purpose, namely, the construction of the railway. This being so, no Act of the provincial Legislature could affect the water upon the lands. Nor, in their Lordships' opinion, does the Water Clauses Act of 1897 purport or intend to affect them; for, by clause 2, the Act expressly excludes from its operation waters under the exclusive jurisdiction of the Dominion Parliament.
>
> The Lordships will humbly advise His Majesty that the appeal should be dismissed with costs.[17]

The situation in the Railway Belt, which had been merely confusing and troublesome prior to this judgment, now became alarming in its implications. The holders of provincial water records in the Belt were, or thought they were, protected by law. When news spread that the hundreds of records within the Belt had no legal standing, each interested party began looking out for himself and water-grabbing became the order of the day.[18] Rivalry, formerly keen, became bitter in its intensity. The situation was further aggravated by the extreme dryness of the 1911 and 1912 seasons.

The newly created Board of Investigation could do nothing in the face of the decision transferring water administration in the Belt to dominion authorities. The inheritance of the Dominion was not enviable, for, unlike land grants, each water grant is entirely dependent upon all previous grants. The chief stumbling block to dominion regulation was that it had had no control over the granting of water records prior to 1884.[19] The early records granted by

[17] The Exchequer Court of Canada gave the initial judgment on May 10 (1909) 12 Ex. C.R. 295, in favour of the Dominion. British Columbia appealed the case to the Supreme Court of Canada, which gave its judgment dismissing the appeal on February 15 [(1910) 43 S.C.R. 27].

[18] Carson, *Railway Belt Hydrographic Survey*, p. 29.

[19] Grants made by the province prior to April 19, 1884, were declared valid by the Court of Appeal in British Columbia on November 5, 1912, in *George* v. *Mitchell* (1912) 17 B.C.R. 531. This was just one of the many court cases arising from the confusion after 1910.

the province would practically control the situation throughout the Railway Belt in view of the accepted principle "first in time, first in right" applicable to all water records granted in British Columbia since 1859. Dominion-provincial co-operation in solving the dilemma was essential, particularly as no new water licence, however carefully defined, could remain anything but indefinite until all prior rights had been assessed for their validity, and this the Dominion had no authority to do.

Before the matter was finally settled in 1916 it was discovered that ten different kinds of water rights had been in existence in the Railway Belt, the legality of each of which had to be determined. There were first those records which had been granted prior to 1884 by the province; then records granted after the transfer of the Belt but appertaining to old provincial lands; records granted from 1884 to 1909 on lands formerly belonging to the Dominion but for one reason or another transferred back to the province; records granted by the province to unpatented dominion lands; records granted by the Indian Reserve Commissioners for Indian reserves; records granted for Indians reserves by the province; rights to the use of or affecting the use of water granted by the Dominion; incompleted water power projects under contract with the Dominion to which water rights were clearly incidental; rights granted by the Dominion to timber interests; and finally, indefinite and unestablished riparian rights.[20]

A further embarrassment arose from the realization that streams having their source in the province and flowing into the Belt, and vice versa, could not be dealt with by one government without affecting the rights and interests of the other. Nor could water rights be administered independently of the land, since power rights required land for power sites and reservoirs, and irrigation rights required land as rights of way for canals and storage facilities.

Because of these insurmountable difficulties and because the establishing of an entirely different administrative procedure for the Railway Belt would have been a cumbersome and needless duplication of effort, the dominion government passed an Order in Council on December 20, 1911, transferring the administration of water rights in the Belt to the province pending such action as

[20] Carson, *Railway Belt Hydrographic Survey*, p. 30.

the Dominion might take later, and without prejudice to any existing rights.[21]

On April 1, 1912, the Dominion passed the Railway Belt Water Act,[22] which vested all ungranted water rights in the Crown and put a stop to any further riparian privileges accruing as a result of the purchase of land. The legislation was helpful, but it provided no machinery for adjusting the numerous conflicting claims within the Belt. It did not supply any system under which these claims could be settled by the Dominion; neither did it transfer the adjudication of the existing rights and claims to the provincial authorities. It left the holders of the numerous grants made by the province since 1884 and of the riparian interest of certain dominion grants without any procedure by which they could have their claims validated or rescinded. This oversight left the provincial Board of Investigation with nothing to do but assess the rights of water record holders outside the Railway Belt and those who held valid provincial records obtained before 1884 within the Belt. Since records held by residents in the Lower Fraser Valley and the South Thompson area, both in the Railway Belt, were the most contentious records in the province, the usefulness of the Board was seriously impaired.

Section 5 of the dominion act dealt with future or pending applications and was phrased as follows:

> The water so vested and reserved to the Crown . . . shall, during the pleasure of the Governor-in-Council, be administered under and in accordance with the provisions of the "Water Act, 1909" of British Columbia.

The only difficulty was that the provincial Water Act had already been repealed. The dominion legislation did apply to any provincial act to come into effect after the passing of its own act, but this authority did not extend to any provincial act passed between 1909 and 1912. The result was that the only act then in force in British Columbia, the Consolidated Act of 1911, could not apply to the

[21] H. W. Grunsky, "Water Rights in the Railway Belt," p. 181. The Order in Council was a direct and immediate outcome of the mission to Ottawa of Premier McBride, W. J. Bowser, and W. R. Ross, in November 1911. They had made urgent representations to the Dominion for transfer of the water rights' administration to the province. (See B.C., *Sessional Papers*, 12th Parl., 2d sess., 1912, p. N7.)

[22] Canada, *Statutes*, 1912, 2 Geo. V, c. 47.

Railway Belt, which would have to be administered under a statute no longer in force.

The difficulty was resolved the next year by the enactment of the new dominion Railway Belt Water Act of 1913.[23] Under section 5, all waters within the Railway Belt were to be administered by British Columbia and all records issued by the province were to be regarded as valid grants. Section 6 stated that all provincial water acts were to apply to the Railway Belt even though they had been enacted for the provincial lands alone. In this way, subject only to grants made by Canada during the period, all records issued by the province within the Belt since 1884 were held to be as valid as though they had been issued for territory outside the Railway Belt, and the provincial Water Consolidation Act of 1911, with its amendments, was to apply to all land in the province irrespective of where it was located. Consistency of administration was now possible.

After 1913 a further adjustment was made between the two governments to permit landowners to co-operate in the construction and operation of water systems, but the major difficulties had been resolved. Although the dominion government reserved the right to abrogate the agreement at any time, for all intents the provincial government had become guardian or trustee of the Dominion's interest in the water within the Railway Belt. The Dominion continued to exercise a careful check on activities within the Belt by virtue of its control of the lands, since it had to protect the extensive timber interests within the Belt. The lands were controlled and administered under the Railway Belt Act of 1906[24] and under section 9 of the 1930 Water Act, which expressly reserved to the Dominion control over all its land.

Settlement of the dispute served to strengthen the authority of the Board of Investigation by permitting it to proceed with its interrupted investigation of every record, regardless of when issued or by whom. The Board set June 1, 1916, as the final date for the filing of riparian owners' claims. Once they were settled, the entire province was again to be covered by the record or licence system of diverting water for beneficial use begun in 1859 by Governor Douglas.

[23] Canada, *Statutes,* 1913, 3-4 Geo. V., c. 45.
[24] Canada, *Revised Statutes,* 1906, c. 59.

CHAPTER 8

The Railway Belt to 1884

The promise to link British Columbia with Canada by a railway was made during the Confederation negotiations in Ottawa, and Article 11 of the Terms of Union provided in part that:

> The Government of the Dominion undertake to secure the commencement simultaneously, within two years from the date of Union, of the construction of a railway from the Pacific towards the Rocky Mountains, and from such point as may be selected, East of the Rocky Mountains towards the Pacific, to connect the seaboard of British Columbia with the railway system of Canada; and further, to secure the completion of such railway within ten years from the date of the Union.[1]

Because optimism prevailed and because it was believed that British Columbia would not be interested in Union without provision for a transportation link, little concern was felt about the practicality of implementing this clause, either in Victoria or in Ottawa. And when, in addition, public thinking about the completion of this grandiose scheme was crystallized by the dominion government itself as of:

> vast importance, not only to the political and commercial interests of Canada, as tending to the closer union of its several Provinces, but also to the British Empire at large, as affording rapid and direct communication through British Territory with her Australian and Asiatic possessions . . .[2]

1 Canada, *Statutes*, 1872, 35 Vict., p. xcii.

2 From the preamble to the original act of incorporation of the Canadian Pacific Railway, ibid., c. 73.

it was fully expected that if the financial burden were to prove excessive for Canada's meagre resources, British assistance would be forthcoming.

Before he left Washington in May of 1871 after maintaining his watching brief on the writing of the Treaty of Washington, Sir John A. Macdonald was reasonably sure of obtaining this aid. He had discovered that Britain had no intention of compensating Canada, nor of pressing the American government to do so, for the losses suffered from the Fenian raids. When it was intimated to him that Britain would proffer some unofficial balm to Canada's wounded pride, Macdonald is said to have "stiffly refused," and to have suggested how much more convenient for Canada it would be, and how distinctly more compatible with national dignity, were the British government to guarantee a large loan for the construction of the transcontinental railway.[3]

The aid was given as Macdonald expected. When the loan of £2,500,000 was being discussed in the British House of Commons on June 24, 1873, it was suggested that it was in the form of a bribe for Canada's concessions in regard to the fisheries clause of the Treaty of Washington, but Prime Minister Gladstone hotly denied the accusation, saying that the money had no connection with the treaty. Its object, he explained, was not to give Canada a certain amount of hush-money, but simply to recognize her just demands on England on account of the Fenian raids.[4]

Lulled by the buoyant spirit of the day, it was ten years before the dominion government fully realized what a tremendous obligation had been assumed. Difficulties over the building of the line brought down Macdonald's government within a year of the passing of his first Canadian Pacific Railway Company Act. The same difficulties led to very strained relations between the provincial and the federal governments, as well as between the mainland and island sections within the province. Before all problems were resolved and the railway an actuality, three Governors General had come to British Columbia in connection with railway matters — Earl Dufferin, the Marquis of Lorne, and the Marquis of Lansdowne. Had the federal authorities not realized that railroad union alone could make the political union a fact, and that the transcontinental line would be a vital link in the "all-red route" between

[3] J. B. Brebner, *North Atlantic Triangle* (Toronto: Ryerson, 1945), p. 193.
[4] Great Britain, *Hansard's Parliamentary Debates*, 3d ser. (1873), 1326-27.

Britain and the Orient and Antipodes, British Columbia might have remained a British colony.

The construction of the line, however, was not a provincial problem. That was up to the federal government. All that was required of the province was to fulfil the bargain contained in the remaining portions of section 11:

> And the Government of British Columbia agree to convey to the Dominion Government, in trust, to be appropriated in such manner as the Dominion Government may deem advisable in the furtherance of the construction of the said railway, a similar extent of public lands along the line of the Railway, throughout its entire length in British Columbia, not to exceed, however, Twenty (20) Miles on each side of the said line, as may be appropriated for the same purpose by the Dominion Government from the public lands in the North-West Territories and the Province of Manitoba. Provided, that the quantity of lands which may be held under pre-emption right or Crown grant within the limits of the tract of land in British Columbia shall be made good to the Dominion from contiguous public lands; and, provided, that until the commencement within two years, as aforesaid, from the date of the Union, of the construction of the said Railway, the Government of British Columbia shall not sell or alienate any further portions of the public lands of British Columbia in any other way than under right of pre-emption, requiring actual residence of the pre-emptor on the land claimed by him.

The government members in Ottawa were pressed closely for an explanation of how they proposed to pay for a railroad through such a "sea of mountains" as British Columbia was reported to be if reliance had to be placed on a strip of land, however wide, in such a wilderness. The financial details were gone over in the House every day the matter came up for discussion, and on every occasion the government sought to impress upon doubtful members the fact that the utmost cost would be a mere $100,000,000, all of which would be paid out of the land grant. Sir George E. Cartier, government leader in the absence of Macdonald, said that:

> While this clause was under discussion between the delegates and the Government it was proposed by the Dominion that the colony should hand over a forty mile strip of land towards the construction of the railway. That would be 24,000 square miles of land, or 50,360,000 acres of land, not merely agricultural land, but mineral land. Placing that land at $1.00 per acre it would

> equal a grant of $50,360,000 towards the construction of the railway.[5]

Cartier assured the House not only that the cost would be a manageable one for the country, but also that there would be no increase in taxation. Although this announcement was greeted with cheers, it was all the ministry could do to scrape by on several motions put during the debate.[6] When questioned concerning the value of the lands to be conveyed by the province, Alexander Morris, minister of inland revenue, said that:

> He could state on the undisputable authority of Mr. Trutch, the Surveyor General of British Columbia, that taking the whole of British Columbia and Vancouvers Island fully one third, or about 50,000,000 acres was good farming land, while the whole acreage of Ontario was 77,000,000 acres.[7]

In view of the amazing amount of misinformation that came out in the debate concerning British Columbia, and in view of the magnitude of the task ahead of the federal government, it is not surprising that to many disinterested persons in 1871, the agreement seemed almost impossible to fulfil. The fate of the resolution might have been very different had the government not agreed that the undertaking should be carried out by private enterprise not the dominion government and that it should be assisted by such liberal grants of land and such subsidy in money or other aid, without increasing the rate of taxation, as Parliament should determine.[8]

Whatever the opposition in Ottawa may have been to the terms, they were accepted in good faith in British Columbia. The statutory authority under which British Columbia had been able to make the contract was to be found in section 49 of the Land Ordinance, 1870, the "Free Grants" section:

5 Canada, *Parliamentary Debates* (1871), 662. The 50,360,000 acre figure, although quoted twice, must surely have been a clerical error. The figure should read 15,360,000.

6 Although the government usually could rely on a three-to-one majority, one motion against acceptance of the Terms was lost by only ten votes. The numbers were seventy-five to eighty-five. Eighteen regular supporters of the ministry voted for the motion of non-acceptance and many other declined to vote. (See: Canada, Parliament, House of Commons, *Journals*, 1st Parl., 4th sess., 1871, pp. 161-67.)

7 Canada, *Parliamentary Debates*, 26 (1871), 714. This was not to be the only instance in which either through ignorance or design Trutch was to mislead the federal government. See chapters 11 to 13 for his role in the disposition of Indian reserves.

8 Canada, *Journals*, 1st Parl., 4th sess., 1871, pp. 264-65.

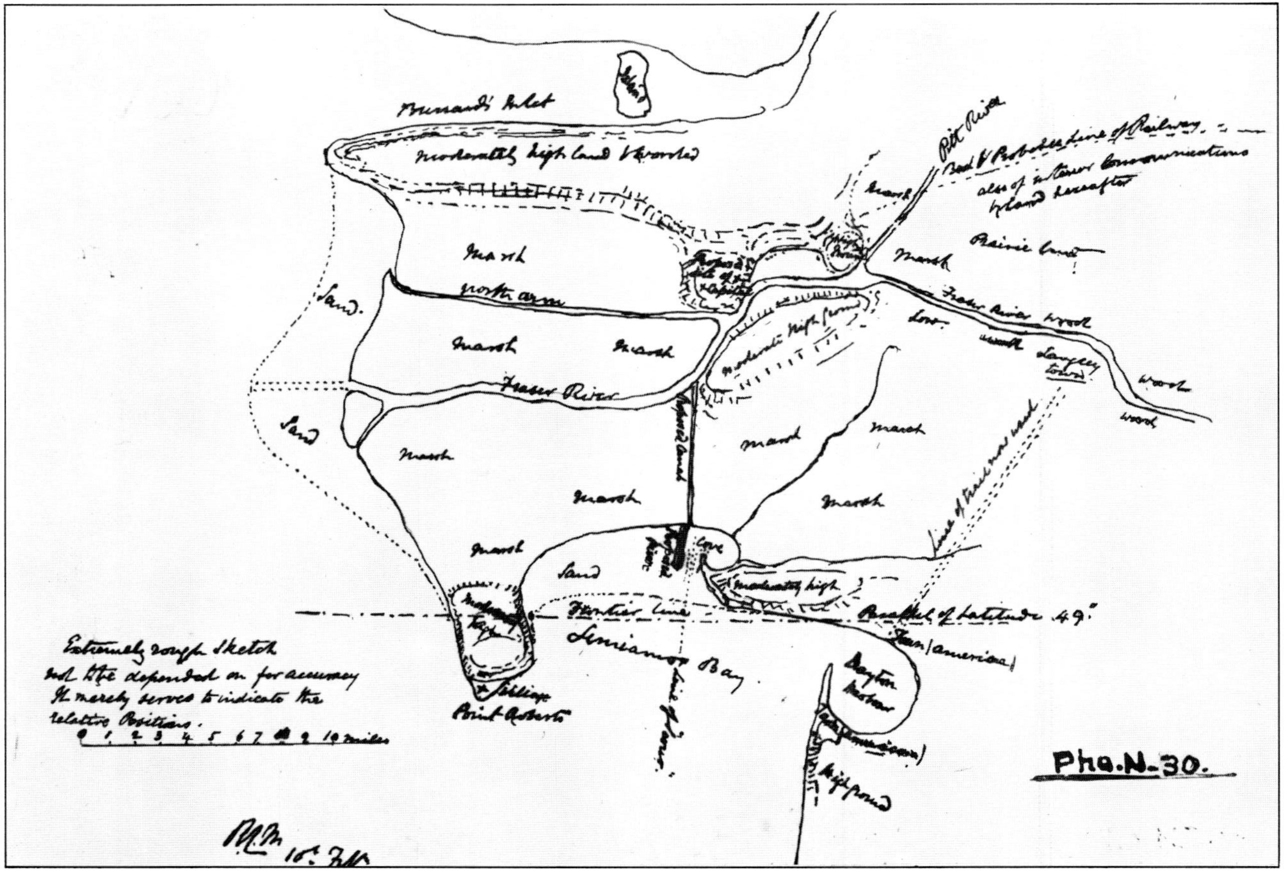

Plate 1. Sketch of the Lower Mainland by Colonel R. C. Moody, presumably in 1863.

PLATE 2. Lord Edward Bulwer Lytton.

PLATE 3. Colonel R. C. Moody.

PLATE 4. Sir James Douglas Taking the Oath of Office as Governor of British Columbia, November 19, 1858.

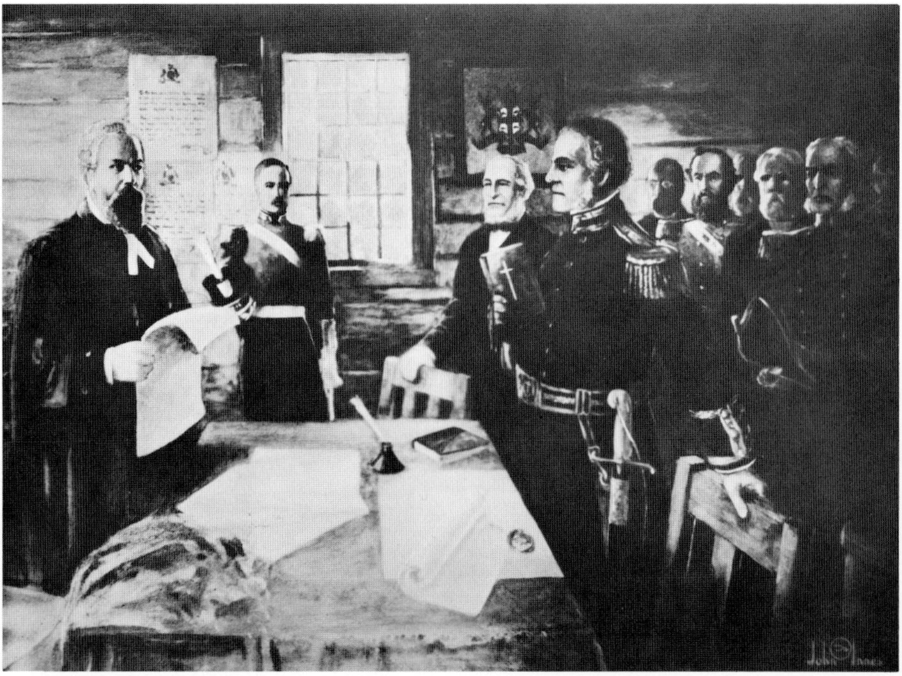

PLATE 5. Reputedly the *D. L. Clynch*, the First Ocean-going Vessel to Enter the Fraser River at New Westminster.

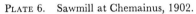

PLATE 6. Sawmill at Chemainus, 1902.

Canadian Pacific Railway Company

CITY OF VANCOUVER

- PRICE LIST OF CITY LOTS -

IN LOT 541, FORMERLY KNOWN AS THE GRANVILLE TOWN SITE

Granville Street,	Corners,	(North of Nelson St.),	$1250 :	Others,	.. ..	$1000
"	"	" (South of Nelson St.),	1000	"	.. ..	750
Hastings	"	"	1250	"	.. ..	1000
Cordova	"	"	1250	"	.. ..	1000
Pender	"	"	1000	"	.. ..	750
Dunsmuir	"	"	$750 ;	Inside Lots, between	Dunsmuir and Lane ..	500
Georgia	"	"	750	" " "	Georgia and Dunsmuir ..	500
Robson	"	"	750	" " "	Robson and Georgia ..	500
Smithe	"	"	750	" " "	Smith and Robson	500
Nelson	"	"	600	" " "	Nelson and Smith ..	400
Helmcken	"	"	600	" " "	Helmcken and Nelson ..	400
Davie	"	"	600	" " "	Davie and Helmcken ..	400
Drake	"	"	500	" " "	Drake and Davie	250
Pacific	"	"	400	" " "	Pacific and Drake ..	250

CONDITIONS OF SALE

Payments one-third cash, one-third in six months, and one-third in twelve months, with interest at 6 per cent. per annum.

A discount from the purchase price will be allowed if buildings are erected by the purchaser within one year as follows:

For buildings on each lot, worth $2000 or over, 20 per cent.
For buildings on each lot worth $5000 or over, 30 per cent.

Rebates to be deducted from the payment first succeeding the completion of the buildings; but in case two or more lots are taken, only the lot or lots actually built upon shall be entitled to the rebate.

Parties erecting permanent buildings to the satisfaction of the Agent of the Trustees, will be accorded an extension of time on the second and third payments at his discretion, but not exceeding two years.

For lots that have been cleared by the Company the purchaser will be required to pay the net cost of clearing in addition to the list price.

The Agent of the Trustees claims the right to depart at any time from this schedule of prices and conditions of sale.

H. ABBOTT
AGENT FOR TRUSTEES

VANCOUVER, June 1st, 1886.

PLATE 7. C.P.R. Price List for City Lots in the Granville Townsite.

Plate 8. The Mint, New Westminster, 1862.

Plate 9. The Land Registry Office, New Westminster.

Plate 10. D. B. Charleson's Camp near Fraser Mills, 1890.

Plate 11.
Gold-Washing, 1868.

PLATE 12. H.M.S. *Cormorant* in Esquimalt Graving Dock in 1887.

PLATE 13. Hudson's Bay Company Store at Yale, 1883.

PLATE 14. Songhees Indian Reserve, Victoria Harbour, Esquimalt and Nanaimo Railway Trestle in Background.

PLATE 15. Testing of the Howe Trestle of the Crow's Nest Railway, December 12, 1897.

PLATE 16. Arrival of First Transcontinental Train at Vancouver, May 23, 1887.

PLATE 17. Joseph W. Trutch.

PLATE 18. Kootenay Indians, Chief Isadore and Council.

PLATE 19. Okanagan Indians, Goastamana, Son of Chief Kalamalka, Long Lake Reserve.

PLATE 20. Okanagan Indians, Mrs. Josephine Gregoire and Children, Long Lake Reserve.

Plate 21. Peter O'Reilly.

Plate 22. Dr. I. W. Powell.

Plate 23. Cartoon of Yale in Construction Days, probably by Harry Fairfax, 1883.

> It shall be lawful for the Governor in Council to make such special free or partially free grants of the unoccupied and unappropriated Crown lands of the Colony, for the encouragement of immigration or other purposes of public advantage.

Not without some justification, the dominion government considered this clause to be inadequate authority for a grant as extensive as that proposed. Hence the 1875 Land Act authorized the reserve of any lands not otherwise lawfully held "for the purpose of conveying the same to the Dominion Government, in trust, for ... railway purposes, as mentioned in Article 11 of the Terms of Union."[9] To facilitate the progress of provincially incorporated lines, an additional clause in 1891 authorized the grant of a right of way not to exceed 100 feet in width, through crown lands, to any railway company incorporated within the province. Any land needed for terminal purposes, stations, sidings, wharves, warehouses, bridges, culverts, drains and other works could also be granted to the company.[10]

Even before the Dominion questioned the authority under which the province could undertake to convey lands, and two years before the province authorized the grant of the Island Railway Belt from Esquimalt to Nanaimo,[11] trouble arose between the two governments over the projected land grant. The first session of the British Columbia legislature had appointed a select committee to investigate the legality of certain land sales made since 1870.[12] Section 20 of the 1865 Land Ordinance had permitted any owner of 160 acres to pre-empt a further 480 acres of waste crown land contiguous to his own land at the reduced price of two shillings, one penny an acre. The second section of the 1870 Ordinance repealed this clause, but it stated that "such repeal shall not prejudice or affect any rights acquired or payments due ... prior to the passing of this Ordinance."[13] Subsequently, several assistant land commissioners had permitted holders of 160-acre settlements to purchase the additional acreage at fifty cents an acre. On July 2, 1872, Premier

[9] B.C., *Statutes*, 1875, 38 Vict., no. 5, s. 60.

[10] B.C., *Statutes*, 1891, 54 Vict., c. 15, s. 17.

[11] B.C., *Statutes*, 1875, 38 Vict., no. 13. This grant was repealed by B.C., *Statutes*, 1882, 45 Vict., c. 16.

[12] "Report of a Select Committee ... in respect to legalizing Sales of Land in the Province, since 1870," B.C., *Journals*, 1st Parl., 2d sess., 1872-73, appendix, *Sessional Papers.*

[13] See Appendix A, s. 2.

and Attorney-General J. F. McCreight gave his opinion that these recent acquisitions were illegal. The government immediately notified all purchasers that their lands must be surrendered and that their money would be returned. McCreight suggested an appeal to the legislature, but A. Rocke Robertson, chairman of the select committee, said that "the Provincial Government holds itself disabled by the 11th Article of the Terms of Union to pass an Act legalizing the purchases made under the circumstances above set forth."[14]

This was the first concrete instance of the problems which developed in British Columbia as a result of the reservation placed on its lands. Lieutenant-Governor Trutch's speech from the throne to the second session of the legislature which opened on December 17, 1872, pin-pointed the difficulty.

> In consequence of the Railway clause of the terms of union preventing free grants of lands and other equally insuperable difficulties, no practical result in the way of introducing new settlers into the Province has been attained.[15]

But hopes were still high in the new province that with the promise of a railway immigration would increase, business would prosper, and labour would be in great demand. So convinced of this was the province that on February 21, 1873, the legislature passed an act imposing a tax of four cents an acre on all wild land in the province. William Smithe, one of the two members for Cowichan, had introduced the bill in the first session early in 1872. In moving the bill, he said that the tax should be imposed on "unoccupied and uncultivated Country Lands, with a view to preventing speculation therein."[16] However, McCreight, a good lawyer if not a first-rate rough-and-tumble politician, reserved the bill for the consideration of the Governor General on the grounds that it could apply to "land hereafter appropriated for Railway purposes."[17]

Sir John A. Macdonald, as minister of justice, disallowed the act when it reached Ottawa. Although the tax did not apply to lands vested in or held in trust for the Crown or for public uses of the

[14] "Report of a Select Committee . . . [on] Sales of Land," s. 6.

[15] B.C., *Journals*, 1st Parl., 2d sess., 1872-73, p. 2.

[16] B.C., *Journals*, 1st Parl., 1st sess., 1872, p. 17.

[17] "Return . . . relative to the four Acts of last Session which were reserved . . . ," B.C., *Journals*, 1st Parl., 2d sess., 1872-73 appendix, *Sessional Papers.*

province, Macdonald felt that the act would tend to discourage private capital on which he depended for the building of the railway. He said:

> The Government of Canada are taking active steps to endeavour to induce capitalists to engage in the great undertaking of constructing a Railway to connect the two Oceans.
>
> The chief inducement to such capitalists, is the promise of a large grant of Land in aid of the enterprise, and the imposition of such a Tax upon these Railway Lands, would greatly diminish the prospect of a Company being formed.[18]

A new act was passed in 1873 levying the same rate of tax on lands of non-residents, but exempting all property then or later to be held as railway lands.[19] The looked-for rush of settlers did not develop, and in spite of the somewhat meagre returns to the Treasury from the Wild Land tax, the government increased the tax in 1876 to five cents an acre on top of the rate levied on all land. The collapse of the railway negotiations in the mid-seventies, the depression that settled on the province, and the serious financial problems which the government had to face made any source of revenue, however small, highly desirable. In spite of road expenditures amounting to 57 per cent of the total cost of government in 1875,[20] the interior remained almost empty. Some of the blame for this stagnant condition was laid on the dominion government for not having begun the railway construction. In an effort to lighten the burden of road construction, the government had been levying a toll on all goods entering the mining and cattle regions over the Cariboo road. The free grant policy appeared of dubious value to the settler if the taxation on his land had to be sufficiently heavy to carry the building costs of roads in such a territory as the Fraser Canyon. Although the federal government pointed out in 1876 that the collection of the half cent a pound on all goods entering the Fraser Canyon was infringing on its prerogative of regulating trade and commerce, Edward Blake, the minister of justice, refrained from disallowing the legislation. He was too well aware of the hostility already prevalent in British Columbia toward the

18 Ibid, p. 8.

19 B.C., *Statutes*, 1873, 36 Vict., no. 11. Railway land was not specifically named until the new act of 1876.

20 Total government expenditure in 1875 was $833,396.79; of this, road maintenance and construction was allotted $413,160. (See "Report of the Chief Commissioner of Lands and Works ... 1875.")

Mackenzie government's railway policy. He contented himself with pointing out that, in effect, the toll charge was placing the chief burden of constructing the public roads of the province upon consumers of imported goods.[21]

It was a different matter, however, when the provincial government proposed to raise the toll charge to one cent a pound in 1878.[22] The correspondence between the Canadian Pacific officials, the dominion government, and the provincial government which preceded the passing of the act reflected the atmosphere surrounding the building of the railway so long as Walkem was premier of British Columbia and Mackenzie prime minister of Canada. The province, implacable in its demands to have the railway built on schedule and determined that the contractors should contribute handsomely to help pay for the roads to the interior made necessary by the non-existence of a railroad, adopted what proved to be both an untenable and a short-sighted policy.

From his reading of the *Victoria Colonist* in the spring of 1878 while the bill was being discussed in the legislature, John Robson, then paymaster and surveyor for the Port Moody to Kamloops section of the Canadian Pacific, knew that the proposed road tolls were large enough to cripple the railway construction. On August 9 he wrote to Premier Walkem that the imposition of such a toll as proposed by the bill would not fail to impede seriously, "if, indeed, it would not render . . . practically impossible," work to begin next spring just beyond the toll gate. He asked for an exemption on all railway material.[23]

Walkem's reply two days later was hardly reassuring:

> In reply to your letter of the 9th inst., recommending the inconvenience of applying the Road Tolls Act to railway plant, or material passing the Yale toll gate, I have to assure you that whenever construction is commenced, the government will afford every facility for its being carried on expeditiously, and so far as they are concerned, as cheaply as possible, arrangements just to the Dominion and province, can then be made.[24]

Robson felt that Walkem's conception of justice in this case would

[21] Hodgins, *Dominion and Provincial Legislation*, 1:1040-41.

[22] The charge was raised to one cent per pound under authority of the Cariboo Waggon Road Tolls Amendment Act, B.C., *Statutes*, 1878, 41 Vict., c. 37, s. 2.

[23] Hodgins, *Dominion and Provincial Legislation*, 1:1069-70.

[24] Ibid., 1070.

not be to his liking. He had read the speech from the throne, written by Walkem, for the opening of the legislature on July 29, 1878, which had said "I would remind you that the time has come when delay in the construction of the work, both on the mainland and the island, can no longer be justified," and that the time had come "to take measures much more decisive than the mere entry of protest" which had been "systematically disregarded" by the Dominion. Robson had also read Walkem's lengthy address to the Queen in which, after outlining the injurious effects which the constant delays were having, he had moved the secession resolution.[25]

In his reply, Robson pointed out as diplomatically as he could that Walkem's assurances were not "altogether satisfactory." Because, he said, the Yale section was to be placed under contract the next spring, the one cent per pound toll would exert a "most serious influence upon tenders," since the contractors would make allowances for the toll charges, charges which "it seems hardly necessary to add ... must amount to something enormous" on all railway plant and supplies. Warming to his subject, he continued:

> I beg, therefore, most respectfully to submit that however willing your government might be to meet the Dominion government in a fair and liberal spirit "whenever construction is commenced," the remedy would have come too late, as the tenders would have been sent in and the contract awarded at the greatly increased price, or what is far more likely to happen, the tenders would be rejected on account of undue appreciation in prices thus occasioned, and instead of the province "making a haul" out of the Dominion, its interests and revenues would suffer on account of consequent delay in railway construction.[26]

For these reasons, Robson asked for the insertion of a clause exempting railway supplies and materials.

Convinced that he could look for no remedy from the province in the mood then prevailing, Robson forwarded all correspondence to the federal Department of Public Works on August 17. That department lost no time in bringing Walkem to task. On September 4, Robson was able to report that a partial concession had been made and that the bill had been sent back to the House for the insertion of an exemption clause. He pointed out, however, that the exemptions were only on "plant and material" used by the

[25] B.C., *Journals*, 2d Parl., 3d sess., and 3d Parl., 1st sess., 1878, pp. 105-7.
[26] August 13, 1878, in Hodgins, *Dominion and Provincial Legislation*, 1:1070.

railway company itself, that the exemption did not apply to supplies employed or consumed in construction, and that the modicum of relief offered was made dependent on a revocable Minute of the Executive, "rather insecure ground it is to be apprehended for contractors to go upon in tendering for the work." The charge of twenty dollars a ton on all contractors' supplies to be used "within the shadow of the toll gate" he considered not only enormous but unjust.[27] Because he had reason to suspect that the measure was a deliberate attempt to operate prejudicially against construction at Yale, Robson asked that the measure be disallowed two days after it had passed the provincial House on September 2, 1878.

The Minister of Justice, James Macdonald, disallowed the bill not only because it imposed unfair charges on the dominion exchequer, but also because it interfered with trade and commerce.[28] When Robson was asked to give reasons for his suspicions that the Tolls Act was a deliberate attempt to frustrate construction of the railway, he explained that he had definite proof that the words "and supplies" had been erased from the exemption clause when it had come before the legislature, and that a full discussion had taken place in the House as to whether supplies should have been included or not. However, the imposition of such a tax on the contractors' supplies had almost become a point of honour with Walkem. Exactly the same bill which had been disallowed once was re-introduced and passed through the House a second time on May 8, 1880.[29] Moreover, a second act was passed setting the toll on all rice carried over the road at two cents, double the levy on all other goods.[30] Both acts were disallowed.[31] It is only fair to add that Walkem had not begun the agitation against the Chinese and that, although the heavy toll placed on rice was aimed directly at the Chinese labourers imported by the Canadian Pacific Company, he was simply giving expression to the general attitude toward Chinese.

Still unwilling to let the dominion government proceed unmolested, Walkem continued. He registered protests over the failure of

27 Robson to Department of Public Works, September 4, 1878, ibid., 1:1071.

28 *Canada Gazette*, October 4, 1879, p. 471.

29 Cariboo Waggon Road Tolls Amendment Act, B.C., *Statutes*, 1880, 43 Vict., c. 28.

30 An Act respecting Tolls on the Cariboo Waggon Road, ibid., c. 29.

31 *Canada Gazette*, July 29, 1881, p. 143.

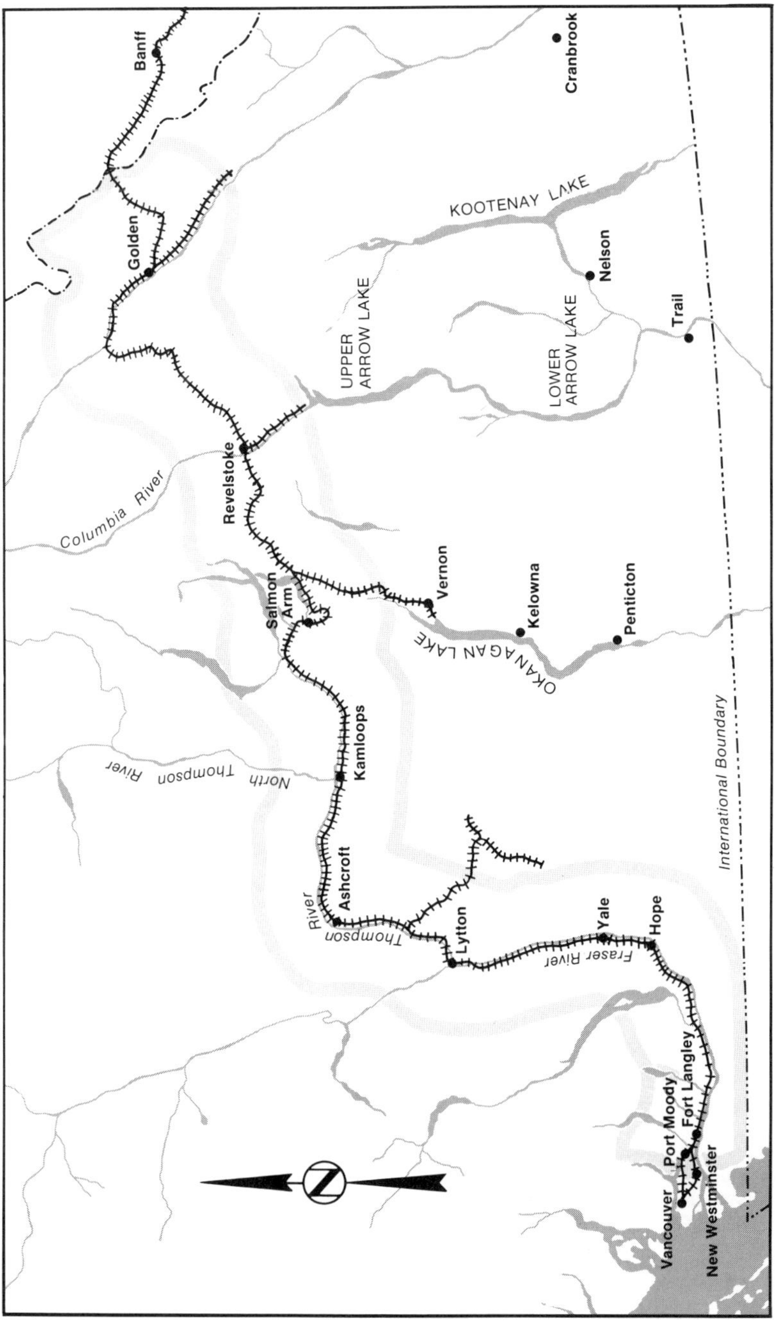

The Canadian Pacific Railway Belt

the Dominion to open the lands in the Railway Belt to settlement. These lands had been reserved by the province since August 3, 1878; since their transfer to the Dominion in 1880, no regulations had been issued to facilitate their settlement. The failure to do so, Walkem protested, had resulted in great injury to provincial development. Both in 1881 and 1882 he complained bitterly to Ottawa about the situation, and asked that the Belt be opened immediately to settlement.[32] Finally with the selection of the Kicking Horse Pass route in 1882 and the establishment of Port Moody

[32] B.C., *Sessional Papers*, 3d Parl., 4th sess., 1881, p. 146, and B.C., *Sessional Papers*, 4th Parl., 1st sess., 1883, p. 349. Typical of the complications which arose from the Dominion's delay in constructing the railway was a dispute over reclaimed lands in the lower Fraser Valley. On April 10, 1878, four months before the reserve was replaced on the railway lands on the mainland, the provincial government authorized E. L. Derby, an engineer from California, to construct a line of dykes in the Chilliwack-Sumas-Matsqui area to reclaim some 50,000 acres of land subject to periodic overflow from the Fraser River. As a statute in effect since 1873 empowered the government to grant crown lands to anyone willing to undertake a reclamation scheme (The Drainage, Dyking, and Irrigation Act. B.C., *Statutes*, 1873, 36 Vict., no. 10.), the 1878 act was simply to stipulate the amount of land Derby should receive in return for his dyking. Providing he should "well and effectually dyke all the said Lands" by July 1, 1880, he was to be given 45,000 acres in the Chilliwack-Sumas region, including Sumas Lake, and 6,000 acres at Matsqui. (Sumas Dyking Act. B.C., *Statutes*, 1878, 41 Vict., c. 6.) Derby did not meet his commitments, and the Matsqui section, the only one on which any work was done, gave way each spring. Finally, in 1881, Derby assigned his entire interest to G. B. Sword, who later in the year received a crown grant of the 6,000 acres at Matsqui. When Derby failed to dyke the eastern portions of the land, a group of twelve men, including such public figures as C. A. Vernon, B. W. Pearse, J. R. Hett, R. G. Tatlow, J. D. Pemberton, and C. E. Pooley, requested authority to undertake the reclamation of the land they described as "cranberry marsh, continually flooded, and worthless until reclaimed." (See B.C., *Sessional Papers*, 5th Parl., 1st sess., 1887, pp. 365-66, for the correspondence.) The syndicate asked for and received permission to buy all the land they reclaimed at one dollar an acre.

Without any authority from the dominion government, the province had sanctioned the grant of 45,037 acres of dominion lands in the lower Fraser Valley in 1878 to Derby. It was argued, of course, that the original agreement had been made before the railway reserve had been gazetted. But by a new act in 1885 (An Act to amend the Sumas Dyking Act of 1878, B.C., *Statutes*, 1885, 48 Vict., c. 9.), the province had cancelled the Derby agreement and offered the lands for sale to anyone willing to undertake the project. The minister of justice in Ottawa promptly disallowed it, arguing that when the act had been passed on March 5, 1885, the lands were described as crown land. But these lands automatically become dominion property the moment the Derby agreement was rescinded, since the Settlement Act of 1884 had transferred all public lands in the Railway Belt to the Dominion. The provincial act was disallowed on March 16, 1886. But Robson, provincial secretary and minister of finance and agriculture, managed to get around the disallowance by persuading the Dominion to reconvey the disputed acreage to the province "to make valid certain titles and interests which the province had undertaken to create therein" (An Act to provide for the conveyance of certain lands in British Columbia, Canada, *Statutes*, 1889, 52 Vict., c. 7).

as the terminus, British Columbia was called upon to convey to the Dominion the Railway Belt. This conveyance had been made in 1880, but as the route chosen at that time was through the Yellowhead Pass, a new instrument of transfer became necessary.[33] By the time the route across the mountains had definitely been selected, a further complication had developed as the result of Prime Minister Mackenzie's Railway Act of 1874.[34] The findings of the preliminary surveys made by dominion surveyors had led to the inclusion in the act of a clause stating that the lands to be conveyed must be of "fair average quality." It had been ascertained by then that not so much of the province was good land as members of the Macdonald government had led the House to suppose.

To settle all the questions which "have so long agitated the public mind, and have tended to embitter the relations existing between the two Governments,"[35] the newly elected Smithe government attempted early in 1883 to adjust all difficulties connected with the Island Railway, the Esquimalt Graving Dock, the railway lands on the mainland, and compensation for delay in the building of the Canadian Pacific Railway. Walkem's elevation to the bench as a judge of the Supreme Court in May of 1882 ended the provincial policy of "fighting Canada" and cleared the way for settlement of dominion-provincial differences. In May, 1883, the Smithe ministry passed "An Act relating to the Island Railway, the Graving Dock, and Railway Lands of the Province."[36] In their rush to settle all problems left by the Walkem regime, members of the Smithe government drew up the act too hastily. After a visit from Sir Alexander Campbell, minister of justice, the act was re-drafted and passed by the provincial legislature on December 19, 1883.[37]

33 The Railway Belt through the Yellowhead Pass was conveyed by An Act to grant Public Lands on the Mainland to the Dominion in aid of the Canadian Pacific Railway (B.C., *Statutes*, 1880, 43 Vict., c. 11). The lands along the route finally chosen were conveyed by an Act relating to the Island Railway, the Graving Dock, and Railway Lands of the Province (B.C., *Statutes*, 1884, 47 Vict., c. 14), known as the Settlement Act. For the history of the route changes, see F. G. Roe, "An Unsolved Problem of Canadian History," in Canadian Historical Association, *Annual Report* (1936), 65-77. For reasons why it had not been located farther south, see W. K. Lamb, "A Bent Twig in British Columbia History," ibid. (1948), pp. 86-92.

34 Canada, *Statutes*, 1874, 37 Vict., c. 14, s. 8(4). See Chapter 12, n. 23.

35 "Papers relating to the Island Railway, the Graving Dock, and Railway Lands," B.C., *Sessional Papers*, 4th Parl., 1st sess., 1883, p. 459.

36 B.C., *Statutes*, 1883, 46 Vict., c. 14.

37 B.C., *Statutes*, 1884, 47 Vict., c. 14.

This act came to be known later as the Settlement Act. The forty-mile strip containing 10,976,000 acres was conveyed to the Dominion for the third time together with a block of land of 3,500,000 acres[38] in the Peace River area. In addition 1,900,000 acres on Vancouver Island[39] was conveyed to the Dominion, to be turned over to some company which would undertake to build the line from Esquimalt to Nanaimo.[40] The Dominion was also to pay $750,000 in cash to this company. Further, the Dominion was to take over and complete the partly-built Esquimalt Graving Dock and to pay the province $250,000 for expenses already incurred on that project.

When the act came up for discussion in the federal House, it was ably defended by Sir Charles Tupper, minister of railways and canals, supported by the members from Victoria, Noah Shakespeare and E. Crowe Baker. It is probable that Sir Charles expected little debate on his bill, since Smithe himself, who was in Ottawa, had assured him that his government was as anxious to clear up the whole problem as was the federal government. Also the provincial administration had already passed the province's version of the bill. Two mainland members J. A. R. Homer of New Westminster and D. W. Gordon of Vancouver, objected strenuously to the terms by which the Dominion government would receive such large and valuable tracts of British Columbia land. Sir Charles Tupper opened the debate, discussing at length the Railway Belt and the "in lieu of" lands in the peace River.

> It was found, owing to the location of the land by the the gorges of the Fraser, that a question arose as to whether the land was to be horizontal or perpendicular, as in many cases you would pass a mile or a long distance from the railway without reaching any land available for cultivation. Those questions were presented and made the subject of discussion between Mr. Trutch, the agent of the Dominion Government, and the Government of British Columbia, and that Government finally made a proposal to the Government of Canada for the solution of these various

38 The selection of the lands in the Peace River block was not made until 1907.

39 See Vancouver Land and Railway Company Act, B.C., *Statutes*, 1882, 45 Vict., c. 15, s. 18, for the legal description of the land.

40 On the advice of Victoria, "His Excellency the Governor-General was pleased" to name Robert Dunsmuir, John Bryden, James Dunsmuir, Charles Crocker, Charles F. Crocker, Leland Stanford, and Collis P. Huntington as a "body corporate and politic," under the name of the "Esquimalt and Nanaimo Railway Company" to construct the line. (See Canada, *Statutes*, 1884, 47 Vict., c. 6, Schedule, pp. 63-68.)

questions. That was in 1883, and the result of those proposals was that a new Act was passed, again appropriating the land in the twenty mile belt on each side of the line, on a new arrangement.

Turning to the problem of the Island railway, Sir Charles continued:

> ... I am sure we all recognize the great importance of the construction of a railway between Nanaimo and Esquimalt. It is well known that although it is somewhat rocky and precipitous, and, to a considerable extent, barren country, there are valuable coal mines contained within that area; and I have been told by some of our friends from British Columbia that they have objected to the terms of this proposal because it was handing over to a company the development of these mines. But it must not be forgotten that, valuable as are these coal areas in Vancouver Island, they have lain for a long time in a comparatively undeveloped state. With the exception of Mr. Dunsmuir's mine, and another one which has not been very successful, I believe that up to this moment, practically, very little has been done in developing those coal areas. We have reason to believe — in fact I am informed by the able Premier of British Columbia, who is now here, that he has applications for large tracts of coal mining areas believed to possess very valuable coal mines outside the section that is covered by these resolutions.[41]

Tupper's speech was answered by J. A. R. Homer of New Westminster. Undoubtedly both Homer and Gordon knew that their opposition would not delay the bill for more than an hour or so, but it was characteristic of both men to oppose what they felt to be wrong. Homer said:

> It is with regret, Mr. Speaker, that, owing to the conditions contained in the agreement on which the resolution is based, I cannot give it my support. It was supposed that after twelve months' deliberation on the negotiation between the Dominion Government and the Government of British Columbia, the result would have been some compensation to that Province for the delay which has occurred in carrying out the terms of Union. But, Sir, instead of that Province receiving any compensation according to this agreement, it is being relieved of property consisting of lands, timber, coal, and other minerals to the value of $20,000,000, for which the Province is to receive a railway, seventy miles in length, involving a cost of above $2,250,000. ... With regard to this railway to which we are asked to give 2,000,000 acres of land on Vancouver Island, including 450 square miles of coal land, it

41 Canada, House of Commons, *Debates*, 1884, pp. 1024-25, March 21, 1884.

> is true that a small portion of these lands have been alienated, but the greater portion of that which has been alienated is owned by one of the members of the present Company, thus creating the greatest coal monopoly in existence. They do not expect to realize their money from the railway, but out of the coal mines; and in addition to the Dominion Government granting this enormous monopoly, they are to receive $750,000.... With regard to the 3,500,000 acres of land on the Peace River, according to the terms of Union, the Government of the Dominion of Canada will receive from the Government of British Columbia a belt of land 20 miles wide on each side of the line, or in all, a belt forty miles wide along the entire line running through British Columbia, and for all the lands which were alienated from that belt previous to its being reserved, they are to receive other lands contiguous thereto. Now, it has been stated by the Minister of Railways that there are 800,000 acres of land alienated, but I think the honourable gentleman is under the mark. I think I am nearer correct when I say, that there are 1,000,000 acres of land alienated, previous to the reserve being placed on it, so that, as I contend, they are receiving 2,500,000 acres more than they were entitled to under the terms of the Union, thereby enabling them to subsidize this company with $750,000.[42]

In support of Homer's objections, Gordon of Vancouver informed the House that the Dominion geological surveyor had computed productive coal measures to amount to 300 square miles in the Comox area alone, containing an estimated 4,800,000,000 tons of coal.[43] He felt this to be entirely too lavish a grant, particularly when considered along with the other clauses of the bill, notably the clause granting the acreage in the Peace River.

Gordon was then castigated by Noah Shakespeare of Victoria for his opposition to the bill.

> In almost every instance, when any large question has come before this Parliament, if it has been on the Island, the Mainland has opposed it; if it has been on the Mainland the Island, has opposed it.[44]

Shakespeare had ample grounds for his exasperation, since the petty bickering between island and mainland was a frequent impediment to the progress of provincial affairs. Victoria members,

[42] Ibid., pp. 1026-27.
[43] Ibid., p. 1027.
[44] Ibid., p. 1029.

intensely aware of the islanders' almost fanatic determination to have a railway, could not be expected to see the whole problem as objectively as could those from the mainland.

Speaking in support of the bill, E. C. Baker, also of Victoria, suggested that as this bill had already passed the provincial legislature by a vote of fifteen out of twenty-five, he could see little reason for lengthy discussion in Ottawa. He reported that he had been in the local legislature when the vote had been taken and noticed that only seven members voted against the bill, that two — Dunsmuir and the member from Cassiar — abstained, and that the twenty-fifth person was the Speaker. In an attempt to help the Dominion recoup the $750,000 which it was going to have to pay the new company, he suggested that the Peace River block could readily be sold to a "colonization scheme," the directors of which would gladly pay fifty cents an acre.[45]

Still feeling it his duty as a member from Vancouver Island to convince the House that the Dominion would be losing nothing were the measure to be passed, Baker pointed out the probable value to the company of the lands they would receive for building the line on the island. From the grant of 2,000,000 acres, the company could derive $4,631,100; coal lands, $2,160,000; timber lands, $1,346,100; agricultural lands, $1,125,000. As the line from Esquimalt to Nanaimo would be seventy miles long, Baker drew the attention of the House to the fact that the company would receive forty square miles of land per mile of railway, or 25,600 acres, which, based on his calculation of one dollar per acre for timber land and five dollars per acre for agricultural land, was tantamount to a cash subsidy of $61,000 per mile.

Homer, well aware of the extreme generosity of the dominion's grant to the company for building the Island line, concluded the debate with a word of prophecy:

> As I said before . . . the Government should hesitate before they give away all this valuable property, as they will find in five or ten years that the Local Government will have to come back to them for assistance, instead of being able to open up various resources of the country.[46]

Shortly thereafter the vote was called and the Settlement Act became law.

45 Ibid., p. 1034.
46 Ibid., p. 1038.

With its passage the Esquimalt and Nanaimo Railway Company received not only a substantial land grant and the $750,000; it also received all the coal, coal oil, ores, stones, clay, marble, slate, mines, minerals, and "substances whatsoever in, or under the lands so to be granted"; the foreshore rights in all its lands; the privilege of mining under the foreshore and the sea opposite and of retaining for their own use all coal and minerals under the foreshore; all the timber; and exemption from taxation on all property until alienated. Homer and Gordon's speeches show clearly that, even before it became law, some British Columbians realized the prodigality of the terms of the Settlement Act.

It would seem that Trutch, by now the dominion's confidential agent in British Columbia, was solely responsible for the inclusion of the Peace River block. Since the provincial government had alienated approximately 900,000 acres of Railway Belt lands between 1871 and 1883,[47] it was reasonable that it should be expected to make substitution elsewhere. But the dominion government went well beyond a reasonable expectation when it insisted that since much of the land within the Belt was not of "fair average quality," British Columbia must convey an equivalent in good lands elsewhere. R. E. Gosnell, the originator of the Better Terms movement in British Columbia and the man who worked for over twenty-five years to have the Railway Belt lands returned to the province, says that Trutch raised "an issue never heard of before, namely, that as the Railway Belt was largely useless, or unfit, for agricultural purposes, it should be supplemented by fertile lands elsewhere."[48] This was indeed strange behaviour for the man who had assured the dominion government in 1870 that at least 50,000,000 acres of land in British Columbia was good agricultural land and who, acting as though much of this acreage would be included in the Railway Belt, had written every word contained in article 11 of the Terms of Union himself.[49] Trutch's assurance had allayed any fears as to the quality of British Columbia land, so much so that

47 This is the figure Gosnell used in 1913 in *A History of British Columbia*, 2:125; writing in 1927, he lowered the figure to 800,000. (See R. E. Gosnell, *Memorandum for the Hon. Mr. Justice Martin, Commissioner in re Railway Lands of British Columbia, Re Conveyance of Railway Belt and Peace River Lands to British Columbia* [Ottawa, 1927], p. 19.)

48 Gosnell, *Memorandum for Mr. Justice Martin*, p. 11.

49 Ibid.

Cartier in 1871 had spoken not only of agricultural land for the settlers who would be enticed into the province, but also of mineral land as an added inducement to immigrants. The quality of land in the Railway Belt had not been a consideration at the time of Union, and the province was in no way bound to supplement it by land of a better quality.

Wherever responsibility lay for the terms of the Settlement Act, the opinion held in British Columbia twenty years later was summed up by Premier McBride:

> By the terms of the "Settlement Act" the Province, tired of delays and wearied with fruitless negotiations, agreed to transfer 3,500,000 [acres] of the best land in the Peace River District in lieu of expenditures on the part of the Dominion, amounting in all to about $1,100,000. These lands, worth now, at the lowest valuation, $17,500,000, were parted with to secure a railway from Esquimalt to Nanaimo, costing less than $3,000,000, which, under the Carnarvon Terms, the Dominion Government had pledged itself to build without cost to the Province. The value of such concession was not then foreseen. The Treaty of 1871, as revised in 1884, was made in misapprehension of the possibilities of British Columbia and the development to accrue from the building of the Canadian Pacific Railway.[50]

But these second thoughts lay in the future. Now that the long-negotiated Settlement Act had finally been passed, the Smithe government determined to do what it could to make up for the delays of the past decade. Its first action was to remove the reserve which had remained since 1873 on crown lands in the province. On May 9, 1884, the Dominion relinquished all claim to the land west of Port Moody; the next day, a provincial Minute in Council cancelled the reserve which had been still in effect on these lands and threw them open for sale and pre-emption.[51]

But these lands west of Port Moody did not remain open long, for it soon became obvious that the eastern end of Burrard Inlet was not a satisfactory terminus for the Canadian Pacific Railway.

[50] "Memorandum Re British Columbia's Claims for Special Consideration," in "Report on Mission to Ottawa," B.C., *Sessional Papers*, 12th Parl., 3d sess., 1912, p. N9.

[51] "Return to an Address for ... all correspondence between the Provincial and Dominion Governments ... relating to the reversion of the lands and townsite of Granville," B.C., *Sessional Papers*, 5th Parl., 1st sess., 1887, pp. 325-6.

A government reserve was placed on the lands on August 7. With more liberality than good sense, the Smithe government readily agreed on February 23, 1885, to grant an additional 6,000 acres west of Port Moody to the Canadian Pacific Railway,[52] plus a number of sizeable lots in Granville, for the extension of its line into Coal Harbour, or Vancouver, as it was then being called. In addition, the company received from private owners a gift of one-third of their holdings.[53] For this twelve-mile extension of a line which, in its own interest, the Canadian Pacific Company would have to construct anyway within a year or so, the gift of these 6,275 acres by the Smithe government of what shortly became valuable land, was indeed a liberal gesture and one to which this same government was subsequently held to very strict account. These lots, previously held under timber lease by the Hastings Sawmill Company, soon comprised the most valuable acreage in Vancouver. In all justice to Smithe and his colleagues, however, it should be explained that they had ample precedent, and that these acres, like all other lands in the province, not only had been reserved from sale since 1878, but also had been reserved specifically for railway purposes, and even tentatively had been transferred to the Dominion to this end. In the next year — 1886 — the government continued its generous policy toward the Canadian Pacific Railway by granting it a bonus of $75,000 and a free right of way to construct its nine-

52 For the full text of the agreement between the province and the C.P.R., see B.C., *Sessional Papers*, 5th Parl., 2d sess., 1888, pp. 545-46. Under section 2 of the agreement the extension was to be completed by December 31, 1886; if not, the province could claim $250,000 from the company. The line was not finished on time; on January 13, 1887, the province asked for the surrender of the bond. C. Drinkwater, secretary of the C.P.R., admitted that the line had not been completed on schedule, but charged that this was so "solely in consequence of the active interference of the judiciary of the Province." The case was taken before Chief Justice Begbie of the B.C. Supreme Court, who gave his decision in favour of the province, (ibid., pp. 549-51). It is not without interest that only five days before the Minute in Council had been passed asking for the forfeiture of the $250,000 bond, H. Abbott, general superintendent of the C.P.R., had had to ask the provincial legislature for the $37,500 bonus promised by the government for the completion of the New Westminster branch line. A Minute in Council of 21st April, 1886, had agreed to pay the bonus, but the C.P.R. never received the money.

53 E. O. S. Scholefield and F. W. Howay, *British Columbia, from the Earliest Times to the Present* (Vancouver: S. J. Clarke Publishing Co., [1914]), 2:431. It was not long before litigation arose over the ownership of many lots in the Granville townsite. The C.P.R. protested that certain lots were being held by squatters, but in vain. (For the evidence regarding ownership, see B.C., *Sessional Papers*, 6th Parl., 4th sess., 1894, 1143-48.)

mile branch line from Vancouver to New Westminster.[54] In law, the extension from Port Moody into Vancouver and the line to New Westminster are still branch lines.

[54] "Return ... for ... all ... correspondence ... between the Government of British Columbia ... and the Canadian Pacific Railway Company [1887]," p. 321.

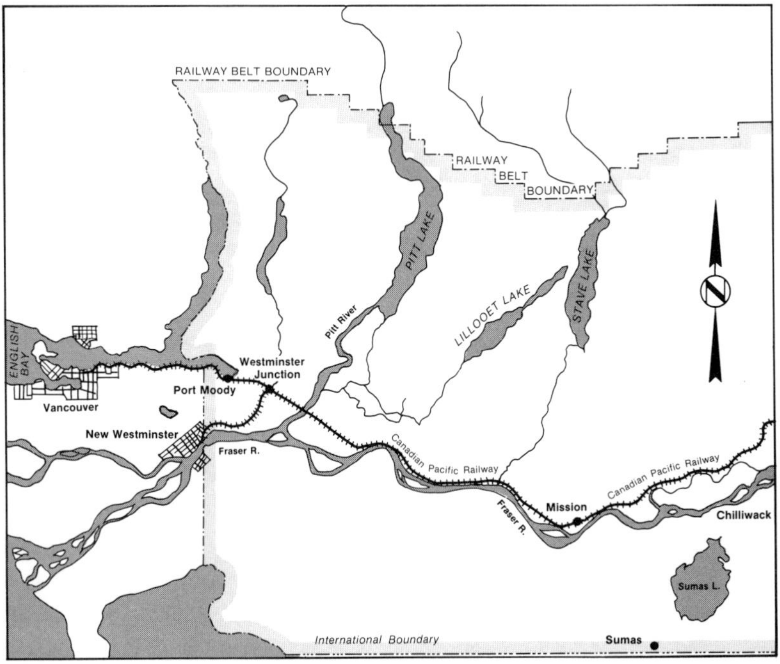

Railway Belt Boundaries in the Lower Mainland

CHAPTER 9

The Railway Belt after the Settlement Act

Once the Settlement Act had been passed, British Columbia anxiously awaited the advent of the railroad and settlers. Expecting that most settlers would take up land near the railway, British Columbia's representatives had insisted on the insertion of a clause in the act by which the Dominion undertook "with all convenient speed" to offer for sale on liberal terms the land within its Railway Belt on the mainland. As time passed the dominion government required constant prodding, and there is no doubt that its failure to fulfil this clause did retard settlement. The Dominion now owned outright much of what would then have been considered the most desirable acreage in the province. The situation proved to be somewhat analogous to that of the Clergy Reserves in Upper Canada. Settlers had their choice of squatting on dominion land in the vain hope of having their claims to the land dealt with expeditiously, or of literally taking to the hills.

The problem became so acute that in the spring session of Parliament in 1886 Noah Shakespeare, M.P. for Victoria, moved the tabling of all correspondence between the British Columbia and dominion governments concerning the opening of the lands in the Railway Belt to settlement. He complained that although British Columbia had lived up to its obligations under the Settlement Act "to the very letter," the dominion government had done "little or nothing" to carry out its obligations.

> The lands referred to are practically withheld from settlement, and actual settlers, who have located, some of them, on these lands in good faith, are still unable to obtain the patents to which they are justly entitled. I am informed that some 3,000

> applications are on record in the office of the Agent of the Dominion Government in British Columbia, and not one, that I am aware of, has received any satisfaction.... Nothing has tended to retard settlement in that Province more than the withholding of the patents to these lands from people who have located upon them. Many of these people became so discouraged that they left the Province.[1]

Thomas White, the minister of the interior, did his best to extricate the government from an uncomfortable position. He regretted "as much as the hon. gentleman does the delays that have taken place," and promised to rectify matters by moving the agent, J. W. Trutch, and his assistant from New Westminster to Victoria, "where he would be of more easy access to settlers who desired to get their patents."[2]

J. A. R. Homer of New Westminster followed this conciliatory statement with a few remarks which clearly demonstrated the inevitable divergence of opinion between island and mainland members. Though he did not deny Shakespeare's allegations, he defended the Dominion's slowness to act on the grounds that such a policy had prevented speculation in land, a problem which was soon to become a very real one.

> The policy pursued by the Government in relation to land in the railway belt of British Columbia has been, although one of delay, the means of placing those lands in the hands of actual settlers. ... If a different policy, or a more hasty policy had been pursued by which those lands would have been put on the market for sale, the probability is they would now have been in the hands of a few speculators, and that result would have proved very detrimental to the settlement of the Province. No doubt there are some grievances ... but, whatever those grievances are, I feel confident that under the energetic administration of the Minister of the Interior they will be speedily removed.[3]

Three weeks later White moved leave to introduce Bill 120, whose object was to bring the lands in the Railway Belt under the jurisdiction of the Dominion Lands Board. Until now, he explained, these lands had been administered by Trutch, the dominion government's agent, "but, as he will cease to hold that office after the

1 Canada, House of Commons, *Debates*, 1886, p. 496.

2 Ibid.

3 Ibid., p. 497.

end of this year,[4] and we now have railway communication which will enable us to reach British Columbia easily," the lands should be administered by the Dominion Lands Board. To facilitate matters for settlers wishing to obtain patents on their land, he had already ordered Trutch's assistant, Aikman, to move to New Westminster. Having questioned White closely regarding Trutch's fate, Edward Blake, leader of the opposition, made sure of the area to be administered by the dominion board. "This will include," he asked, "in addition to the 40-mile railway belt, the lands given in the Peace River district?" White replied that it would embrace all lands of the Dominion in British Columbia.[5]

In spite of the new administration promised for the Railway Belt lands, troubles continued to develop. In February of 1885 the dispute over jurisdiction of minerals in the Belt had led to a test case being taken to the courts.[6] In April, the province complained bitterly of the Dominion's regulations for disposing of Railway Belt land, since these regulations differed in so many respects from those

4 During the discussion on the bill, some interesting comments were made concerning Trutch. Peter Mitchell, former premier of New Brunswick (1865), and an ex-senator from that province (1867-74) who had resigned his senatorship so he could enter the House of Commons (1874-78, 1882-96), insinuated that the whole dominion land administration policy in the Railway Belt was being subverted by Trutch. When the bill was introduced, he expressed his delight at Trutch's removal and tendered his congratulations to White, saying, "and so will all who know the circumstances connected with the management of lands in British Columbia and the administration of Mr. Trutch. I am sure the change will be a great improvement," (ibid., p. 912). When the bill came up for second reading on May 11, 1886, White repeated that "Mr. Trutch's services are to be dispensed with." Edward Blake, leader of the Liberal opposition, then asked, "What is to become of Mr. Trutch, because I believe his services are very dear to the people of that Province, as we know they have been to the country. Is he to be superseded altogether?" With White's answer that he would require notice of that question, Blake was content, but not Mitchell. "I should like to ask the Minister of the Interior," said Mitchell, "whether there is any provision in the Bill for the pet of the Administration . . . because I think it would be very unfair, after he has been petted and pampered by the Government so long, that he should not be provided for." Blake interjected, "He will be," and Mitchell added, "No doubt." White said nothing (ibid., p. 1202). As the minister of marine and fisheries in Macdonald's government during the visit of the B.C. Confederation Delegation in 1869, Mitchell may have met Trutch and formed a dislike of him, and it may be that, as a private member in 1886, he could voice opinions White, as a member of the cabinet, could not.

5 Ibid., p. 1202. This is the first positive indication in the debates following the Settlement Act that the federal government had retained all the unalienated portion of the Railway Belt in spite of having received the "in lieu of" lands in the Peace River.

6 See p. 84.

in force on contiguous provincial land.[7] In 1887 the problem of defining the northern and southern boundaries of the Belt throughout the width of the province arose. The first method to be used was outlined by the Dominion in an Order in Council of May 27. A second one was proposed by British Columbia in its Minute in Council of August 24.[8] But by December of 1887, the local government had had enough of the endless complications arising from dominion jurisdiction over the most thickly settled strip of land in the province. The Executive Council passed the following Minute:

> The Committee ... submit that, apart from the impracticality of establishing satisfactory boundary lines, very great inconvenience and ever-recurring complications will arise from the administration by the Dominion Government of a narrow and extremely irregular strip of land extending through the entire mainland part of the Province, while the whole of the public domain, with the exception of said strip, is administered by the Provincial Government.
>
> The Committee believe that it would be for the convenience of both Governments, as well as in the general interests of the country, that the belt along the line of railway should be exchanged for such an area of the public lands of the Province ... as might be considered equivalent in value.[9]

It was suggested that 15,000,000 acres be accepted in lieu of the existing Railway Belt.

The Minute was referred to Edgar Dewdney, now the minister of the interior in the dominion cabinet, for consideration and report. Dewdney recommended that the question should not be considered at that time; "It does not appear that such consideration would serve any useful purpose so long as the right to the minerals in the Railway Belt is still unsettled."[10] When the *Precious Metals Case* was settled in favour of the province in 1889, nothing further was heard of the proposal for exchanging land.

One problem at least was settled when the northern and southern boundaries of the Belt were determined in 1895.[11] In the same year

[7] See pp. 85-87. For the Orders in Council, correspondence with British Columbia or with Trutch, the Dominion's agent, as well as for a summary of lands appropriated in the Railway Belt from June 30, 1873 - October 25, 1880, see Canada, *Sessional Papers*, 4th Parl., 3d sess., 1880-81, no. 21(k), pp. 23-51.

[8] These are listed in the preamble to the Railway Belt Act, B.C., *Statutes*, 1895, 58 Vict., c. 18.

[9] B.C., *Sessional Papers*, 5th Parl., 4th sess., 1890, p. 401.

[10] B.C., *Sessional Papers*, 5th Parl., 3d sess., 1889, p. 165.

[11] B.C., *Revised Statutes*, 1911, 2 Geo. 5, c. 195.

provincial legislation made it possible for pre-emptors and purchasers of land in the Belt to secure titles to their land which could be registered under the provincial Registry Act.[12] Since the Dominion could not register any titles to land within the Belt, residents on these lands had been unable to obtain their patents.

Though some problems had been settled, others took their place. In 1906 the water rights case developed over the province's granting of a water record in the Railway Belt to the Burrard Power Company at Lillooet Lake. And by the time it was settled in the province's favour in 1910 new problems had appeared.

The McBride ministry forwarded a resolution to Ottawa pointing out the "urgent necessity of some action being taken looking to the better settlement of lands in the Dominion Railway Belt throughout the Province." The reply stated that although it had been found necessary to place a reserve on the lands in the Columbia Valley and Shuswap Lake areas in 1909, these lands would soon be released once more for settlement. Meanwhile, it was pointed out, all other lands were open.[13]

Finally in 1906 the western boundary of the Railway Belt was drawn. In terms comprehensible to surveyors only, the sinuosities of the boundary were outlined in detail. One more vexatious and contentious issue was laid to rest.[14]

Then later in 1911 came a near settlement of all the problems. Though Robson's offer in 1887 to exchange the Belt for 15,000,000 acres in the Peace River had proved abortive, the province still sought a definitive solution to the steadily increasing problems. The publicity programme carried on through the office of the agent general in London, combined with the efforts of the provincial bureau of information in Victoria, had resulted in the arrival of thousands of settlers. As population increased, so did the complications of divided land jurisdiction. On a mission to Ottawa with the Attorney-General, W. J. Bowser, and the Minister of Lands, W. R. Ross, Premier McBride offered to purchase the Railway Belt and the Peace River lands. McBride's note to Prime Minister Borden on November 6, 1911, said:

12 Railway Belt Act, B.C., *Statutes*, 1895, 58 Vict., c. 18.

13 "Reply . . . to . . . a respectful Address . . . [on] the urgent necessity of some action being taken . . . to the better settlement of lands in the Dominion Railway Belt . . . ," B.C., *Sessional Papers*, 12th Parl., 2d sess., 1911, p. M29.

14 Railway Belt Definition Act., B.C., *Statutes*, 1906, 6 Edw. 7, c. 37.

> As the settlement of British Columbia proceeds, it becomes more and more patent, we submit, that the development of the interests held by the Dominion Government in these districts, in the way of settlement and occupation, can best be forwarded by administration through the local authorities. We are prepared, on behalf of British Columbia, to purchase outright the rights of the Dominion in these properties. Pending a final settlement, the Province will undertake to administer the lands under local laws and to account for all moneys received, less cost of administration, to the Federal Government.[15]

Had the war not intervened, the case would have been settled by a royal commission.

In 1927, Mr. Justice Martin of the Quebec Supreme Court was appointed Royal Commissioner to investigate the merit of the case McBride had presented in 1911. In his brief to Martin, R. E. Gosnell frankly admitted that "from the strictly legal point of view, the Province has not a leg to stand on, because whatever legal status she possessed prior to 1884, the Act of Settlement of that year places British Columbia definitely out of court." He added, however, that it was "not a question of law but of equity, the undoing of a constitutional injustice."[16] To lend weight to the argument, Gosnell presented statistics to show that from 1871 to 1926, the dominion revenue for homesteads, sales of land, parks, and timber in the Belt had amounted to $5,798,205. The expenditures for the same period for administrators' salaries, surveys, forestry, parks, and water power investigations had amounted to $7,637,826.[17] Here was proof indeed that the province did not want the lands for the sake of their revenue but merely to remove administrative complications. In 1930 the Dominion turned the unalienated portions of the Railway Belt and Peace River block lands back to the province.[18] Of the total area of 10,976,000 acres in the Belt, the Dominion had disposed of 4,920,500 acres; hence the province received back 6,055,500 acres together with the Peace River lands.[19] It is ironic that nearly fifty years of inconvenience, dispute, and litigation had to precede this simple solution.

15 B.C., *Sessional Papers*, 12th Parl., 3d sess., 1912, p. N2.

16 "Memorandum for Mr. Justice Martin," p. 1.

17 Ibid., p. 16.

18 The Railway Belt and Peace River Block Act, Canada, *Statutes*, 1930, 20-21 Geo. 5, c. 37.

19 The acreage alienated within the Belt had been disposed of as follows:

Homesteads .... 732,400 acres

Even if the C.P.R. lands had been the only ones granted, opposition in the province could still hardly be blamed for deploring what it termed the "give-away" policy of the government. During the election campaign of 1886 it did so vociferously. But the voters so heartily endorsed that policy that they returned the government with nineteen out of twenty-seven members. Obviously the male property owners of British Columbia considered it good business to construct rail lines by subsidizing them with crown land. It was, apparently, a matter of no concern that by 1886, as the opposition charged, the government had given away the Graving Dock, 3,500,000 acres in the Peace River, 1,900,000 acres on Vancouver Island, 750,000 acres including the mineral rights to the Columbia and Kootenay Railway Company,[20] 60,000 acres for a useless road,[21] 78,000 acres for a worse than useless canal,[22] and 6,000 acres for an extension which the Canadian Pacific would have been obliged to make for its own protection.

So far, however, none of these land grants could truthfully be said to have been made to companies whose motives were purely speculative. Certainly the invitation was there and was soon to be accepted by dozens of companies with their government's blessing.

Sales (including mining lands)	171,800 acres
Parks	747,500 acres
Timber berths	1,057,300 acres
Grazing leases	325,200 acres
Forest reserves	1,713,700 acres
Indian reserves	172,600 acres
Total	4,920,500 acres

(See Gosnell, *Memorandum for Mr. Justice Martin*, p. 15.)

20 Columbia and Kootenay Railway and Transportation Company Act, B.C., *Statutes*, 1883, 46 Vict., c. 25.

21 Granted to G. B. Wright, 1883, in the Yale and Kootenay Districts, for building the Eagle Pass Wagon Road, a twelve-foot road from Shuswap Lake to the Columbia River to aid in the construction of the C.P.R. in the Columbia region.

22 Built by W. A. Baillie-Grohman, 1883-1888, across Canal Flat to turn the Kootenay River into the Columbia, thereby reclaiming land which was under water every spring. To build the canal, which was to be 45 feet wide and 6,700 feet long, Baillie-Grohman was granted 48,000 acres of rich alluvial soil lying along the Kootenay River. Fearful of danger to the C.P.R., the federal government required the insertion on the canal of a lock. For the extra work and expense, 30,000 acres of picked land in the upper Kootenay Valley were granted. To climax the absurdity of the project, within twelve months of its completion, the local government voted Baillie-Groman $2,500 to have his canal closed. (See: "Lease. Kootenay Reclamation and Colonization," B.C., *Sessional Papers*, 5th Parl., 1st sess., 1887, pp. 315-19.)

CHAPTER 10

Intraprovincial Railways

All that any enterprising group of men had to do to form an incorporated company was to subscribe their names to a printed memorandum of association, name the termini of their line — which had to be within the province — and indicate the location of their registered office. Only one man's name had to appear in the Act of Incorporation.[1]

It was as simple as that. The liability of the company was limited to the amount, if any, "unpaid on shares respectively subscribed for and held by them," i.e. the subscribers to the memorandum of association. Shares were regularly $100. In order to persuade the public in British Columbia, eastern Canada, or abroad of the company's sincerity, each director usually bought a block of shares, although he was not required to do so. No doubt if the company intended to proceed with its undertaking, each director would buy a sizeable number of shares in the expectation of reaping rich rewards from the completed line. The directors of those companies whose sole interest lay in speculation in public lands or public money perhaps bought equally heavily of their own stocks, but only to convince the public of their good intentions. How many millions of dollars went into the pockets of directors of stillborn railway companies cannot be known, but the capitalization of such defunct companies in British Columbia amounted to the huge sum

[1] B.C., *Revised Statutes*, 1911, 2 Geo. 5, c. 194, part 2, s. 8. Though the act to incorporate railway companies received minor emendations from time to time, the 1911 act was little different from those of the previous thirty years.

of \$343,715,000 for Canadian and \$4,400,000 for English companies.[2]

Usually two separate acts were required to get a line underway. The Act of Incorporation, introduced by a private member, constituted the company under the private acts of the session, and a Subsidy Act, introduced by one of the ministers, stipulated the number of acres the government would grant to the company under the public acts of the legislature. Each subsidy act ensured the protection of the rights of pre-emptors. Once the government had set aside a reserve of land from which the company could choose its portion, no further sections could be alienated from the reserve. All these provisions, the model for which was article 11, became standard practice in the provincial subsidy acts.

Once a road was built and running to the satisfaction of the Lieutenant-Governor in Council,[3] the lands selected by the company were conveyed to it. Only then was the unused portion of the government reserve opened again for pre-emption. Since many companies petitioned the legislature for at least one, if not more, time extensions,[4] there were further delays in freeing land from reserve. With the passage each year of more acts to incorporate railway companies, more and more land was reserved from settlement.

Although Premier James Dunsmuir abandoned the land grant

2 These figures were compiled from all the provincial acts incorporating railroads which were never built. The capitalization may not be too significant, as it meant only that the directors were authorized by statute to issue shares up to the figure specified in their act of incorporation, and not that they did so or that they had that amount available. It is more than likely that many of these companies sold very few shares and, conversely, that some sold shares up to the statutory limit. In the latter case, it is doubtful that any money was ever returned to subscribers. (For the list of all the defunct companies, their names, capitalization, and date of incorporation, see Appendix C, Item 1.)

3 This was done by having a government engineer inspect the line and submit a detailed report on it to the chief commissioner of lands and works. If the engineer approved the line, the chief commissioner notified the company that it could begin operations and that its subsidy lands would be released to it. After 1900, the plan of releasing a certain fraction of subsidy lands per mile of construction was adopted. The engineers' reports appeared annually during the 1890's. The Trail-Robson section of the Columbia and Western, for example, was reported on by H. B. Smith to G. B. Martin on October 12, 1897. Smith gave the 19.3 miles in the division his approval. (See B.C., *Sessional Papers*, 7th Parl., 4th sess., 1898, pp. 411-17.)

4 See Appendix C, Item 2, "Railways Incorporated under Acts of the Legislature of British Columbia since 1883," in which there are listed numerous companies whose original charters were amended. Invariably, the amendment extended the date for beginning construction.

policy in favour of cash subsidies after 1900,[5] discouraged immigrants still complained bitterly of the extensive land reservations. The fact that at this time land in the Railway Belt was not readily available for settlement because of administrative and jurisdictional difficulties did not help the situation.[6] The most potent weapon of the opposition in the legislature continued to be loud denunciation of the government's "give-away" land policy.

In 1883 the Smithe government began the policy of granting public land to aid the construction of railways and other public works. Up to 1889 this policy expanded almost annually. With "An Act to authorize the granting of a certain Land Subsidy for and in aid of the Canadian Western Central Railway" of that year,[7] the A. E. B. Davie Ministry reached the height of the land grant spree. This company, incorporated on April 6, 1889,[8] was to begin construction within six months after filing its plan on a line "from a convenient point near the eastern boundary of the Province to the northernmost terminus of the Esquimalt and Nanaimo Railway."[9] For the railroad, beginning no one knew where and ending at a similar destination, the company was to receive a grant of land extending thirty-two miles on each side of the proposed railway, or approximately 14,000,000 acres of British Columbia's public domain. The only stipulation in the act, other than the usual time limit for beginning construction, was that the line "shall be continuously prosecuted to completion with reasonable diligence." As work progressed, the land was to be conveyed to the company in alternate blocks of 20,000 acres on each side of the line. Moreover, the lands, once conveyed, were not to be taxed until the company had used them for other than railway purposes. All stock and property was to be free from provincial and municipal taxation for ten years.[10]

5 B.C., *Journals*, 8th Parl., 2d sess., 1900, p. 2.

6 As late as 1910, the provincial government was still urging the Dominion to take action "looking to the better settlement of the lands in the Dominion Railway Belt throughout the Province." (See B.C., *Sessional Papers*, 12th Parl., 2d sess., 1911, p. M29.)

7 B.C., *Statutes*, 1889, 52 Vict., c. 20. The line was to use the old Yellowhead route and connect with the Esquimalt and Nanaimo and, through some contortion, to pass through Barkerville.

8 Ibid., c. 34. See Appendix C, Item 2, nos. 39 and 40.

9 Ibid., c. 20, preamble.

10 The general attitude toward railway building at the expense of crown lands may be gauged from the fact that the bill to incorporate this company passed

In view of this liberal but customary treatment accorded a company, it is interesting to note the names of the six directors, who capitalized their company at $50,000,000. They were Robert Paterson Rithet and Thomas Earle, both merchants of Victoria; Frank Stillman Barnard and Edward Gawler Prior, both Members of Parliament; Henry Purdom Bell, a civil engineer; and James Reid, a senator. It was not in any way unusual for them to receive a land grant for the construction of their railway, telegraph, and telephone lines. But it was somewhat beyond the ordinary, even in that age of grandiose schemes, for the legislature to incorporate a railroad company with so few specifications in the act concerning its termini and other details. Nor was it customary to grant so much land — as much in this case as in the Railway Belt and the Peace River block combined. Perhaps it is significant that each of the men seems to have been on intimate terms with Davie himself. Fortunately for British Columbia the line, designed to go where the Canadian Pacific Railway had originally been intended to go and where the Canadian Northern twenty-five years later did go, was never built. The Canadian Northern received no such princely grant.

In justice to the governments of British Columbia in the eighties and nineties, it must be remembered that in an era of annual deficits, land was the only asset the province had to grant as a bonus. Their only alternative would have been to borrow money to give such companies. Before 1900 neither Ottawa nor Victoria ever seemed to question the need for lines they approved or the ability of the directors to carry out construction. It is significant that the largest subsidies in cash or lands or both were granted to well-known public figures,[11] but all who asked, received.

> The attitude of the Dominion, which was shared by the province, was that the granting of a subsidy was not to be considered as

---

the House without a division. (See B.C., *Journals*, 5th Parl., 3d sess., 1889, pp. 76-78.) The act to incorporate the line entailed no obligation, but every member would have been aware of the land subsidy bill about to be presented. Lobbying was keen.

11 There is ample evidence that even cabinet ministers were involved in land grants. In 1903, Premier Prior requested and received the resignations of W. C. Wells, chief commissioner of lands and works, and D. M. Eberts, attorney-general, who were involved in the provincial land grant to the Columbia and Western. These lands contained valuable coal deposits. The evidence gathered by the investigating committee indicated that the complicated situation extended back over several years and implicated members of four preceding administrations. (See: Scholefield and Gosnell, *A History of British Columbia*, 2: 154-55.)

> the expression of an official opinion with reference to the probable success of the railway.[12]

The reckless granting of aid did hurt Canadian credit, since the bondholder, often English, naturally regarded the government which was granting the subsidy as a "partner in the enterprise, not as a careless distributor of largesse."[13]

Between the years 1890 and 1900 eighty-seven railway companies were incorporated in British Columbia. By 1890 a number of promising mineral strikes had been made in the Okanagan and in the Kootenays, and the mining promoters were anxious to secure railway communication with the outside world. They cared little whether the railway they sought would be economically sound or whether the outlets arrived from Vancouver or from the United States, but the Robson government, constituted in August, 1889, following the death of A. E. B. Davie, cared a great deal. Attempting to forestall American interests, the Robson ministry instituted the policy or bonusing railways begun and completed on time to the extent of 20,000 acres per mile.[14]

The province continued to realize that it should give its assistance to lines which would keep industrial products at home rather than force them across the international boundary. To this end in 1897 the government voted $2,500,000 "for the purpose of aiding the construction of Railways and other Public Works." The preamble to the act stated in part that:

> Whereas the existence of extraordinary mineral wealth has been substantiated in many parts of the Province, and there are valid reasons for believing that there are numerous districts in the Province as yet unprospected, which will also prove rich in mineral wealth, and that an extensive immigration and increase of population may be anticipated if means of communication are afforded by railways, roads, and other works for developing the natural wealth which exists both in minerals, timber and farming land:

12 S. J. McLean, "National Highways Overland," in *Canada and its Provinces*, Shortt and Doughty, eds., 10: 448.

13 Ibid.

14 B.C., *Statutes*, 1890, 53 Vict., c. 40. This was an act called "An Act in aid of certain Railways." The preamble to the act stated that the construction of these lines "would materially advance the welfare of the Province, and it is expedient to offer inducements for the construction of such lines." There is nowhere a clearer statement than this of the government's attitude toward granting substantial land subsidies to railway companies.

> And whereas it is expedient that the Trade and Commerce of British Columbia accompanying such development and increase in population should, as far as possible, be retained in the Dominion of Canada, which will be best effected by the early construction of such railways, roads and public works.[15]

These clauses demonstrate clearly the prevailing optimism in British Columbia at the turn of the century. Mineral, timber, and farming lands were present in abundance in the province if only they could be made available to immigrants, and railways provided the only practical transportation for settlers and their goods. But the lavish land grants, reserving extensive acreage, soon constituted a serious obstacle to the rapid settlement of the interior of the province. A return tabled in 1898, for example, showed that by then 2,719,087 acres had already been conveyed and a further 9,656,040 acres were under government reserve for railway grants to provincial companies.[16] Settlement, with its resulting revenue to the government, was imperative if the government was to pay cash subsidies to railways. But since railroad lands were generally tax-exempt for from five to ten years, the more land that had been promised to railroad promoters, the less was available immediately for taxation purposes. In the valleys of British Columbia distant from the main line of the Canadian Pacific the best land was not available. It was a serious dilemma. Immigrants needed railroads, but they also needed the land tied up by subsidies to railroads. It is obvious why the government abandoned its land subsidy policy in the late 1890's in favour of cash subsidies, which it in turn abandoned for bond guarantees after 1903.

The land settlement problem in the remoter valleys of the province would have been less serious if lands along the main line of the Canadian Pacific had been readily available to settlers. But for a multitude of reasons lands in the Railway Belt were difficult to acquire, as the local government discovered soon after the passing of the Settlement Act in 1884. A series of unforeseen complications developed, until British Columbia was thoroughly weary of its Railway Belt bargain and determined to trade the Belt for other land.

15 British Columbia, Provincial Bureau of Information. *Manual of Provincial Information: Province of British Columbia 1930* (Victoria: King's Printer, 1930), p. 181.

16 British Columbia Public Works Loan Act, B.C., *Statutes*, 1897, 60 Vict., c. 24.

Of the eighty-seven lines promoted, thirty-four were to have been constructed in the Kootenays. The Canadian Pacific, which was later to lease in perpetuity the lines which were eventually built, would have built them in the first place. It was prevented from doing so owing to the widespread fear of creating a monopoly in western Canada similar to those formed among railway promoters in the United States. Voters in British Columbia wanted either independent or government lines. Whether the government was as sensitive to the people's wishes as it pretended is doubtful, since a good many public men were directors of companies incorporated by the government to build lines in the Kootenays and since all those companies received sizeable land grants. During the 1890's five railway companies received grants as follows: 580,783 acres to the Nelson and Fort Sheppard in 1891; 250,022 acres to the Kaslo and Slocan in 1892; 188,593 acres to the Columbia and Kootenay in the same year; 3,755,733 acres to the British Columbia Southern in 1893, and 1,348,225 acres to the Columbia and Western in 1896.[17]

Because the promoters of these lines were practically assured of rich rewards from their lines, every one was built. No better proof exists in all the complications of British Columbia's railroad history that the development of mining provided the stimulus for the building of the railroads. The directors of those lines, among whom were F. Augustus Heinze and his brother Arthur P., F. W. Aylmer, Lieutenant-Governor Edgar Dewdney, William Fernie, and Robert G. Tatlow, seem to have assessed remarkably well the permanent nature of the Kootenay mining operations.

F. A. Heinze, builder of the first smelter at Trail, is a classic example of a promoter who built his line entirely from loans and shares acquired by using his land and cash subsidies as security. In 1897 his line, the Columbia and Western, was built from Rossland to Trail and thence to Robson. It was leased to the C.P.R. in 1898 and used by the C.P.R. to carry ore to the smelter and minerals and fertilizer back to the Kettle Valley line at Castlegar. The line no longer carries passengers. Elsewhere in British Columbia many companies were failing to act upon their charters.

> To carry on generally the business of an exploration company, and for that purpose to organize and maintain from time to time

[17] "Return for . . . 5. Number of acres set apart for subsidizing railways within the Province," B.C., *Sessional Papers*, 7th Parl., 4th sess., 1898, p. 1101.

> parties of surveyors, engineers or scientific men, and to do all things necessary or conducive to the comfort and success of such expeditions.[18]

In the lands acquired, the company was not to have any mineral rights.

In not building their lines, these two colonization companies were by no means unique. When the provincial legislature finally enacted out of existence all the defunct railway companies, 127 were dissolved as legal entities.[19] Of the 210 railway companies incorporated in the province up to 1913, only 34 built their lines, and only 5 earned their land grants.[20]

Although the land grant policy was not officially terminated until 1900, it became an accepted rule after 1897 under the Turner ministry to grant no further lands.[21] Between 1894 and 1898 the public debt had increased from $2,398,767 to $4,845,414, so that the opposition's cry of waste could not go unheeded by any government. And when this charge was coupled with that of squandering public lands, Premier Turner concluded that he could no longer afford to make grants, particularly of the type made to lines in the Kootenays. The ministry was subjected to very severe attacks in the legislature as a result of the 10,240 acres of land per mile made in 1896 in aid of construction of the Columbia and Western. Turner was attacked even more vigorously for the unconditional extension of time awarded the British Columbia Southern, a branch of the Canadian Pacific, in which to earn its subsidy of 20,000 acres per

18 B.C., *Statutes*, 1898, 61 Vict., c. 63, s. 8(7).

19 B.C., *Statutes*, 1926-1927, 17 Geo. 5, c. 55. For the complete list, see Appendix C, Item 1.

20 Although incorporated in British Columbia, the Esquimalt and Nanaimo Railway Company received its land grant from the Dominion. It is not included, therefore, as one of the five companies receiving land grants from the province.

21 Land grants were made hereafter to transcontinental lines holding federal charters, but of inconsequential amounts. On March 10, 1905, Premier McBride granted 10,000 acres at Kaien Island to the Grand Trunk Pacific for its terminus. For papers dealing with the land grant from part of the Indian reserve at Prince Rupert, see B.C., *Sessional Papers*, 11th Parl., 1st sess., 1907, pp. F33-43. The letters appear in "Return . . . of all correspondence . . . between the Government and the Grand Trunk Pacific Railway Co.," B.C., *Sessional Papers*, 11th Parl., 3d sess., 1909, pp. G51-58. McBride's 1909 agreement with the Canadian Northern included free right of way through crown lands as well as the grant of certain areas for townsite purposes.

mile in the coal fields of the Crow's Nest Pass.[22] Further, the aid amounting to 700,000 acres promised to the Cassiar Central in 1897[23] caused no little dissension among the government's own supporters. In 1898, shortly before the legislature was dissolved, D. W. Higgins, speaker of the house since 1890, handed in his resignation as a protest against this prodigality.

In the late 1890's the provincial government adopted the dominion policy of granting cash instead of land subsidies to railway companies. Having been persuaded in 1882 that land was not sufficient inducement to railway promoters, Sir John A. Macdonald's government had begun giving cash subsidies of $3,200 per mile, the cost of the 100 tons of steel at $32.00 a ton needed for each mile of track. By 1894 the Dominion had altogether abandoned its policy of making land grants, since these grants hindered rapid settlement and caused taxation difficulties. The provincial government followed suit a few year later and adopted the cash subsidy system which, however, it had already been using to a certain extent along with or instead of land subsidies. Unfortunately, it also adopted the Dominion's practice of granting these subsidies indiscriminately to any group which made application.

The following statistics[24] show the land grants for railway purposes by provincial governments and by the Dominion, and the cash subsidies paid by British Columbia and by all the provinces. They provide a basis for comparison of the situation in British Columbia with that elsewhere in Canada.

22 See B.C., *Statutes*, 1894, 57 Vict., c. 39 and c. 53; 1896, 59 Vict., c. 4 and c. 53; 1897, 60 Vict., c. 33. These were all acts to extend the time-limit in which the subsidy could be earned. When it was completed, the 202-mile line from Nelson to the Crow's Nest Pass was leased in perpetuity to the C.P.R., but before the line was completed the company had granted 50,000 acres of valuable coal lands to the dominion government in return for a cash subsidy of $10,000 per mile. The matter of the provincial land grant of 3,755,733 acres was protested by the province when the C.P.R. leased the line and the case was eventually taken to the Privy Council. (For the report on the case, see B.C., *Sessional Papers*, 9th Parl., 1st sess., 1900, pp. 439-62.)

23 B.C., *Statutes*, 1897, 60 Vict., c. 52.

24 Canada, Department of Railways and Canals, *Railway Statistics of the Dominion of Canada, for the year ended June 30, 1917*, pp. xii-xiii. This also appears in Canada, *Sessional Papers*, 13th Parl., 1st sess., 1918, no. 206.

Land Grants to Railways

*By the Dominion Government	31,864,074 acres
By Quebec	1,681,690 acres
**By British Columbia	8,119,221 acres
By New Brunswick	1,647,772 acres
By Nova Scotia	160,000 acres
By Ontario	624,232 acres
Total acreage	44,096,989 acres

* 18,206,986 acres of this went to the Canadian Pacific for its main line.

** This figure includes the acreage granted the Dominion for transfer to the Esquimalt and Nanaimo Railway Company.

Cash Subsidies Paid

Year	*By British Columbia*	*All Provinces*
1893	$ 37,500	$23,460,507.70
1899	37,500	28,039,412.31
1905	37,500	32,304,304.61
1911	798,209	36,506,695.04
1915	1,284,572	37,437,895.16

Although an insignificant amount of land was received by railway companies in British Columbia after 1900, the results of Premier Dunsmuir's cash assistance policy may be seen from the 1915 figure given above. The requirement that the lines had to be built and approved before the subsidy was paid explains why no appreciable amount of money was paid out under this policy before 1911. By 1900, however, most intraprovincial roads receiving land subsidies had been constructed.

Meanwhile promoters had discovered the dominion government to be another source of ready cash assistance to intraprovincial lines. The Federal Railway Act of 1883 stated that all main lines were "works for the general advantage of Canada," and that any branch line of these main lines, the Intercolonial and the Canadian

Pacific, "connecting with or crossing them ... is a work for the general advantage of Canada"; and that any branch lines to be built in the future should also come under the act. Section 6 argued that this dominion jurisdiction would lead to "better and more uniform government of all such works," and would result in "greater safety, convenience and advantage of the public."[25] In reality, the act provided justification for subsidies which the Dominion had already given to various intraprovincial railways. Although Ontario and Nova Scotia objected that the Dominion was infringing on their rights, British Columbia did not. More and more roads in British Columbia sought dominion charters,[26] partly because of their desire for financial assistance from the federal treasury and partly because of the better status such a charter would give them in disposing of their bonds. Indeed, in 1887 there is the unusual spectacle of the British Columbia ministry itself petitioning the Dominion for a subsidy for the Shuswap and Okanagan line, already incorporated under a federal charter.[27] The argument British Columbia used was that not only would the line be of advantage to the provincial mining interests, but also that it would be of advantage to Canada in the event of war![28]

To eliminate the ambiguity in the 1883 Federal Railway Act under which arose the jurisdictional conflict, the federal government clarified its position in 1903 by enacting that:

> Where any railway, the construction or operation of which is authorized by a Special Act passed by the Legislature of any province, is declared, by any Special Act of the Parliament of Canada, to be a work for the general advantage of Canada, this Act shall apply to such railway, and to the company constructing or operating the same, to the exclusion of such of the provisions of the Special Act of the Provincial Legislature as are

25 Canada, *Statutes*, 1883, 46 Vict., c. 24.

26 The five companies which completed their lines and received their land grants also received cash subsidies from the Dominion. The Columbia and Kootenay, the Nelson and Fort Sheppard, the Kaslo and Slocan, and the Columbia and Western received $3,200 per mile. The B.C. Southern received $10,000 per mile, but only because it gave the Dominion 50,000 acres of coal land.

27 Not only did the line receive a federal cash subsidy; it also received $200,000 from the province. This cash subsidy was later changed to a guarantee of interest at 4 per cent for twenty-five years on $1,250,000. (See B.C., *Statutes*, 1890, 53 Vict., c. 42, s. 4.)

28 McLean, "National Highways Overland," p. 446.

> inconsistent with this Act, and in lieu of any General Railway Act of this province.[29]

Land speculators in British Columbia did not miss the potentialities for personal gain under this act. As there was nothing to prevent any company from seeking a federal charter, thirty-two British Columbia companies had done so by 1913. Seventeen of them were built, a considerably higher percentage than prevailed among the provincially incorporated companies.

After 1903 a new development of the cash subsidy policy across Canada was the guaranteeing of interest on bonds rather than the making of an outright gift. In this matter, as in so many others, the provinces followed the example set by the Dominion. The bond guarantees made by the Dominion and the provinces up to 1913 were as follows:[30]

Bond Guarantees

Dominion	$ 91,983,553
Manitoba	20,899,660
Alberta	55,489,000
Saskatchewan	32,500,000
Ontario	7,860,000
British Columbia	38,946,832
New Brunswick	1,893,000
Quebec	476,000
Nova Scotia	5,022,000
Total	$245,070,045

These bond guarantees representing contingent liabilities had a much wider appeal among the electorate after 1900 than did the former subsidy policy. Bond guarantees did not sound quite so prodigal as the outright subsidies, and if the government were ever called upon to redeem the bonds, it did not need to enact a special statute with all its attendant publicity. Moreover, the burden of the redemption of those guarantees would become the heritage of a later administration.

During the railway building spree, successive British Columbia governments were considerably less reckless in granting mineral rights to the companies than they were in making grants of land or

[29] Canada, *Statutes*, 1903, 3 Edw. 7, c. 58, s. 6.

[30] McLean, "National Highways Overland," p. 469.

cash. Though the grant of 750,000 acres to the Columbia and Kootenay in 1883 had included "all mines, minerals, and substances of whatever kind,"[31] it proved to be a temporary lapse from long established policy. Later land grants to railway companies in the 1880's included a separate clause specifically reserving mineral rights on subsidy lands to the Crown. Then in 1890 the British Columbia Railway Act excepted all mines of iron, slate or minerals under any land purchased by railway companies "except only such parts thereof as shall be necessary to be dug or carried away, or used in the construction of the works, unless the same shall have been expressly purchased; and all such mines, excepting as aforesaid, shall be deemed to be excepted out of the conveyance of such lands, unless they shall have been expressly named therein and conveyed thereby."[32] In reserving mineral rights from land grants to railway companies, the British Columbia government departed from the Dominion example, which it otherwise followed so closely in the matter of land and cash subsidies and bond guarantees to railways.[33]

During the thirty years of railway promotion and construction up to 1913, British Columbia seems to have been concerned chiefly with incorporating railroads which were never built and granting generous land and cash subsidies to those that were. To a degree, this was true. Once the main line of the Canadian Pacific to the seaboard had been built, the problem was to provide outlets from remote corners of the province to join it. But unfortunately the problem was not seen in this light until the Great Northern and the

[31] B.C., *Statutes*, 1883, 46 Vict., c. 25, s. 17. The land grant to this company, whose line was to run from Nelson to Castlegar, covered the rich silver-bearing veins of the Slocan and Nelson districts. Fortunately the company failed, its grant lapsed, and its $25,000 deposit was forfeited. Interest in the line revived in1889. (See B.C., *Statutes*, 1889, c. 21 and c. 35; and 1890, c. 41.) The new company was to receive 200,000 acres. It finally got 188,593 acres.

[32] B.C., *Statutes*, 1890, 53 Vict., c. 39, s. 21.

[33] Like most policies, that of reserving minerals to the Crown from railway lands had its exception, although in this case it was a minor one. Under section 13 of B.C., *Statutes*, 1890, 53 Vict., c. 40, An Act to aid certain Railways, four lines — the Canadian Western Central, the Crow's Nest and Kootenay Lake, the Ashcroft and Cariboo, and the Okanagan and Kootenay, none of which was built — were to receive the right for twenty-five years after their completion to exact and collect a royalty of 5 per cent on all gold and silver subsequently found on their lands. Kootenay miners were not slow to protest this royalty levied on all ores shipped from mines in these railway lands. (See "Petition," B.C., *Sessional Papers*, 5th Parl., 4th sess., 1890, p. 465.)

Spokane Falls and Northern for a few years drew the trade of the Kootenays away from Canadian outlets.

The railway history of the Kootenay region was largely a struggle for control between the American interests and the Canadian Pacific, both of which were anxious to secure control of traffic from the mining regions. The competition provided by James J. Hill's Great Northern became severe, and when D.C. Corbin of the Spokane Falls and Northern began securing not only charters but also land subsidies, the Canadian Pacific was nearly forced out. Corbin's company, the Columbia and Kootenay Railway and Transportation Company,[34] was to receive 750,000 acres of tax-free land along its right of way from Nelson to Castlegar, as well as along its steamboat route up the Arrow Lakes, but the federal government disallowed the act. This action was taken ostensibly on the strength of a vigorously worded protest from the citizens of Victoria, who objected to the act on the grounds that it was giving American lines control of the trade in the most valuable areas of the province; that it was unfair to the Canadian Pacific; that it would establish a "mischievous monopoly"; and above all, that it would "convey to three Americans 750,000 acres of the best land in the Province."[35] How much of this opposition was spearheaded by the Canadian Pacific officials is open to question. Instead of Corbin, it was Harry Abbott, a director of the Canadian Pacific, who in 1890 was one of the successful petitioners for a charter to build the Columbia and Kootenay line. Later in the year the Canadian Pacific leased the road for 999 years. Within the next ten years the Canadian Pacific acquired all the major lines in the Kootenays including, along with the Columbia and Kootenay, the Columbia and Western in 1898, the British Columbia Southern in 1898 and 1901, and the Kettle Valley in 1913. That the Canadian Pacific finally achieved supremacy in the Kootenays is owing in some measure to the resolution passed by the provincial government in March, 1898, requesting the Dominion to grant no further railway charters having for their object the diversion of traffic into the United States.[36] Along with the leases of the Kootenay lines, the

[34] Incorporated originally by B.C., *Statutes*, 1883, 46 Vict., c. 25.

[35] F. W. Howay, W. N. Sage, and H. F. Angus, *British Columbia and the United States*, ed. H. F. Angus (Toronto: Ryerson, 1942) p. 250.

[36] B.C., *Journals*, 7th Parl., 4th sess., 1898, pp. 75-76.

Canadian Pacific acquired the land grants amounting to 5,292,551 acres.

But as the situation stood in 1913, the province had alienated more crown land for railway purposes than for mining, forestry, and agricultural activities combined. The following tabulation shows how these railway lands were alienated:

Grants to Provincially Incorporated Railways

Esquimalt and Nanaimo	2,110,054 acres
Nelson and Fort Sheppard	580,783 acres
British Columbia Southern	3,755,733 acres
Columbia and Western	1,348,225 acres
Kaslo and Slocan	250,022 acres
Columbia and Kootenay	188,593 acres
Total	8,233,410 acres
Repurchased 1912 from Columbia and Western and British Columbia Southern	4,065,076 acres
Permanently alienated for intraprovincial lines	4,168,334 acres

Grants to Dominion for Railway Purposes

Railway Belt	10,976,000 acres
Peace River block	3,500,000 acres
Crow's Nest Pass Coal Lands	50,000 acres
Total	14,526,000 acres
Total lands alienated for railway purposes	18,694,334 acres

As indicated, 8,233,410 acres were granted in aid of intraprovincial lines, including the Esquimalt and Nanaimo. This total represents the land actually alienated. The total acreage granted at one time or another by the legislature as subsidies to railway companies amounted to at least four times this figure. That only slightly more than 8,000,000 acres were taken up was no fault of the legislature. Either its members knew with a fair degree of certainty that many of the lines to which they had made a land grant were entirely speculative or, more damning still, they did not care. Fortunately for the province, however, as part of his railway policy Premier

McBride was able to repurchase 4,065,076 acres from the Columbia and Western and the British Columbia Southern though he had failed in his larger plan of buying back the lands in the Railway Belt.[37] This action left 4,168,334 acres permanently alienated for lines within the province which, with the 14,526,000 acres granted to the Dominion, made a total of 18,694,334 acres alienated for railway purposes.

Of British Columbia's 234,000,000 acres, approximately 6,500,000 acres, is classified as arable or as potentially arable land. Since the railway companies were permitted to select their subsidy lands from within the much larger land area reserved by the government for them, it is reasonable to assume that the best land in the reserve was selected by the companies. Had all the companies receiving land subsidies built their roads, there can be little doubt that every acre of arable land in the province would have been permanently alienated as the price of securing railway communication. As matters stood, the 18,694,334 acres alienated by 1913 must have included most of the arable land within the province.

It is still debatable whether the people of British Columbia received a fair return for their lands. Transportation was vital to the development of the province within the framework of Confederation, but the price was high.

37 The repurchase, authorized by An Act respecting the Repurchase by the Crown of certain Railway Subsidy Lands (B.C., *Statutes*, 1912, 2 Geo. 5, c. 37), permitted the government to buy the unalienated subsidy lands of the two lines at forty cents an acre.

CHAPTER 11

Imperial Colonial Indian Policy

From the time of the first settlement in the New England colonies, the English Crown always reserved to itself the right to deal directly with the Indians for the surrender of their lands. Moreover, the aboriginal title of the Indians to the lands they occupied was conceded, and in Ontario and the Northwest compensation was granted for the surrender of their hunting grounds. Pursuing this policy after the conquest of Canada, the formulators of the "Articles of Capitulation of Montreal 1760" provided in Article XL that "The savages or Indian allies of his most Christian Majesty, shall be maintained in the lands they inhabit, if they chuse to remain there."[1]

This policy respecting the Indians and their lands was reaffirmed in the "Royal Proclamation, 7 October, 1763," the latter part of which reveals the constitutional authority on which the Dominion policy was to be based and which at the time of the Union the Dominion naturally assumed had also been followed in British Columbia:

> And whereas it is just and reasonable, and essential to our Interests, and the Security of our Colonies, that the several Nations or Tribes of Indians with whom We are connected, and who live under our Protection, should not be molested or disturbed in the Possession of such Parts of our Dominions and Territories as, *not having been ceded to or purchased by Us, are reserved to them*, or any of them, as their Hunting Grounds. — We do therefore, with the Advice of our Privy Council, declare it to be our Royal Will and Pleasure, that no Governor or Com-

[1] W. P. M. Kennedy, *Statutes, Treaties and Documents of the Canadian Constitution* (Toronto: Oxford University Press, 1930), p. 29.

mander in Chief in any of our Colonies of Quebec, East Florida, or West Florida, do presume, upon any Pretence whatever, to grant Warrants of Survey, or pass any Patents for Lands beyond the Bounds of their respective Governments, as described in their Commissions; as also that no Governor, or Commander in Chief in any of our other Colonies or Plantations in America do presume for the present, and until our further Pleasure be known, to grant Warrants of Survey, or pass Patents for any Lands beyond the Heads or Sources of any of the Rivers which fall into the Atlantic Ocean from the West and North West, or upon any Lands whatever, which, *not having been ceded to or purchased by Us as aforesaid, are reserved to the said Indians, or any of them.*

And We do further declare it to be Our Royal Will and Pleasure, for the present as aforesaid, to reserve under our Sovereignty, Protection and Dominion, for the use of the said Indians, all the Lands and Territories *not included within the Limits of* Our said Three new Governments, or within the Limits of *the Territory granted to the Hudson's Bay Company,* as also all the Lands and Territories lying to the Westward of the Sources of the Rivers which fall into the Sea from the West and North West as aforesaid;

And We do hereby strictly forbid, on Pain of our Displeasure, *all our loving subjects from making any Purchases or Settlements* whatever, or taking Possession of any of the Lands above reserved, without our especial leave and Licence for that purpose first obtained.

And, we do further strictly enjoin and require all Persons whatever who have either wilfully or inadvertently seated themselves upon any Lands . . . which, not having been ceded to or purchased by Us, are still reserved to the said Indians as aforesaid, forthwith to remove themselves from such settlements.

And whereas great Frauds and Abuses have been committed in purchasing Lands of the Indians to the great Prejudice of our Interests and to the great Dissatisfaction of the said Indians; in order therefore, to prevent such Irregularities for the future, and to the end that the Indians may be convinced of our Justice and determined Resolution to remove all reasonable Cause of Discontent, We do, with the advice of our Privy Council, strictly enjoin and require, that *no private Person do presume to make any Purchase from the said Indians of any Lands reserved to the said Indians,* within those parts of our Colonies where, We have thought proper to allow Settlement; *but* that, *if* at any Time any of *the said Indians should be inclined to dispose of the said Lands, the same shall be purchased only for Us in our Name,* at some public Meeting or Assembly of the said Indians, to be held for that purpose by the Governor or Commander in Chief of our Colony respectively within which they shall lie; and in case they shall lie within the limits of any Proprietary Government, they shall be purchased only for the Use and in the name of such Proprietaries, conformable to such Directions and Instruction as we or they shall think proper to give for that Purpose.[2]

The explicit language of this document permitted no misinterpretation, and from it derived the entire dominion treaty policy with the Indians living on dominion crown land. The essential elements of the policy have always been the recognition of Indian title and of the need to secure its cession in return for adequate compensation. It was natural enough for Ottawa to assume in 1871 that British Columbia had followed the word and spirit of this proclamation. In fact, however, between Douglas's retirement and British Columbia's union with Canada colonial officials both spoke and acted in direct opposition to these principles. The failure of the Dominion to appreciate the wide difference in British Columbia and Imperial policies at the time of union and the intransigence of the provincial government in the face of Indian and dominion efforts to secure permanent settlement of aboriginal claims in the forty years following Confederation have led to the still inconclusive position.

During Douglas's tenure, there was little deviation from Imperial policy in British Columbia, and treaties might well have been secured had he been able to continue the Indian policy he had begun in 1850 in his role as chief factor and governor of "Vancouver's Island." The insistence of the British government on colonial self-sufficiency made it impossible for him to do so. Between 1850 and 1854, Douglas made the fourteen agreements with various tribes of Indians inhabiting the southern portion of Vancouver Island which remain the only treaties made with B.C. Indians. In consideration of money payments made to them at once, the Indians relinquished their "possessory rights" to the area about Fort Victoria. The payments averaged £2.10.0 per head of a family for the southern 100 square miles of the Island.[3]

The first of these agreements was made with the Teechamitsa

[2] Ibid., p. 37. Italics added.

[3] Douglas to Newcastle, March 25, 1861, in "Papers Connected with the Indian Land Question," B.C., *Sessional Papers*, 2d Parl., 1st sess., 1876, p. 179. These papers were also separately published with different pagination (Victoria: Richard Wolfenden, Government Printer, 1875). See: Wilson Duff, "The Fort Victoria Treaties," *B.C. Studies*, 3 (Fall 1969), 3-57. Indians in the Peace River area did sign treaties with the dominion government in the early years of this century. See p. 237.

Tribe on April 29, 1850, for all lands lying between Esquimalt and Point Albert. It read as follows:

> Know all men, we, the chiefs and people of the Teechamitsa Tribe, who have signed our names and made our marks to this deed on the twenty-ninth day of April, One thousand eight hundred and fifty, do consent to surrender, entirely and forever, to James Douglas, the agent of the Hudson's Bay Company in Vancouver Island, that is to say, for the Governor, Deputy Governor, and Committee of the same, the whole of the lands situate and lying between Esquimalt Harbour and Point Albert, including the latter, on the Straits of Juan de Fuca, and extending backwards from thence to the range of mountains on the Saanich Arm, about ten miles distant.
>
> The condition of or understanding of this sale is this, that our village sites and enclosed fields are to be kept for our own use, for the use of our children, and for those who may follow after us; and the lands shall be properly surveyed hereafter. It is understood, however, that the land itself, with these small exceptions, becomes the entire property of the white people forever; it is also understood that we are at liberty to hunt over the unoccupied land, and to carry on our fisheries as formerly.
>
> We have received, as payment, Twenty-seven pounds, ten shillings sterling.
>
> In token whereof, we have signed our names and made our marks, at Fort Victoria, 29th April, 1850.[4]

Altogether, during his incumbency, 358 square miles on Vancouver Island were ceded by the Indians to Douglas.

Had the Colonial Office granted the request in 1861 for a loan of £3,000 to complete the extinction of the Indian title to the 1,600 square miles of public lands remaining on Vancouver Island, the cost would have been approximately one dollar per square mile. In his despatch asking for the loan Douglas stated that he had "made it a practice up to the year 1859, to purchase the native rights in the land, in every case, prior to the settlement of any district," but that, owing to lack of funds, he had not been able to continue. He wrote that the Indians "have distinct ideas of property in land, and mutually recognize their several exclusive possessory rights in certain districts," and would, he believed, feel a sense of injury were white settlers to occupy lands where the Indian title had not been extinguished. Since all settled districts with the exception of the Cowi-

[4] "Papers Connected with the Indian Land Question," p. 165. The other treaties appear pp. 166-71 inclusive.

chan, Chemainus, and Barclay Sound areas had already been bought out, he felt justified in asking for the loan, particularly as he offered to repay it from the sale of public lands, the price of which had only two months previously been reduced from ten to four shillings twopence per acre.[5] Unfortunately for the plans both of Douglas and of his Legislative Assembly, Newcastle was not receptive and replied that "the acquisition of the title is a purely colonial interest."[6]

In the course of time, Douglas gave blankets, trade goods, and even cash payments to tribes in other sections of Vancouver Island. Later, Joseph W. Trutch was convinced, or at least he was to argue, that all these presents were made for the purpose of securing the friendship of the Indians to the Company and not in acknowledgment of any general title of the Indians to the lands occupied by them.[7] Whatever Douglas's intent was,[8] it is now evident that the Indians never really understood what was happening. To them, the legal concept of individual ownership in land was meaningless. As Douglas suggested, they did understand the principle of usufruct, and the rival chieftains thought they were yielding to the white interlopers only the right to use the land, not the right to anything called "exclusive private ownership." It was this misunderstanding which gave rise to the request from the Indians throughout the province as years went by for an increase in the size of their reservations.

Partly in the interests of humanity, partly because it was good business, and partly because he had been instructed to do so by the Colonial Office, Douglas regarded the Indians as the special wards of the Crown. In his Address to the first Legislative Assembly on Vancouver Island on August 12, 1856, he said that he proposed to

5 "Proclamation, no. 1, A.D. 1861," in B.C., [*Proclamations and Ordinances, 1858-1864*].

6 Newcastle to Douglas, October 19, 1861. "Papers Connected with the Indian Land Question," p. 180.

7 "Report of the Government of British Columbia on the Subject of Indian Reserves," B.C., *Sessional Papers*, 2d Parl., 1st sess., 1876, p. 67. This report also appears in Canada, *Sessional Papers*, 3d Parl., 3d sess., 1876, no. 9.

8 The Hudson's Bay Company account against the colony presented to Governor Blanshard in 1851 included the assertion "that they have expended $2,735, of which $2,130 are for goods paid to Indians to extinguish their title to the land about Victoria and Soke harbours." Blanshard signed the account "with protest." See: Vancouver Island, Governor, *Despatches: Governor Blanshard to the Secretary of State, 26th December 1849, to 30th August, 1851* (New Westminster: Printed at the Government Printing Office, n.d.), no. 8, February 12, 1851.

treat the Indians "with justice and forbearance, and by rigidly protecting their civil and agrarian rights; many cogent reasons of humanity and sound policy recommend that course to our attention." He went on to remind the Assembly of the benefits to be derived from the friendship of the Indians, "while it is no less certain that their enmity may become more disastrous than any other calamity to which the colony is directly exposed."[9]

In 1858 in response to a despatch from Lytton enjoining him to "consider the best and most humane means of dealing with the Native Indians" and to see that "in all bargains or treaties with the natives for the cession of lands possessed by them, that subsistence should be supplied to them in some other shape," Douglas outlined his policy in full. He envisioned the settlement of Indians on reserves where, among other benefits, they would be secure against the encroachment of white settlers, and the possibility of "having the native Tribes arrayed in vindictive warfare against the white settlement" would be lessened. Any land on the reserve not being utilized by the Indians was to be leased to the highest bidder, the proceeds of the lease to be applied to the exclusive benefit of the Indians.[10] Where land was valuable, Douglas assured Lytton this arrangement would relieve the colony of any financial burden arising from the care and maintenance of the natives; where the land was of no value, the Indians could be left to pursue their course unmolested. On the reserves, each family was to have a distinct portion for its own use, but Indians were to be denied the power to sell or alienate the land. With this project in mind, reserves were to be made for the benefit and support of the tribes in all districts of British Columbia inhabited by natives. "Those reserves should in all cases include their cultivated fields and village sites, for which from habit and association they invariably conceive a strong attachment, and prize more, for that reason, than for the extent or value of the land."[11]

9 Bancroft, *History of British Columbia*, pp. 322-23, n.11.

10 Lytton to Douglas, July 31, 1858, no. 6, Gt. Brit., *Papers Relative to British Columbia*, 1: 44-46. Douglas actually began this procedure. A return tabled by Robert Beaven on January 13, 1873, showed that 13.94 acres of the Songhees reserve in the middle of Victoria were being leased at a rental of $222 by five people, among them George Hills, bishop of Columbia, who leased lot 51 for a mission School. B.C., *Journals*, 1st Parl., 2d sess., 1872-73, appendix, *Sessional Papers*, appendix 1, p. 4.

11 Douglas to Lytton, March 14, 1859, "Papers Connected with the Indian Land Question," pp. 176-77.

The procedure outlined by Douglas was more or less adhered to by the colonial government throughout the next twelve years and remained in effect at Confederation. In assigning reserves, Douglas and his officials followed no consistent pattern other than that of including within a larger reserve, if possible, all Indian settlements, graveyards, gardens, hunting lodges, berry patches, or fishing stations, or of making one or all of them separate smaller reserves. The only principle adopted was to placate the Indians and keep them out of the way of incoming settlers by granting each tribe a definite reservation of land. In his Address to the newly elected first Legislative Council of British Columbia at New Westminster on January 21, 1864, Douglas said:

> The Native Tribes are quiet and well-disposed. The plan of forming Reserves of land embracing the village sites, cultivated fields, and favorite places of resort of the several Tribes, and thus securing them against the encroachment of settlers, and forever removing the fertile cause of agrarian disturbance, has been productive of the happiest effects on the minds of the natives.
>
> The areas thus partially defined and set apart in no case exceed the proportion of *ten acres for each family* concerned, and are to be held as the joint and common property of the several tribes, being intended for their exclusive use and benefit, and especially as a provision for the aged, the helpless, and the infirm.[12]

This was no hastily conceived scheme, for Douglas had three years before requested Moody, the chief commissioner of lands and works, to mark out distinctly the sites of all proposed towns and Indian reserves throughout the mainland colony. He further directed that such reserves were to be defined exactly as the Indians themselves pointed them out.[13] Despite Douglas's directions and his own efforts, however, there was no codified system for the reservation of lands for the use and benefit of the various tribes at the time of his retirement. The rights of the Indians to hold lands were totally undefined, although the 1865 Land Ordinance specifically withheld

[12] B.C., Legislative Council, *Journals*, 1st Parl., 1st sess., 1864, p. 2.

[13] Douglas to Moody, March 5, 1861, "Papers Connected with the Indian Land Question," p. 181. After 1864, the British Columbia government chose to interpret the "ten acres for each family" statement as policy. But when Douglas put his views in writing in 1874, he said there had never been an official limitation. (See Appendix D, Item 4.)

from pre-emption all Indian reserves or settlements, as Douglas himself had wished.[14]

In order to prevent anyone from buying land directly from the Indians and in keeping with the Proclamation of 1763, Douglas inserted a notice in the Victoria *Gazette* in 1859 stating that land was the property of the Crown and that the Indians were incapable of conveying a legal title.[15] But no reserves of land intended as Indian reservations were made by official notice in the *Gazette* until 1866,[16] after Douglas had retired and after Trutch had become commissioner of lands and works. Even then, only half the existing surveyed reserves were gazetted. Trutch reported in 1867 that since he was unable to find any written directions on the subject in the correspondence in his office,[17] most of the reserves made before 1865 must have been made in furtherance of verbal instructions from Douglas. It would appear that in many cases lands which Douglas intended to be appropriated for reserve purposes were set apart and made over to the Indians on the ground by Douglas personally. These "on-the-spot" reservations were for the most part small, comprising usually a potato garden adjoining a village, a burial ground, or a berry patch. Few reserves had been staked off or in any way practically defined. After a thorough search through his office

[14] Every subsequent land law in British Columbia has contained such a clause, but none has ever defined an "Indian settlement." Had the Indians wished, they could have been most difficult about this point, but the only complaint uncovered during this study was that of William Smithe to the Indian Superintendent, Dr. I. W. Powell, in a letter of November 24, 1884. Powell had requested the provincial government to reserve 100 acres for fifty-four Indians on the west shore of Okanagan Lake opposite the present city of Kelowna, even though reserves of nearly 50,000 acres had been established at the north end of the lake. Already furious at the size of the main Okanagan reserves, Smithe remarked that "No doubt families of Indians were found scattered over the district, and when the Commissioners appeared they gathered in detachments from far and near to swell the number applying for a tribal reserve," and went on to imply that the Indians then scattered and asked "for additional and independent reserves at their nomadic homes or places of temporary abode" (B.C., *Sessional Papers*, 4th Parl., 3d sess., 1885, p. xiv, following p. 410). On December 9, 1884 Powell replied that until he had read Smithe's letter he had never heard of such a thing happening and added that "nor does it appear reasonable that vague reports, or rumors of such deception, should control or influence the action of the Government in withholding for so many years their final approval and confirmation of Indian lands which have been so long in a state of uncertainty," (ibid., pp. xx-xxi).

[15] Douglas to Lytton, February 9, 1859, "Papers Connected with the Indian Land Question," p. 175.

[16] Ibid., pp. 324-27.

[17] Trutch to Acting Colonial Secretary, August 28, 1867, ibid., pp. 201-203.

Trutch could find a record of only nine: three lots at the mouth of the north arm of the Fraser River, an island at the mouth of the Coquitlam River, two lots on its banks, one lot opposite New Westminster, and two lots at Keatsie (Hatzic). It is possible that Douglas avoided committing his decisions to paper because he was too busy; it is also possible that he thought no such formal procedure necessary at that stage in the development of the colonies. What is more likely, however, is that he was constantly mindful of a despatch from Carnarvon in May, 1859, cautioning him against laying out and defining reserves in those localities where they might impede progress of white colonists in the future.[18] Genuine as its solicitude for the natives undoubtedly was, the Colonial Office in London was also acutely aware that British Columbia, like all other colonies, must finance itself, and that it could do so provided the immigrants pouring into the colony could be induced to remain as settlers after the gold fever had abated.

Before Douglas retired, two interesting incidents involving Indians and lands occurred which were to be the genesis of the still unresolved aboriginal title disputes. Both incidents suggest that even at that early date the Indians were not completely satisfied with their reserve allotments.

At a public sale of lots in New Westminster held in May, 1862, Colonel Moody, who was conducting the sale, was so perturbed when an Indian named Snat Strouten wanted to buy a lot just as the white settlers were doing that he felt it necessary to write William A. G. Young, the colonial secretary, for instructions. After pondering Strouten's unusual request and consulting with the governor, Young wrote back three weeks later to say that "there can be no objection." Strouten was probably unaware that when he received his lot he was setting a precedent. Douglas had long since declared that the Indians were "rational beings, capable of acting and thinking for themselves," but when it came to acknowledging the fact in practice, three weeks' cogitation was required.[19]

In June of the same year Moody encountered another problem, somewhat more serious and not so simple of solution. The 1860 Land Ordinance reserved Indian settlements from pre-emption, but

18 Carnarvon to Douglas, May 20, 1859, ibid., p. 178.

19 Moody to Young, May 27, 1862, ibid., p. 183; Young to Moody, June 8, 1862, ibid., p. 184; Douglas to Lytton, March 14, ibid., p. 177.

it did not forbid Indians to pre-empt.[20] Moody said he "understood" that all along the Fraser River up to Hope, Indians were pre-empting "precisely as a white man could" and were doing so to a considerable extent, and he observed that the practice was likely to increase rapidly.[21] Moody referred the problem to Young and was told that legislation containing a provision permitting Indians to pre-empt under certain conditions[22] was being drawn up to deal with just such a contingency. The clause presaged by Young was passed in 1865 and stipulated that Indians could pre-empt only with the prior consent of the governor.[23] When an Indian finally did succeed in obtaining permission to pre-empt, a Minute in Council was required to authorize the transaction.[24]

The action of the Indians along the Fraser River was no doubt prompted by a reasonable desire to secure as large tracts of land as possible before it was all pre-empted in 160-acre blocks by white settlers. In addition, such a location along the river was ideal for their purposes, since it provided hay meadows for their horses and cattle and suitable fishing sites. However there is no record of their ever having received crown grants to any of these lands. Even had the reserves been allotted to them and had they been large enough, it is unlikely that the Indians would have fully realized what ownership of land meant. The failure to allot reserves officially, the ten-acre restriction imposed after 1864, and the fact that land was only of value to the Indians for what use could be made of it at the moment were all factors boding ill for the future.

Douglas's own generous attitude is reflected in one other instance the year before his retirement. When he received information early in 1863 that the Indians of the Coquitlam River reserve were dissatisfied with their fifty acres of land, he wrote personally to Colonel Moody in peremptory fashion. After outlining the Indians' complaint, he said:

20 "Proclamation," of January 4, 1860 in B.C., [*Proclamations and Ordinances, 1858-1864*].

21 Moody to Young, June 11, 1862, "Papers Connected with the Indian Land Question," p. 185.

22 Young to Moody, July 2, 1862, ibid.

23 B.C., Legislative Council, *Ordinances Passed by the Legislative Council of British Columbia during the Session from January to April, 1865*, no. 27, April 11, 1865.

24 "Report on Indian Reserves," Appendix A, p. 65.

> I beg that you will, therefore, immediately cause the existing reserve to be extended in conformity with the wishes of the Natives, and to include therein an area so large as to remove from their minds all causes of dissatisfaction.
>
> Notwithstanding my particular instructions to you, that in laying out Indian Reserves the wishes of the Natives themselves, with respect to boundaries, should in all cases be complied with, I hear very general complaints of the smallness of the areas set apart for their use.
>
> I beg that you will take instant measures to inquire into such complaints, and to enlarge all the Indian Reserves between New Westminster and the mouth of the Harrison River, before the contiguous lands are occupied by other persons.[25]

The subsequent correspondence indicates that Moody was not as negligent as Douglas's letter suggests, but the letter does emphasize the policy that prevailed so long as Douglas was governor. The correspondence reveals also that the Indians were not slow to learn the white man's methods in obtaining the desired ends. They too could play both ends against the middle and they did so admirably in this instance.[26] Moody suggested that the missionaries were showing the Indians how to take advantage of gaps in the legislation pertaining to pre-emption. Referring to assistance the Indians were receiving from Roman Catholic priests, Moody said, "It is a growing question that will have to be met."[27] Moody's objection reveals that his sympathies did not lie entirely with the Indians in their claims for larger reserves, nor with Douglas in his policy of permitting the Indians to designate the size of their reserves.

Actions of the government officials shortly after Douglas's retirement illustrate clearly that Moody's attitude was not unique in the colony. So long as Douglas was governor, the Indians had only to ask to receive additional land; once he was safely retired, a concerted effort was made to reduce the larger Indian allotments, particularly in Kamloops-Shuswap and Lower Fraser River areas.

The most outstanding case of this kind involved reserves marked out in 1864 by a surveyor named McColl who, acting on instructions from the Surveyor General Brew, proceeded to the Fraser

25 Douglas to Moody, April 27, 1863, "Papers Connected with the Indian Land Question," p. 187.

26 On more than one occasion Trutch or the surveyors in his department suspected that the Indians had altered the location of the boundary stakes on the reserves. (See ibid., p. 192.)

27 Moody to Douglas, April 28, 1863, ibid., pp. 187-88.

River, where he marked out the reserves from New Westminster to Harrison River. Before leaving Victoria, McColl received additional verbal instructions from Douglas that all lands claimed by Indians were to be included in their reserves, that the Indians were to have as much land as they wished, and that in no case should any reserve contain less than 100 acres.[28] According to Trutch's comment on the incident three years later when the successful attempt to reduce these reserves was being made, McColl had proceeded to act on the "indefinite authority" given him by Douglas, rather than on his written instructions from Brew which had specified what the new administration called the "ten-acre per family" rule.[29] The surveyor then "marked out reserves of most unreasonable extent, amounting, as estimated by himself, to 50, 60, 69, 109, and even to as much in one case as 200 acres for each grown man in the tribe." As the surveyor general in 1866, Trutch was aghast that McColl seemed merely to have walked over the ground, putting in posts where directed to do so by the Indians and estimated the acreage. Because these lands were not all being used by the Indians and because they contained rich pastures or readily cultivable portions, "greatly desired for immediate settlement," and, at the moment, were "utterly unprofitable to the public interest," Trutch believed that in almost every case these reserves should be "materially reduced."

The two suggestions Trutch made for regaining these lands for public purposes demonstrate the colonial Indian land policy which the dominion government fell heir to in 1871. Trutch recommended to A. N. Birch, colonial secretary and administrator of the government during the absence of Governor Seymour, that McColl's authority could be absolutely disavowed in view of the "extravagant extent" of the reserves laid out by him in defiance of the ten-acre rule. The surveys could be made anew. Alternatively, negotiations could be undertaken with the Indians with a view to securing a surrender of the greater portion of the area. The latter procedure, he made clear, would be tantamount to buying the lands back from the Indians. Negotiations with the Indians Trutch found repugnant, asserting that the tribes "have really no right to the lands they claim . . . and I cannot see why they should either retain these lands to the prejudice of the general interests of the Colony, or be allowed to

[28] McColl to Chartres Brew, May 16, 1864, ibid., p. 203.

[29] Brew to McColl, April 6, 1864, ibid.

make a market of them either to Government *or to individuals*."[30] Trutch seems temporarily to have forgotten that the sale of any portion of their reserves by the Indians to any agency other than the Crown had never been countenanced in the colony,[31] although it was debatable whether there was any legal barrier to such sale. Trutch suggested that disavowing McColl's authority was the more judicious course. There was good precedent. Only the year before, in 1866, similar negotiations had been undertaken over the tract of land extending more than forty miles along the South Thompson River which Douglas had granted to the Kamloops and Shuswap Indians. By notice in the *Gazette* of October 5, 1866, Trutch proclaimed that the claims of the Kamloops and Shuswap Indians "have been adjusted." The adjustment made it possible to open by far the greater portion of the river-bottom lands to pre-emption on January 1, 1867.[32]

In recommending a similar course with respect to the reserves on the Lower Fraser River, Trutch advised caution; in his words, "very careful management of the dispositions of the Indian claimants would be requisite to prevent serious dissatisfaction; firmness and discretion are equally essential . . . to convince the Indians that the Government intend only to deal fairly with them and the whites who desire to settle on and cultivate the lands which they (the Indians) have really no right to and no use for."[33]

In his reply to Trutch, the colonial secretary enunciated another aspect of the colony's Indian land policy which was to be of considerable interest and import after 1871. He agreed with Trutch that the reservations should certainly be "amply sufficient" for the actual requirements or wants of the Indians but that in no case should the allotment "be of such extent as to engender the feeling in the mind of the Indian that the land is of no use to him, and that it will be to his benefit to part with it." With this consideration in mind, Trutch was instructed to effect a severe reduction in the acreage of the reserves. "'The Indians have no right to any land

30 Trutch to Acting Colonial Secretary, August 28, 1867, ibid., pp. 201-203. For a recent survey of Trutch's role see: Robin Fisher, "Joseph Trutch and Indian Land Policy," *B.C. Studies*, 12 (Winter 1971-72), 3-33.

31 William A. G. Young, colonial secretary, was soon to remind him. See "Papers Connected with the Indian Land Question," p. 205.

32 Ibid., p. 324. Birch personally undertook this mission. For details of the settlement with the Indians, see ibid., pp. 189-99.

33 Ibid., p. 202.

beyond . . . their actual requirements," said Young, nor "for they really have never actually possessed it," can they have any "claim whatever to any compensation."[34]

To bring about the surrender, Trutch visited the tribes, telling them that since McColl had acted under improper authority, his decisions were extra-legal. The disclosure did not discomfit the Indians. They only complained bitterly of the intrusion of white settlers on land they considered to be their own, "evidently," reported Trutch, "regarding such settlements as unauthorized intrusions on their rights."[35] When Stipendiary Magistrate Ball surveyed the new reserves the next summer he wrote that the Indians appeared perfectly satisfied with the procedure.[36]

At the very time Ball was making the surveys, the delegates to the Yale Convention were condemning the government's Indian policy. Having resolved that "religion, humanity, and public opinion demand that due and proper consideration be paid to the Indian population, with a view to their preservation, and the improvement of their moral, intellectual, and material condition," the delegates, led by Amor De Cosmos, berated the government for having done nothing for the Indians "beyond making reservations of land." These reservations, the resolution stated, were of large and valuable tracts of agricultural land which were not being utilized by the Indians and were in districts where settlers would cultivate them. The resolution concluded by demanding that the government "establish such regulations as would utilize the Indian reserves, and appropriate the proceeds to the benefit of the Indians."[37] The delegates, however, were not critical either of the size or of the quality of the reserves. Their criticism was simply that these lands were lying in an unproductive state.

These outright refusals by the new Legislative Council to recognize any aboriginal title to the land, as specified in the 1763 Proclamation, are attested by numerous statements, the earliest official one being that of Trutch in a memorandum included by Governor Musgrave to Earl Granville, then secretary of state for the colonies,

[34] Young to Trutch, November 6, 1867, ibid., p. 205.

[35] Trutch to Young, November 19, 1867, ibid., p. 206.

[36] Ball to Governor Seymour, October 17, 1868, ibid., p. 212.

[37] Resolution XXXI, *Papers on the Union of British Columbia with the Dominion of Canada*, p. 25, in [Gt. Brit.], *Miscellaneous Papers Relating to British Columbia.*

in a despatch of January 29, 1870. Trutch's memorandum was intended to answer criticism of the colony's Indian policy, and in it he outlined the position of the colonial government in British Columbia:

> It is not true . . . that in this Colony we have no "Indian Policy whatever;" that "there are no Indian Agents;" and that "the only friends the Indians have in the Colony are the Missionaries." On the contrary, for the past ten years at least, during which I have resided in this Colony, the Government appears to me to have striven to the extent of its power to protect and befriend the Native race, and its declared policy has been that the Aborigines should, in all material respects, be on the same footing in the eye of the law as people of European descent, and that they should be encouraged to live amongst the white settlers in the country, and so, by their example, be induced to adopt habits of civilization. . . .
>
> This policy towards the Indians has been consistently carried out so far as I am aware, by successive Governors. . . .
>
> The Magistrates, too, throughout the Colony, are the especially constituted protectors of the Indians against injustice. They are, in fact "Indian Agents" in all but the name, and I am confident that they have so performed this well-understood branch of their duty, that as full a measure of protection and general advantage has been bestowed on the Indians through their agency by Government, out of the pecuniary means at its disposal for this purpose, as could have been afforded to them through the medium of a special Indian Department.
>
> The Indians have, in fact, been held to be the special wards of the Crown, and in the exercise of this guardianship Government has, in all cases where it has been desirable for the interests of the Indians, set apart such portions of the Crown lands as were deemed proportionate to, and amply sufficient for, the requirements of each Tribe; and these Indian Reserves are held by Government, in trust, for the exclusive use and benefit of the Indians resident thereon.[38]

Trutch's defence of his Indian policy, written especially for the Colonial Office, may have served to allay any fears Granville had, but it would not have met with the approval of the Indians. Trutch knew that the Indians were not necessarily content with "such portions of the Crown lands as were deemed proportionate to, and amply sufficient for, the requirements of each Tribe." A clear indication of British Columbia governmental policy towards Indians

[38] Trutch to Musgrave, January 28, 1870, "Report on Indian Reserves," pp. 67-68.

and land at the time of Confederation is found later in the memorandum:

> the title of the Indians in the fee of the public land, or of any portion thereof, has never been acknowledged by Government, but, on the contrary, is distinctly denied. In no case has special agreement been made with any of the Tribes of the Mainland for the extinction of their claims of possession; but these claims have been held to have been fully satisfied by securing to each tribe, as the progress of the settlement of the country seemed to require, the use of sufficient tracts of land for their wants for agricultural and pastoral purposes.[39]

[39] Ibid., pp. 66-69.

CHAPTER 12

Indian Land Policy after Confederation

In drafting article 13 of the Terms of Union, it is possible that neither the dominion nor the provincial negotiators intended to be anything less than candid. Certainly Trutch, Carrall, and Helmcken, the delegates from British Columbia, had full knowledge of the Dominion's Indian policy in the reservation of land. In the light of subsequent difficulties and disclosures, it is doubtful whether the Committee of the Privy Council acting on behalf of Canada possessed equally accurate information concerning the Indian policy of the colonial government in British Columbia. Trutch certainly could have given a complete summary of that policy. He had been chief commissioner of lands and works in the colony since 1864, and more recently surveyor general as well. In both functions he had been responsible for severely altering Douglas's principles. Less than three years after Union, the Dominion was to discover that the meaning which it abstracted from article 13 was the opposite of that read into it by the province. The clause reads as follows:

> The charge of the Indians, and the trusteeship and management of the lands reserved for their use and benefit, shall be assumed by the Dominion Government, and a policy as liberal as that hitherto pursued by the British Columbia Government shall be continued by the Dominion Government after the Union.
>
> To carry out such policy, tracts of land of such extent as it has hitherto been the practice of the British Columbia Government to appropriate for that purpose, shall from time to time be conveyed by the Local Government to the Dominion Government in trust for the use and benefit of the Indians, on application of the Dominion Government; and in case of disagreement between the two Governments respecting the quantity of such tracts of

> land to be so granted, the matter shall be referred for the decision of the Secretary of State for the Colonies.

The wording is reminiscent of Trutch's 1870 memorandum and suggests that he had much, if not everything, to do with the framing of article 13. The evidence leads to the conclusion that he deliberately put in those two contentious and ambiguous phrases, "a policy as liberal as that hitherto pursued by the Government of British Columbia," and "tracts of land of such extent as it has hitherto been the practice of the British Columbia Government to appropriate." It seems likely that these two vague clauses were not discussed in Ottawa in 1870, for Sir George E. Cartier found it unnecessary to amplify them when he was introducing the Terms of Union into the House of Commons.[1] The assumption by the Dominion of responsibility for Indian affairs was merely a re-statement of the duty already assumed under Article 91, section 24 of the British North America Act. Since responsible government was not in operation in the colony, it at first appeared that there was no need to include this article in the Terms of Union. In his despatch of August 14, 1869, to Governor Musgrave, Earl Granville, secretary of state for the colonies, stated that "the Constitution of British Columbia will oblige the Governor to enter personally upon many questions — as the condition of the Indian tribes ... with which, in the case of a negotiation between two Responsible Governments, he would not be found to concern himself."[2] Acting on his instructions, Governor Musgrave "purposely omitted any mention of [Indians] in the terms proposed to the Legislative Council" in 1870.[3] Musgrave felt the subject should be handled either by himself under direction of the secretary of state for the colonies, or by

1 If Trutch wrote this clause without making a full explanation of his government's denial of Douglas's policy of permitting the Indians to designate their own reserves, and if he made no mention of the recent successful attempts of his government to reduce drastically in size such large reserves as had been defined and gazetted, he was guilty of duplicity, and, as will be seen, of doing his colony-province a grave disservice.

2 Granville to Musgrave, August 14, 1869, "Despatches from the Secretary of State, No. 6," *Papers on the Union of British Columbia with the Dominion of Canada*, pp. 30-31.

3 Musgrave to Sir John Young, governor general, February 20, 1870, Canada, Senate, *Journals*, 16th Parl., 1st sess., 1926-27, appendix, Special Joint Committee ... [on] Claims of Allied Indian Tribes of British Columbia, *Report and Evidence*, (Ottawa: F. A. Acland, 1927) pp. 4-5.

the latter officer in direct negotiation with the government of Canada.

For this reason, no mention of Indians appears in the original union resolutions of the British Columbia Legislature. Article 13 was added later in what proved to be a vain attempt to effect a satisfactory division of responsibility between the two governments, and the Imperial Government acquiesced to this section on May 16, 1871.[4]

In attempting to honour its obligations, the dominion government soon discovered that the Indian land policy "as it has hitherto been the practice of the British Columbia Government" was not "as liberal as" the dominion policy pursued in Manitoba and the North-west Territories, nor "as liberal as" the centuries-old policy pursued by England in her other colonies in North America. As a result, the setting aside of reserves in British Columbia by the officers of the dominion government appointed for that purpose became a difficult and contentious matter, and over the years gave rise to a further problem which has become known as the "reversionary interest" in lands abandoned by the Indians. Out of these two problems came a still unresolved third, that of "aboriginal title."

The British North America Act itself was the source of some of these problems. Under Article 146, provision was made in 1867 for the possible entry of, *inter alia*, British Columbia "into the Union"; under Article 10 of the Terms of Union, the remaining portions of the British North America Act became operative. Article 109 of the British North America Act reads:

> All Lands, Mines, Minerals, and Royalties belonging to the several Provinces ... and all Sums then due or payable for such Lands, Mines, Minerals, or Royalties, shall belong to the several Provinces ... in which the same are situate or arise, subject to any trusts existing in respect thereof, and to any interest other than that of the Province in the same.[5]

4 The report of the debate in the House of Commons occupies 57 pages, and the report of the discussion of the Senate occupies 128 pages. Yet, so completely unaware were the members of any possible difficulty with reference to article 13 that a single sentence sufficed to dispose of the subject. In introducing the whole matter of the Terms of Union in the House, Sir George E. Cartier said: "A certain portion of the public lands had been reserved for the Indians, and the only guarantee that is necessary for the future good treatment of the Aborigines was the manner in which they had been treated in the past." Canada, *Parliamentary Debates* (1871), 663.

5 Kennedy, *Documents of the Canadian Constitution*, p. 629.

The application of this article, by which all crown lands and their natural resources became the property of the Crown in the right of the government of British Columbia, placed British Columbia in a unique position among the newly acquired areas of the federation.

Under authority of the 1868 Rupert's Land Act, the Dominion had been empowered "to accept a Surrender of all or any of the Lands, Territories, Rights," of government in the entire area previously controlled by the Hudson's Bay Company. The surrender was accepted by an Imperial Order in Council on June 23, 1870 which formally transferred Rupert's Land and the Northwest Territories to Canada. With the acquisition of the title to the Hudson's Bay Company's preserve, the Dominion also applied to it the Indian land policy followed since 1760 in British North America.

When Manitoba became a province in 1870, all ungranted lands were vested in the Crown for dominion purposes. Section 31 of the Manitoba Act of 1870 specifically stated that in order to extinguish the Indian title to the lands of the province, the province was to select 1,400,000 acres of land for division among the native population of Manitoba "on such conditions . . . as the Governor General in Council shall from time to time determine."[6]

The failure of the dominion government to make equivalent provision in the case of British Columbia reinforces the belief that they were ignorant of the actual situation. One contemporary at least tried to warn them that British Columbia's Indian land policy was not all it might be. Immediately prior to the colony's entry into Confederation, the Bishop of Columbia, George Hills, registered a strong protest with Joseph Howe, the secretary of state, urging immediate reform.[7] After union, his complaint was passed on to Trutch. In his new capacity as Lieutenant-Governor, Trutch summarized in general terms once again the policy hitherto pursued by the colony. Admitting that the policy was not based on any written code, he assured Howe that the government's policy had nonetheless been both " 'definite and tangible,' — a well considered system ably devised by experienced men specially interested in favour of the Indians . . . consistently carried out so far as the pecuniary means at command would admit of." As proof, Trutch stated that the colony had been remarkably free from Indian disturbances,

[6] Ibid., p. 643.

[7] Rev. George Hills, bishop of Columbia, to Howe, May 27, 1871, B.C., "Papers Connected with the Indian Land Question," pp. 257-58.

scattered as was the meagre white population over "this immense territory" among some 50,000 Indians. If the colonial government had not done all it should in defining and gazetting reservations, its inaction was not to be attributed to callousness or indifference, but rather to lack of funds "to take charge of, and apportion out under careful regulation, the lands which have been or may be set apart as Indian Reserves."

These tasks were now the responsibility of the dominion government, and in answer to Howe's request for specific information on the number of reserves that were surveyed, their area and location, and the title under which they were held, Trutch could answer that the governor had, by virtue of the authority conferred on him by his commission and the royal instructions, and later by the land ordinances, caused notices to be inserted in the Government *Gazette*, "or in such manner as was held to be sufficient advertisement of such notice previous to the establishment of the Government *Gazette*."[8] B. W. Pearse, the first chief commissioner of lands and works, was asked for a report on the subject, and this was forwarded to Howe.

Pearse's letter supported Trutch's contention that there were many reserves throughout the province which had been assigned to the Indians but never surveyed because of the government's policy of making surveys only when settlers reached the area. This system, observed Pearse, had been found effective and far less costly than that of surveying the reserves altogether, since they were "naturally scattered and often at great distances apart." As it was necessary to keep expenditures on surveys to a minimum and the price of land low, many reserves had never been gazetted, and numerous areas in the province which were remote from any settlement had never been visited in order that reserves might be made. This was true of the entire west coast of Vancouver Island, the east coast of the island above Comox, and the whole coast of the mainland above Burrard Inlet, as well as the interior of the province north of the Fraser River. Finally, Pearse stated that the area of those reserves which had been surveyed amounted to 28,437 acres and that the Indians had at no time been issued titles. Furthermore, the policy had been to prevent the Indians from alienating any portion of their reserves.[9]

8 Trutch to Howe, November 3, 1871, ibid., pp. 259-62.
9 Pearse to Trutch, October 16, 1871, ibid., pp. 262-63.

The list of reserves prepared by Pearse and submitted to Howe by Trutch indicated that there were in 1871 a total of seventy-six reserves of which official notice could be taken.[10] These comprised the hardly liberal area of less than one acre per Indian. Of the reserves, fifteen were on Vancouver Island, twenty-one were in the New Westminster area, one was near Lytton, and thirty-seven, representing much the largest acreage of 19,561.5 acres, were in Yale district.

After receipt of this information, the Dominion took no further step toward assuming its obligation to the Indians of British Columbia until the appointment in November, 1872 of Lieutenant-Colonel I. W. Powell, M.D., a strong proponent of Confederation, as superintendent of Indian affairs in the province.[11] Trutch, who had originally opposed Confederation, protested strongly to Sir John A. Macdonald when Powell's name was proposed for the position and intimated that the support of the navy, hitherto enlisted from time to time to aid the civil authorities in the suppression of what Trutch called "outrageous crime" committed by "utter savages living along the coast," would be given only reluctantly to "one having no experience among them." Nor did Trutch content himself with this tirade concerning Powell's unfitness for the new position. He went on to castigate the entire plan outlined by Macdonald. "I may tell you that I am of opinion, and that very strongly, that for some

10 Not all of these had been gazetted. On October 5, 1866, the large reserve at Kamloops and the two at Shuswap had appeared in the *Gazette*; on July 4, 1867, the Cowichan reserves appeared, and those at Chemainus the day before; on December 18, 1868, those at Lytton were listed; and on November 25, 1869, three reserves were gazetted for the New Westminster district. (See ibid., appendix, "Gazette Notices of Indian Reserves," pp. 324-27.)

11 The action was not taken until after an Address from the Legislative Assembly in British Columbia had been received in Ottawa, praying the Dominion to move immediately to establish an "Indian policy for this Province, and a proper adjustment of Indian reserves." (See B.C., *Journals*, 1st Parl., 1st sess., 1872, p. 27.) Powell's father had been a Tory member of parliament prior to Confederation. Dr. Powell, the son, came to British Columbia in 1862 after graduating from McGill. He soon entered politics, becoming a member of the Legislative Assembly in September, 1863, where he continued until he and De Cosmos were defeated on the Confederation issue by J. S. Helmcken and M. T. Drake in August, 1866. After 1871, Sir John A. Macdonald offered Powell first the position of first Lieutenant-Governor of the new province, and then a place in the Senate. Powell refused both. The position of Indian superintendent must also have been regarded as a rich political "plum," and it is probable that there were others in the province who would have liked the office, which may in part account for the un-co-operative attitude Powell encountered early in his incumbency. (See: B. A. McKelvie, "Lieutenant-Colonel Israel Wood Powell, M.D., C.M.," *British Columbia Historical Quarterly*, 9 (1947), 33-54.

time to come at least the general charge and direction of all Indian affairs in British Columbia should be vested in the Lt. Governor ... and that instead of one there should be three Indian Agents, one for Vancouver Island, one for the Northwest coast and the third for the interior of the mainland."[12]

If the Indians were as satisfied with government policy as Trutch had led both Granville and Howe to believe, there seems little reason why the details and subsequent implementation of this policy could not have been conveyed to Powell with a modicum of disturbance among the Indians. The evidence does not prove that Trutch himself was not convinced that the Indian policy of the province was anything but in the best interests of both the Indians and the white settlers, but it does suggest that he was not anxious to have the details of that policy known to the dominion authorities.

However, Powell had been appointed before Trutch's views reached Macdonald. He acted alone in the province until a second superintendent, James Lenihan, was appointed a year later for the New Westminster area. The second appointment temporarily vindicated Trutch's view that not one but several agents should have been appointed. The Indian Board established by the dominion government in 1874 consisting of Trutch and the two Indian superintendents was, however, soon discovered to be impracticable. No less an authority on Indian affairs in the province than William Duncan, a lay missionary whose work since 1857 with the Tshimshian Indians of the Port Simpson area had been praised all over the continent, recommended the abolition of the Board as being "so palpably defective and misdirected" in its labours as to be useless.[13] Partly on the strength of Duncan's criticism, the Annual Report of the Department of the Interior for 1875 admitted the failure of the Board, largely because the Lieutenant-Governor now regarded his position on it as placing him in an anomalous situation.[14] The Report for 1876 announced that after February 1, 1876, the Indian

12 For the complete text of the letter see Appendix D, Item 2. Its content throws considerable light on subsequent developments.

13 Duncan to David Laird, minister of the interior, May, 1875, "Report on Indian Reserves," appendix C, p. 69.

14 Canada, *Sessional Papers*, 3d Parl., 2d sess., 1875, no. 8, p. 7. Trutch's feeling can be understood, for as lieutenant-governor he was constitutionally bound to uphold the policies of his government, which were unalterably opposed to the policies of the Indian Affairs Branch of the Department of the Interior. For evidence of Trutch's attempts to disrupt the workings of the Board, see Fisher, "Joseph Trutch," pp. 25-26.

Boards in both British Columbia and the Northwest Territories were to be abolished. For them would be substituted the superintendents and agencies which had proved so successful in Ontario.[15] British Columbia was to have two superintendents, Dr. Powell in Victoria to assume charge of the coast Indians and James Lenihan at New Westminster to assume charge of the interior tribes. Further reorganization was carried out in 1880 with the appointment of district agents who were to live among the Indians and be accessible to them. The agents were to serve under a single superintendent responsible to the minister of the interior.[16] By Order in Council of April 3, 1881, six local agents were appointed, three for Vancouver Island and one each for the Lower Fraser River, Kamloops (Henry Cornwall), and "O'Kanagan" (A. E. Howse) areas.[17] Powell throughout retained his position as superintendent in spite of Trutch's disapproval.

It was not an easy task Powell assumed. Immediately he was the victim of antagonism, since members of the provincial ministry held differing views as to the meaning of article 13 of the Terms of Union. From the beginning Powell found his activities obstructed on all sides by the local government. Not having been supplied by Ottawa with anything other than notification of his appointment, he directed letters to G. A. Walkem, chief commissioner of lands and works in the last days of the McCreight government, and to A. R. Robertson, provincial secretary, asking for a statement of previous Indian policy and a list of all reserves. Both men replied that the necessary information had been forwarded to Howe by Trutch the previous January. Finally, Powell requested and received copies from Trutch.

No sooner had Powell been appointed than he was besieged with requests from Walkem and his successor as chief commissioner, Robert Beaven, to proceed at once to the Chilcotin country to define the Indian reserves there. Trouble was brewing, Walkem said, because white settlers were ignoring the government reserves on the land and pre-empting land which the Indians held to be their own

15 Canada, *Sessional Papers,* 3d Parl., 3d sess., 1876, no 9, p. xiii.

16 Canada, Department of the Interior, "Report of the Department of the Interior," Canada, *Sessional Papers,* 4th Parl., 2d sess., 1880, no. 4, p. xiv.

17 Canada, Department of Indian Affairs, "Report of the Department of Indian Affairs," Canada, *Sessional Papers,* 4th Parl., 4th sess., 1882, no. 6, p. xi.

territory.[18] Powell did what he could, which was little enough. He had still not received instruction concerning the active duties of his office. Having no idea of how many acres to allot per family on each reservation, his hands were tied; yet Beaven kept urging that, since the settlers were entering the Cariboo, Alberni, and Cowichan regions, the Indians lands must be set aside at once. The "agrarian discontent" foreseen nine years before by Governor Douglas had materialized. Finally Beaven wrote to Powell explaining the necessity for immediate action:

> I have the honour to inform you that constant complaints are being made to me by parties desirous of pre-empting land at Alberni, that the Indians in that locality claim the lands as their property, and threaten to molest parties occupying said land. Now it is almost impossible to prevent some parties going in there, and I have therefore to call your attention to the imperative necessity of at once having all Indian land claims settled, not only in Alberni, but in other parts of the Province. There are at present numerous parties desirous of settling in British Columbia, but the fact of the Indians being located in almost every District where white settlers would wish to locate is preventing many from doing so, and is consequently retarding the settlement of the Province. I must, therefore, most respectfully but urgently, request your earliest attention to this subject, as delay at this juncture may be a very serious matter to this Province.[19]

As it was now nearly two years since the Dominion had assumed control of Indian affairs in the province, Beaven had every right to urge action. Settlers were arriving, although not in the numbers Beaven implied. With the prospect of a railroad and the hopes its completion aroused, no doubt every member of the De Cosmos-Walkem ministry foresaw clashes over land between the Indians and the incoming settlers. But Powell was still powerless, anxious to help as he might have been. He had to content himself with continuing his search for all available data pertinent to his position and sending his findings on to Ottawa as he proceeded. He was not missing very much. In the copies of the letters Trutch sent him containing both Trutch's and Pearse's memoranda, Powell noticed that Pearse had mentioned $1,984.82 deposited in the Treasury to the credit of the

18 This correspondence may be found in "Papers Connected with the Indian Land Question," pp. 267 ff.

19 Beaven to Powell, April 16, 1873, ibid., p. 273.

Songhees Reserve lease fund.[20] To retrieve the money for present uses, he asked John Ash, the provincial secretary, for an accounting. One can see Ash's delight at being able to reply that the money had been so deposited in the Treasury to form part of the assets of the colony at Confederation, and therefore it had been taken over by the Dominion in 1871.[21]

As isolated incidents, none of these petty annoyances was significant; as part of a series, they seemed a conspiracy to frustrate the activities of the new superintendent. But if Powell found these incidents annoying, they were nothing compared to the storm which broke around him following his letter to Beaven on April 17, 1873.[22] In his letter he included the operative sections of a dominion Order in Council of March 21, 1873, outlining at last the action Powell was to take in British Columbia.

Having studied Powell's correspondence to the Department of Indian Affairs in which he had cited several instances of attempted pre-emption of Indian lands by white settlers, the dominion government was now of the opinion that action as recommended by Powell was imperative. Accordingly, the following instructions were issued and sent to Powell. He, in turn, informed the provincial government.

> The Deputy Superintendent General accordingly suggests that each family be assigned a location of 80 acres of land of average quality, which shall remain permanently the property of the family for whose benefit it is alloted.
>
> That it is a matter of urgent importance to convince the Indians of that Province that the Dominion Government will do full justice to the rights of the Indian population, and thus remove any spirit of discontent which in various quarters appears to prevail.
>
> That authority be at once given to Mr. Powell to confer with the Local Government in regard to Indian Reserves already set apart, which may require to be extended and the outlines marked out in survey, also for setting apart such additional reserves, as in his judgment he may deem to be important, for the purpose of fulfilling the just expectations of those Indians.[23]

20 Pearse to Trutch, October 16, 1871, ibid., p. 262.

21 Powell to Ash, February 4, 1873; Ash to Powell, February 5, 1873, ibid., p. 272.

22 Powell to Beaven, April 17, 1873, ibid., p. 274.

23 The presence of the phrase "of average quality" in this Order in Council passed by the Macdonald Ministry on March 17, 1873, disproves the frequent statement that it was first introduced into legislation by the Mackenzie ministry over the Railway Belt difficulties stemming from the Terms of

The contents of this Order in Council took the local government by surprise. In order to stall for time, Beaven asked Powell the next day to supply him with statistics concerning each individual in every Indian family in all tribes in the province, as well as "specifying also the name and locality of all Indian Reservations, and the acreage of such reservation claimed by you on behalf of the various tribes; distinguishing (in the manner requested above) Indians whose present abode is on land other than known Indian Reservations, and the acreage desired for them."[24]

All Powell could do in reply was to state what Beaven already knew—that he had no possible way of knowing any of this information. The only figure he could give was for the total Indian population, which he had estimated to be 28,500.[25] On April 30, Beaven informed Powell that the ministry "consider that 80 acres is far too large an average for each family," and that, using Powell's own estimate of the Indian population and the acreage of the then established reserves, the present average per family was six acres. As this was not an official statement of the government's views, Powell could do nothing other than try to reach the ear of the ministry until such a statement was forthcoming. That he did so is reflected in the Executive Council Minute of July 25, 1873, setting forth the stand taken by the local government. It stated that, in the opinion of the government, eighty acres was "greatly in excess of the grants considered sufficient by previous governments of British Columbia, and recommend that throughout the province Indian Reserves should not exceed a quantity of twenty acres of land for each head of a family of five persons."[26] With his success in raising the amount from ten to twenty acres Powell had to be content, and so he advised his superiors in Ottawa.[27] He had little choice. The July 25 Minute had pointed out that twenty acres, being a larger amount than had been previously granted to the Indians of British Columbia, was, therefore, more than the government was bound to consent to under article 13.

Union, article 11. It does appear in the Canadian Pacific Railway Act of 1874, "the said lands to be of fair average quality" (Canada, *Statutes*, 1874, 37 Vict., c. 14, s. 8[4]), but it is not original there.

24 Beaven to Powell, April 18, 1873, B.C., *Sessional Papers*, 2d Parl., 1st sess., 1876, p. 274.

25 Powell to Beaven, April 19, 1873, ibid., p. 275.

26 B.C., *Sessional Papers*, 1st Parl., 4th sess., 1875, p. 666.

27 "Papers Connected with the Indian Land Question," p. 290.

To resolve the difference so that reserves might be assigned at once and generally to lessen tension which was characterized in 1927 as great enough to have disrupted Confederation,[28] David Laird, minister of the interior in the Mackenzie government, submitted a memorandum to the federal cabinet on March 1, 1874, advising the lowering of the acreage from eighty to twenty. At the same time, he took the opportunity to deplore the attitude being adopted in British Columbia and suggested that in view of the provision in the 1870 Land Ordinance permitting white settlers east of the Cascades to pre-empt 320 acres, Powell should try to persuade the local government to permit Indians in that area to have forty acres.[29]

Had the question of acreage been the only point at issue, innumerable additional difficulties might have been avoided and there probably would not have arisen the serious threat of an Indian war. Although the province persisted throughout the next ten years in maintaining that at Confederation the Indians were perfectly satisfied with such reservations as had been assigned for their use and benefit,[30] the fact that Powell was besieged by urgent requests from the government as soon as he had been appointed to move quickly to assign additional reserves suggests that all was not as well as the government stated. The Indians, in fact, had been complaining for several years that the lands upon which they had settled and which they had cultivated had been taken from them without compensation and pre-empted by white settlers. In some cases, they said, even their burial grounds had been pre-empted. In addition, there were numerous complaints that white settlers took advantage of the law in reference to pastoral land to drive cattle and horses belonging to the Indians from the open range country and obtain large pastoral leases for themselves.[31]

[28] Special Joint Committee, *Report and Evidence*, p. 148.

[29] B.C., *Sessional Papers*, 1st Parl., 2d sess., 1875, p. 672.

[30] C. F. Cornwall, a British Columbia senator, remarked in the Senate in 1878 that at Confederation "there was not the slightest ill-feeling in any Indian breast in that country . . . but since Confederation, from some cause or other — I should say from the unwise interference and meddling of the Dominion Government — irritation has sprung up." He went on to say that as another result of the unfitness of the present government for its position "there has been a change and British Columbia has been put to considerable expense and no little alarm has been caused by the slack, procrastinating and injudicious policy of this government" (Canada, Senate, *Debates*, 3d Parl., 5th sess., 1878, p. 547).

[31] Powell drew one case to Walkem's attention in which an Indian at Cache

The Indians were feeling for the first time the inconvenience of being hemmed in by white settlers and losing the land for pastoral purposes. They were learning what white men meant by ownership of land. Also, the Indians were beginning to understand the value of agriculture and to desire land for cultivation. The Indians of British Columbia had also learned of the liberal land policy recently extended by the dominion government to the natives in the Northwest Territories. Three treaties, No. 1 of August 3, 1871; No. 2 of August 21, 1871; and No. 3 of October 3, 1873, reserved to the Indians tracts of land ranging in size from 160 to 640 acres for each family of five and granted each Indian an annuity of from three to five dollars.[32] In view of these circumstances, it should have required considerably more patience than the Indians of British Columbia possessed to be anything but restless.

That the government of British Columbia had little interest in settling the Indian land question in accordance with dominion policy was made apparent in the new Land Act of 1874.[33] When the act reached Ottawa the Minister of Justice, Telesphore Fournier, disallowed it. The consternation in Victoria must have been great when, in the course of his remarks on the act, Fournier pointed out that the act had defined " 'Crown lands' " as being "all lands of this Province held by the Crown in free and common socage."[34] Such definition implies freehold under grant from the Crown, and could therefore have meant that if the Crown were indeed tenant by freehold, the British Columbia legislature was admitting by its own statute the Indian sovereignty to all lands of the province. Doubtless what had been meant was "in fee simple," and "in free and common socage" had been an inadvertent slip;

Creek had been assessed damages in court "for alleged trespass upon lands which were not fenced, but held under a lease from the Government for pastoral purposes" (Powell to Walkem, January 12, 1874, B.C., *Sessional Papers*, 1st Parl., 4th sess., 1875, p. 670). Walkem assured Powell that the action was perfectly legal. Under s. 30 of the 1870 Land Ordinance the lessee had the right to "maintain ejectment or trespass in the same manner as if he were the owner." In addition, under English Common Law, in effect in British Columbia, owners did not have to fence their property, but the owners of animals were bound to keep them off private property (Walkem to Powell, January 13, 1874, ibid., p. 671).

32 Canada, Department of Indian Affairs, "Report of the Deputy Superintendent-General of Indian Affairs," Canada, *Sessional Papers*, 14th Parl., 2d sess., 1923, no. 14, pp. 11-12.

33 B.C., *Statutes*, 1874, 37 Vict., no. 2, s. 86.

34 Ibid., s. 2.

but the significance of the error becomes apparent when it is seen how strongly opposed the provincial government was at all times to admitting any title whatever held by the Indians, equitable or legal, and how reluctant the province was to part with a single acre more than was absolutely necessary for the use of the Indians.

But it was not on the basis of its definition of crown lands that the act was disallowed. In truth, nothing would have pleased the dominion government more than to have had British Columbia recognize the Indian title by statute. The act was disallowed because it made no provision for any Indian reservations nor of lands for that purpose; nor were the Indians accorded in it any rights or privileges in respect to land — neither could they pre-empt nor purchase land except by applying to the Lieutenant-Governor in Council for a special dispensation to permit them to do so.

Although Fournier said he did not wish to become involved in the merits of the aboriginal title claim, he did feel it his duty to call attention to the legal position of the public lands in British Columbia, particularly in view of what he termed the

> known, existing, and increasing dissatisfaction of the Indian tribes of British Columbia at the absence of adequate reservation of lands for their use, and at the liberal appropriation for those in other parts of Canada upon surrender by treaty of their territorial rights, and the difficulties, which may arise from the not improbable assertion of that dissatisfaction by hostilities on their part.

To substantiate his statement that "there is not a shadow of a doubt, that from the earliest times, England has always felt it imperative to meet the Indians in council, and to obtain surrender of tracts of Canada, as from time to time were required for the purposes of settlement," Fournier quoted sections of the 1763 Proclamation. He also noted the presence of the phrase "Indian territories" used in the Imperial act of 1849 providing for the administration of the colony of Vancouver Island. Because there had never been a cession of the Indian title in British Columbia, because the Indians had already expressed themselves as greatly dissatisfied with the reserves assigned them arbitrarily by the province and were "not averse to hostilities in order to enforce rights which it is impossible to deny them," and because of the express denial to the Indians in the act of any land rights, the minister of justice felt he had no choice but to recommend that the 1874 act be disallowed. British Columbia, he held, was attempting to legislate with respect to the public lands as though those lands were its absolute property, an assumption ignoring the honour and good faith always shown the Indians elsewhere in Canada since 1763.

Fournier also noted that Article 109 of the British North America Act, 1867, conveyed the public lands to the province "subject to any trust existing in respect thereof, and to any interest other than that of the province, in the same." He felt that what was ordinarily spoken of as the "Indian title" must, of necessity, have consisted of some species of interest in the public lands of the province, and that if it were not a freehold in the soil, it surely must have been a usufruct, a right of occupation or possession for the Indians' use. In that case, if the land of the province were not subject to a "trust existing in respect thereof," at least it was subject "to an interest other than that of the province alone."[35] Fournier's decision was used repeatedly over the years by the Indians and their advisers in their attempts to demonstrate to the province the legal basis of their claims to a beneficial interest to all the land of the province.

The unrest evident among the Indians was also noted by the Minister of the Interior, David Laird, in a memorandum of November 2, 1874. In it he outlined the policy of his department toward the British Columbia Indians:

> In laying the foundation of an Indian policy in that Province, on the same permanent and satisfactory basis as in other portions of the Dominion, the Government of the Dominion feel they would not be justified in limiting their efforts to what, under the strict letter of the Terms of Union, they were called upon to do. They feel that a great national question like this, a question involving possibly in the near future an Indian War with all its horrors, should be approached in a very different spirit, and dealt with upon other and higher grounds. Actuated by these feelings, the Government of the Dominion in its dealings with the Indians of British Columbia has acted . . . in a spirit of liberality far beyond what the strict terms of the agreement required at its hands; and they confidently trust that on a calm review of the whole subject in all its important bearings, the Government of that Province will be prepared to meet them in a spirit of equal liberality.[36]

The threat of war was echoed by Father C. J. Grandidier of Okanagan Mission, by the Roman Catholic Bishop of British

[35] Hodgins, *Dominion and Provincial Legislation,* 1:1025.

[36] B.C., *Sessional Papers,* 1st Parl., 4th sess., 1875, pp. 684-86.

Columbia, Rev. L. J. d'Herbomez, by Powell,[37] and even by Walkem. But Walkem did not attribute the disturbance to any unrest caused by the failure to settle reservations. He drew Powell's attention to the fact that the Indians at Cache Creek "had assumed a hostile attitude," but blamed this solely on Powell's failure to visit them, making them "feel they have been neglected by the Indian Department."[38]

Powell was less concerned with the Indians' feelings than with a restriction placed upon the local government's offer of twenty acres per family. He had received a letter on July 28, 1873, three days after the receipt of an Order in Council outlining policy for the province, which informed him that "all future reserves for Indians will be adjusted on the basis of twenty acres of land for each head of a family of five persons."[39] At first Powell had no intimation of the significance of the word "future." In the three days intervening between the passing of the Order and Ash's sending the letter to Powell, Walkem and his colleagues had realized that as their Minute stood, Powell could increase all *present* reserves to the limit of twenty acres per family of five. Acting on the authority vested in him under the Order in Council of March 21, 1873, Powell had sent survey crews into the province to begin surveying present reserves as well as to define new reserves.

One of the crews had gone to the Musqueam reserve at the mouth of the north arm of the Fraser River. Here it was discovered that in order to allot twenty acres to each family,[40] 1,197 additional acres would be required for the seventy families, since the present reserves contained only 314 acres, of which 114 were quite useless. On July 31, 1874, Powell applied to Beaven, chief commissioner of lands and works, for the additional acreage.[41]

[37] Ibid., pp. 680-81, 679, 673.

[38] Walkem to Powell, December 26, 1873, ibid., pp. 667-68. A telegram from Clinton on January 9, 1874, however, informed the government that in a Council of Chiefs, seven were for war and only two for peace. The message added that Father Grandidier, a confidant of the Indians, "gave it as his opinion that the Indians were liable to commence hostilities at any moment" ("Papers Connected with the Indian Land Question," p. 286).

[39] Ash to Powell, July 28, 1873, "Papers Connected with the Indian Land Question," p. 279.

[40] By repeated representations to Walkem, Powell had persuaded the government to alter its Order in Council of July 25, 1873, to read "twenty acres of land to each head of a family" instead of to each head of a family of five persons (enclosure in Ash to Powell, July 21, 1874, ibid., p. 293).

[41] Ibid., p. 294.

After much correspondence, it became apparent to Powell that his worst fears were being confirmed. To determine precisely the interpretation that the local government was placing on the Order in Council of July 25, 1873, he sent the following letter:

> As many of the present reserves do not contain *five* acres of land to each head of a family, the injustice with which Indians having such reserves would be treated in case they were not extended, and the serious complications which would at once be consequent upon such treatment are so great, that I sincerely trust the interpretation seemingly conveyed by the Honourable Chief Commissioner's letter, of confining the grant to new reserves, is not that intended by the Government in lieu of *all* reserves containing twenty acres to every head of a native family.[42]

But it was. Pending official notification, Powell discharged the survey parties, warned the government again of the serious consequences attendant upon such a policy, and drew to their attention the fact that the action was a gross breach of good faith. On September 28, Powell was informed that the operation of the Minute of July, 1873, was "altogether confined to cases in which, at the time of Confederation, aboriginal tribes or communities were not provided with lands set apart for their separate and exclusive use."[43]

By now Lenihan, the New Westminster superintendent, had also registered his protest and pointed out in two letters that since the province was deriving some considerable financial advantage each year in the form of annual subsidies based on population, it might well adopt a more liberal attitude toward Indian land grants.[44] In answer to his first letter, Lenihan was informed by the provincial secretary that the province was being quite "reasonable and just" in honouring its obligations under the Terms of Union.[45]

A voluminous correspondence was now carried on between Powell and the local government, and between the local government and the Dominion — "an awful amount of correspondence," as Andy Paull said when he presented his evidence before the Special Joint Committee in 1927.[46] The conclusion is inescapable that the prov-

42 Powell to Ash, August 15, 1874, ibid., p. 299.
43 Ash to Powell, September 28, 1874, ibid., p. 303.
44 Lenihan to Ash, October 15, 1874, ibid., pp. 148-50.
45 Ash to Lenihan, October 12, 1874, ibid., p. 305.
46 Special Joint Committee, *Report and Evidence*, p. 95.

ince was carrying over into its dealings with the officers of the federal Indian department much of the frustration and bitterness engendered by the railway problem. Powell as an appointee of the Dominion and the Indians as its wards were suffering from the "fight Canada" attitude. No other explanation for the obstructionist tactics offers itself. If the dominion government was bending every effort to dishonour certain provisions of the railway clause, then the provincial government would retaliate by exerting all its resources to adhere as closely as possible to the letter of the law under the Indian clause. Scarcity of land could hardly have weighed heavily as a factor at that time, although in a lengthy memorandum to the Dominion on August 18, 1875, Walkem did object to the stipulation that the Indians' land should be of "average quality." To buttress his argument that British Columbia could ill afford the extensive acreages of arable lands requested by the Dominion, Walkem presented the following table which he based on an assumed Indian population of 40,000:

1st. — Terms of Union — 10 acres to each Indian family	80,000 acres
2nd.—21st March, 1873 — Request by Dominion for 80 acres of average quality for each family of five persons, and old Reserves to be regulated accordingly, equal to	640,000 acres
3rd. — In reply the Province offered 20 acres to each head of a family of five persons, which the Indian Department was authorized by the Dominion Authorities to accept, equal to	160,000 acres
4th. — 15th May, 1874. — In lieu of the above, a further request was made for 20 acres to each head of a family or, as understood, for each Indian adult, (the adults being about three-tenths of the Indian population), equal to	240,000 acres

This was assented to in the case of future Reserves; but the Provincial Government declined to include past Reserves in this agreement. They, however, offered to consider any special claim which might arise in respect of the latter.

NOTE: From each of the above quantities, the acreage of the old Reserves must, of course, be deducted. The amount cannot be stated with accuracy in the absence of complete surveys. It, however, represents but a very small fraction of the quantities stated.[47]

[47] "Report on Indians Reserves," p. 62.

Walkem went on to state that in dealing with large tracts of agricultural land which were vitally needed for settlement purposes, his government felt "fully justified in hesitating to accede to propositions which might not only retard the future settlement of the Province but prove to be both ill-judged and ill-timed, in the interests of the present settlers and of the Indians themselves." In presenting what was a well reasoned argument, he said the request from the Dominion "for any reasonable and discriminating acreage of cultivable land for the use of the Indians" would not have been refused, if for no other reason than the very practical one that "as large consumers and as labourers" the Indians were entitled to "kind and liberal treatment." His government, he continued, had granted the request for twenty acres for each family, which was more than they were obliged to do, but felt they could not agree that this should apply to present reserves. "With great reluctance," he added, his government "felt compelled to differ in opinion from the Dominion Government." He considered, however, that the local government could not justly be held responsible for the impasse now reached. "The real causes of this failure are attributable to the want of proper information on the part of the Dominion Government of the physical structure of this country and of the habits of the Indians."[48]

In this statement there was much truth. The Dominion planned to follow the procedure which had been so successful on the extensive prairie lands of the Territories. The way of life of the Indians of British Columbia differed essentially from that of the prairie Indians. But because of the animosity existing between Victoria and Ottawa, the local government did not at any time convey this information to Ottawa.

With the aid of arguments supplied by William Duncan of the Metlakatla colony,[49] Walkem then proceeded in his memorandum to demonstrate effectively that his government was not merely being difficult. He incorporated Duncan's suggestions "in order that erroneous impressions may be removed, unnecessary complications be avoided, a practical land scheme be devised, and the Indian question finally settled to the mutual satisfaction of both Governments."[50]

48 Ibid., p. 61.

49 Ibid., appendix C, pp. 69-71.

50 Ibid., p. 65.

All these views were attached to a Minute of the Executive Council of British Columbia on August 18, 1875, and forwarded to Ottawa. The Indian department gave the Minute close study. On November 10, an Order in Council was passed outlining the views of R. W. Scott, acting minister of the interior during Laird's absence in British Columbia. He recommended that with a view to the prompt and final settlement of the Indian lands question, an Allotment Commission of three men be appointed, one by each government and the third jointly, "to visit, with all convenient speed, ... each Indian nation ... in British Columbia, and, after a full enquiry on the spot into all matters affecting the question, to fix and determine for each nation, separately, the number, extent, and locality of the Reserve or Reserves to be allowed to it."[51]

The remaining clauses of the Order in Council incorporated the recommendations contained in Walkem's memorandum which, in turn, had been based entirely upon Duncan's suggestions. Duncan's influence becomes apparent from a close reading of the last sentence in clause 5 from which originated the vexatious problem of the reversionary interest in Indian lands.

> That each Reserve shall be held in trust for the use and benefit of the nation of Indians to which it has been allotted, and, in the event of any material increase or decrease hereafter of the numbers of a nation occupying a Reserve, such Reserve shall be enlarged or diminished, as the case may be, so that it shall bear a fair proportion to the members of the nation occupying it. The extra land required for any Reserve shall be allotted from Crown Lands, and any land taken off a Reserve shall revert to the Province.

In conclusion, Scott recommended that each commissioner be paid by the government appointing him, and that the expenses and salary of the joint commissioner, who was to be allowed ten dollars a day, should be borne jointly.[52] Even the method of paying the joint commissioner was to have unpleasant repercussions.

Meanwhile, increasing unrest was apparent among the Indians throughout the province. This unrest, in turn, caused a growing fear among the white settlers that an Indian war was a distinct and immediate possibility. When the surveys had been discontinued in

51 "Papers Connected with the Indian Land Question," pp. 220-23.

52 Ibid., pp. 320-23.

the summer of 1874, the discontent and alarm among the Indians were greatly aggravated. That there had been no war that year, Powell attributed solely to the lack of unity among the Indians and not in any way to the absence of sufficient provocation.[53] Powell was not being alarmist; some white settlers and missionaries shared his views. Until the land grievances were settled, no money grants or presents would have placated the Indians. Powell stated that the Nicola and Okanagan Indians, the most seriously disaffected, refused to accept his customary gifts, fearing that by taking any they might be thought to be waiving their claim for compensation for the injustice they felt was being done them.

The Indians along the Lower Fraser River, equally aggrieved, adopted the white man's procedure and on July 14, 1874, presented a petition to the government through the medium of Dr. Powell.[54] The Indians were chagrined at the recalcitrance of the provincial government in denying them eighty acres per family and annoyed at the pre-empting of their pastures by white settlers. The petitioners were quite aware that the government had to record the pre-emptions. They were also aware that under the 1870 Land Ordinance they themselves were at liberty to pre-empt large acreages after obtaining the written permission of the Lieutenant-Governor in Council. However, they also knew that the provincial government was not granting such permission, and had not been since 1872, pending location of the railway lands.[55] Even if this had not been the case, they had a shrewd suspicion of the probable result if the chief commissioner of lands and works received many applications for pre-emptions from Indians. Further, unless an Indian had money to purchase provisions and implements and to sustain himself over a long period of time, it is doubtful that he could have fulfilled the pre-emption residence requirements of ten months annually on the claim. In all likelihood, he would have found it necessary to work elsewhere to finance his holding. But he could not arrange for another Indian to live on his claim, since

53 As reported by David Laird, minister of the interior, in his "Memorandum," November 2, 1874, Canada, *Sessional Papers*, 3d Parl., 3d sess., 1876, no. 9, pp. xli-xlv.

54 See Appendix D, Item 3, for the complete text.

55 This was one reason given by the British Columbia government. The other one voiced by Walkem was that the practice of permitting Indians to pre-empt had been discontinued "lest it should interfere with the Dominion policy of concentrating the Indians upon Reserves," a policy he was to denounce severely. (See: "Report on Indian Reserves," p. 59.)

under the 1873 Land Amendment Act no one could engage an Indian to live on a pre-emption while he himself was absent.[56]

With all these facts in mind, it is remarkable that the petitioners refrained from adding anything other than the veiled threat that "we cannot say what will be the consequence" if what they sought were not granted, and soon. Such moderation was no doubt advised by the missionaries active among the tribes, but the note of warning was not lost on Powell or the dominion officials. The easterners had not forgotten the rebellion at Red River three years before, the origin of which had been a set of circumstances very similar to those now developing in British Columbia.

The two governments exchanged thinly disguised accusations. Each was certain that its position was correct. The Dominion took the position that when the framers of the Terms of Union had inserted the provisions requiring the Dominion to pursue a policy as liberal toward the Indians as that which British Columbia had followed until 1871, they could hardly have been aware of the marked contrast between the Indian policy which had always been pursued in Canada and the policy being enforced in British Columbia. The ten-acre grant, or even the twenty, could hardly compare with the Canadian allotment of eighty acres, and the same contrast prevailed in regard to schools and agricultural assistance. Laird was moved to declare that under such circumstances "the insertion of a policy as liberal as was pursued by the local government seems little short of a mockery" of the Indian claim.[57] The provincial government struck what it considered a telling blow by pointing out that the very fact of Powell's acknowledgement that many of the existing reserves did not allow of twenty acres per family was conclusive proof that the province, in agreeing to furnish twenty acres in the future, was being more liberal than required under the Terms of Union.[58]

56 British Columbia, *Land Laws of British Columbia: together with Land Office Forms and Regulations* (Victoria: R. Wolfenden, 1873), p. 8. Both Indians and Chinese were forbidden to act as "occupiers" for anyone pre-empting the land. Because of the stringent regulations of section 16 of the 1870 Ordinance requiring "continuous *bona fide* personal residence of the pre-emptor on his pre-emption claim," the 1873 Amendment permitted an "agent." Section 16 was aimed directly at speculators, or those whose appetite for land was larger than their ability to use it all.

57 Canada, *Sessional Papers*, 3d Parl., 3d sess., 1876, pp. xli-xlv.

58 Beaven to Powell, August 10, 1874, B.C., *Sessional Papers*, 1st Parl., 4th sess., 1875, p. 676.

Out of this duel-by-letter was nurtured, if not born, the problem of aboriginal title, even before the Allotment Commission had gone into the field. The Indians and their sympathizers were not slow to appreciate that the federal Indian policy, based on Imperial policy, offered the perfect basis for their claim to all lands in the province. No official action was taken for many years in the formal presentation of this claim, but it was to be troublesome to the Allotment Commission among the Tshimshian tribe of the Skeena and Nass regions. On the first visits of the Commission this tribe refused to permit any reserves to be set aside, fearing that, by accepting them, they would be foregoing their larger claim.[59] These, however, were problems for the future. The more immediate task was to set apart reserves. The way was cleared on January 8, 1876, when the provincial government agreed to the formation of the Joint Allotment Commission, as recommended by dominion Order in Council of November 10, 1875. In their Minute accepting all the terms the local government pointed out that "strictly speaking, the Province should not be responsible for any portion of the expenses connected with the charge or management of Indian Affairs which are entrusted by the Terms of Union to the Dominion Government."[60] In May, 1876, the Dominion appointed Alexander C. Anderson of North Saanich as its representative. British Columbia took no action until August, at which time it appointed Archibald McKinlay of Lac la Hache, and recommended Gilbert Malcolm Sproat as the joint commissioner. On August 15, Sproat's appointment was confirmed.[61] In the instructions sent to Anderson and Sproat on August 23, they were told to assure the Indians of the dominion government's anxious desire to deal with them "justly and liberally"; to do nothing that would militate against the existing friendly relations between the Dominion and the Indians; to refrain from disturbing the Indians in the possession of their villages, fishing stations, fur-trading posts, settlements, or clearings; to confer in all matters with the two superintendents, Powell and Lenihan; and to work as rapidly as possible. By a proclamation of December 23, 1876, three

59 Canada, Department of Indian Affairs, "Report of the Superintendent-General of Indian Affairs," Canada, *Sessional Papers*, 6th Parl., 1st sess., 1887, No. 6, pp. x-xi.

60 "Papers Connected with the Indian Land Question," pp. 328A-328B.

61 Canada, Department of the Interior, "Report of the Department of the Interior," Canada, *Sessional Papers*, 3d Parl., 4th sess., 1877, no. 11, p. xvi.

months after the commissioners had entered upon their formidable task, they were empowered to deal absolutely and at once with any question that might arise without reference to either government.

To indicate that the dominion government was cognizant of the native title claim and was not disposed to deny it, the Order in Council establishing the Commission concluded by stating that the question of the rights of the Indians in all lands in British Columbia where those rights had not been extinguished by treaties was still unsettled.

CHAPTER 13

The Reserve Allotment Commissions

The work of the commissioners was necessarily slow, and it was not speeded when they were forced to discharge their secretary after objections from Victoria to the expense. Beginning at the mouth of the Fraser River, the commissioners visited each existing reserve. They went on to Burrard Inlet, up the coast to Jervis Inlet, across to Comox, and down to Victoria the first winter, 1876-1877. In each area they were required to establish accurately the population of the tribe or band for which the reserve was to be either confirmed, created, or extended. At Burrard Inlet, for instance, they discovered that no further land could be allotted because of settlement on all sides and the presence of sawmills. As the commissioners for the Dominion had been especially instructed not to disturb existing settlement, it was necessary to look elsewhere for land. Because the Squamish tribe living on Burrard Inlet had fishing stations on Howe Sound and because it was desirable to set aside as large tracts as possible in unsettled areas with a view to having the Indians settle permanently, the commissioners eventually went to Howe Sound. After alloting two reserves, one of 2,000 acres and a second of 14,000 acres, "the highest satisfaction at the result of our proceedings was expressed by the Chiefs."[1] At Comox a reserve of fourteen acres was allotted to include "scattered graves."[2] At Cowichan,

1 "Report of Alexander C. Anderson, Dominion Commission Indian Reserves," Canada, *Sessional Papers*, 3d Parl., 5th sess., 1878, no. 10, special appendix D, pp. li-lxiv.

2 In his report for the year, Powell noted when the Comox chief came down to Victoria to report on the activities of the Allotment Commission, the chief expressed approval of all that had been done but wondered "when I thought

Anderson reported that the large reserves given by Douglas[3] had been cut down by successive governors, "(especially . . . by the late Governor Seymour)," but in accord with his instructions, Anderson "informed the Indians at the outset that, while the Dominion Government in unison with the Provincial Government, were solicitous to promote the interest of the Indians, and to satisfy them in every reasonable way, no interference with the vested interests of the White settlers could be permitted."[4]

The commissioners' problems on the coast were nothing in comparison with those encountered in the interior, where they went in June, 1877. The coast Indians could and did hire themselves out as labourers. Hence their land was not as economically important to them as to those tribes who relied almost exclusively upon their cattle and horses for livelihood. After working in the southern interior in the neighbourhood of Osoyoos and up Lake Okanagan for three months, Sproat expressed alarm at the feeling among the Indians. He found that the action of the colonial government in cutting down their former extensive reserves, the unextinguished title to all lands, the delay since 1871 in attending to their complaints, and the presence of an Indian outbreak immediately south of the border had all contributed to a situation in which any unusual event, even a rough quarrel between an Indian and a white man, might have "an unusually bad effect." To his knowledge, he reported, messengers were being sent constantly back and forth across the border. The two bands were of the same tribe, separated by a political line which was meaningless to them. He said there was valid evidence that the interior tribes, the "O'Kanagans" and the Shuswaps, had agreed to settle their land claims in their own way, and that they were plentifully supplied with ammunition.[5]

---

it likely they would be paid for their title to all other land in Comox occupied by white people?" (Powell to David Mills, minister of the interior, October 18, 1877, ibid., p. 47). In a return tabled April 24, 1901, the smallest reserve listed is one of 3/100 of an acre for a graveyard at Sooke, allotted by the Reserve Commission June 11, 1877 (B.C., *Sessional Papers,* 9th Parl., 2d sess., 1901, pp. 589-601).

3 After seeking legal advice, Sproat reported that he had been assured the reserves established by Douglas were perfectly legal (Sproat to Sir John A. Macdonald, November 11, 1879, Canada, *Sessional Papers,* 4th Parl., 2d sess., 1880, no. 4, pp. 142-45).

4 Canada, *Sessional Papers,* 3d Parl., 5th sess., 1878, no. 10, special appendix D, p. l.

5 Sproat to Mills, December 1, 1877, ibid., special appendix E, pp. lxv-lxxvi. Mill's report to the Governor General, Lord Dufferin, on this critical situation is found, ibid., p. xix.

Sproat was so disturbed by the effect on the Indians of newspaper stories criticizing the excessive acreage the commissioners were rumoured to be granting that he wrote to the *Colonist* on October 20, 1877. He pointed out that "the Indian question overshadows every other practical question which we have to deal with at the present time." He added that there could be no substantial railway progress in British Columbia until the Indian land question had been finally and completely settled. The commissioners, he said, were attempting to give the Indians enough, but not too much, land; and it was to the credit of the province generally that the commissioners were finding that where there had been any trespassing, the Indian was usually the offender. Finally, he wrote, they were instructing the Indians everywhere to withdraw any extravagant claims to supposed prior grants made by the colonial government.[6]

The general alarm gradually subsided as the commissioners made their visits. It is clear, however, that the white settlers' fears of a general war were not unfounded. In June it was discovered that the Shuswaps had decided to call a great general meeting at Okanagan Lake. Such a large meeting spelled trouble. Moreover, the interior tribes were in constant communication with Chief Joseph and his tribe in Washington Territory, who were currently engaged in a bloody battle against troops of the United States' Army. While the Indians were meeting at Okanagan Lake, the reserve commissioners were detained in Victoria awaiting the outcome of another disagreement between the two governments. As soon as dominion officials learned of the critical situation, they directed the commissioners to proceed at once to the scene of the expected trouble. It is possible that without the timely arrival of the commissioners on the spot to adjust reserves, British Columbia might have found itself engaged in an Indian war.

On the surface, it seemed to the Indians that the local government was directly responsible for the crises that arose both in 1874 and in 1877. There could be no doubt that the colonial government, at the very least, was careless in its handling of Indian reserves before 1871, since it had made little effort to survey the reserves that had been assigned. To the Indian the terms "colonial" and "provincial" were indistinguishable. Further, agents of the dominion government, acting under a misapprehension but with all good

6 Quoted ibid., special appendix E, p. lxxv-lxxvi.

intentions, had promised the Indians eighty acres of land as well as further considerations.[7] And when news reached the Indians of the liberal treatment of the prairie tribes through dominion treaties, they had no doubt as to which government was their benefactor.

The provincial government would not accept the proposition that the Royal Proclamation of 1763 applied to any territory west of the Rockies. Hence it felt under no obligation to secure the cession of the Indian title by treaty. Since three-quarters of the Indian population lived along the coast in the 1870's, the British government felt that the treaty system should not be used in a country where a fishing economy was so predominant among the Indians.[8]

Premier Smithe expressed the same opinion to Prime Minister Macdonald in 1884. After noting that "the administration of Indian affairs is in anything but a satisfactory condition," and suggesting radical changes in the treatment of the Indians in his province, he laid the entire blame on the Indian Act, which he said was "framed especially to provide for the protection and government of the native race in Eastern Canada and the North-West Territories, where the habits and customs, and character of the people are entirely dissimilar to those found among the tribes of British Columbia," and therefore "would appear to be, in many respects, quite inapplicable to the Indians in the Pacific Province."[9]

Trutch had made the further telling point in 1872 that should the dominion government now attempt to buy out the Indian title to the land in British Columbia "you would go back of all that had been done here for 30 years past and would be equitably bound to compensate the tribes who inhabited the districts now settled farmed

[7] In complaining about this matter, Premier Walkem probably had Powell in mind, for Powell's actions had undoubtedly placed the province in an embarrassing position. (See: "Report on Indian Reserves," p. 61.)

[8] Walkem put the number of Indians gaining their livelihood from fishing and hunting along the coast at 30,000. He added that, should the treaty system of placing Indians on large tracts of land, as in Ontario, be adopted in British Columbia, "a serious injury will be inflicted upon the Indians and the Province," and that such a system would be "'fraught with mischief for the Province at large." As an alternative, he suggested that no uniform acreage be decided upon, but rather that each tribe should be assigned land as its circumstances dictated — fishing stations, hunting areas, settlements, and farming areas. This was another of William Duncan's suggestions. (See: Duncan to Laird, May, 1875, "Report on Indian Reserves," pp. 69-71.)

[9] Smithe to Macdonald, March 7, 1884, B.C., *Sessional Papers*, 4th Parl., 3d sess., 1885, pp. 1-2.

[*sic*] by white people equally with those in more remote and uncultivated portions. Our Indians are sufficiently satisfied and had better be left alone as far as a new system towards them is concerned."[10]

The Allotment Commissioners discovered that the Indians were not as aware of the satisfaction between themselves and the local government as Trutch.[11] Wherever there was dissatisfaction, however, the visit of the commissioners to assign lands generally met with the approval of the Indians. Notification of the exact size and location of the allotted land was forwarded to the chief commissioner of lands and works in Victoria. Notice then was to have appeared in the *Gazette* to indicate the government's official confirmation of the reserve.

In fact, however, no such notice ever did appear in the *Gazette* for reserves assigned by the Joint Allotment Commission. In spite of Smithe's protestations that "the British Columbia Government are anxious to deal justly and generously with the Indians of the Province," and that "the Province is ready to give such areas of Crown land for Indian Reserves as are necessary and reasonable,"[12] he labelled the Joint Commissioners as "notoriously prodigal" in their allotment of land and castigated them for having set apart reserves "with such reckless extravagance."[13] Smithe became so vitriolic when Powell begged him in his capacity of chief commissioner of lands and works to have the reserves gazetted — something Smithe had no intention of doing — that he accused the Allotment Commissioners of setting themselves above the law and of encouraging the Indians to do likewise.

10 See Appendix D, Item 2.

11 Cornelius O'Keefe's holdings exemplified the kind of delicate problem they could encounter. They discovered that on April 29, 1873, O'Keefe had pre-empted 320 acres of an Indian settlement and that he had done so before receiving a crown grant for a previous 480-acre pre-emption which had been recorded in 1871. Both actions were illegal under the Land Ordinances of 1865 and 1870. After discussing the case at some length in his report, Sproat added, "Mr. Keefe is not a poor ignorant settler, but a wealthy intelligent cattle farmer, already in possession of 640 acres." O'Keefe discovered that he had urgent business to attend to in England immediately prior to the visit of the commissioners. He left his assistant, Mr. Greenhow, in charge. (See: B.C., *Sessional Papers*, 2d Parl., 3d sess., and 3d Parl., 1st sess., 1878, pp. 715-28 for the full correspondence.)

12 Smithe to Deputy Superintendent-General Vankoughnet, April 11, 1884, B.C., *Sessional Papers*, 4th Parl., 3d sess., 1885, p. 13.

13 Smithe to Powell, November 24, 1884, ibid., p. xiv, following p. 410, and Smithe to O'Reilly, November 29, 1884, ibid., p. xvi.

> The Commissioners would undoubtedly have done service to all concerned in the good government of the country if they had taught the Indians that they were entirely subject to the law of the land, and not superior to it; by explaining that they themselves were subject to the law and could not grant rights and privileges to water or anything else in the teeth of the express provisions of the Act upon the subject.[14]

Powell's repeated requests to the government to recognize the reserves set aside by the Allotment Commissioners were in vain, and the province continued to dishonour its obligations under the 1875-1876 Agreement. Powell said that the delay was very unfortunate "as tending to unsettle the minds of the Indians in the good faith of the Government after they have been informed that the Commissioners were regularly authorized Chiefs, whose decisions were to be final, and after these lands have been duly pointed out to the natives by the Commission as permanent reservations." Moreover, the white settlers were beginning to disregard any Indian reservation and to pre-empt such lands at a rapid rate.[15] Smithe's only answer was that, after seeing such reserves as the two at the north end of Okanagan Lake — one of 24,742 acres (including the Commonage above Vernon) and the other of 29,392 acres (including the range west of Vernon), "separated from the first by a narrow strip of water only," and both "lying in a wild, waste condition without any attempt being made to improve it" — he felt

> an almost criminal wrong had been done in withdrawing from settlement so large a tract of fertile land. A wrong, particularly apparent at this time, when there is such a demand for the land by white settlers, who are entering the country in search of homes. Constantly applications are being made to me for just such lands as are locked up in these reserves by men who would invest large means in their development, and make them productive of wealth to the state.[16]

This was more than Powell could accept, particularly as Smithe had accused the Department of Indian Affairs of gross dereliction of duty in not teaching the Indians to use their lands to better advantage. Powell pointed out to Smithe that, although in all those 50,000 acres there was much grazing land on the Commonage, it

[14] Smithe to Powell, December 5, 1884, ibid., p. xviii, following p. 410.

[15] Powell to Smithe, November 11, 1884, ibid., p. viii, following p. 410.

[16] Smithe to Powell, November 24, 1884, ibid., p. xiii, following p. 410.

was "common ground" on which white settlers pastured twenty times as many cattle as did the Indians, and that there was very little cultivable land. He continued:

> You will pardon me for stating that your impression as to "the immense area of land lying in a wild, waste condition" is, in my opinion, calculated to mislead in a correct consideration of this matter. Nor can I understand, under such circumstances, the justice of your reflections upon this department in the settlement "that no effort is being made to train Indians to utilize the broad acres set apart for them" — lands which the Provincial Government have refused to confirm as reserves, notwithstanding the length of time which has elapsed since they were set apart by a Commission whose decisions were, by agreement between the two Governments, to have been final.
>
> It is also important to remember that great doubt and uncertainty have been caused as to the intentions of the Provincial Government with regard to all reserves of the interior, on account of their action in alienating and receiving moneys for reserve lands which were gravely promised and given to the Indians by the Joint Reserve Commission.[17]

Although on many of the reserves the Indians were left in undisputed possession, it was only because the lands were not being sought by settlers. Not a single reserve set aside by the Joint Commission was ever accepted by the provincial government.

At first the commissioners had no intimation of any such complications. They were not permitted, however, to proceed far before objection was voiced in the local legislature to the "time and expense involved over many years if the present Joint Commission were to continue its work." A. C. Elliott, premier and provincial secretary, the instigator of the motion, recommended to his Executive Council on January 27, 1877, that because of the expense, the commission should restrict its activities "to places where the whites and natives are living in close proximity" as well as to those areas where dissatisfaction was being voiced. Expressing an opinion the opposite of that used earlier by Walkem in an effort to speed up surveys, Elliott said that throughout the greater portion of the province "the Indians are, and will be for many years to come, completely isolated, having little or no intercourse with the whites; and in these remote places no difficulties are likely to be experienced." With this in

17 Powell to Smithe, December 9, 1884, ibid., pp. xx-xxi, following p. 410, No. 2.

mind, he advised the dissolution of the Joint Commission in favour of a single commissioner at the end of 1877, and did so with the full approval of Powell.[18] The reduction was reluctantly concurred in by the Dominion, and an Order in Council to that effect was passed on February 23, 1877.[19]

A return tabled in 1878 indicated that the cost to the province of the Joint Commission from its inception in 1876 to the end of 1877 was $12,024.68.[20] At this period of disenchantment over the railway and of mounting deficits, this sum seemed an unreasonable amount, particularly if it were to continue indefinitely. Especially irksome to the local government, of course, was the fact that Indian affairs were legally the responsibility of the Dominion, as had been carefully noted in the Minute accepting the Allotment Commission.

By Order in Council of March 8, 1878, Sproat became the single commissioner. In the course of his first year's work, he reported to Sir John A. Macdonald that rather than objecting to the reduction in size of the commission, the Indians appeared better pleased to be dealing with "one white chief than with three, the respective duties and positions of whom . . . they did not understand."[21] He took up his duties in the Lower Fraser River area, where he found the greatest problem to be squatters on Indian lands in the Railway Belt, but he reported that he had exhausted every effort to provide for the Indians without unnecessarily disturbing any of those settlers. Having allotted all the reserves along the proposed railway line to a distance fifty miles up the North Thompson from Kamloops, he moved his operations to the northern end of Vancouver Island. When his plans became known to the provincial authorities, he discovered that the government was attempting to prevent the investi-

18 Elliot to Laird, January 27, 1877, B.C., *Sessional Papers*, 2d Parl., 2d sess., 1877, pp. 433-34.

19 Ibid.

20 "Return of Expenditures on Account of Indian Commission for the year 1876 to 31st December, 1877," B.C., *Sessional Papers*, 2d Parl., 3d sess., and 3d Parl., 1st sess., 1878, p. 499. The figure represents the province's share only. Each year the Reserve Commission was costing the dominion government close to $50,000. (Canada, *Sessional Papers*, 4th Parl., 2d sess., 1880, no. 4, p. 249.) In 1877 provincial expenditures exceeded receipts by $175,-466, and in 1878 the deficit increased to $191,213 ("Table of Expenditures and Receipts, 1872-1901," B.C., *Sessional Papers*, 9th Parl., 2d sess., 1901, p. 566).

21 "Annual Report of the Department of the Interior," Canada, *Sessional Papers*, 4th Parl., 1st sess., 1879, no. 7, pp. ix-x.

gation and adjustment of reserves in that district, "for reasons which I cannot surmise."[22]

Sproat went ahead with his plans, but at the price of his job. He found the conditions among the Indians so deplorable that he felt constrained to report directly to Dr. Powell in Victoria what he had found, in order to give Powell the opportunity to advance any contrary views before Sproat's report was submitted to the department in Ottawa. In his letter to Powell, which was subsequently included in his annual report, he said that the "pot-lach" custom had increased, that sick Indians had to travel all the way to Victoria for care, that cannibalism was not extinct, that prostitution was unchecked, that drinking was as bad as ever, and that he could not find that "any particular remedy has been applied."[23]

Having been so outspoken about his findings so close to Powell's headquarters, and having ignored the veiled threat from the provincial government that it would be "impolitic" for him to visit the northern end of the island, Sproat could hardly have expected commendation. Powell and Sir John A. Macdonald were personal friends, and Sproat was probably asked for resignation. At any rate, he tendered it in March, 1880.

In his place Peter O'Reilly, a judge of the county court and a stipendiary magistrate, was appointed. As a judge, he was unable to take up the duties of his new office until he could be relieved of his other duties in the autumn. The work of surveying, however, went on all summer, since the two survey parties had never been able to keep up with the commissioners, or even with the single commissioner.[24] Since Elliott's memorandum in 1877 dealing with the expense of the commission, the provincial government had scrutinized more closely the commissioner's reports and insisted that the allotments be approved not only by the chief commissioner of lands and works but also by the Executive Council. Until then, no notice could appear in the *Gazette*.

For the next eighteen years O'Reilly went up and down the province, first to complete the work of allotting reserves where none had existed before and then to go back to certain reserves to enlarge

22 Sproat to Vankoughnet, November 24, 1879, Canada, *Sessional Papers*, 4th Parl., 2d sess., 1880, no. 4, pp. 141-44.

23 Sproat to Powell, November 11, 1879, ibid., pp. 146-48.

24 Powell to Macdonald, November 15, 1880, Canada, *Sessional Papers*, 4th Parl., 3d sess., 1880-81, no. 14, pp. 118-20.

them or to settle some difficulty which had arisen with white settlers. The latter problem was not common, although he did encounter serious trouble in the Cariboo and Kootenay districts. In 1884 he visited the Indians around Soda Creek, Canoe Creek and Alkali Lake, none of whom had ever had any reserves but who now asked the provincial government to provide land — somehow, someplace. All land in the vicinity had been pre-empted. In view of its responsibility for seeing that every Indian band in the province was supplied with enough land for its purposes, the local government was asked to locate a satisfactory area of land previously reserved by the government.[25] This request had repercussions in the legislature. In a motion designed to remove Indians from their valuable agricultural and timber lands, G. B. Martin and C. A. Semlin sought also to censure the Smithe ministry for acceding to the request of the reserve commissioner for such large tracts of land. They succeeded neither in having the Indians transferred to "wild land equally suitable for the purpose for which they require them," nor in censuring the government.[26] Though the motion failed, it did start ugly rumours circulating among the Indians. These rumours persisted for years and O'Reilly found them exceedingly troublesome.

The provincial government refused to provide the necessary land at Soda Creek and Alkali Lake. It was partly to discuss the injustice felt in British Columbia over this and other Indian matters that Smithe made a special trip to Ottawa in the spring of 1884, just a year after he had become premier. While in Ottawa he expressed his views on the subject of Indians and their lands as follows:

> The Indians at Alkali Lake, as well as at Soda and Canoe Creeks, certainly would seem to have urgent claims for relief at the hands of the Dominion Government; and I cannot but think that that Government have not fully realized their responsibilities in respect of the Indians who are in their charge. It is manifestly wrong that the Indians, whose guardianship the Federal Government assumed at Confederation, should be left, in some instances, to starve, simply because the Provincial Government cannot afford to do that which never ought to have been expected, never asked for at their hands, that is, to purchase improved property at high prices, and give it to the Dominion Government for Indian pur-

25 "Annual Report of the Department of Indian Affairs," Canada, *Sessional Papers*, 5th Parl., 3d sess., 1885, no. 3, p. lv.

26 B.C., *Journals*, 4th Parl., 2d sess., 1884, p. 31.

> poses. The Indians are a heavy burden to the Province as it is. It would not be an exaggeration to say that the cost of administration of justice is doubled to the Province on Indian account, and yet as wards of the Dominion they contribute nothing to the Provincial Treasury. It is quite different however with the Federal Government in that regard. The Indians are large consumers of goods upon which heavy duties are paid to the Dominion; and if there were no other or better reason, the fact that the Indians contribute more to the Exchequer of the Dominion than is expended on their behalf, ought to be sufficient to induce the Dominion Government to make such expenditure in the interest of their Indian wards as the circumstances demand ... it is not fair to expect that [the Province] can take of its small and inadequate revenue and purchase improved farms for either the Indians or the Dominion Government.[27]

Rather than attempt to force the issue, Powell purchased for the Indians a tract of 1,464 acres from the estate of A. S. Bates. From this land the Indians obtained "a large supply of both hay and grain."[28]

The rumours which circulated as a result of the defeated motion of 1884, coupled with the fact that O'Reilly was incapacitated for some months in 1885 by a serious accident, gave rise to a much more alarming situation in the Kootenays. As early as 1883 A. S. Farwell, a special agent for the provincial government, had warned Victoria that for years the Kootenay Indians had been anxiously awaiting the arrival of the commissioner to define their reserves and so put a stop to the extensive encroachment of pre-emptors on lands the Indians conceived to be their own. He warned that because these Indians were constantly moving back and forth across the border and were consequently aware of the "vast extent" of the American Indian reservations, the commissioner would probably meet with more difficulty than he would anywhere else in the province. A week later, on January 7, 1884, a similar warning was received from G. M. Sproat, now a provincial land surveyor.[29]

The trouble came in the summer of 1887. It was of sufficient magnitude to prompt the British Columbia government to send seventy-five North West Mounted Police under Major Steele to

[27] Smithe to Vankoughnet, April 11, 1884, B.C., *Sessional Papers*, 4th Parl., 3d sess., 1885, p. 13.

[28] Powell to Smithe, December 9, 1884, ibid., p. xxi.

[29] A. S. Farwell, B.C., *Sessional Papers*, 4th Parl., 3d sess., 1884, pp. 325-27; G. M. Sproat, ibid., p. 323.

quell the disorder.[30] The A. E. B. Davie government was so alarmed that it set up a special commission consisting of F. G. Vernon, chief commissioner of lands and works, Judge O'Reilly, and Dr. Powell. When further lands were allotted to the Indians the alarm subsided.[31]

In many cases the Indians seemed perfectly satisfied with the manner in which O'Reilly had treated them, and he generally experienced no difficulty in having his allotments confirmed by the Executive Council.[32] But this was not because the local government was in any way relaxing its vigilance. Sir John A. Macdonald complained in 1886 that, to add to "the existing complications in connection with Indian management in this Province," the province was now refusing to allow Indian Agents acting in their capacity as magistrates, the use of courthouses, jails, and services of constables.[33] The provincial government had taken this action because the agents had refused to pay over to it fines imposed and collected from Indians for infractions of the Indian Act.

The matter of law enforcement among the Indians had been discussed at length by Smithe on his mission to Ottawa in 1884. On behalf of the British Church Missionary Society, Bishop Ridley had dismissed William Duncan of Metlakatla for his failure to teach

30 "Annual Report of the Department of Indian Affairs," Canada, *Sessional Papers*, 6th Parl., 2d sess., 1888, no. 15, p. x.

31 For report of the Special Commission, see ibid., pp. xci-xcvii.

32 Not even for the reserve of 8,552 acres, all of Hope Island in the Queen Charlottes, which he allotted September 17, 1886, and which the government confirmed May 18, 1889. (See: B.C., *Sessional Papers*, 9th Parl., 2d sess., 1901, pp. 589-601.) An exception was the Kootenays, where he encountered opposition first from the Indians and later from the government. On November 29, 1884, Smithe wrote to O'Reilly saying that "since you have assumed the work of laying out reserves, I am bound to say that a much fairer and more accurate appreciation of the duties and responsibilities of the office has been displayed," but he added that "in the Kootenay you have over-estimated the requirements of the Indians and under-estimated those of the whites" (B.C., *Sessional Papers*, 4th Parl., 3d sess., 1885, p. xvi, following p. 410). O'Reilly had set aside 38,630 acres on four reserves for 441 Indians, a per capita allotment of 87.6 acres (ibid., p. 410). In his reply to Smithe on December 10, 1884, O'Reilly justified the size of the reserves by saying that "I had the utmost difficulty in persuading the Kootenays to agree to the boundaries fixed on by me, and which they looked upon as meagre in the extreme, compared with the millions of acres set apart by the United States Government for American Indians, a few miles south of the line. Moreover, I think it important, for Provincial and International reasons, that Indians living on the frontier should have no reasonable ground of complaint, and in this view I feel sure you will concur" (ibid., p. xxi, following p. 410).

33 Canada, *Sessional Papers*, 5th Parl., 4th sess., 1886, no. 4, p. lvi.

orthodox Anglican rites to the Indians in 1881. Disturbances so threatening that the province found it necessary to swear in special constables to preserve order followed. Since the Indians were wards of the Dominion, Smithe maintained that the Dominion should never have allowed the disturbances, as he said:

> to continue to the extent of seriously jeopardizing the interests of the white community or of imposing upon the Provincial Authorities the necessity of incurring heavy expenditure for the administration of justice and the maintenance of law and order among a people who contribute nothing to the Provincial revenue. The Dominion Government have taken the management of Indians on the reserves into their own hands, and I submit that there must be something radically wrong when a number of refractory wards, openly and avowedly resisting Federal authority, are allowed to flaunt with bravado before other tribes their successful defiance of the Indian Office.[34]

Smithe then requested Ottawa to pay the salary of a stipendiary magistrate at Metlakatla. Macdonald agreed but said he would have to consider the matter of turning all Indian fines over to the local government.[35] On this point Smithe argued that "it is most desirable that a change should be made in the Act in order to remove the present unfair and anomalous condition of things under which fines are required to be paid to the Dominion, but when not paid by those who have violated the Act the expense of their conveyance to, and maintenance while in, gaol is required to be borne by the Province."[36]

Because the province had refused to sanction Sproat's allotments on the grounds of their improvidence,[37] O'Reilly had spent part of the summer of 1885 re-allotting reservations on Vancouver Island and on the southern mainland. During the year the first provincial statistics were tabled in the legislature showing what work the Joint Allotment Commissioners and the single reserve commissioners, first Sproat and then O'Reilly, had been doing. The return, tabled by Smithe as chief commissioner of lands and works on February 20,

34 Smithe to Macdonald, March 7, 1884, B.C., *Sessional Papers*, 4th Parl., 3d sess., 1885, p. 2.

35 Macdonald to Smithe, April 10, 1884, ibid., p. 10.

36 Smithe to Vankoughnet, April 11, 1884, ibid., pp. 13-14.

37 "Annual Report of the Department of Indian Affairs," Canada, *Sessional Papers*, 6th Parl., 1st sess., 1887, no. 6, p. lix.

1885, showed all lands set apart for the Indians subsequent to the list tabled on January 13, 1873.[38]

It was a most comprehensive tabulation, as it not only indicated the names of the tribes and the number of Indians for whom each reserve had been made, but also listed all the reserves to which the chief commissioner had refused his assent. In addition, it listed the location of the tribes, the date on which the reserve commissioner's decisions had been received, and the date on which the Executive Council had given its approval. It also indicated whether the reserve had been surveyed, anything unusual about the reserve, and the acreage. Nothing was overlooked which might have been of interest to the legislature, and it is certain that the list was subjected to the severest scrutiny, particularly from Smithe himself, as well as from the other members of his ministry — A. E. B. Davie, John Robson, and M. W. T. Drake. The return showed that by 1877 when the Joint Commissioners were released they had set aside 145 reserves for 5,158 Indians and had allotted 186,704.99 acres, a per capita grant of 36.19 acres.[39]

In allotting the reserves the commissioners had faced many complications such as the one in connection with the reserve of 33,600 acres at Osoyoos.[40] A settler's bad faith and a clerk's error combined to cause loss of lands to the Indians and much correspondence for the officials. In 1875, J. C. Haynes had applied to purchase 4,245 acres known to be used by the Indians but not at that time officially reserved to them. Owing to several delays, Haynes's final survey was not completed until 1877, immediately prior to the arrival of the Allotment Commissioners. The commissioners duly allotted most of the land in Townships 50 and 51 to the Indians, although it included the acreage Haynes wanted. In transcribing the commission's Minute of decision, however, a clerk carelessly entered Townships 5 and 6 as reserved, instead of 50 and 51. Meanwhile Haynes had gone ahead with his claim for a crown grant in Townships 50 and 51. When the surveyors' notes were checked and found correct, a notice was inserted in the *Gazette* and the newspapers, advising that anyone with prior claim to the land should submit the claim

38 See Appendix D, Item 1, for the 1873 list.

39 "Return ... of all lands set apart for Indians ... subsequent to the return ... on 13th January, 1873 ...," B.C., *Sessional Papers*, 4th Parl., 3d sess., 1885, pp. 392-95.

40 Ibid., p. 395.

in writing. Since none was presented, Walkem accepted Haynes's purchase money and issued him a crown grant.[41]

In drawing the whole matter to Smithe's attention on November 11, 1884, Powell quoted from a letter written by Sproat when he was reserve commissioner, to Walkem, then chief commissioner of lands and works, stating that "Mr. Haynes was perfectly aware that the land purchased by him had been reserved for the Indians" and implied that Haynes, aware of the clerk's blunder, had taken advantage of it.[42] Powell then asked for Smithe's serious and sympathetic consideration of the needs of the Indians at Osoyoos, particularly as the circumstances in the district were such that they could lead to a troubled situation if the obvious injustice was not rectified.

After outlining for Powell what appeared to him to be the facts of the case, Smithe concluded:

> Everything having been done in this office in strict accordance with the law, it would be quite impossible now to attempt to disposses Mr. Haynes of the land, to which he has got a Crown grant in perfectly regular manner. Whatever fault there is in connection with the affair seems to attach to the Indian Commissioners.[43]

Powell must have known the futility of argument, but he was not one to give in until all avenues of settlement had been explored. In this case he was not slow to point out to Smithe that "In attaching blame to the Indian Commission, it should be observed that one of its members was a paid officer of the Province, and the Local Government paid a moiety of the expense in maintaining the Commission, and, if a mistake was made, it was in a great measure due to its own agent."[44]

No further correspondence occurred on the subject, and as the return discloses no further allotments in the Osoyoos area, presumably the Indians had to manage with the 29,000 acres of bench lands remaining. Powell had to deal with this type of problem constantly, and that he could do so for eighteen years without once displaying any bitterness or animosity in his official correspondence is indeed a tribute to his patience and understanding.

41 Smithe to Powell, December 4, 1884, ibid., p. x, following p. 410.

42 Ibid., p. viii, following p. 410.

43 December 4, 1884, ibid., p. x, following p. 410.

44 December 10, 1884, ibid., p. xix, following p. 410.

Under the column headed "Date of Approval by C.C.L. & W." in the return on the work of the Joint Allotment Commission there is not a single entry. Sproat's reserves as sole commissioner fared equally badly.[45] None of his 257 reserves was approved. In addition, the thirty-one reserves of 81,500 acres he had alloted for 522 Indians in the Nicola Valley were noted as "Not accepted, April 10, '80." Apart from these reserves, he had allotted only 23,962.38 acres on 226 reserves to 3,044 Indians located on the Fraser River and along the northern coast of Vancouver Island.

With O'Reilly it was a different matter. His allotments of 216,-840.90 acres on 239 reserves to 8,634 Indians were all accepted by the government, including those 38,630 acres in the Kootenays to which Smithe had objected.[46] His per capita grant of 25.1 acres apparently did not alarm the government. Yet O'Reilly did not escape his share of condemnation. On several occasions Smithe accused him of an unwarranted assumption of authority, and he was once reprimanded for making reserves on his own.[47]

By 1885, then, 621 reserves had been allotted. Of these, only 239 had been approved by the local government and only 477 had been surveyed. The area allotted to the 17,358 Indians visited by commissioners was 427,608.27 acres, exclusive of the acreage not accepted in Victoria.

O'Reilly's most persistent difficulty was the demands made by the northern tribes for more land than their already extensive reserves contained. The Tsimshian tribe laid claim to all land, not only that contained in their reserves. As in the Kootenay trouble of the year before, rumours stemming from the motion put by Martin and Semlin and defeated in 1884 played their part. The Indians feared that they were to be herded back into the hills, charged for the wood they cut, and forbidden to fish.[48] When, in February, 1887, an Indian delegation waited upon the government

45 Ibid., pp. 396-402.

46 Ibid., pp. 402-12.

47 Smithe to Vankoughnet, April 11, 1884, ibid., pp. 12-14; Smithe to O'Reilly, December 3, 1884, ibid., pp. xvii-xviii, following p. 410.

48 There is no doubt that William Duncan of Metlakatla was behind a good deal of this agitation. (See Sir John A. Macdonald's letter to Senator Macdonald, pp. 239-40.) The provincial government established a Royal Commission to investigate the disturbances on October 28, 1884, with A. E. B. Davie, H. M. Ball, and A. C. Elliott as Commissioners. Their report is found ibid., pp. 131-36 and pp. i-lxxxii, and all the correspondence on the subject is found ibid., pp. 277-91 and pp. 317-21.

in Victoria, Smithe tried to allay their fears as best he could.[49] Still the trouble persisted. Finally a joint dominion-provincial commission was set up to investigate.

Clement F. Cornwall acted for the Dominion and J. B. Planta, stipendiary magistrate of Nanaimo for the province.[50] Having made a thorough investigation on the spot, the commission assured the Indians once again that no one would disturb them in possession of their land or customary rights and privileges. The commissioners discovered that William Duncan was the prime mover behind the disturbance. But the Indians, not to be put off so easily, persisted in stating that unless a treaty were made extinguishing their title in return for a lump sum payment or the privilege of selecting 160 acres of their own choice, they would go on talking about their title until a treaty was made.

In 1891, Edgar Dewdney, now superintendent general of Indian Affairs in Ottawa, reported that the aboriginal title agitation, "one time so strong . . . appears to have subsided." Dewdney chose his verb well. The Indians, he wrote, "had been falsely informed by unprincipled, and probably self-interested parties."[51] This information had been conveyed to him by A. W. Vowell, the new Indian superintendent in British Columbia who had been appointed in 1890 after Dr. Powell retired.[52] By 1894 the funds provided by the dominion government for surveying reserves were exhausted. With numerous allotments still to be defined, O'Reilly had to discharge the survey crews.[53]

There was still work for O'Reilly to do throughout the province even without surveys to oversee. Owing to the awakening of the Indians to the value of agricultural pursuits, their increasing herds of cattle, their growing reliance on irrigation, and the presence of so many Chinese labourers in fields formerly occupied by them,

49 "Report of Conferences . . . 3rd and 8th February, 1887," B.C., *Sessional Papers*, 5th Parl., 1st sess., 1887, pp. 253-72.

50 Their report appears in Canada, *Sessional Papers*, 6th Parl., 2d sess., 1888, no. 15, pp. xcviii-cvii. Their report and the papers connected with the commission may also be found in British Columbia, *Papers Relating to the Commission Appointed to Enquire into the Condition of the Indians of the North-West Coast* (Victoria: Richard Wolfenden, Government Printer, 1888).

51 "Annual Report of the Department of Indian Affairs," Canada, *Sessional Papers*, 7th Parl., 1st sess., 1891, no. 18, p. xxxi.

52 Vowell to Dewdney, November 5, 1890, ibid., p. 187.

53 O'Reilly to T. Mayne Daly, superintendent general, September 24, 1894, Canada, *Sessional Papers*, 7th Parl., 6th sess., 1896, no. 14, pp. 206-207.

interior and coast tribes were requesting additional land. Where good agricultural land was available, O'Reilly gave it to them. He tried always to do so in sections where ultimate conflict with white settlers might be avoided.

After Clifford Sifton took charge of Indian affairs in the Laurier government in 1897, the first dominion figures for twenty years on the work of the Reserve Commission appeared. For the nine Indian agencies by then established in British Columbia, Sifton tabled the following information:[54]

Agency	*Area of Reserve*	*Area Under Cultivation*
Cowichan	19,634 acres	2,496 acres
Kwawkewlth	17,052 acres	10.5 acres
West Coast	4,288 acres	4 acres
North-West Coast	149,347 acres	147.5 acres
Fraser	47,492 acres	3,705 acres
Kamloops-Okanagan	319,998 acres	2,552 acres
Kootenay	42,061 acres	350 acres
Williams Lake	74,065 acres	1,265 acres
Babine	44,631 acres	197 acres
Total	718,568 acres	10,727 acres

The total acreage was a vast increase on the 28,437 acres which the Indians had at Union. It had taken a quarter-century of struggle and misunderstanding to get so far but at last the Indians, by and large, appeared to be satisfied. The 10,727 acres under cultivation may have been only a small fraction of their lands, but a comparable percentage for land cultivated by white settlers contrasted with that under pre-emption would not have shown a higher figure. The wonder is not that the area cultivated was so small; rather it was that it had increased so much in twenty-five years. Their acceptance of the settler's ways, however, had very serious effects on their mortality rate. A steady decline in the total native population was noticed for years. Within twenty years the population had

[54] Compiled from "Annual Report of the Department of Indian Affairs," Canada, *Sessional Papers*, 8th Parl., 2d sess., 1897, no. 14, pp. 68-83.

been reduced to exactly half what it had been estimated at in 1871, 23,620.[55] If the white man's ways were civilized, his diseases and assorted vices proved anything but civilizing.

After eighteen years as Indian Reserve Commissioner, Judge O'Reilly retired on February 28, 1898. He was succeeded by Vowell, who now assumed this role in addition to that of Indian superintendent.[56] Until 1908 Vowell's activities were confined to re-defining present reserves and allotting small areas as fishing stations, hay meadows, and gardens.

In 1908 the work of the reserve commissioner was brought to an abrupt halt on orders from R. G. Tatlow, chief commissioner of lands and works in the McBride government. In a statement to Vowell, Tatlow said that "Owing to the unsatisfactory state of affairs between the Dominion and the Province in relation to the question of Indian Reserves, the Executive considers it inadvisable in the meantime to make further allotments, but will be prepared to consider any application by the Department for purchase, or deal with suitable exchanges."[57]

When Vowell received this message, the three strands of the Indian lands problem in British Columbia became inextricably tangled. Tatlow's statement brought into the open the legal battle being waged between the local and the federal governments over the question of reversionary interest in Indian lands. Since the provincial government had arrested all further allotments, a decision as to the reversionary interest had to be sought first. While the litigation was on, the Indians availed themselves of the confusion to push their aboriginal title claim. Doubtless they or their "rascally advisers" hoped that in the chaos they might possibly get someone in authority to listen to their claim. And indeed they might have had they asked for anything less than what they did — recognition of their beneficial interest in all the land in the province.

What the province sought was somewhat less ambitious but nonetheless of great importance. It was attempting to establish its

55 "Annual Report of the Department of Indian Affairs," Canada, *Sessional Papers*, 7th Parl., 1st sess., 1891, no. 18, p. xl.

56 Vowell to Sifton, November 5, 1898, Canada, *Sessional Papers*, 8th Parl., 4th sess., 1899, no. 14, pp. 248-49.

57 Quoted in Vowell to Frank Pedley, deputy superintendent-general of Indian Affairs, April 3, 1908, Canada, *Sessional Papers*, 11th Parl., 1st sess., 1909, no. 27, p. 273.

right of reversionary interest in reserve lands abandoned by the Indians.

In 1904 E. V. Bodwell of Victoria, on behalf of an unnamed client known to be the Grand Trunk Pacific Railway Company, had written to R. F. Green, chief commissioner of lands and works, to ask if the government would give consideration to selling him, on behalf of his client, 10,000 acres of reserved crown land on the side of Tuck Inlet opposite the Tshimshian Indian reserve. Bodwell pointed out that under section 32 of the Land Act, the government would retain one-quarter interest in this land if it were designated a townsite. If his client chose the other side of the Inlet, the side on which the Indian reserve was located, he reminded Green that his client would be dealing directly with the dominion government. In that case, he said, "no direct benefit will be obtained by the Province."[58] By Minute of Council of May 4, 1904, the provincial government accepted the offer, settling on one dollar an acre as the price.[59]

Requiring a portion of the Indian reserve also, Bodwell the following spring asked Green what price the government would set on its reversionary interest should his client be able to make suitable arrangements with the dominion government first.[60] In reply McBride reminded Bodwell that if his client considered acquiring a portion of the Tshimshian Indian reserve on Kaien Island for railway purposes, action could not be taken unless and until the Dominion removed the Indians from all parts of the reserve. He indicated his government's willingness to deal with the company upon a satisfactory termination of its dealings with the Department of Indian Affairs.[61]

On April 2, 1906, a dominion Minute in Council asked the province to waive its reversionary interest. The request was promptly refused.[62] The province based its refusal on the statement in the Order in Council of November 10, 1875, recommending the Allotment Commission, that "any land taken off a Reserve shall revert

[58] January 19, 1904, B.C., *Sessional Papers,* 10th Parl., 3d sess., 1906, p. F20.

[59] Ibid., pp. F13-14. For a copy of the Indenture, see p. F15.

[60] February 21, 1905, ibid., p. F19.

[61] McBride to Frank W. Morse, vice-president and general manager, Grand Trunk Pacific Railway, March 17, 1905, ibid.

[62] The two minutes are found in B.C., *Sessional Papers,* 11th Parl., 1st sess., 1907, pp. F33-34.

to the Province." British Columbia had acceded to this Order by Minute in Council of January 8, 1876. The two together had become known as the 1875-76 Agreement. The province took strong objection to the assumption by the Dominion of the right to surrender portions of the Tshimshian reserve, as it had done on September 21, 1906, by Order in Council, to facilitate construction of the terminus and wharf accommodation for the Grand Trunk Pacific, a railway project to which the Laurier government had lent both moral and financial support. A provincial Minute in Council of March 11, 1907, pointed out that the moment the Dominion assumed to surrender part of the Indian reserve, the property then became the Crown's in the right of British Columbia.[63] That was all there was to the matter so far as the province was concerned, but the Department of Indian Affairs asked an opinion of the Department of Justice.

Before it was obtained British Columbia proceeded under section 80 of its Land Act to alienate various portions of its reversionary interest in Indian reserves.[64] This alienation was possible by virtue of certain amendments to the Land Act, the first of which had been effected in 1899 in anticipation of just such a contingency as was arising at Kaien Island. To the provision which had empowered the government to reserve lands for conveyance to the Dominion in trust for the use and benefit of the Indians was added a sentence authorizing the government "in trust to re-convey the same to the Provincial Government in case such lands at any time cease to be used by such Indians."[65] This clause became section 80 of the Consolidated Land Act of 1908. In 1911 a further proviso was added to the effect that the Executive Council should always be at liberty

63 Attorney General F. J. Fulton to James Dunsmuir, lieutenant-governor, March 9, 1907, B.C., *Sessional Papers*, 11th Parl., 2d sess., 1908, p. D47.

64 In 1909 three people bought 161 acres at the rate of $2.50 per acre, for all of which crown grants were issued. One of these areas was Long Lake Reserve No. 5, containing 128 acres, sold to John Kennedy. A crown grant was reported to have been issued February 8, 1909 (B.C., *Sessional Papers*, 12th Parl., 1st sess., 1910, p. H49), but there is no trace of this grant in the *Gazette*. The commissioners who visited this area in 1915, known as Lot 3, 888 of Osoyoos district, were completely unaware of Kennedy's purchase or crown grant, and proceeded to deal with it as any other reserve. Fortunately for Kennedy, this was one of the reserves classified as of no further use to the Indians, and hence it could be sold by the province. In 1921, 5.48 acres of this reserve were sold for $458 ("Annual Report of the Department of Indian Affairs," Canada, *Sessional Papers*, 13th Parl., 5th sess., 1921, no. 27, p. 74).

65 B.C., *Statutes*, 1899, 62 Vict., c. 38, s. 72.

to dispose in any way of its interest, "reversionary or otherwise," in any Indian reserve or portion thereof. A return of all such transactions was to be submitted at the next sitting of the legislature within fifteen days of its opening.[66]

The presence of this legislation still further complicated the situation. The reversionary interest created by the 1875-76 Agreement had established a joint ownership which made it impossible for the Dominion to dispose of any agricultural or timber lands reserved for but not required by the Indians without the concurrence of the province. As a result, no excess Indian lands had ever been sold in British Columbia. Elsewhere throughout Canada excess lands were being sold annually.

The incident involving the Grand Trunk Pacific terminus created an impossible situation, particularly after the announcement by the Indian Department in 1908 that the policy in connection with the sale of agricultural and timber lands, where such lands were beyond the possible requirements of the Indians, would be relaxed. The department had always firmly opposed such sale so long as no particular harm or inconvenience arose from the Indians' holding of vacant lands beyond their requirements, and so long as no profitable disposition of the land was possible. But now, because of the large influx of settlers into the western provinces, the department felt some relaxation of its policy was in order. In addition, excess Indian lands would fetch a price sufficiently high to reduce materially the costs of administration of Indian affairs.[67] Under the Indian Act, however, the consent of the Indians themselves was necessary before any lands could be sold.

Concurrently with the development of the reversionary interest dispute there once again emerged in British Columbia the old problem of the size and extent of reserves. The first official intimation the Dominion received that the provincial government wanted reserves cut down came in 1901 when Premier James Dunsmuir presented the claim of his government for "Better Terms." A section of his memorandum asked that some step be taken to re-assess Indian holdings. Dunsmuir's suggestion was that many of the reserves in British Columbia should be cut down, since "very valuable agricultural lands are held by a very small number of In-

66 B.C., *Revised Statutes*, 1911, 2 Geo. 5, c. 129, s. 127.

67 "Annual Report of the Department of Indian Affairs," Canada, *Sessional Papers*, 11th Parl., 1st sess., 1909, no. 27, p. xxxv.

dians."[68] After the many years spent both in securing adequate reserves and in extending to British Columbia the benefits of an Indian policy prevailing east of the Rockies in regions where there had been a cession of the Indian title, the Department of Indian Affairs was chagrined.

No action was taken by the department in the next ten years to honour Dunsmuir's request. Following the presentation of a similar request by McBride in 1912, this time more strongly worded, action became imperative, since McBride's memorandum associated the two problems of reversionary interest and excessive acreage in the same message. McBride wrote as follows:

> The title of the Crown in the right of the Province to Indian reserve lands in British Columbia was never questioned until within the past few years.... We still maintain that the reversionary interest ... is the property of the Province, and that it is essential in the public interest that the attitude of the Province be maintained. It may be well, in this connection, to refer to the large excess acreage held on account of Indian reserves in British Columbia, and to the necessity, in view of the rapid increase in white population, of having an immediate readjustment of all reserves, so that the excess acreage may be released to the Province.[69]

And to add to these difficulties the third problem — aboriginal title — became a live issue. By 1912 the Indians, by no means inactive on their own behalf, had secured reinforcements through an organization formed in Victoria in March, 1910, called the Conference of Friends of the Indians of British Columbia. They had also obtained the support of a Toronto group called the Moral and Social Reform Council of Canada, and to advance their cause and consolidate their support they had secured Rev. A. E. O'Meara as a full-time legal advisor.[70]

King Edward VII had been interviewed by a deputation of Indians in 1906, a petition had been presented to His Majesty's Government in 1909, and a "Statement of Facts and Claims" had

68 Dunsmuir to Sifton, February 2, 1901, B.C., *Sessional Papers*, 9th Parl., 2d sess., 1901, p. 581.

69 British Columbia Mission (Sir Richard McBride, premier, W. J. Bowser, attorney general, W. R. Ross, minister of lands) to Prime Minister Borden, November 6, 1911, B.C., *Sessional Papers*, 12th Parl., 3d sess., 1912, p. N2.

70 Special Joint Committee, *Report and Evidence*, p. 53. Between 1886 and his ordination as priest of the Church of England in 1906, O'Meara practised law in Toronto.

been forwarded to the federal Department of Justice in January, 1910.[71] Meanwhile, the petition to England had been referred back to Canada. The Department of Justice recommended that judicial decision should be sought for the claims of the Indians. To facilitate a decision from the courts, the Dominion began negotiations with British Columbia. The dominion and Imperial governments, both sympathetic to the Indian claim, were perfectly willing that the case should go before the Judicial Committee of the Privy Council.[72] Since this procedure was precisely what the Indians wanted, they seemed well on their way to having their forty-year old claim adjudicated by a court which had hitherto, under similar circumstances, rendered decisions in favour of natives.

In May, 1910, the chief civil law officers of Canada and British Columbia met in Ottawa and drew up a list of ten questions for submission to the Supreme Court of Canada. The intention was that the questions should then be presented to the Privy Council. The first three dealt with the matter of Indian title, and the other seven were concerned with the size of reserves. The Indian claim was that many of the reserves were grossly inadequate for their needs. All the questions received the approval of the deputy attorney-general of Canada, counsel for the province of British Columbia, and of O'Meara for the Indian tribes.[73]

The questions were then submitted to Sir Richard McBride. His answer was a categorical no if the first three questions were to be included. So far as he was concerned and so long as he headed the government of the province, the Indians had no title to the public lands of British Columbia. The Laurier government was by now fully aware that should a case be contrived which could be taken to court, the province of British Columbia would be the defendant.[74]

[71] Ibid., pp. 133, 52, 53.

[72] Ibid., pp. 10-11.

[73] Ibid., p. 53.

[74] To a deputation on behalf of the Indians which waited on him on April 26, 1911, Sir Wilfrid Laurier had said, "The matter for us to immediately consider is whether we can bring the Government of British Columbia into Court with us. We think it is our duty to have the matter enquired into. The Government of British Columbia may be right or wrong in their assertion that the Indians have no claim whatever. Courts of Law are just for that purpose — where a man asserts a claim and it is denied by another. But we do not know if we can force a Government into Court. If we can find a way, I may say we shall surely do so . . . . The Indians will continue to believe they have a grievance until it has been settled by the Court that they have a claim, or that they have no claim" (ibid., p. 11).

Despite the refusal of British Columbia to consent to a stated case, Ottawa twice passed enabling legislation altering the Indian Act to permit the presentation of such a case to secure a judicial decision.[75]

At the general election in the autumn of 1911 the Laurier government was defeated. Immediately a more conciliatory attitude was adopted in Ottawa, and direct negotiation with British Columbia was resumed in an effort to settle all three of the troublesome questions concerning Indian lands. By Order in Council of May 24, 1912, Dr. J. A. J. McKenna of Winnipeg was appointed as special commissioner "to investigate claims put forth by and on behalf of the Indians of British Columbia, as to lands and rights, and all questions at issue between the dominion and provincial governments and the Indians in respect thereto, and to represent the government of Canada in negotiating with the government of British Columbia a settlement of such questions."[76]

The first problem investigated by Dr. McKenna was the aboriginal title claim. After making an exhaustive study, he presented a lengthy memorandum to McBride on July 29, 1912. It said, in part:

> I understand that you will not deviate from the position which you have so clearly taken and frequently defined, i.e., that the province's title to its lands is unburdened by any Indian title, and that your government will not be a party, directly or indirectly, to a reference to the Courts of the claim set up. You take it that the public interest, which must be regarded as paramount, would be injuriously affected by such reference in that it would throw doubt upon the validity of titles to land in the province. As stated at our conversations, I agree with you as to the seriousness of now raising the question, and, as far as the present negotiations go, it is dropped.[77]

In this way two politically compatible friends could accomplish to their mutual satisfaction in two months what had been dividing the two governments for years. McKenna, however, carefully avoided any reference to his own views on the validity of the Indians' claim.

With the aboriginal title claim removed from the realm of practical politics, McKenna tackled the problem of reversionary interest. His visits to the Indians throughout British Columbia and his studies

[75] Ibid., p. 12.

[76] Ibid., p. 8.

[77] Ibid., p. 9.

of the historical background of the difficulty led him to state in his report of October 26, 1912, that one of the greatest sources of dissatisfaction among the Indians was the provincial interest in their lands stemming from the 1875-76 Agreement. As the Indians learned more of the settler's laws they realized that the tenure to their lands in the right of the Dominion was considerably less secure in British Columbia than elsewhere in Canada. In contrasting the treatment they had received by the two governments since 1871, it was apparent to the Indians that British Columbia had displayed much less sympathy with their claims than had the Dominion. Consequently, the insecurity by which the Dominion held the reserve lands distressed them greatly.

British Columbia's position "was that the title of Indians to lands reserved for them was a mere right of use and occupancy; that under [article 13 of the Terms of Union] no beneficial interest in such lands was to be taken by the Dominion as guardian of the Indians; and that, whenever the Indian Right to any such lands ... became extinguished through surrender, or cessation of use or occupation, or diminishment of numbers, the land reverted, unburdened, to the province."[78] So far as the province was concerned reverted Indian lands were in exactly the same position as were Railway Belt lands once any portion of them had been alienated by the Dominion.

McKenna agreed with the Indians on reversionary interest, and he was quite unable to resolve the difficulty with British Columbia. His decision was that only a Royal Commission comprised of representatives from both governments could settle the two problems of reserve acreage and reversionary interest. To this proposal McBride was amenable and the McKenna-McBride Agreement, which laid down the terms of reference for the commission, was drawn up on September 24, 1912.[79] The location and extent of all reserves was to be settled by five commissioners. Where any reserve land was found to be in excess of actual requirements, the land was to be subdivided and sold at public auction by the province, with half the proceeds going to the Department of Indian Affairs. Should additional land be required, or new reserves, the province was to "take all such steps as are necessary to locally reserve the additional lands." Finally, when the reserves were definitely determined to the

[78] McKenna to Department of Indian Affairs, October 26, 1912, ibid.

[79] See Appendix D, Item 5, Part I.

satisfaction of the five commissioners, the lands were all to be conveyed by the province to the Dominion. The federal government was to have full power to deal with the lands in any manner, even to selling them. The only interest to be retained by the province was in the case of a reserve unoccupied because the tribe had become extinct. The land in such a case was to revert to the province.

Both governments accepted the terms of reference and on April 23, 1913, the letters patent were issued constituting the Royal Commission.[80] By Order in Council of March 31, 1913, N. W. White of Nova Scotia and Dr. James A. J. McKenna of Winnipeg were designated as the dominion appointees; J. P. Shaw, M.L.A. of Shuswap and D. H. Macdowall of Victoria were appointed for British Columbia. On April 12, E. L. Wetmore, former chief justice of Saskatchewan, was selected as the chairman.

As recorded in their final report, the commissioners at once considered how best to settle all outstanding differences between the two governments. After careful study of all the pertinent documents and correspondence, extended visits to reserves throughout the province, and numerous meetings with the Indians and public organizations, the commission presented a massive report in four volumes to both governments on June 30, 1916. During the three years of their work the commissioners submitted ninety-eight interim reports and five progress reports. Their final full report reviewed the whole question of reserves in detail. Certain specific recommendations, preceded by a statistical analysis, were made regarding each of the 1,103 reserves found in the province.[81] In some cases the existing reserves were confirmed as previously allotted; in other, reserves were reduced either because the land was not all needed or because it was worthless; in still others, reserves were disposed of as being no longer required for Indian use and occupancy.

80 [Canada], [Royal Commission on Indian Affairs], *Report of the Royal Commission on Indian Affairs for the Province of British Columbia*, 4 vols. (Victoria: Acme Press, 1916), I:8.

81 No one authority seems to know exactly how many reserves there were in the province. The Geographic Board of Canada stated in 1913 that there were 934; of these, the largest was one of 44,175 acres in the Port Simpson reserve, and the smallest one of .15 acres on the Squamish River. The Geographic Board's *Handbook* required twenty-five pages to list the reserves in British Columbia, but only nine to list those throughout the rest of the Dominion. The total number in the rest of the provinces in 1913 was: Nova Scotia, 35; Prince Edward Island, 2; Ontario, 156; Manitoba, 54; New Brunswick, 24; Quebec, 20; Saskatchewan, 80. Canada, Geographic Board, *Handbook of Indians of Canada* (Ottawa: C. H. Parmelee, 1913), pp. 515-49.

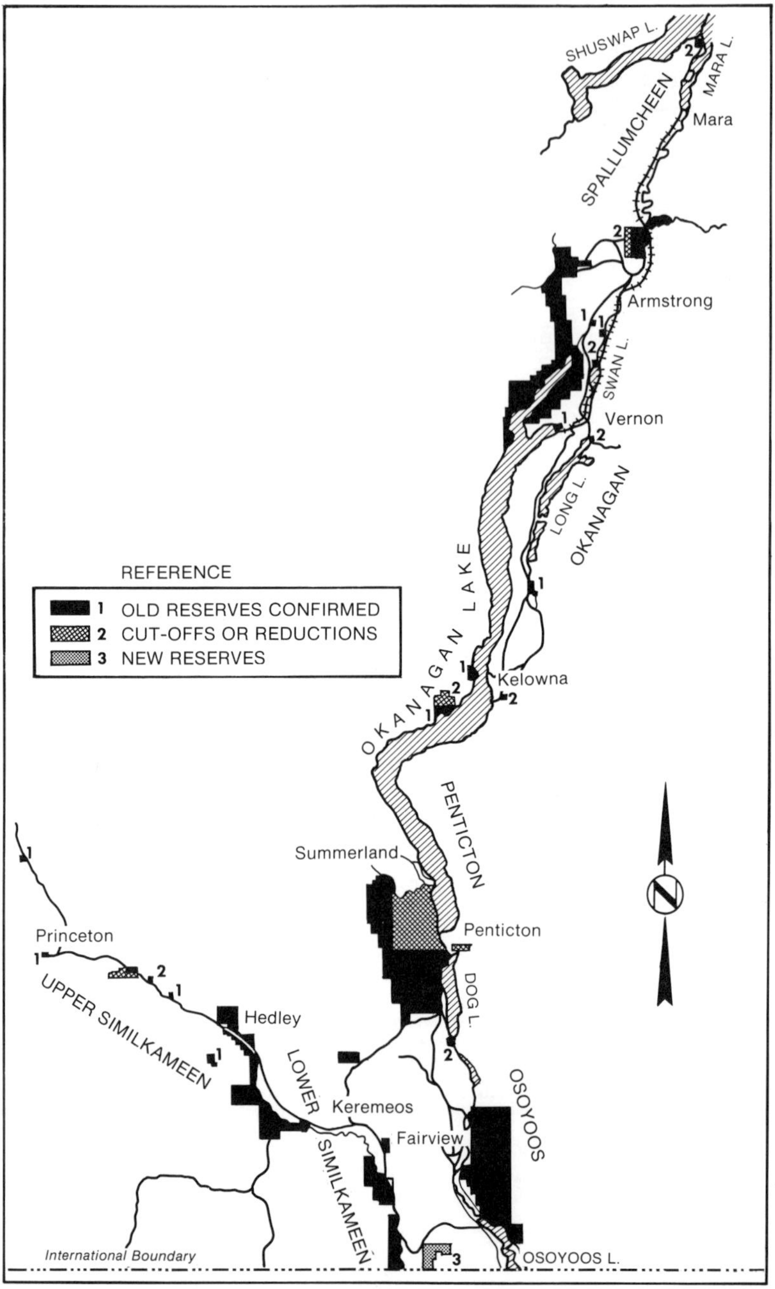

Indian Reserves in the Okanagan Agency, 1916

In 1919 British Columbia passed the enabling legislation necessary for the adoption of the report, and in 1920 the Dominion also cleared the way for acceptance.[82] Acting on the authority provided by this legislation, the *Report of the Royal Commission on Indian Affairs for the Province of British Columbia*, as revised and amended since 1916, was adopted by British Columbia in August, 1923, and by the Dominion the following July.[83]

The joint ratification settled two of the problems which had been bedevilling Indian affairs in the province since 1871; namely, size, location, and nature of the reserves, and the reversionary interest in them. The 1,103 reserves found already in existence by the commissioners were increased by 456, bringing the total to 1,559. The acreage was increased from 666,640.25 to 773,642.83. The work of the commissioners gave each Indian on the average an increase of 3.58 acres, calculating from the Indian population of 21,489 as determined by the commission.[84]

Interim Report No. 91 of February 1, 1916, dealt with lands reserved for the Indians in the Peace River district. The Slaves and Sicanees of the Fort Nelson area had signed an adhesion to Treaty No. 8 with the dominion government on August 15, 1910.[85] This action removed 104,400 square miles of territory east of the Rockies from the jurisdiction of the British Columbia government.[86] The treaty allotted one square mile of land to each Indian. The commissioners did not visit the area, but they did stipulate that if the 75,147 acres in the five existing reserves were found after a dominion census to be less than the square mile per head, the province was to make good the deficiency.[87]

So far as the two governments were concerned, all three problems were now settled, one as a preliminary to the McKenna-McBride Agreement of 1912 and two by the 1916 Report. Laying the ghost

82 The Indian Affairs Settlement Act, B.C., *Statutes*, 1919, 10 Geo. 5, c. 32, and The British Columbia Indian Lands Settlement Act, Canada, *Statutes*, 1920, 11 Geo. 5, c. 51.

83 Special Joint Committee, *Report and Evidence*, pp. xix-xx.

84 See Appendix B, Table 10, "Summary of Data, 1916 Royal Commission on Indian Affairs."

85 "Annual Report of the Department of Indian Affairs," Canada, *Sessional Papers*, 14th Parl., 2d sess., 1923, no. 14, pp. 13-14. The Crees, Beavers, and Chipewayans of what is now northern Alberta signed Treaty No. 8 on June 21, 1899.

86 Special Joint Committee, *Report and Evidence*, p. 3.

87 *Royal Commission on Indian Affairs*, 1:126-28.

of reversionary interest was a source of much satisfaction to the two governments, but it delighted the Indians even more. They now could feel secure on their lands, a security never before possible. The Indian Act had always permitted disposal of reserve land for purposes of public necessity in exactly the same manner as that in which the Land Act authorized the taking of any other land, crown-granted or otherwise. As portions of their lands had increased in value commensurate with the progress of the province, the Indians were relieved to have their land, some of which was in highly desirable locations for provincial government purposes, transferred irrevocably to the Dominion.

Now that agreement had been reached between Ottawa and Victoria on all three issues, it is interesting to compare the areas of Indian reserves in the various provinces, as well as to note the number of acres per head, the value of the Indian lands, and the number of acres under cultivation in each province.

Indians and Indian Lands in Canada, 1924[88]

Province	*Indian Population*	*Total area of Reserves*	*Per capita area*	*Under cultivation*	*Value of lands in reserves*
		Acres	*Acres*	*Acres*	
Alberta	8,990	1,307,343	145.4	58,543	$17,368,117
B.C.	24,316	733,891	30.2	29,154	13,507,881
Manitoba	11,673	415,477	35.6	13,018	2,934,862
N.B.	1,606	34,507	21.5	377	71,008
N.W.T.	4,543	No information supplied			
N.S.	1,827	21,504	11.8	1,333	102,409
Ontario	26,706	1,045,037	39.1	63,959	4,946,005
P.E.I.	315	1,527	4.8	397	20,000
Quebec	13,191	175,220	13.3	9,751	1,429,020
Sask.	10,271	1,195,674	115.9	42,540	14,344,490
Yukon	1,456	No information supplied			
Totals	104,894	4,930,180		219,072	$54,723,792

88 Compiled from "Annual Report of the Department of Indian Affairs," Canada, *Sessional Papers*, 14th Parl., 4th sess., 1925, no. 14, pp. 60-69.

With the second largest population, British Columbia Indians in 1924 had the fourth highest total acreage and per capita allotment in Canada. The Indians, however, were anything but pacified by the Royal Commission's Report of 1916. At no time did they accept it as a final award and settlement. The agitation which had been present among them since before Union now broke forth in a veritable deluge of petitions, statements, and memoranda directed at the local, federal, and Imperial governments, and guided throughout by O'Meara. He served for sixteen years to keep alive the protest from the Indians and in this respect was simply carrying on the work begun by William Duncan after his replacement by the Church Missionary Society in 1881. Some harsh words had been said about Duncan; more were said about O'Meara. As the following letter from Sir John A. Macdonald to Senator Macdonald of Toronto indicates, there is little doubt that it was really Duncan, whose village had once been the model native colony on the continent, who was behind the agitation of the earlier era.

> As I learn from the enclosed letter from Mr. Duncan, that you take an interest in his course, I send you some papers concerning it, which please read and return. From my personal communications with Mr. Duncan, I have satisfied myself that he is an ambitious man, brooking no control, and refusing to obey the laws of the land. I believe that when first sent to Metlakahtla he did a great deal of good among the Indians, but afterwards he had become so accustomed to unrestrained power that he lost his head altogether.
>
> Some years ago I happened to be in England before Mr. Duncan left for Alaska, and I did what I could to bring him and the Church Missionary Society together. I must say that that body showed every desire to act cordially with him. I went so far, being their Superintendent-General of Indian Affairs, as to offer him the appointment of Indian Agent at Metlakahtla district if he would carry into effect as an Agent must do, the statutes relating to Indians and Indian reserves. This offer he declined, and did everything he could on his return to the district to prevent the carrying of the law into effect. Of this the British Columbia government complained again and again, and his conduct in disturbing the minds of the Indians caused so much trouble that the Provincial Government was obliged to appoint a stipendiary magistrate for the purpose of seeing the law obeyed — the Dominion Government paying the salary of that functionary. I am convinced that if he had not left the country we should have had armed resistance from some of the Indians of the

> Metlakahtla district. I send you these papers for your information only.[89]

Since the turn of the century, the Nishga tribe from Duncan's district have spear-headed the drive to have the Indian claims adjudicated first by the Judicial Committee and now by the Supreme Court of Canada. It was they who laid the claim before the Imperial government in March 1909 and placed a "Statement of Facts and Claims" in the hands of the Justice Department; in January, 1910 a memorial was presented to Laurier, and delegations waited on all three governments. In each case their plea was for a ruling on their aboriginal title claim by the Privy Council.[90] Nor did the activity abate during the period 1913-1916 while the Royal Commission was active. Indeed, it increased, since the McKenna-McBride Agreement had set aside the whole matter of aboriginal title. The deputy minister of justice, in answer to the request for an interpretation of "final adjustment of all matters relating to Indian Affairs in the Province of British Columbia" as contained in the McKenna-McBride Agreement, had given as his official opinion that the words meant precisely what they said and would therefore "exclude claims by either government for better or additional terms."[91] The Indians were spurred on to greater efforts.

Wishing to clear the way for a settlement, the Dominion passed an Order in Council in 1914 advising that "the [Indian] claim be referred to the Exchequer Court of Canada with the right of appeal to the Privy Council" guaranteed, providing that the Indians "shall, by their Chiefs or representatives, in a binding way, agree, if the Court, or on appeal, the Privy Council, decides that they have a title to lands of the Province, to surrender such title," receiving in return "benefits . . . in accordance with past usage of the Crown."[92] O'Meara refused to agree to the surrender asked for in the 1914 Order in Council.[93]

89 Sir John Pope, ed., *Correspondence of Sir John Macdonald: Selections from the Correspondence of the Right Honourable Sir John Alexander Macdonald, G.C.B., First Prime Minister of the Dominion of Canada* (Toronto: Oxford University Press, 1921), p. 459.

90 Special Joint Committee, *Report and Evidence*, pp. 52-54, 58-60.

91 Ibid., p. 10.

92 Ibid., p. 55.

93 When he learned of the Indians' refusal and received yet another letter from O'Meara on October 26, 1914, stating the desire of the Indians to bypass

In November, 1919, in response to a request from the provincial government, the Indians presented still another in a long list of statements to the local government. Included in the statement were their reasons for refusing to accept the findings of the 1916 Commission and a list of twenty "Conditions proposed as a basis of Settlement."[94] For the next three years, conferences were held between the executive of the Allied Tribes, an Indian organization formed to press their claims, and both governments, including a meeting with the Superintendent General of Indian Affairs, Charles Stewart, and a meeting with D. C. Scott who had come to British Columbia to confer on Indian problems. No agreement was reached.[95]

When the estimates for the Indian Department came up in the House of Commons in 1925, Arthur Meighen wanted to know what the "present position of this long standing controversy over the title to Indian lands" was. If the Indians wanted to present their case to the Privy Council, he could see no reason why that step should not be permitted.[96] Stewart, as minister of the interior and therefore the responsible official, rose to explain that although the McKenna-McBride agreement had been carried out, it had in no way satisfied the Indians, "but inasmuch as the provincial government were threatening to cancel the arrangement altogether if we did not take action," that agreement and the ensuing report had had to be ratified.

No better summation of the utter frustration of the dominion government is available than Stewart's remarks. With rare candour for a minister of the Crown, he admitted that he had no idea where to turn next.

> Regarding the controversy over the aboriginal title, I have been trying for the past three years to find out just what the Indians

---

Canadian courts and go directly to the Privy Council, C. J. Doherty, minister of justice, included the following sentence in his reply, "If, therefore, it be possible for me to make any statement here which can consistently with the amenities of official correspondence, impress you with the futility of urging upon this government a reference direct to the Judicial Committee, I beg you to consider that statement incorporated in this letter" (ibid., p. ix).

94 See Appendix D, Item 7, for these two statements. The Special Joint Committee report discussed each in turn (ibid., pp. xi-xvii).

95 Ibid., p. 14 and pp. 65-71. See also: Forrest E. LaViolette, *The Struggle for Survival* (Toronto: University of Toronto Press, 1961), pp. 136-37, and George Edgar Shankel, "The Development of Indian Policy in British Columbia" (Ph.D. Diss., University of Washington, 1945), p. 152 ff.

96 Canada, House of Commons, *Debates*, 14th Parl., 4th sess., 1925, p. 4993.

mean by this. Do they lay claim to all lands in British Columbia in view of the fact that in ninety per cent of the cases no treaty had been signed between the tribes and representatives of the crown? After a great deal of discussion I found that they did not lay claim to the land in its entirety, but they do say that before an adjustment can take place they should have certain specified and unspecified provisions made for them by the government of Canada. This is all so vague and difficult of understanding that it is very hard to arrive at any concrete definition of what their claims are. On behalf of the government I have informed them that we are prepared to do for them everything that was done for treaty Indians in any other part of Canada. As a matter of fact we are giving them the same consideration as we have given every other Indian in Canada. Still that does not seem to be enough; certain claims are made for compensation and so on. A gentleman whose name is no doubt known to most hon. members, Mr. O'Meara, spends his whole time investigating this very vexed question and preparing briefs for consideration. My hon. friend says, why not send it to the Privy Council?

Mr. Meighen: Why do you not let them take it?

Mr. Stewart: They want the government of Canada to pay their expenses.

Mr. Meighen: Oh, I see.

Mr. Stewart: I must confess that I do not see very much hope. I have joined with me in the investigation the Speaker of the Senate and the Minister of Public Works (Mr. King, Kootenay) in an endeavor to see whether or not we can get on common ground. We have asked the Indians to prepare a brief and they have done so. Their representatives were here some months ago and the deputy superintendent general is now getting ready a brief in reply to theirs. But one of the difficulties we have to meet is the vagueness of their demands. I defy anyone to get them down to a concrete basis, as, for example, so much for education, so much for relief and so forth. That is one great difficulty and it looks hopeless to me. I believe the Privy Council would only come to one decision. They are quite likely to follow precedent and to say to the Indians, "You are entitled to the same consideration as has been given other tribes throughout Canada." That the government is prepared to give them, and for the life of me I do not know what to recommend. It seems to be an unending difficulty, and I do not see that the government would be warranted in paying expenses of representatives of the Indians to go over and argue the case before the Privy Council unless we have something very concrete presented to us.[97]

A Special Joint Committee of the House and the Senate with Hewitt Bostock, speaker of the Senate, as chairman, was convened

[97] Ibid., p. 4994.

on March 22, 1927, "to enquire into the claims of the Allied Indian Tribes of British Columbia." The committee soon discovered that the Indians themselves were not in agreement as to the nature of their claims. The spokesmen of the interior tribes made no claim to any land based on aboriginal title, yet the representatives of the Allied Tribes of the coast rested their whole case upon such a title.[98] Through it they claimed beneficial interest to 251,000 square miles of the province, or all but the 358 square miles ceded to Douglas in the 1850's, and the 104,000 square miles included in Treaty No. 8.

In presenting its report, the Joint Committee took occasion to deplore the "mischievous" agitation "often carried on by designing white men," by which the Indians "are deceived and led to expect benefits from claims more or less fictitious."[99] After dealing with every claim, the committee arrived at the conclusion that the Indians in British Columbia were receiving benefits in excess of those granted to "treaty" Indians elsewhere in Canada. The members were of the unanimous opinion that "the petitioners have not established any claim to the lands of British Columbia based on aboriginal or other title" and that "it is the further opinion of your Committee that the matter should now be regarded as finally closed."[100]

Thus ended for nearly 50 years what Trutch in 1872 had had the prescience to label "the most delicate and presently momentous responsibility of the Dominion Government within the Province."[101] The bitterness engendered between the two governments in the 1870's over implementing article 11 of the Terms of Union had established in British Columbia a pattern of thinking towards article 13 that was never changed. Personal animosities played their part, as did political expediency and individual duplicity. But through the sixty years of debate over article 13 surveyed here, the Indians of the province, left to themselves, conducted themselves with restraint and patience while awaiting a settlement of what they considered to be their legitimate grievances. That settlement has yet to come.

98 It is perhaps significant that O'Meara was counsel for the Allied Tribes but that the interior tribes declined his assistance.

99 Special Joint Committee, *Report and Evidence,* p. viii.

100 Ibid., p. x.

101 See Appendix D. Item 4, last paragraph. The aboriginal title controversy is not yet closed. For later developments see Douglas Sanders, "The Nishga Case," *B.C. Studies,* 19 (Autumn 1973), 3-20.

Conclusion

The least spectacular phase of the development of British Columbia from 1871 to 1913, but clearly the most significant, was the evolution of a land policy. Size alone presented numerous problems in legislating for the disposal of public lands, but the rough and mountainous terrain, the presence of minerals, and the existence of vast timber stands complicated the problems enormously. More recently, water resources as a source of hydroelectric power have compounded the difficulties in assuring miners' water rights.

When British Columbia entered Confederation in 1871, the basis of land legislation had already been laid. Ordinances and proclamations issued from 1858 until 1864 by Governor Douglas had been revised and amended several times by 1871. The Gold Mining Act of 1869 regulated the activities of free miners and the operation of their claim. The Land Ordinance of 1870 made provision for preemptions, sale of land, both surveyed and unsurveyed, leases for various purposes, and water rights, but there was no legislation covering timber. With those two acts as the foundation, provincial governments added to them, altered, and discarded as the occasion required, and by 1913, separate acts dealt with land itself, minerals, timber, surveys, railways, and water.

Under various sections of the acts, British Columbia had alienated approximately 31,000,000 acres of crown land by 1913. This figure seems insignificant, but for the paucity of arable or potentially arable land. The acreage alienated was disposed of for the following purposes:

Mineral and coal lands	500,000 acres
Indian reserves	666,240 acres
Agricultural lands	2,500,000 acres
Timber lands	8,500,000 acres
Railway lands	18,694,334 acres
Total	30,860,574 acres

There were three constant factors in framing legislation for disposing of the land; the wish to encourage settlement, the desire to prevent speculation in public lands, and the acute need to provide an adequate revenue with which to administer such a large territory. Soon after assuming office as governor of British Columbia, Douglas was advised by the Colonial Office to make land readily available, even to aliens who indicated their desire to become British subjects. At the same time as he was instructing Douglas to encourage settlement, the Colonial Secretary, Sir Edward Bulwer Lytton, spoke strongly of the need to take immediate steps that would prevent speculation in public lands. Finally, Douglas was warned repeatedly that he must so frame his land legislation as to secure to the colony a revenue adequate to provide all the public services that would be demanded in so large and so new a territory.

The encouragement of settlers, the prevention of speculation, and the securing of a revenue were provided for in every land act after 1871. But there was nothing unique about this. What was unusual, however, was the opportunity to apply these principles in an uncharted wilderness, inhabited only by scattered bands of Indians. For that reason, Lytton directed Douglas to embody in his proclamations the further lesser principles of reserving to the Crown certain rights, of providing for the sale of land only by auction, of requiring prompt cash payment for the land, of surveying all land before sale, and of assuring beneficial use of the land before alienating it for any purpose.

Lytton was giving him the benefit of the long experience the Colonial Office had had with the disposal of crown lands in other territories. Realizing the value of the advice and having neither American nor Canadian example before him, Douglas at once implemented the five policies in his land proclamations. By 1871 the policy of beneficial use had been so thoroughly implanted in land legislation that it was never thereafter abandoned. Settlers who pre-empted land were required to "prove up" within a specified time; leaseholders, whether of timber, hay, mineral, or coal lands were required to use the land for the purposes stated in the lease; purchasers were under the obligation of improving the land before they could buy any more.

However praiseworthy the legislation, it was only as effective as the supervision required to ensure compliance with the law. To limit the amount of land that could be bought to 640 acres until improvements had been made to the original value of the land, as was done in 1891, was good theory. In practice, however, the law, like so many others, became a dead letter. To require pre-emptors under the law to "prove up" within two years, as was done in 1875, was admirably fitted to speed the development of the province, but until inspection was provided, it too was unenforceable.

Douglas also had to abandon the practices of sale by auction, prompt cash payments, and survey of the land before alienation. Neither Douglas nor provincial governments could afford to follow the theory. Settlers early discovered that by waiting until after the land auction they could acquire the land at the upset price rather than at an advanced price. And if Douglas wished to retain within the colonies any of the miners who were coming down from the Cariboo after 1860, he had to forego the requirement that they pay cash for their land. So far as surveying the land before alienation was concerned, Douglas reluctantly had to admit to the Colonial Office that the expense was too heavy. Fully aware of what was at stake, Douglas asked the home government repeatedly for loans with which to cover expenses involved in surveying and providing communication services, only to be curtly informed that Vancouver Island and British Columbia, like any other colonies, had to be financially independent. The result was the end of planned settlement throughout the two colonies, the easing of restrictions to the point where agricultural lands were alienated wholesale, and the granting of natural resources to anyone willing to pay the modest price. Had the British government seen fit to underwrite the paltry sums Douglas required, the history of land disposal in British Columbia might well have been very different.

In view of the constant deficits experienced by every provincial government down to 1905, British Columbians may be justly thankful that more public lands and natural resources were not permanently alienated than was the case by 1913. Land, being the most readily available asset, was disposed of in large tracts on easy terms to all comers for over thirty years. The majestic timber stands on Vancouver Island and the coast of the mainland were alienated with similar abandon. The only reason the Crown in British Columbia retained all but the approximately 1,000,000 acres which had been bought outright of the provincial timber lands was that until 1900 standing timber was looked upon with a jaundiced rather than a glinting eye. It was a nuisance, a brake on settlement, and a hindrance to communication. After 1905, when the timber stands of the province were thrown open to licensees, the rush from all over the continent was so great that the McBride government took stock of the situation and decided to place all unalienated timber lands under government reserve where they have remained ever since.

Another early result of the financial stringency prevailing in colonial days was that Governor Douglas had to abandon his plan of buying out the Indian title to all the lands of the colonies. His policy then was to set aside for Indian reserves any lands used by the Indians or requested by them. In 1876 when the Joint Allotment Commission took to the field to establish reserves throughout the province, the railway difficulties had so embittered dominion-provincial relations that the province placed every conceivable obstacle in the path of a quick, equitable, and final settlement of Indian reserves. The result has been that the original problem of the size of reserves was further confused by the addition of what came to be known as the province's reversionary interest and the Indians' claim of aboriginal title.

Thirdly, lack of money for surveying has meant that British Columbia achieved the dubious distinction of being the only Canadian province in which land was alienated prior to survey. Throughout the province there were for years innumerable plots of legally acquired land the location of which was not definitely known on the maps in the Lands Office in Victoria. This embarrassing situation arose because private surveyors were hired to do much of the surveying that was done before 1900. Many of these surveys were hastily and inadequately done, and while frequently the discovery of incorrect surveys is more frustrating and annoying than significant, expensive litigation has sometimes followed. In addition, the government's failure to survey led to a wide scattering of settlement with settlers receiving no direction as to where their efforts at farming would be most likely to succeed. With provincial reserves placed on so much land held for subsidizing railroads after 1883 and with no information as to where best to locate, settlers took up marginal lands that should not have been pre-empted and where the provision of transportation services became an added burden on the province.

By 1900 settlers were scattered throughout the province with no regard for either probable success or communication facilities. Their isolation made expenditures for public works even more expensive than would normally have been the case. Beginning with Premier Dunsmuir in 1901 and continuing to the present, governments in

British Columbia have repeatedly appealed to the federal government for special financial consideration. The basis of the argument for "Better Terms" has been that provision for public services, particularly transportation services, is more expensive on a per capita basis than elsewhere in Canada. The history of provincial settlement would indicate, however, that the expense has been materially increased as a result of indiscriminate settlement permitted by former provincial governments.

To provide the transportation facilities demanded by miners and settlers, the Smithe ministry began the practice in 1883 of subsidizing railway companies with large blocks of crown lands. The reservation of so much land at one time for railway purposes seriously hampered settlement, but by the 1890's provision of railway facilities at any cost was considered of more importance than securing suitable lands to settlers. Protests against locking up this land under government reserve came in from various sections of the province, but in vain. With the example of the Railway Belt before them, as well as the American example of granting millions of acres of public lands for railway purposes, the government accorded railway promoters preferential treatment. When the heyday of land subsidies to railways had passed, over 4,000,000 acres of subsidy lands were repurchased at forty cents an acre by the McBride government in 1912, and the unalienated portions of the Railway Belt lands were returned to the province in 1930. Neither event, however, alters the fact by 1913, a total of 22,759,410 acres of provincial lands had been granted to provide railways.

British Columbia was following the American example, as adopted by eastern Canada, by subsidizing railways with large acreages of crown lands. British Columbia also adopted the American practice of granting pre-emptions. There, the pre-emption system, had been found to work well as a method of peopling the west. It proved to be satisfactory on the Canadian prairies as well, but in British Columbia, with the exception of the years 1875 to 1879, land was never free. While homesteads were still available on the prairies, settlers coming to British Columbia discovered that they must either buy the land or pay for it on the installment plan by pre-empting.

Framing legislation for such diverse activities as farming and ranching, mining and lumbering, as well as for the construction of railways and the allotting of Indian reserves was a monumental task fraught with innumerable obstacles and hazards. That the province could by 1913 boast of the best mining laws on the continent, timber legislation as enlightened as any to be found in the world, and the most advanced water legislation is a credit to the many pioneer legislators who had a part in the work. More especially is this the case when it is appreciated that to the immensity of the original task was added the further complication of the presence of a forty-mile strip of land through the heart of the province granted to the dominion government in 1871 in return for rail connections with eastern Canada. Had either the province or the Dominion had any intimation of the frustrations that lay in the future regarding mineral rights, water rights, foreshore rights, pre-emption claims and other jurisdictional conflicts, both governments would have hesitated a long time before sanctioning article 11 of the Terms of Union. Sorting out rights took sixty years during which appeals were made constantly to the Privy Council. An attitude of dislike and mistrust arose in British Columbia toward the dominion government that is even yet not entirely dispelled.

Appendix A

Land Ordinance, 1870

An Ordinance to amend and consolidate the Laws affecting Crown Lands in British Columbia.

[*June 1st*, 1870.]

WHEREAS it is expedient to amend and consolidate the Laws affecting Crown Lands in British Columbia;

Be it enacted by the Governor of British Columbia, with the advice and consent of the Legislative Council thereof, as follows:

I. In the construction and for the purposes of the Ordinance (if not inconsistent with the context or subject matter), the following terms shall have the respective meanings hereinafter assigned to them: "The Governor" shall mean the Governor of British Columbia, or any person for the time being lawfully exercising the authority of a Governor of British Columbia;

"Chief Commissioner of Lands and Works and Surveyor General" shall mean and include the Chief Commissioner of Lands and Works and Surveyor General and any person for the time being lawfully acting in that capacity.

"Commissioner" shall mean the Chief Commissioner of Lands and Works and Surveyor General of this Colony, or the person acting as such for the time being, and shall include every Stipendiary Magistrate for the time being in charge of any District, and every person duly authorized by the Governor to act as and for the Chief Commissioner of Lands and Works and Surveyor General, as Assistant Commissioner of Lands and Works in any District in which the Land that may be referred to lies, other than that in which the Chief Office of the Lands and Works Department is situated, and any other District or Districts for which no such Assistant Commissioner of Lands and Works as aforesaid has been appointed.

"Supreme Court" shall mean the Supreme Court of British Columbia;

"The Crown" shall mean Her Majesty, Her Heirs and Successors;

"Crown Lands" shall mean all Lands of this Colony held by the Crown in fee simple;

"Act" shall mean any Proclamation or Ordinance having the force of Law in this Colony;

Words importing the singular number shall include more persons, parties, or things than one, and the converse.

II. The following Acts, Ordinances, and Proclamations relating to the disposal and regulation of the Crown Lands of the Colony are hereby repealed:—

An Act dated February 14th, 1859;
An Act dated January 4th, 1860;
An Act dated January 20th, 1860;
The "Pre-emption Amendment Act, 1861;"
The "Country Land Act, 1861;"
The "Pre-emption Purchase Act, 1861;"
The "Pre-emption Consolidation Act, 1861;"
The "Mining District Act, 1863;"
The "Land Ordinance, 1865;"
The "Pre-emption Ordinance, 1866;"
The "Pre-emption Payment Ordinance, 1869;" and
The "Vancouver Island Land Proclamation, 1862;"

but such repeal shall not prejudice or affect any rights acquired, or payments due, or forfeitures or penalties incurred prior to the passing of this Ordinance in respect of any Land in this Colony.

PRE-EMPTION

III. From and after the date of the proclamation in this Colony of Her Majesty's assent to this Ordinance, any Male person being a British Subject, of the age of eighteen years or over, may acquire the right to pre-empt any tract of unoccupied, unsurveyed, and unreserved Crown Lands (not being an Indian Settlement) not exceeding Three Hundred and Twenty Acres in extent in that portion of the Colony situated to the Northward and Eastward of the Cascade or Coast Range of Mountains, and One Hundred and Sixty Acres in extent in the rest of the Colony. Provided that such right of pre-emption shall not be held to extend to any of the Aborigines of this Continent, except to such as shall have obtained the Governor's special permission in writing to that effect.

IV. Any Chartered or Incorporated Company may acquire such right by obtaining a special permission in writing from the Governor to that effect, but not otherwise; and the Governor may grant or refuse such permission at his discretion.

V. Any person desiring to Pre-empt as aforesaid, shall first apply to and obtain from the Commissioner permission in writing to enter upon such Land, which must be fully described in writing by the applicant, and a plan thereof must be deposited with the Commissioner, and such description and plan shall be in duplication.

VI. After such permission has been obtained, and within such time, not exceeding thirty days thereafter, as shall be specified by the Commissioner in such permission, such person shall enter into possession of the Land so described, and place at each corner thereof a post marked with his name or other distinguishing sign, and thereupon shall apply in writing to the said Commissioner to have his claim recorded to such tract of Land not exceeding Three hundred and twenty Acres or One hundred and sixty Acres, as the case may be, as hereinbefore provided.

VII. If such Land has not been previously recorded, the Commissioner shall, upon the fulfilment by the applicant of the preceding requirements, and upon payment by him of a fee of Two Dollars, record such Land in his favour as a Pre-emption Claim, and give him a Certificate of such Pre-emption Record, in the Form A. in the Schedule hereto; and such Record shall be made by the Commissioner in triplicate, the original to be handed to the Pre-emptor, a duplicate to be retained by the Commissioner for local reference, and the triplicate to be forwarded forthwith to the head office of the Lands and Works Department, to be there examined, and if found in all respects (or if necessary after having been amended by the Chief Commissioner of Lands and Works and Surveyor General so as to be) in accordance with the provisions of this Ordinance, to be finally registered in the Land Office Pre-emption Register.

VIII. Every piece of Land sought to be acquired as a Pre-emption Claim under the provisions of this Ordinance shall, save as hereinafter excepted, be of rectangular shape, and the shortest line thereof shall be at least two-thirds of the length of the longest line. Such lines shall run as nearly as possible North and South, and East and West.

IX. Where such Land is in whole or in part bounded by any mountain, rock, lake, river, swamp, or other natural boundary, or by any public highway, or by any pre-empted or surveyed Land, such natural boundary, public highway, pre-empted or surveyed Land, may be adopted as the boundary of such Land; and it shall be sufficient for the claimant to shew to the Commissioner that the form of the Land conforms as nearly as circumstances permit to the provisions of this Ordinance.

X. The Chief Commissioner of Lands and Works and Surveyor General may, however, in carrying out any Government Survey, if in his opinion circumstances require it, survey Pre-emption Claims or Purchased Lands recorded previous to the date of this Ordinance, by such metes and bounds as he may think proper; and every survey so made and certified by him in writing shall be binding upon all parties affected thereby, and the survey so certified shall be deemed in any Court of this Colony to have been done in compliance with the provisions of this Ordinance.

XI. A Pre-emptor shall be entitled to receive from the Commissioner a Certificate, to be called a "Certificate of Improvement," in the Form B. in the Schedule hereto, upon his proving to the Commissioner, by the declarations in writing of himself and two other persons, that he has been in occupation of his Pre-emption Claim from the date of the Record thereof, and has made permanent improvements thereon, to the value of Two Dollars and Fifty Cents per Acre. Such Certificate shall be in triplicate, the original to be handed to the Pre-emptor, the duplicate retained by the Commissioner for local reference, and the triplicate transmitted forthwith to the head office of the Lands and Works Department; and it shall be the duty of the Commissioner to note the issue of such Certificate on the original Pre-emption Record, which must be produced to him at the time of applying for the Certificate by the Pre-emptor, and on the duplicate thereof retained in the Commissioner's Office.

XII. Every such declaration shall be subscribed by the person making the same, and shall be filed with the Commissioner, who is hereby fully authorized and empowered to take the same, and such Declaration shall be in the Form C. in the Schedule, and shall be made before such Commissioner, under and subject to the provisions and penalties of the "Oaths Ordinance, 1869."

XIII. After the grant of the Certificate of Improvement, but not before, the Pre-emption right to the Land referred to in such Certificate may be transferred to any person entitled to hold a Pre-emption Claim under this Ordinance, subject, however, to the continuance of all the provisions of this Ordinance as to occupation, forfeiture, and payment of purchase money due or to become due to the Crown.

XIV. Every such transfer must be made in writing, signed by the person making the same, or his attorney in fact, in the Form D. in the Schedule, or in words to that effect, and in the presence of the Commissioner, and if not so made shall be void; and such transfer shall be in triplicate, the original to be retained by the person in whose favour the transfer is made, the duplicate to be retained as a record in the Office of the Commissioner, and the triplicate forwarded forthwith to be registered in the head office of the Lands and Works. Upon the examination of such transfer in the manner and form so prescribed, and on payment of the fee of Two Dollars the Commissioner shall cancel the previous Record of such Pre-emption Right, and Record the same anew in the maner prescribed in Section VII. in the name of the person in favour of whom such transfer shall have been made, subject to the completion of the period of occupation required by this Ordinance, and to all other the terms and conditions thereof.

XV. Whenever any Pre-emptor shall permanently cease to occupy his Pre-emption Claim, save as hereinafter provided, the Commissioner may in a summary way, upon being satisfied of such permanent cessation, cancel the claim of the Pre-emptor so permanently ceasing to occupy the same, and all Deposits paid, and all Improvements and Buildings made and erected on such land, shall be absolutely forfeited to the Crown, and the said land shall be open to Pre-emption and may be Recorded anew by the Commissioner as a Pre-emption Claim, in the name of any person satisfying the requirements in that behalf of this Ordinance.

XVI. The occupation herein required, shall mean a continuous *bona fide* personal residence of the Pre-emptor on his Pre-emption Claim.

Provided, however, that the requirement of such personal occupation shall cease and determine after a period of Four Years of such continuous occupation shall have been fulfilled.

XVII. Every holder of a Pre-emption Claim shall be entitled to be absent from his claim for any one period not exceeding Two Months during any One Year. As an ordinary rule he shall be deemed to have permanently ceased to occupy his claim when he shall have been absent, continuously, for a longer period than Two Months, unless leave of absence have been granted by the Commissioner, as hereinafter provided.

XVIII. If any Pre-emptor shall show good cause to the satisfaction of the Commissioner, such Commissioner may grant to the said Pre-emptor leave of absence for any period of time, not exceeding Four Months in any One Year, inclusive of the Two Months' absence from his claim, provided for in Clause XVII. Such leave of absence shall be in the Form E. in the Schedule hereto, and shall be made out in duplicate, the original to be handed to the Pre-emptor, and the duplicate to be retained of record in the office of the Commissioner.

XIX. If any Pre-emptor shall show good cause to the satisfaction of the Commissioner, he may grant him a "License to Substitute," for any period not exceeding six calendar months, in the Form F. in the Schedule hereto, in duplicate, the original to be handed to the Pre-emptor, and the duplicate to be retained of record in the Office of the Commissioner. The continuous personal residence of the person named in such License (such person not being or becoming subsequently to the date of the License a claimant of land under any Law or Proclamation regulating the Pre-emption of land within the Colony) shall, during the continuance of the License, and after the record thereof with the Commissioner, be as effectual as the continuous personal residence of the claimant himself.

XX. No person shall be entitled to hold, at the same time, Two Claims by Pre-emption; and any person so pre-empting more than One Claim shall forfeit all right, title, and interest to the prior claim recorded by him, and to all improvements made and erected thereon, and deposits of money paid to Government on account thereof; and the Land included in such prior claim shall be open for Pre-emption.

XXI. When the Government shall survey the land included in a Pre-emption Claim, the person in whose name the said claim stands registered in the Pre-emption Register of the Land Office, shall, provided a Certificate of Improvement shall have been issued in respect of such land, and that the condition of Four Years occupation required by this Ordinance has been duly fulfilled, shall be entitled to purchase the said land at such rate not exceeding One Dollar per acre as may be determined upon by the Governor for the time being, payable by four equal annual instalments, the first instalment to be paid to the Commissioner at his office within three calendar months from the date of the service on the said Pre-emptor of a notice from the Chief Commissioner of Lands and Works and Surveyor General requiring payment for the said land, or within six calendar months after the insertion of a notice to such effect to be published for and during such period in the *Government Gazette*, or in such other newspaper published in the Colony, as the Commissioner may direct.

If the purchase money for such land be not paid according to the terms of such notice, the Pre-emption Claim over such land may at the discretion of the Commissioner be cancelled, and all such land and the improvements thereon, and any instalments of the purchase money paid thereon, may be forfeited absolutely to the Crown.

XXII. The Crown Grant to a Pre-emption Claim will not be issued unless it shall have been proved to the Commissioner that written or printed notices of the intended application for such Grant have been posted for a period of Sixty Days prior to such application, upon some conspicuous part of the said Pre-emption Claim, and upon the adjacent claims (if any), and upon the Court House of the District wherein the Land lies.

XXIII. Upon payment of the whole of the purchase money for such land, and upon production to the Chief Commissioner of Lands and Works and Surveyor General of a Certificate in Form G. in the Schedule hereto, from the Commissioner of the District in which such land is situated, that the notices of intended application for a Crown Grant of such land have been duly posted as required in the previous Section without any objection to the issue of such grant having been substantiated, a Crown Grant or Conveyance in the Form H. of the Schedule hereto of the fee simple of the said land shall be executed in favor of the purchaser.

Provided that every such Crown Grant shall be deemed to include among the reservations therein contained, a reserve in favor of the Crown, its assignees, and licensees, of the right to take from any such land without compensation, any gravel, sand, stone, lime, timber, or other material which may be required in the construction, maintenance, or repair of any Roads, Ferries, Bridges, or other Public Works.

XXIV. In the event of the death of any Pre-emptor under this Ordinance, his heirs or devisees (as the case may be) if resident in the Colony, shall be entitled to a Crown Grant of the Land included in such Pre-emption Claim if lawfully held and occupied by such Pre-emptor at the time of his decease, but subject to payment of the full amount of purchase money for such land then due or to become due; but if such heirs or devisees be absent from the Colony at the time of such decease, the Chief Commissioner of Lands and Works and Surveyor General is hereby authorized and empowered to make such disposition of the Pre-emption Claim, and such provision for the person (if any) entitled thereto or interested therein, as he may deem just and proper.

XXV. Every person lawfully occupying a Pre-emption Claim situated to the Northward and Eastward of the Cascade or Coast Range of Mountains, at the date of the passing of this Ordinance, if less than Three hundred and twenty Acres, may, with the permission of the Commissioner, pre-empt Land liable to pre-emption, and immediately contiguous to or abutting on his said existing claim, so as to make up the total amount of his claim to Three Hundred and twenty Acres, and thereupon such total claim shall be deemed to have been and to be taken up and held under the provisions of this Ordinance.

LEASES

XXVI. Leases of any extent of unpre-empted and unsurveyed Land may be granted for pastoral purposes by the Governor in Council, to any person or persons whomsoever, being *bona fide* Pre-emptors or Purchasers of Land in the vicinity of Land sought to be leased, at such Rent as such Governor in Council shall deem expedient. But every such Lease of Pastoral Land shall, among other things, contain a condition making such Land liable to Pre-emption, Reserve for public purposes, and purchase by any persons whomsoever, at any time during the term thereof, without compensation, save by a proportionate deduction of Rent; and to a further condition, that the Lessee shall, within Six Months from the date of such Lease, stock the property demised in such proportion of animals to the One hundred Acres, as shall be specified by the Commissioner.

XXVII. Leases of unoccupied and unsurveyed Land, not exceeding Five hundred Acres in extent, may be granted by the Governor in Council, for the purpose of cutting Hay thereon, to any person or persons whomsoever, being *bona fide* Pre-emptors or Purchasers of Land, at such Rent as such Governor in Council shall deem expedient. The term of such Lease shall not exceed Five Years; but every such Lease shall, among other things, contain a condition making such Land liable to Pre-emption, Reserve for public purposes, and purchase by any persons whomsoever, at any time during the term thereof, with such compensation for improvements made thereon, to be paid to the Leaseholder, as shall be fixed by the Commissioner of the District.

XXVIII. Leases of any extent of unpre-empted Crown Lands may be granted by the Governor in Council, to any person, persons, or corporation duly authorized in that behalf, for the purpose of cutting spars, timber, or lumber, and actually engaged in those pursuits, subject to such rent, terms, and provisions as shall seem expedient to the Governor in Council; provided, however, that any person may hereafter acquire a Pre-emption Claim to or upon any part of such Leased Land, by complying with the requirements of this Ordinance. Such Pre-emptor shall, however, only be entitled to cut such timber as he may require for use upon his claim; and if he cut timber on the said Land for sale, or for any purpose other than for such use as aforesaid, or for the purpose of clearing the said Land, he shall absolutely forfeit all interest in the Land acquired by him, and the Commissioner shall cancel his claim thereto.

XXIX. The application for any such Lease must be in writing, in duplicate, addressed to the Commissioner, who shall retain the original in his office, and transmit the duplicate through the head office of the Lands and Works, to the Governor in Council, who shall alone decide on any such Lease.

WATER

XXX. Every person lawfully entitled to hold a Pre-emption under this Ordinance and lawfully occupying and *bona fide* cultivating Lands, may divert any unrecorded and unappropriated water from the natural channel of any stream, lake, or river adjacent to or passing through such Land, for agricultural and other purposes, upon obtaining the written authority of the Commissioner of the District to that effect, and a record of the same shall be made with him, after due notice as hereinafter mentioned, specifying the name of the applicant, the quantity sought to be diverted, the place of diversion, the object thereof, and all such other particulars as such Commissioner may require; for every such record the Commissioner shall charge a fee of Two Dollars; and no person shall have any exclusive right to the use of such water, whether the same flow naturally through or over his land, except such record shall have been made.

XXXI. Previous to such authority being given, the applicant shall, if the parties affected thereby refuse to consent thereto, post up in a conspicuous place on each person's Land through which it is proposed that the water should pass, and on the District Court House, notices in writing, stating his intentions to enter such Land, and through and over the same to take and carry such water, specifying all particulars relating thereto, including direction, quantity, purpose, and term.

XXXII. Priority of right to any such water privilege, in case of dispute, shall depend on priority of record.

XXXIII. The right of entry on and through the Lands of other, for carrying water for any lawful purpose upon, over, or under the said Land, may be claimed and taken by any person lawfully occupying and *bona fide* cultivating as aforesaid, and (previous to entry) upon paying or securing payment of compensation, as aforesaid, for the waste or damage so occasioned, to the person whose Land may be wasted or damaged by such entry or carrying of water.

XXXIV. In case of dispute, such compensation or any other question connected with such water privilege, entry, or carrying may be ascertained by the Commissioner of the District in a summary manner, without a Jury, or if desired by either party, with a Jury of Five men.

XXXV. Water privileges for mining or other purposes, not otherwise lawfully appropriated, may be claimed, and the said water may be taken upon, under, or over any Land so pre-empted or purchased as aforesaid, by obtaining a Grant or Licence from the Commissioner of the District; and, previous to taking the same, paying reasonable compensation for waste or damage to the person whose Land may be wasted or damaged by such water privilege, or carriage of water.

XXXVI. All Assignments, Transfers, or Conveyances of any Preemption Right, heretofore or hereafter acquired, shall be construed to have conveyed and transferred, and to convey and transfer, any and all recorded water privileges in any manner attached to or used in the working of the Land pre-empted.

XXXVII. Every owner of a ditch or water privilege shall be bound to take all reasonable means for utilizing the water taken by him; and if he shall wilfully take and waste any unreasonable quantity of water, it shall be lawful for the Commissioner to declare all rights to the water forfeited.

EJECTMENT

XXXVIII. Any person lawfully occupying a Pre-emption Claim, or holding a Lease under this Ordinance may, in respect thereof, institute and obtain redress in an action of ejectment or of trespass in the same manner and to the same extent as if he were seised of the legal estate on the Land covered by such claims; but either party thereto may refer the cause of action to the Stipendiary Magistrate of the District wherein the Land lies, who is hereby authorized to proceed summarily, and make such order as he shall deem just. Provided, however, that if requested by either party, he shall first summon a Jury of Five persons to hear the cause, and their verdict or award on all matters of fact shall be final.

JURY

XXXIX. It shall be lawful for any Magistrate, by an order under his hand, to summon a Jury of five persons for any purpose under this Ordinance, and in the event of non-attendance of any persons so summoned he shall have the power to impose a fine not exceeding Twenty-five Dollars.

APPEAL

XL. Any person affected by any decision of a Magistrate or Commissioner under this Ordinance may within One calendar month after such decision but not afterwards, appeal to the Supreme Court in a summary manner, and such appeal shall be in the form of a petition, verified by affidavit, to any Judge of such Court, setting out the points relied upon; and a copy of such petition shall be served upon the Commissioner whose decision is appealed from, and such time shall be allowed for his answer to the said petition as to the Judge of the Supreme Court may seem advisable; but no such appeal shall be allowed except from decisions on points of law.

XLI. Any person desirous of appealing in manner aforesaid, may be required, before such appeal be heard, to find such security as may be determined by the Commissioner whose decision is appealed from, and such appeal shall not be heard until after security to the satisfaction of the Commissioner shall have been given for the due prosecution of such appeal and submission thereto.

SURVEYED LANDS

XLII. The Governor shall at any time, and for such purposes as he may deem advisable, Reserve, by notice published in the *Government*

Gazette, or in any newspaper of the Colony, any Lands that may not have been either sold or legally pre-empted.

XLIII. The upset price of Surveyed Lands, not being reserved for the Sites of Towns or the Suburbs thereof, and not being reputed to be Mineral Lands, shall be One Dollar per Acre; and the upset price of Town and Suburban Lots shall be such as the Governor may in each case specially determine.

XLIV. Except as aforesaid, all the Land in British Columbia will be exposed in lots for sale by public competition, at the upset price above mentioned, after the same shall have been surveyed and made ready for sale. Due notice shall be given of all such sales; notice at the same time shall be given of the upset price and terms of payment when they vary from those above stated, and also of the rights specially reserved (if any) for public convenience.

XLV. All Lands which shall remain unsold at any such auction may be sold by private contract at the upset price and on the terms and conditions herein mentioned, on application to the Chief Commissioner of Lands and Works and Surveyor General, or other person for the time being duly authorized by the Governor in that behalf.

XLVI. Unless otherwise specially notified at the time of sale, all Crown Lands sold shall be subject to such public rights of way as may at any time after such sale be specified by the Chief Commissioner of Lands and Works and Surveyor General, and to the right of the Crown to take therefrom, without compensation, any stone, gravel, or other material to be used in repairing the public roads, and to such private rights of way, and of leading or using water for animals, and for mining and engineering purposes, as may at the time of such sale be existing.

XLVII. Unless otherwise specially announced at the time of sale, the conveyance of the land shall include, except as provided in Section XXIII, all trees and all mines and minerals within and under the same (except mines of gold and silver.)

FREE MINERS' RIGHTS

XLVII. Nothing herein contained shall exclude Free Miners from entering upon any land in this Colony, and searching for and working minerals; provided that such Free Miner prior to so doing shall give full satisfaction or adequate security to the satisfaction of the Commissioner, to the Pre-emptor or Tenant in fee simple, for any loss or damage he may sustain by reason thereof. If the amount of compensation (if any) cannot be agreed upon, the Stipendiary Magistrate or Gold Commissioner of the District wherein the land lies, with the assistance, if desired by either party, of a Jury of Five persons to be summoned by him, shall decide the amount thereof, and such decision and award shall be final. If there be no such Stipendiary Magistrate or Gold Commissioner in the said District, the Supreme Count shall have jurisdiction in the matter.

FREE GRANTS

XLIX. It shall be lawful for the Governor in Council to make such special Free or partially Free Grants of the unoccupied and unappropriated Crown Lands of the Colony, for the encouragement of Immigration or other purposes of public advantage, with and under such provisions, restrictions, and privileges, as to the Governor in Council may seem most advisable for the encouragement and permanent settlement of Immigrants, or for such other public purposes as aforesaid.

L. Nothing in this Ordinance contained shall be construed so as to interfere prejudicially with the rights granted to Free Miners under the "Gold Mining Ordinance, 1867."

LI. The Schedule hereto shall form part of this Ordinance.

LII. Each Commissioner appointed under this Ordinance, shall keep a book or books in which he shall enter the date and particulars of every Pre-emption Record, Certificate of Improvement, License to Substitute, Transfer, or other document relating to or in any manner affecting any Pre-emption Claim within his District.

LIII. All fines and fees payable under this Ordinance shall be deemed to be made payable to the use of the Crown.

LIV. This Ordinance shall not take effect until Her Majesty's assent thereto shall have been proclaimed in the Colony.

LV. This Ordinance may be cited for all purposes as the "Land Ordinance, 1870."

Appendix B

Table 1.

Pre-emption Records, 1873-1913

	Victoria	Cowichan	Nanaimo	New Westminster	Yale	Lillooet	Cariboo	Omineca	Kootenay	Kamloops	Osoyoos	Cassiar	Esquimalt	Comox	Coast (1912-13 Vancouver)	Alberni	Atlin	Telegraph Creek	Golden	Cranbrook	Slocan	Revelstoke	Nelson	Fairview	Vernon	Nicola	Ashcroft	Clinton	Barkerville	Prince Rupert	Hazelton	Fort George	Total
1873	56	35	33	206	76	22	10	3																									441
1874		14	16	106	34	14				8	6	10																					208
1875	5	6	8	152	9	6	1			6	2	3																					198
1876	4	4	7	119	12	8	4			27	2	1																					188
1877	7	9	12	214	17	7			3	31	13	7																					320
1878	6	15	22	141	9	11	4		2	28	5	2																					245
1879	15	7	20	19	3	9	3			20	4																						100
1880	3	5	5	1	3	2	2			7	35	1																					64
1881	18	8	5	6		6	7			13	21	1																					85
1882	14	18	17	1		4	1			7	15																						77
1883	3	28	9	1	2	5	8		7	38	78		15		6																		200

1884	13	239	235	49	2	12	3		15	34	68		33	2	2																		707
1885	10	164	181	25	1	19	11		22	24	107		31	40	3																		638
1886	4	113	154	52		18	13		35	52	69		12	63	4																		589
1887	6	36	6	90		17	15		21	27	67		16	1	1																		303
1888	9	38	5	284		15	12		14	36	94		13	19	9																		548
1889	27	27	8	217	1	12	16		15	26	137		10																				496
1890	45	27	6	228		22	14		46	25	158		37	1	7																		616
1891	80	25	8	347		68	21		62	35	230		59		53																		988
1892	151	21	14	134	1	21	43		150	50	204	2			78																		869
1893	195	14	6	63		45	24		141	34	257	1	8		44																		832
1894	108	15	11	44	2	24	38		109	34	295	2			27																		709
1895	112	14	5	31		32	54		80	28	236	2			36																		630
1896	61	3	6	24		36	45		89	26	177	2			17																		486
1897	50	6	5	19		27	28		148	15	139	6			19																		462
1898	41	2		14		26	12		134	27	181	3			27																		467
1899	54	1	8	9		20	30		164	38	281				11																		616
1900	55		1	31		33	24		218	42	309	2			7																		722
1901	48	3		26	3	34	21		129	56	300	5			21																		646
1902	63	2	3	18	8	42	24		164	58	253	3			17																		655
1903	60	7	4	86	8	31	31		141	33	308	10			39																		758
1904	52			38	12	31	34		151	59	395	8			105																		885
1905	48	11	2	65	7	53	23		155	97	323				171																		955
1906	53	12	13	68	4	64	24		185	149	240	26			210																		1048
1907	41	9	11	49	4	58	42		172	79	293	6			172																		936
1908	77	9	9	64	4	68	62		164	113	448				517																		1535
1909	86	5	6	59	1	102	95		146	125	437				558																		1620
1910	140		16	72						152						130	1	1	20	40	5	9	34	154	221	99	8	144	244	197	362		2049
1911	152		12	70						178						247		3	31	39	10	2	52	169	149	77	19	104	123	337	359	250	2383
1912	109		24	146						250					191	435			81	84		10	61	144	126	116	25	158	184	538	342	631	3655
1913	31		13	13						206					391	315	4	1	62	19		4	45	144	109	160	12	367	279	442	167	1071	3855
Totals	2112	952	926	3401	223	1024	799	3	2882	2293	6187	103	234	126	2743	1127		5	194	182	15	25	192	611	605	452	64	773	830	1514	1230	1952	33,784

Notes: 1. Figures include 970 pre-emptions in Island Railway Belt, 1884-1886.
(Compiled from the annual reports of the chief commissioners of lands and works, 1873-1913.)

Table 2.

Certificates of Improvement, 1873-1913

	Victoria	Cowichan	Nanaimo	New Westminster	Yale	Lillooet	Cariboo	Omineca	Kootenay	Cassiar	Kamloops	Osoyoos	Esquimalt	Comox	Coast (1912-13 Vancouver)	Alberni	Atlin	Telegraph Creek	Golden	Cranbrook	Slocan	Revelstoke	Nelson	Fairview	Vernon	Nicola	Ashcroft	Clinton	Barkerville	Prince Rupert	Hazelton	Fort George	Total
1873	13	4	15	21	15			1																									69
1874	6	12	20	23	9	1				1																							72
1875	1	10	5	22	5	3				1	12																						59
1876	2	5	7	12	10	1	1		1			3																					42
1877	3	5	8	43	4							2																					65
1878																																	
1879	6		1	48	1				2																								58
1880			9	45																													54
1881	6	3	7	28	2				1	1	6	1																					55
1882			2	24		3																											29
1883		3	3	22		2					11	16			3																		60

1884	4	19	40	31		3					8	9	3		2																	119
1885	2	51	36	31	2	5	1		4		10	14	2	5																		163
1886	3	50	34	20	2	5					10	10	2	5																		141
1887		13	17	15	2	1			1		3	16		5																		73
1888	1	15	10	92		3			1		15	11	4	1	4																	157
1889	4	11	3	80	1	3			3		13	13	1																			132
1890	3	21	8	82		5	3		4	1	9	19	9	1	4																	169
1891	11	16	11	146		7	1		6		16	29	13	2	2																	260
1892	32	22	8	106	1	9	13		7		25	49																				272
1893	27	13	7	32	1	12	4		14		9	50		1	3																	173
1894	27	7	3	21		5	6		9		6	26			7																	117
1895	29	10	14	14		5	3		17		7	22			2																	123
1896	42	9	5	5		4	5		26	2	1	37		1	5																	142
1897	13	2	2	85		19	6		27	1		43			6																	204
1898	23	4	3	3		9	13		28		8	47			6																	144
1899	10	2	2	2		16	11		18		3	48			1																	113
1900	17	2	1	3		5	2		16		8	58			1																	113
1901	15	2	1	8	2	16	13		37	1	16	53			4																	168
1902	10		2	2		8	10		37		11	58			5																	143
1903	8		1	9		4	2		32		8	59																				123
1904	21			10	1	4	8		43		15	101			6																	209
1905	18	2	2	16	3	6	4		85		10	42			1																	189
1906	19	1	2	17	1	15	6		52	6	15	41			5																	180
1907	24	6		17	1	20	12		64		16	86			16																	262
1908	19	1		20	1		8		80		12	99			16																	256
1909	21	2		24	7	19	11		68		38	89			10																	289
1910	41			20							24					13		11	16	4	3	12	63	89	16	4	40	20	63			439
1911	38		5	14							38					34	1	16	24	3	1	26	60	106	33	7	40	14	56	92	16	624
1912	43		2	8							46				24	24		10	41		3	20	36	91	37	2	53	31	70	135	39	715
1913	16		6	2							44				71	65		13	17			9	70	107	39	5	55	51	100	116	176	962
Totals	578	323	302	1223	71	218	143	1	683	14	473	1151	34	21	204	136	1	50	98	7	7	67	229	393	125	18	188	116	289	343	231	7737

Notes: 1. Figures include 195 certificates of improvement in Island Railway Belt, 1884-86.
(Compiled from the annual reports of the chief commissioners of lands and works, 1873-1913.)

Table 3.

Certificates of Purchase, 1873-1913

	Victoria	Cowichan	Nanaimo	New Westminster	Yale	Lillooet	Cariboo	Omineca	Kootenay	Kamloops	Osoyoos	Esquimalt	Comox	Coast (1912-13, Vancouver)	Cassiar	Alberni	Atlin	Telegraph Creek	Golden	Cranbrook	Slocan	Revelstoke	Nelson	Fairview	Vernon	Nicola	Ashcroft	Clinton	Barkerville	Prince Rupert	Hazelton	Fort George	Total
1873	5	12		121	4																												142
1874	5	6	14	122	2		5																										154
1875	4	3	11	178	2	1																											199
1876	11	36	17	76		22																											162
1877	1	18	10	140	3	80				9																							261
1878	16	32	20	198	7	2	3			30	25																						317
1879	59	28	23	199	7	2				61	9																						404
1880	33	25	22	107	4	4			2	29	10																						236
1881	40	17	17	80	2	3	3			36	7																						205
1882	34	23	21	68	2	6	2			21	24																						201
1883	52	34	29	41	1	8	10		1	34	61	28	9	20																			328

1884	98	32	40	256	1	11	7	2	63	63	26	3	13																			615
1885	31	46	35	110	1	17	3	12	45	27	6	4	3																			340
1886	12	71	47	157	1	25	6	5	48	46	7	8	3																			436
1887	11	25	22	90	3	32	3	7	67	71	13	2	5																			351
1888	15	22	27	126		19	9	11	46	57	7	7	9																			355
1889	21	29	20	251	2	14	16	121	53	44	7																					578
1890	45	52	17	331	1	27	14	183	36	84	23		16																			829
1891	170	20	15	366	3	37	19	45	39	76	50		23																			863
1892	315	38	18	354	2	56	14	26	7	97		2	68	3																		1000
1893	30	7	7	61	1	9	5	62	4	64	3		3	8																		264
1894	20	6	3	23	1	5	1	29	8	44	2		11																			153
1895	63	37	15	50		33	17	57	24	26			11	1																		334
1896	69	49	22	52	2	54	47	235	49	91	1	1	20	2																		694
1897	47	14	5	11	1	166	34	556	32	85			20	6																		977
1898	47	12	3	64		40	60	344	31	85			29	50																		765
1899	34	13	4	61		38	29	121	12	89			1	16																		418
1900	44	9		51	1	37	23	75	18	134			6	1																		399
1901	33	7	2	66	7	36	27	145	23	169			10	6																		531
1902	41	4	3	72	4	37	39	134	56	142			21	12																		565
1903	20	1	3	61	4	17	34	146	39	122			16	47																		510
1904	50	9	2	115	5	19	36	210	82	356			50	35																		969
1905	38	5	4	183	14	59	26	334	61	835			70	8																		1637
1906	58	7	2	191	14	122	64	583	74	104			258	73																		1550
1907	119	10	5	452	17	132	147	1421	95	499			295	13																		3205
1908	116	9		300	3	114	195	702	93	225			678	3																		2433
1909	313	12	1	644	16	143	451	704	147	229			1681	22																		4363
1910	1939		2	204					120						235	1	1	150	166	42	21	148	115	163	135	29	552	1990	971	2097		
1911	1285		14	449					89						302			244	94	82	27	171	140	145	184	166	597	431	676	980	1063	
1912	1264		3	84					65				62		670	1	3	43	153		26	97	74	141	125	65	181	224	480	757	547	
1913	558		5	5					48				426		523	2	3	24	58		6	77	70	84	51	12	127	166	552	434	415	
Totals	7166	780	530	6570	138	1427	1349	6273	1794	4000	173	36	3828	306	1730	4	7	461	471	124	80	493	399	533	495	272	1457	2811	2679	4268	2025	52,679

(Compiled from the annual reports of the chief commissioners of lands and works, 1873-1913.)
Notes: 1. Figures include 113 certificates of purchase in Island Railway Belt, 1884-86.

Table 4.

Crown Grants, 1873-1913

	Victoria	Cowichan	Nanaimo	New Westminster	Yale	Lillooet	Cariboo	Omineca	Kootenay	Kamloops	Osoyoos	Esquimalt	Comox	Coast	Cassiar	Total
1873	9	12	2	14	5											42
1874	23	7	12	57	3		4									106
1875	23	5	8	88	5		26									155
1876	21	14	14	54	2	2	21									128
1877	2	6	7	60	6	2	1			4						88
1878	12	21	6	91	4	5	6		7	9	11					172
1879	7	24	25	128	7	1				14	5					211
1880	11	12	16	70	7	3	3		2	5	3					132
1881	14	11	12	56	2	1	3		1	7	4					111
1882		14	13	66	5	3	1		1	13	6	3	3	1		129
1883	40	23	12	64	4	5	7		1	28	42	23	7	18		274
1884	77	32	16	114	5	19	1		5	29	68	22	2	16		406
1885	29	21	19	124	1	6	4		8	36	50	5	1	2		306
1886	15	24	4	137	1	15	3		11	40	16	5		3		274
1887	12	25	15	92	7	15	6		9	66	60	7	1	5		320
1888	13	27	27	114	1	13	5		26	48	40	9	2	7		332
1889	27	41	15	184	2	15	5		102	34	33	8	2	13		481
1890	70	53	16	221		11	8		99	34	41	18		21	1	593
1891	143	16	10	266	4	24	8		75	28	54	39		18		685
1892	243	24	16	225	3	41	11		104	51	69	1	1	35	4	828
1893	56	12	10	96	5	11	3		122	8	49	4		9	8	393
1894	12	5	7	17		4	14		43	11	36	2		8		159
1895	22	12	8	16	2	17	5		80	12	39	1		1		215
1896	29	20	6	16	2	13	19		228	14	57	1	1	5		411
1897	28	5	6	26	2	66	13		503	13	87			14	3	766
1898	32	11	3	21		45	22		599	24	164			25	5	951
1899	51	6	2	31		38	26		509	4	174			21	6	868
1900	48	5	2	58	8	31	26		620	16	260			6	21	1101
1901	41	13	2	51	8	29	16		440	26	223			42	21	912
1902	87	6	7	46	4	34	19		513	27	257			49	10	1059
1903	97	2	5	54	14	17	17		309	47	238			35	25	860
1904	81	3	5	101	17	29	27		307	32	269			54	28	953
1905	49	33	25	94	25	23	10		347	42	249			154	13	1064
1906	69	4	9	126	10	31	15		334	65	310			132	19	1124
1907	143	7	22	197	7	59	39		524	39	278			119	66	1500
1908	119	11	6	247	10	59	95		604	93	259			149	15	1667
1909	86	5	3	318	10	35	80		479	93	231			339	35	1714
																21,490
1910																1572
1911																2566
1912																2757
1913																2110
Totals	1841	572	393	3740	198	722	569		7012	1012	3682	148	20	1301	280	30,495

Notes: 1. Detailed statistics not given, 1910-1913, inclusive. (Compiled from annual reports of the chief commissioners of lands and works, 1873-1913, inclusive.)

Table 5.

Total Land Transactions, 1873-1913

	Pre-emption Records	Certificates of Improvement	Certificates of Purchase	Crown Grants	Total Transactions for year	Letters received in Land Office	Total acreage deeded by Crown Grant
1873	441	69	142	42	694	2068	*
1874	208	72	154	106	540	3252	*
1875	198	59	199	155	611	4110	17,960.5
1876	188	42	162	128	520	*	17,984.3
1877	320	65	261	88	734	*	9,991
1878	245	*	317	172	734	*	31,210
1879	100	58	404	211	773	*	46,815
1880	64	54	236	132	486	1319	24,115
1881	85	55	205	111	456	1314	23,141
1882	77	29	201	129	436	1617	23,609
1883	200	60	328	274	862	2463	54,637
1884	707	119	615	406	1847	3357	146,197
1885	638	163	340	306	1447	3260	128,811
1886	589	141	436	274	1440	3485	50,472
1887	303	73	351	320	1047	3079	73,950
1888	548	157	355	332	1392	3141	94,278
1889	496	132	578	481	1687	3326	134,169
1890	616	169	829	593	2207	4168	99,334
1891	988	260	863	685	2796	5224	143,455
1892	869	272	1000	828	2969	5321	309,878
1893	832	173	264	393	1662	4339	124,634
1894	709	117	153	159	1138	4018	47,167
1895	630	123	334	215	1302	5079	95,456
1896	486	142	694	411	1733	6532	36,821
1897	462	204	977	766	2409	8034	609,597
1898	467	144	765	951	2327	9126	371,394
1899	616	113	418	868	2015	10993	672,148
1900	722	113	399	1101	2335	12943	104,724
1901	646	168	531	912	2257	13306	4,632,832
1902	655	143	565	1059	2422	13546	87,907
1903	758	123	510	860	2251	14001	83,699
1904	885	209	969	953	3016	15141	107,385
1905	955	189	1637	1064	3845	16609	133,184
1906	1048	180	1550	1124	3902	19661	336,145
1907	936	262	3205	1500	5903	29430	599,420
1908	1535	256	2438	1667	5896	33629	253,542
1909	1620	289	4363	1714	7986	25798	326,230
1910	2049	439	9081	1572	13141	37188	300,588
1911	2383	624	7139	2566	12712	41946	524,325
1912	3655	715	5065	2757	12192	43302	253,141
1913	3855	962	3646	2110	10573	31738	390,036
Totals	33,784	7,737	52,679	30,495	124,695	446,863	11,620,383.8

* No figures available. (Compiled from Tables I, II, III, and IV.)

Table 6.

Land and Natural Resources Receipts, 1871-1913

Government Receipts from Natural Resources Only

Years	Land Sales $	Wild Land (Coal and Timber Lands) $	Survey Fees $	Timber Lease Rentals $	Timber Royalty and Licences $	Free Miners' Certificates $	Mineral Tax $	Mining Receipts General $	Royalty and Tax on Coal $	Total Provincial Revenue, all sources $
1871	8,863					4,760		8,135		191,846
1872	4,269					8,377		7,552		328,160
1873	10,636	950				6,715		4,937		379,782
1874	23,617	2,558				11,187		7,786		567,017
1875	19,417	1,478				8,762		7,009		760,898
1876	16,749	2,118				10,037		7,669		506,162
1877	22,119	7,641				10,087		6,909		436,609
1878	40,092	9,530	991			11,925		8,593		480,512
1879	26,034	6,883	70			4,625		2,676		213,587
1880	22,032	5,218	702	1,263		9,527		5,413		392,484
1881	16,570	6,491	200	667		8,900		5,343		397,035
1882	19,178	5,604	355	472		6,982		4,426		454,621
1883	26,034	5,162	462	593		6,625		3,430		439,400
1884	91,432	5,402	725	1,820		7,607		6,292		891,279
1885	174,579	7,657	430	674		8,155		4,601		602,797
1886	77,502	8,418	270	3,266		18,840		8,535		515,281
1887	88,776	9,154	275	7,319		12,850		6,915		540,398
1888	80,873	13,832	180	14,504		11,280		8,586		608,678

1889	142,818	15,964	180	11,869	13,286	12,795		9,534		706,779
1890	244,529	21,221	100	6,314	18,356	20,625		10,145		845,522
1891	243,551	25,695	145	16,500	25,172	12,861		12,329		964,943
1892	213,519	53,301	220	23,824	20,475	17,903		14,744		1,038,237
1893	179,999	38,113	342	13,426	9,586	27,868		23,232		1,019,206
1894	33,917	35,947	494	24,925	18,725	23,015		25,545		821,660
1895	25,880	34,566	2,228	49,544	16,581	31,190		41,647		896,025
1896	64,003	36,123	1,076	27,876	31,514	54,953	306	76,638		989,765
1897	86,214	41,511	766	40,663	55,631	166,681	29,788	157,408		1,383,048
1898	104,180	61,575	945	46,076	57,647	139,756	36,061	159,432		1,439,623
1899	73,807	47,309	1,024	24,143	64,323	155,104	34,121	186,702		1,531,638
1900	53,267	49,376	787	38,812	97,517	133,765	31,894	194,303	5,933	1,444,108
1901	43,338	48,241	730	28,981	86,613	93,510	95,483	154,270	85,251	1,605,920
1902	86,161	50,938	1,123	45,861	115,210	78,240	84,077	141,382	85,702	1,807,925
1903	64,834	71,340	1,160	84,111	214,106	67,287	78,273	148,722	75,826	2,044,630
1904	118,276	112,233	1,231	116,382	289,366	59,854	65,844	108,270	95,600	2,638,260
1905	141,510	101,607	1,092	76,228	410,288	53,504	114,236	105,192	94,682	2,920,461
1906	189,391	101,308	1,183	100,449	509,043	54,298	161,904	116,895	107,587	3,044,442
1907	663,035	117,900	3,689	95,219	1,155,346	54,241	151,513	117,778	107,310	4,444,593
1908	548,036	193,974	1,855	74,043	2,258,566	53,256	112,567	92,329	125,518	5,979,054
1909	528,604	37,312	2,887	59,085	1,848,254	13,739	81,927	79,502	143,223	4,664,500
1910	2,618,188	210,904	15,871	85,875	2,234,099	53,095	102,608	91,253	222,722	8,874,741
1911	2,431,231	316,130	18,052	106,857	2,357,951	68,937	91,038	105,319	248,332	10,492,892
1912	1,805,390	428,274	17,544	83,066	2,300,263	68,101	100,659	93,461	195,207	10,745,708
1913	2,344,596	546,087	22,053	84,576	2,457,129	62,685	155,163	94,754	302,225	12,510,215
Totals	13,816,746	2,895,045	101,437	1,395,283	16,655,047	1,744,504	1,527,462	2,475,593	1,895,119	93,560,441

Total Government Receipts from Natural Resources only as above: $42,506,236 = 45.4% of Total Provincial Revenue, all Sources. (B.C., *Sessional Papers*, 9th Parl., 4th sess., 1902, p. D21, Table 1; ibid., 12th Parl., 1st sess., 1910, p. B21 Table 2; ibid., 13th Parl., 3d sess., 1915, p. C21, Table 3.)

Table 7.

Private and Government Surveys, 1900-1913

(Acres)

Year	Pre-emptions	Purchases	Mining Claims	Timber Limits	Coal Licences	Leases	B.C. Gov't Surveys	Totals
1900	22,873	4,419	33,441	59		664	10,057	71,513
1901	26,493	16,401	33,400	2,207		593		79,094
1902	35,297	29,652	31,057	1,040	626	1,026		98,698
1903	37,615	26,787	18,115	127,992		2,003	800	213,312
1904	48,124	36,468	20,549	155,279	48,670	3,009	179	312,278
1905	42,660	58,705	15,535	214,841	137,218	806	107	469,872
1906	33,573	66,668	9,894	77,829	41,312	9,566		238,842
1907	50,460	162,218	10,017	83,016	20,367	4,387	113,968	444,433
1908	66,788	147,980	14,607	167,925	9,821	2,580	97,072	506,773
1909	71,316	145,325	10,744	426,121	8,310	15,239	512,373	1,189,428
1910	79,273	455,356	12,499	509,201	43,363	5,864	302,536	1,408,092
1911	89,485	1,352,809	21,325	686,909	120,938	6,500	948,644	3,226,610
1912	99,461	1,011,934	16,645	804,730	99,236	8,560	826,362	2,866,928
1913	55,202	508,062	18,043	1,181,355	72,719	4,740	1,014,366	2,854,487
Totals	758,620	4,022,784	265,871	4,438,504	602,580	65,537	3,826,464	13,980,360

(Adapted from: B.C., Department of Lands, "Report of the Survey Branch . . . 1914," p. D50.)

Table 8.

Timber Statistics

(1) Timber Licences issued, 1883-1911, inclusive.

Year	No. Licences	Year	No. Licences
1883	96	1897	78
1884	2	1898	87
1885	1	1899	87
1886	35	1900	143
1887	42	1901	129
1888	36	1902	525
1889	35	1903	1307
1890	21	1904	1451
1891	21	1905	2166
1892	34	1906	3959
1893	36	1907	10456
1894	23	1908	17700
1895	40	1909	15164
1896	68	1910	12195
		1911	15195
		Total:	81,132

(Source: Forestry inspectors' reports in the reports of the chief commissioner of lands and works 1883-1911.)

(2) Extent and Value of Privately held Timber Lands, 1913.

District	Acreage 1913	Average Value per Acre
Victoria	17,341	$13.30
Cowichan	69,109	14.88
Alberni	44,733	15.45
Nanaimo	84,199	11.05
Comox	219,343	12.54
Rossland	29,385	4.50
Kettle River	6,041	3.00
Slocan	31,768	7.86
Kamloops	4,960	1.13
Vancouver	7,428	15.03
Nelson	182,373	3.82
Vernon	4,692	3.06
Golden	77,947	3.85
Revelstoke	48,598	11.47
Fort Steele	95,031	6.41
Totals	922,948	$ 9.02

(Source: B.C., *Sessional Papers,* 13th Parl., 2d sess., 1914, p. D52.

(3) Provincial Land Areas, Productive and Unproductive, 1913.

Total Land Area

	Square Miles	Acres
Dominion lands	22,647	14,494,000
Provincial lands	331,341	212,058,240
Total	353,988	226,552,240

Productive Area
(Sq. miles)

	Timber	%	Agricultural	%
Dominion lands	4,489	19.8	3,589	15.8
Provincial lands	47,522	14.3	20,700	6.3
Total	52,011	14.7	24,289	6.9

Unproductive Area
(Sq. miles)

	Area	% of total
Dominion lands	14,092	64.6
Provincial lands	263,119	79.4
Total	277,211	78.4

(Adapted from *Forests of B.C.*, Tables pp. 239 and 242.)

Table 9.

Timber Leases Held, 1888

Name	Number of Mills and where situated	Daily Capacity	Location	Date	Term of Years	Acreage	Rental: At which granted	Rental: Revised by Act, 1888
Moodyville Saw-Mill Company	1. Burrard Inlet	105,000	New Westminster District	Jan. 1, 1870	21	11,410	114.10	114.10
			New Westminster District	Jan. 11, 1875	21	10,162	101.62	101.62
			New Westminster District	Nov. 28, 1884	20	1,947	194.70	97.35
			New Westminster District	Feb. 6, 1886	21	7,825	782.50	391.25
			New Westminster District	Jan. 10, 1888	21	1,433	214.95	71.65
			New Westminster District	Mar. 16, 1888	21	800	120.00	40.00
Hastings Saw-Mill Company	2. Vancouver	65,000	Coast District	Mar. 15, 1886	21	8,216	921.40	410.80
			New Westminster District	Nov. 30, 1886	2	704	70.40	
			New Westminster District	Nov. 30, 1886	5	3,220	322.00	161.00
			Coast and Sayward District	Jun. 10, 1887	21	2,301	345.15	115.05
			Sayward District	Feb. 8, 1888	21	1,360	204.00	68.00
			New Westminster District	Mar. 16, 1888	21	1,467	220.05	73.35
Royal City Planing Mills Co.	2. New Westminster	110,000	Sayward District	Feb. 6, 1886	21	6,971	1,045.65	348.55
	1. Vancouver	30,000	Coast and Sayward District	Jun. 10, 1887	21	3,652	547.80	182.60
			Coast and N.W. District	Nov. 10, 1887	21	8,353	1,252.95	417.65
			Sayward District	Jan. 27, 1888	21	1,482	222.30	74.10
Leamy & Kyle	1. Vancouver	50,000	Coast District	Jan. 18, 1887	21	2,500	375.00	125.00
			Coast and Sayward District	Feb. 3, 1888	21	3,749	562.35	187.45
W. P. Sayward	1. Victoria		Coast District	Jun. 18, 1885	21	1,380	138.00	69.00

Name	Number of Mills and where situated	Daily Capacity	Location	Date	Term of Years	Acreage	Rental: At which granted	Rental: Revised by Act, 1888
Wm. Sutton	1. Cowichan	35,000	Cowichan District	Jan. 9, 1879	20	7,069	70.69	70.69
J. Martin and Son			Harrison, Lake, N.W. District	Feb. 1, 1876	21	787	7.87	7.87
Haslem and Lees	1. Nanaimo	70,000	Sayward District	Mar. 16, 1888	21	18,462	2,769.30	923.10
Croft and Argus	1. Chemainus	50,000	New Westminster District	Mar. 16, 1888	21	1,413	211.95	70.65
Leonard G. Little			Sayward District	Feb. 3, 1888	21	4,800	720.00	240.00
Ross & McLaren			Sayward District	Feb. 3, 1888	21	23,600	3,540.00	1,180.00
Knight Brothers	1.	25,000						
Shuswap Milling Company	2. Yale District	32,000						
Muir Brothers	1. Sooke	12,000						
Brunette Saw-Mill Co.	1. New Westminster	30,000						
Fader Brothers	1. Vancouver	75,000						
Port Moody Saw-Mill Co.	1. Port Moody	15,000						
W. H. Johnston	1. Quesnelle	20,000						
I. B. Nason	1. Barkerville	7,000						
Indians	1. Alert Bay	5,000						
Cunningham Company	1. Port Essington	8,000						
G. Williscroft	1. Georgetown	12,000						
N. Hanson	1. Kootenay District	10,000						
Indians (Kincolith)	1. Nass River	3,000						
Vancouver Lumber Co.	1. Vancouver							
Totals						135,063	15,074.73	5,540.83

(Adapted from B.C., *Sessional Papers*, 5th Parl., 2d sess., 1888, p. 153.)

Table 10.

Summary of Data, 1916 Indian Royal Commission Report

Agency	Source in 1916 Report	Indian Population	No. reserves found 1916	Acreage of already confirmed Reserves	Acreage per capita	Acreage cut off 1916	No. reserves added	Total after 1916 Report	Acreage added by 1916 Report	Total Acreage after 1916 Report	Acreage per capita
Babine	1:180	1626	45	30,054.21	18.49	19.59	23	67	5,734.93	35,808.73	22.02
Bella Coola	1:225	1511	65	18,592.93	12.31	4,075.00	46	110	7,050.60	25,643.53	16.99
Cowichan	1:275	1936	66	19,362.55	10.01	517.04	—	59	Nil	19,352.55	9.99
Kamloops	1:306	2340	103	206,959.12	88.44	3,498.53	—	103	1,477.00	171,205.13	73.16
Kwawkewlth	2:380	1183	91	16,466.63	13.92	140.86	29	118	1,902.29	18,228.06	15.43
Kootenay	2:359	598	33	43,771.38	73.20	2,370.00	8	41	8,260.00	52,031.38	87.00
Lytton	2:442	2502	158	51,381.61	20.53	3,100.00	54	211	15,707.65	67,089.26	26.81
Naas	3:550	1799	63	50,945.72	28.32	11,909.19	130	190	5,671.00	56,616.72	31.47
New Westminster	3:626	2487	157	40,923.37	16.45	152.48	18	168	1,168.45	41,939.30	16.30
Okanagan	3:696	797	44	127,391.41	159.84	18,536.80	1	35	2,600.00	129,991.41	163.00
Queen Charlotte	3:724	597	25	3,484.50	5.83	Nil	7	32	360.10	3,844.60	6.44
Stikine	4:745	217	2	415.00	1.90	Nil	26	28	9,638.00	10,053.00	15.73
Stuart Lake	4:767	965	37	21,638.94	22.85	409.00	97	131	14,892.20	36,531.14	31.22
West Coast	4:851	1683	150	11,543.10	6.85	840.00	14	164	661.95	12,200.25	7.24
Williams Lake	4:911	1248	64	60,940.77	48.83	1,490.00	29	92	12,167.00	93,107.77	58.56
Totals		21,489	1103	666,640.25		47,058.49	482	1,559	87,291.17	773,642.83	

Appendix C

Item 1

Defunct Railway Companies Legislated out of Existence, 1927

An Act respecting certain Defunct Railway Companies. B.C., Statutes, 1926-27, 17 Geo. 5, C. 55.

HIS MAJESTY, by and with the advice and consent of the Legislative Assembly of the Province of British Columbia, enacts as follows:—

1. This Act may be cited as the "Defunct Railway Companies Dissolution Act."

2. The corporations named in the first column of Schedule A which were incorporated under the Acts referred to in the second column of Schedule A opposite their respective names shall, for all purposes, be deemed to be dissolved; and all powers and franchises held by the said corporations respectively are hereby declared to have wholly ceased.

3. The dissolution of a corporation under this Act shall not absolve the property of the corporation or any shareholder of the corporation from any charge, obligation, or liability, or prejudice or impair the right of any creditor or person to enforce in any lawful manner whatsoever any claim against the corporation or any shareholder thereof.

4. The Acts specified in Schedule B are repealed.

SCHEDULES

SCHEDULE A.

Corporations Dissolved

Name	Statutes of British Columbia.
Adams River Railway Company	1903, c. 30.
Alberni and Cowichan Railway Company	1903-4, c. 59.
Alice Arm Railway Company, The	1898, c. 46.
Ashcroft and Cariboo Railway Company, The	1896, c. 52.
Arrowhead and Kootenay Railway Company	1898, c. 47.
Ashcroft and Cariboo Railway Company, The	1890, c. 60.
Ashcroft, Barkerville and Fort George Railway Company, The	1906, c. 49.

Name	Statutes of British Columbia.
Atlin Short Line Railway and Navigation Company, The	1899, c. 79.
Atlin Southern Railway Company	1899, c. 80.
Barkerville, Ashcroft and Kamloops Railway Company,	1897, c. 46.
Bedlington and West Kootenay Railway Company, The	1893, c. 46.
Bella Coola and Fraser Lake Railway Company	1906, c. 50.
Bentinck Arm and Quesnelle Railway Company	1907, c. 48.
British Columbia and Alaska Railway Company	1910, c. 56.
British Columbia Central Railway Company	1906, c. 51.
British Columbia Central Railway Company	1910, c. 57.
British Columbia Northern and Alaska Railway Company	1906, c. 52.
British Columbia Northern and Mackenzie Valley Railway Company	1903, c. 32.
Burrard Inlet and Fraser Valley Railway Company, The	1891, c. 54.
Burrard Inlet Railway and Ferry Company, The	1891, c. 53.
Canadian Northern Railway Company, The	1892, c. 48.
Canadian Western Central Railway Company, The	1889, c. 34.
Canadian Yukon Railway Company, The	1898, c. 50.
Cariboo, Barkerville and Willow River Railway Company	1910, c. 62.
Cariboo Railway Company, The	1894, c. 55.
Cassiar Central Railway Company	1897, c. 52.
Chilkat and Klehini Railway and Navigation Company	1901, c. 68.
Chilliwhack Railway Company, The	1891, c. 55.
Coast-Kootenay Railway Company, Limited, The	1901, c. 69.
Coast-Yukon Railway Company, The	1903-4, c. 58.
Columbia and Carbonate Mountain Railway Company, The	1890, c. 61.
Columbia and Kootenay Railway and Transportation Company	1883, c. 25.
Comox and Cape Scott Railway Company, The	1901, c. 71.
Crawford Bay Railway Company, The	1901, c. 72.
Crow's Nest and Northern Railway Company	1908, c. 58.
Delta, New Westminster and Eastern Railway Company, The	1894, c. 57.
Delta Railway Company, The	1887, c. 34.
Downie Creek Railway Company	1898, c. 52.
East Kootenay Railway Company	1897, c. 61.

Name	Statutes of British Columbia.
East Kootenay Valley Railway Company, The	1898, c. 53.
Fernie and Elk River Railway Company, The	1921, c. 75.
Flathead Valley Railway Company	1903, c. 33.
Flathead Valley Railway Company	1909, c. 52.
Fording Valley Railway Company	1905, c. 63.
Fraser River Railway Company	1883, c. 26.
Graham Island Railway Company	1909, c. 54.
Hardy Bay and Quatsino Sound Railway Company	1909, c. 55.
Harrison Hot Springs Tramway Company, Limited, The	1888, c. 47.
Hot Springs and Goat River Tramway Company, The	1891, c. 68.
Hudson Bay Pacific Railway Company	1908, c. 61.
Imperial Pacific Railway Company, The	1901, c. 77.
Island Valley Railway Company	1910, c. 68.
Kamloops and Atlin Railway Company	1899, c. 83.
Kamloops and Atlin Railway Company, The	1901, c. 78.
Kamloops and Yellowhead Pass Railway Company	1906, c. 58.
Kaslo and Lardo-Duncan Railway Company	1897, c. 58.
Kaslo and Slocan Tramway Company, The	1893, c. 52.
Kitimat Railway Company, Limited	1898, c. 54.
Kootenay and Athabasca Railway Company, The	1887, c. 35.
Kootenay and North-west Railway Company, The	1898, c. 55.
Kootenay, Cariboo and Pacific Railway Company	1903, c. 34.
Kootenay Development and Tramways Company	1903, c. 36.
Kootenay Lake Shore and Lardo Railway Company, The	1893, c. 53.
Kootenay Railway and Navigation Company, The	1888, c. 46.
Lake Bennett Railway Company	1901, c. 80.
Lardeau and Kootenay Railway Company, The	1893, c. 54.
Lardeau Railway Company	1897, c. 64.
Liverpool and Canoe Pass Railway Company, The	1891, c. 57.
Meadow Creek Railway Company	1909, c. 56.
Menzies Bay Railway Company	1910, c. 69.
Mid-Provincial and Nechako Railway Company	1911, c. 68.
Midway and Vernon Railway Company, The	1901, c. 81.
Mount Tolmie and Cordova Bay Railway Company, The	1893, c. 55.
Mountain Tramway and Electric Company	1898, c. 56.
Naas and Skeena Rivers Railway Company	1911, c. 69.
Nanaimo-Alberni Company, The	1897, c. 66.

Name	Statutes of British Columbia.
Nanaimo Electric Tramway Company, Limited, The	1891, c. 69.
Nelson and Arrow Lake Railway Company, The	1893, c. 57.
New Westminster and Port Moody Railway Company, The	1882, c. 14.
New Westminster and Vancouver Short Line Railway Company, The	1889, c. 37.
New Westminster Southern Railway Company, The	1883, c. 27.
North Star and Arrow Lake Railway Company, The	1898, c. 58.
Northern Vancouver Island Railway Company	1910, c. 71.
Okanagan and Kootenay Railway Company, The	1890, c. 64.
Osoyoos and Okanagan Railway Company, The	1893, c. 59.
Pacific Northern and Eastern Railway Company	1903, c. 39.
Pacific Northern and Omineca Railway Company	1900, c .50.
Pacific Railway Company	1910, c. 73.
Peace and Naas River Railway Company	1911, c. 73.
Penticton Railway Company	1910, c. 74.
Port Moody, Indian River, and Northern Railway Company	1910, c. 75.
Portland and Stickine Railway Company	1898, c. 59.
Portland Canal Railway Company	1907, c. 56.
Prince Rupert and Port Simpson Railway Company	1909, c. 60.
Quatsino Railway Company	1903, c. 42.
Queen Charlotte Islands Railway Company, The	1901, c. 83.
Queen Charlotte Islands Railway Company	1905, c. 68.
Queen Charlotte Railway Company	1910, c. 76.
Rainy Hollow Railway Company	1907, c. 58.
Revelstoke and Cassiar Railway Company	1898, c. 61.
Rock Bay and Salmon River Railway Company, The	1900, c. 51.
St. Mary's Valley Railway Company	1906, c. 65.
Skeena River and Eastern Railway Company	1898, c. 62.
Skeena River Railway, Colonization, and Exploration Company	1898, c. 63.
South Kootenay Railway Company	1899, c. 88.
South-East Kootenay Railway Company	1898, c. 64.
South-East Kootenay Railway Company	1906, c. 63.
Southern Okanagan Railway Company	1906, c. 66.
Stave Valley Railway Company	1905, c. 70.
Stickeen and Teslin Railway, Navigation, and Colonization Company	1897, c. 71.

Name	Statutes of British Columbia.
Toad Mountain and Nelson Tramway Company, The	1891, c. 70.
Upper Columbia Navigation and Tramway Company, The	1891, c. 50.
Vancouver and Grand Forks Railway Company, The	1901, c. 84.
Vancouver and Lulu Island Electric Railway and Improvement Company, The	1891, c. 61.
Vancouver and Nicola Valley Railway Company	1908, c. 63.
Vancouver and Northern Railway Company, The	1909, c. 64.
Vancouver and Westminster Railway Company	1900, c. 53.
Vancouver Land and Railway Company, The	1882, c. 15.
Vancouver-Nanaimo Railway Transfer Company	1897, c. 74.
Vancouver, Northern, and Yukon Railway Company	1899, c. 89.
Vancouver, Northern, Peace River, and Alaska Railway and Navigation Company	1891, c. 62.
Vernon and Okanagan Railway Company, The	1891, c. 63.
Victoria and Barkley Sound Railway Company, The	1909, c. 65.
Victoria and North American Railway Company, The	1891, c. 64.
Victoria and Saanich Railway Company, The	1886, c. 29.
Victoria and Seymour Narrows Railway Company, The	1902, c. 79.
Victoria, Vancouver, and Westminster Railway Company, The	1894, c. 64.
Yale-Northern Railway Company, The	1901, c. 87.

SCHEDULE B.

Acts Repealed

Hall Mines Limited Tramway Act, 1894	1894, c. 59.
Nanaimo Railway Act, 1881	1881, c. 25.
Victoria and Yellowhead Pass Railway Aid Act, 1902	1902, c. 70.
Wellington Collieries Railway Act, 1883	1883, c. 28.
Yukon Mining, Trading and Transportation Company (Foreign) Act, 1897	1897, c. 77.

Item 2

Railways Incorporated under Acts of the Legislature of British Columbia since 1883

	Cap.	*Year*	*Remarks*
1. Adams River	30	1903	Lapsed
2. Alice Arm	46	1898	Lapsed
3. Ashcroft and Cariboo	40	1890	Lapsed
4. Ashcroft and Cariboo	60	1890	Lapsed
5. Ashcroft and Cariboo	52	1891	Lapsed
6. Ashcroft and Cariboo	52	1896	Lapsed
7. Ashcroft, Barkerville and Fort George	49	1906	Lapsed
8. Arrowhead and Kootenay	47	1898	Lapsed
9. Arrowhead and Kootenay	65	1901	Lapsed
10. Atlin Short Line Railway and Navigation Co.	79	1899	Lapsed
11. Atlin Southern	80	1899	Lapsed
12. Barkerville, Ashcroft and Kamloops	46	1897	Lapsed
13. Bedlington and Nelson	47	1897	Declared for public benefit, c. 53, 1899
14. Bedlington and West Kootenay	46	1893	Lapsed
15. Bentinck Arm and Quesnel	48	1907	Lapsed
16. Bella Coola and Fraser Lake	50	1906	Lapsed
17. British Columbia and Alaska	56	1910	Lapsed
18. British Columbia and Northern	32	1903	Lapsed
19. Mackenzie Valley	53	1906	Lapsed
20. British Columbia Central	51	1906	Lapsed
21. British Columbia Central	57	1910	Lapsed

	Cap.	Year	Remarks
22. British Columbia Northern and Alaska	52	1906	Lapsed
23. British Columbia Southern	36	1893	Amended, c. 47, 1893; repealed, c. 53, 1894; c. 39, 1894; c. 4, 1896; c. 53, 1896; c. 33, 1897. Declared for public benefit, c. 36, 1897
24. British Columbia Electric Railway:			
Vancouver Street Railway	31	1886	Lapsed
Vancouver Street Railway	38	1889	Incorporation
Vancouver Electric Railway and Light Co.	51	1890	Amendment
National Electric Tramway and Light Co.	39	1889	Victoria Electric Railway and Light Co., c. 63, 1894
National Electric Tramway and Light Co.	52	1890	Amendment
Westminster Street Railway	65	1890	
Western and Vancouver Tramway Co.	67	1890	Amendment
British Columbia Electric Co.	49	1890	
British Columbia Electric Co.	71	1891	Act to amalgamate Western Street Railway Company and Western and Vancouver Tramway Co.
British Columbia Electric Co.	51	1894	Amendment Land Grant
Consolidated Railway and Light Co.	56	1894	Incorporation
Consolidated Railway and Light Co.	55	1896	Amendment
Victoria Electric Railway and Light Co.	63	1894	City of Victoria to supply light and power
Victoria and British Columbia Electric Railway Co. Agreement	81	1910	Supply electric light and power in and around City of Victoria

	Cap.	*Year*	*Remarks*
25. British Columbia Yukon	49	1897	Operating
26. Burrard Inlet and Fraser Valley	54	1891	Amended, c. 48, 1893 and c. 59, 1895 Lapsed
27. Burrard Inlet Railway and Ferry Co.	53	1891	Lapsed
28. Canadian North-eastern	74	1911	Lapsed
29. Canadian Northern	48	1892	
30. Canadian Northern	3	1910	Main lines — Agreement (a) Yellowhead Pass to Vancouver completed (b) Victoria to Barkley Sound time extended to Feb. 1st, 1917
31. Canadian Northern Pacific	4	1910	
32. Canadian Northern Pacific	32	1912	Barkley Sound to Nootka Sound, time extended to Feb. 27th, 1917
33. Canadian Northern Pacific	57	1913	Branch Lines: (a) Westminster Bridge to Vancouver, time extended to Feb. 1st, 1917; (b) Westminster Bridge to Steveston completed; (c) Victoria to Patricia Bay, completed
34. Canadian Northern Pacific	58	1913	Amendment to c. 4, 1910
35. Canadian Northern Pacific	59	1913	Terminals—Port Mann, New Westminster, Vancouver, Victoria, Steveston, and Patricia Bay
36. Canadian Northern Pacific	61	1914	Further aid toward construction
37. Canadian Northern Pacific	62	1914	Amendment to c. 57, 1913
38. Canadian Pacific Railway	11	1880	Lapsed
39. Canadian Western Central	20	1889	Land subsidy

	Cap.	*Year*	*Remarks*
40. Canadian Western Central	34	1889	Incorporation. Amended c. 40, 1890; c. 36, 1892; c. 39, 1893; c. 4, 1895; c. 34, 1897. Lapsed
41. Canadian Yukon	50	1898	Lapsed
42. Cariboo, Barkerville, and Willow River	62	1910	Lapsed
43. Cariboo (Ashcroft and Cariboo)	55	1897	Amendment, c. 50, 1897. Lapsed
44. Cassiar Central	35	1897	Crown grant
45. Cassiar Central	52	1897	Incorporation. Lapsed
46. Chilkat and Klehine Railway and Navigation Co.	68	1901	Lapsed
47. Chilliwhack	55	1891	Declared for public benefit, c. 43, 1893
48. Columbia and Carbonate Mountain	61	1890	Lapsed
49. Columbia and Kootenay	21	1889	Land subsidy
50. Columbia and Kootenay	62	1890	Amended, c. 49, 1892; c. 60, 1892. Declared for public benefit, c. 89, 1890
51. Columbia and Kootenay Railway and Transportation Co.	25	1883	Amended, c. 24, 1884; c. 21, 1889; c. 41, 1890. Lapsed
52. Columbia and Western	8	1896	Subsidy Act. Repealed c. 8, 1903
53. Columbia and Western	54	1896	Incorporation. Amended, c. 12, 1898; c. 14, 1899; c. 4, 1900; c. 70, 1901; c. 8, 1903; c. 9, 1906; declared for public benefit, c. 61, 1898
54. Coast-Kootenay	69	1901	Amended, c. 9, 1902; declared for public benefit, c. 199, 1903
55. Coast-Yukon	58	1904	Lapsed
56. Comox and Cape Scott	71	1901	Lapsed
57. Comox Logging and Railway Co.	63	1910	Operating

	Cap.	*Year*	*Remarks*
58. Cowichan, Alberni, and Fort Rupert	59	1904	Amended, c. 54, 1906. Lapsed
59. Crawford Bay	72	1901	Lapsed
60. Crow's Nest and Kootenay Lake	72	1888	Land Grant Incorporation
61. Crow's Nest and Kootenay Lake	44	1888	Amended, c. 63, 1890; c. 56, 1891. Repealed, c. 53, 1894. Lapsed
62. Crow's Nest and Northern	58	1908	Amended, c. 64, 1911. Lapsed
63. Crow's Nest Southern	73	1901	Operating (Great Northern Railway or Vancouver, Victoria, and Eastern Railway)
64. Delta, New Westminster and Eastern	57	1894	Amended, c. 54, 1897. Lapsed
65. Delta	34	1887	Lapsed
66. Downie Creek	52	1898	Lapsed
67. East Kootenay Logging	52	1907	Operating
68. East Kootenay	61	1897	Lapsed
69. East Kootenay Valley	53	1898	Lapsed
70. Eastern British Columbia	60	1908	Operating
71. Esquimalt and Nanaimo	13	1875	Land Grant. Repealed, c. 16, 1882. Amended, c. 28, 1888; c. 45, 1888
72. Esquimalt and Nanaimo	26	1903	Settlers' Rights Act
73. Esquimalt and Nanaimo	33	1912	Agreement. Amended, c. 60, 1913. Declared for public benefit, c. 90, 1905
74. Flathead Valley	33	1903	Lapsed
75. Flathead Valley	52	1909	Lapsed
76. Fording Valley	63	1905	Lapsed
77. Fraser River	26	1883	Lapsed
78. Graham Island	54	1909	Lapsed
79. Graham Island	65	1910	Amendment. Time extended to 1918

	Cap.	*Year*	*Remarks*
80. Grand Trunk Pacific	19	1908	Crown Grant, Amended, c. 22, 1909; c. 34, 1912
81. Grouse Mountain Scenic Incline	16	1911	Time extended to Apr. 1, 1917
82. Hall Mines Ltd., Tramway	59	1894	Lapsed
83. Hardy Bay and Quatsino Sound	55	1909	Lapsed
84. Harrison Hot Springs Tramway Co.	47	1888	Lapsed
85. Hot Springs and Goat River Tramway	68	1891	Lapsed
86. Howe Sound, Pemberton Valley and Northern	53	1907	$5000 deposit with Minister of Finance
87. Howe Sound and Northern	67	1910	Amendment to c. 53, 1907. Amalgamated with the P.G.E.
88. Hudson Bay Pacific	61	1908	Lapsed
89. Imperial Pacific	77	1901	Lapsed
90. Island Valley	68	1910	Lapsed
91. Kamloops and Atlin	83	1899	Lapsed
92. Kamloops and Atlin	48	1900	Lapsed
93. Kamloops and Atlin	78	1901	Lapsed
94. Kamloops and Yellowhead Pass	58	1906	Lapsed
95. Kaslo and Lardo-Duncan	58	1897	Lapsed
96. Kaslo and Slocan	37	1892	Land Grant
97. Kaslo and Slocan	52	1892	Incorporation, Amended c. 41, 1894; c. 61, 1894; c. 36, 1897. C.P.R. was paid $100,000 for reconstructing Kaslo and Slocan (c. 37, 1912). Now operating
98. Kaslo and Slocan Tramway Co.	52	1893	Lapsed
99. Kettle River Valley	26	1910	Agreement
100. Kettle River Valley	35	1912	Ratify agreement Jan. 12th, 1912
101. Kettle River Valley	53	1912	By-law. Operating
102. Kitimat	54	1898	Amended, c. 84, 1899. Lapsed

	Cap.	Year	Remarks
103. Kootenay and North-west	55	1898	Amended, c. 85, 1899. Lapsed
104. Kootenay Lake Shore and Lardo	53	1893	Lapsed
105. Kootenay and Athabasca	25	1887	Land Grant. Lapsed
106. Kootenay and Athabasca	35	1887	Incorporation. Lapsed
107. Kootenay, Cariboo and Pacific	34	1903	Lapsed
108. Kootenay Central	79	1901	Lapsed
109. Kootenay Central	35	1903	Declared for public benefit
110. Kootenay Railway and Navigation Co.	29	1888	Land Grant. Lapsed
111. Kootenay Railway and Navigation Co.	46	1888	Change of title. Lapsed
112. Columbia and Kootenay Railway and Navigation Co.	35	1889	Lapsed
113. Ladysmith Lumber Co. Railway	62	1908	Operating
114. Lake Bennett	80	1901	Lapsed
115. Lardeau and Kootenay	54	1893	Lapsed
116. Lardeau	64	1897	Lapsed
117. Liverpool and Canoe Pass	57	1891	Lapsed
118. Meadow Creek	56	1909	Lapsed. $5000 deposited with Minister of Finance
119. Menzies Bay	69	1910	Time extended to March 28th, 1917
120. Mid-Provincial and Nechako	68	1911	Lapsed
121. Midway and Vernon	81	1901	Amended, c. 45, 1902. Repealed, c. 45, 1902. Amended, c. 36, 1904; c. 60, 1906. Lapsed
122. Midway-Penticton	44	1899	
123. Morrissey, Fernie and Michel	37	1903	Lapsed
124. Mountain Tramway and Electric Co.	56	1898	Lapsed
125. Mount Tolmie Park and Cordova Bay	55	1893	Lapsed
126. Naas and Skeena Rivers	69	1911	Amended, c. 79, 1916, extending time of commencement of construction 1 year from date of Act

	Cap.	*Year*	*Remarks*
127. Nakusp and Slocan	56	1893	Amended, c. 43, 1894. Operated by C.P.R.
128. Nanaimo-Alberni	66	1897	Lapsed
129. Nanaimo Electric Tramway	69	1891	Lapsed
130. Nanaimo Railway Act	25	1881	Lapsed
131. Nelson and Fort Sheppard	58	1891	Amended, c. 42, 1894; c. 37, 1897
132. Nelson and Fort Sheppard	38	1892	Land Grant. Declared for public benefit, c. 57, 1893
133. Nelson and Fort Sheppard	42	1894	Amended, c. 42, 1894; c. 37, 1897
134. Nelson and Arrow Lake	57	1893	Lapsed
135. New Westminster-Port Moody	14	1882	Amended, c. 25, 1884. Lapsed
136. New Westminster and Vancouver Short Line	37	1889	Amended, c. 67, 1892; c. 60, 1896. Lapsed
137. New Westminster Southern	27	1883	Lapsed
138. New Westminster Southern	36	1887	Amended, c. 36, 1889. Operating. Great Northern Pacific purchased from Port Kells to the Bridge, New Westminster
139. Nicola, Kamloops and Similkameen Coal and Railway	47	1891	Amended, c. 38, 1903. Declared for public benefit, c. 164, 1903
140. Nicola Valley	59	1891	Declared for public benefit, Cap. 50, 1892
141. Nicola Valley	37	1893	
142. North Star and Arrow Lake	58	1898	Amended, c. 86, 1899. Lapsed
143. Northern Vancouver Island	71	1910	
144. Northern Vancouver Island	70	1911	Time extended to March 28, 1917. $5000 deposited with Minister of Finance
145. Okanagan and Kootenay	40	1890	Lapsed
146. Okanagan and Kootenay	64	1890	Lapsed
147. Osoyoos and Okanagan	59	1893	Lapsed
148. Pacific Great Eastern	34	1913	Amended, c. 61, 1913; c. 62, 1913; c. 65, 1914

	Cap.	Year	Remarks
149. Pacific Great Eastern	36	1912	Under construction
150. Pacific Northern and Eastern	39	1903	Lapsed
151. Pacific Northern and Omineca	50	1900	Amended, c. 55, 1902; c. 77, 1902; c. 40, 1903; c. 67, 1905; c. 58, 1909. Lapsed. Security deposited with Minister of Finance
152. Pacific Railway	73	1910	Lapsed
153. Peace and Naas River	73	1911	Lapsed
154. Penticton	74	1910	Lapsed
155. Portland and Stickeen	59	1898	Lapsed
156. Portland Canal Short Line	59	1909	Amended, c. 74, 1911. Now called North-eastern Railway. Abandoned
157. Portland Canal	56	1907	Lapsed
158. Port Moody, Indian River and Northern	75	1910	Lapsed
159. Prince Rupert and Port Simpson	60	1909	Lapsed
160. Quatsino	42	1903	Lapsed
161. Queen Charlotte Island	83	1901	Amended, c. 57, 1907
162. Queen Charlotte Island	63	1905	Lapsed
163. Queen Charlotte	76	1910	Lapsed
164. Rainy Hollow	58	1907	Lapsed
165. Red Mountain	61	1893	Declared for public benefit, c. 60, 1895
166. Revelstoke and Cassiar	61	1898	Lapsed
167. Rock Bay and Salmon River	51	1900	Lapsed
168. Saint Mary's and Cherry Creek	64	1906	
169. Saint Mary's Valley	65	1906	
170. Shuswap and Okanagan	26	1887	Amended, c. 30, 1888; c. 42, 1890; c. 37, 1891
171. Skeena River and Eastern	62	1898	Lapsed
172. Skeena River Railway, Colonization and Exploration Co.	63	1898	Lapsed
173. South-east Kootenay	64	1898	Lapsed

	Cap.	*Year*	*Remarks*
174. South-east Kootenay	63	1906	Amended, c. 61, 1909; time extended to Feb. 17, 1917
175. South Kootenay	88	1898	Lapsed
176. South Okanagan	66	1906	Lapsed
177. Stave Valley	70	1905	Lapsed
178. Stickeen and Teslin Railway, Navigation and Colonization Co.	71	1897	Lapsed
179. Toad Mountain and Nelson Tramway Incorporation	70	1891	Amended, c. 44, 1898; c. 40, 1900
180. Toad Mountain and Nelson Tramway	185	1897	Cap. 58, 1901, and Act respecting the Incorporation of Tramway Telephone, Telegraph Companies
181. Tramway Inspection	50	1910	Amended, c. 51, 1911
182. Upper Columbia Navigation and Tramway Co.	50	1891	
183. Vancouver and Grand Forks	84	1901	Lapsed
184. Vancouver and Lulu Island Electric Railway and Improvement Co.	61	1891	Lapsed
185. Vancouver and Lulu Island	60	1891	Amended, c. 73, 1897; c. 52, 1900. Declared for public benefit, c. 86, 1901
186. Vancouver and Nicola Valley	63	1908	Amended c. 80, 1910. Lapsed
187. Vancouver and Northern	64	1909	Lapsed
188. Vancouver and Westminster	53	1900	Amended, c. 78, 1902.
189. Vancouver Island Hydro-Electric Tramway Co.			Incorporated, joint-stock co., Nov. 12, 1912. Lapsed
190. Vancouver Land and Railway Co.	15	1882	Lapsed
191. Vancouver-Nanaimo Railway Transfer Co.	14	1897	Lapsed
192. Vancouver, Northern and Yukon	89	1899	Amended, c. 55, 1900. Lapsed

	Cap.	Year	Remarks
193. Vancouver Northern, Peace River and Alaska Railway and Navigation Co.	62	1891	Lapsed
194. Vancouver, Victoria, and Eastern Railway and Navigation Co.	75	1897	Declared for public benefit, c. 172, 1905
195. Vernon and Okanagan	63	1891	Lapsed
196. Victoria and Barkley Sound	65	1909	Lapsed
197. Victoria and Northern America	64	1891	Lapsed
198. Victoria and Saanich	16	1886	Lapsed
199. Victoria and Saanich	29	1886	Lapsed
200. Victoria and Seymour Narrows	79	1902	Lapsed
201. Victoria and Sidney	39	1892	*Subsidy
202. Victoria and Sidney	66	1892	*Incorporation
203. Victoria and Yellowhead Pass Railway Aid	70	1902	Lapsed
204. Victoria Harbour	44	1911	Lapsed
205. Victoria Terminal Railway and Ferry Co.	85	1901	*Amended, c. 54, 1905
206. Victoria Terminal Railway and Ferry Co.	86	1901	*By-Law
207. Victoria, Vancouver, and Western	64	1894	Amended, c. 76, 1897 Lapsed
208. Wellington Colliery	28	1883	Lapsed
209. Wellington Colliery	44	1911	Operating
210. Yale Northern	87	1901	Lapsed
211. Yukon Mining, Trading, and Transportation Co.	38	1897	
212. Yukon Mining, Trading, and Transportation Co.	77	1897	Lapsed

* Operated by Great Northern.

(Source: British Columbia. Legislative Assembly. Department of Railways. *Report of the Department of Railways of the Province of British Columbia, from 1911 to December 31st, 1916*, 1917.)

Appendix D

Item 1

Indian Reserves in the Province of British Columbia, 1871

	Acreage
ESQUIMALT DISTRICT	
Esquimalt Harbour	47
Songhees Village, near Victoria City	112
SOOKE DISTRICT	
Sooke River	60
SAANICH, N. DISTRICT	
Union Bay	69
Cole Bay	315.02
SAANICH, S. DISTRICT	
Saanich Inlet	494
Bazan Bay	727
COWICHAN AND QUAMICHAN DISTRICTS	
Cowichan River	2,675
Somers Creek	30
Large Island, mouth of Chemainus River	139
Chemainus Creek	100
NANAIMO DISTRICT	
Nanaimo Harbour	40
Nanaimo River, west side	131
Nanaimo River, east side	
CRANBERRY DISTRICT	
Nanaimo River	273
NEW WESTMINSTER	
First Narrows, Burrard Inlet	165
Burrard Inlet	37

Burrard Inlet	37.45
Burrard Inlet	112.46
Near New Westminster	1
Coquitlam River	18.4
Coquitlam River near the Fraser River	6.5
Musqueam, north of North Arm of the Fraser River	342
Chehalis, west bank of Harrison River, four miles from its mouth	626
Fraser River, 1½ miles below the mouth of Harrison River	658
Whanock Reserve, on Fraser River	92
Matsqui Reserve No. 1, on Fraser River	96
Matsqui Reserve No. 2, on Fraser River	52
Katzie Reserve on Fraser River	108
Sumas Reserve, near Chadsey's Slough	43
Sumas Reserve, Upper Forks of Sumas and Slough	440
Sumas Reserve No. 1, Fraser River, Nicoamen Slough	32
Clatwas Reserve, Nicoamen Slough	86
Scowlitz Reserve, Fraser River, at mouth of Harrison River	330
Nicoamen Reserve	109
Squeeam Reserve	73
YALE DISTRICT	
Ohaunil Reserve, on Fraser River ten miles below Hope	488.5
Cheeam Reserve, left bank of Fraser River, twenty miles below Hope	375
Popkum Reserve, left bank of Fraser River, eighteen miles below Hope	369
Squatits Reserve, left bank of Fraser River, thirteen miles below Hope	380
Greenwood Island, opposite Hope	10
Lytton, mouth of Thompson River	14
South-east of the town of Lytton	12
Two miles north of the town of Lytton	18
Nickelpalm Reserve, twenty miles above Lytton	111
Stryem Reserve	297
Shoook Reserve, thirty-six miles on Yale and Lytton Road	204.5
Stan-uja-hamig Reserve, forty-three miles on Yale and Lytton Road	40
Ma-coi-yai Reserve, 1½ miles below Lytton	100
Nohomeen Reserve, 1½ miles above Lytton	30
Skopah Reserve, on Fraser River	58
Kopachicken Reserve, 2½ miles above Boston Bar	205
Boston Bar, twenty-four miles on Yale and Lytton Road	82

Fraser River, seventeen miles on Yale and Lytton Road	81
¼ mile below Alexandra Bridge, ¼ mile from Fraser River	19
Right bank of Fraser River, ten miles on Yale and Lytton Road	110
Two miles below Alexandra Bridge, left bank of Fraser River	51
Similkameen River, Vermillion Forks, right bank	21
Similkameen River, Vermillion Forks, left bank	342
Similkameen Reserve, halfway between Princeton and Keremeos	1,028
Albert Flat, four miles below Yale	163.5
Skowall Reserve, seven miles below Hope	135
Spellumcheen Reserve, one mile from Spellumcheen River	200
Spellumcheen Reserve, left bank of Fraser and Spellumcheen Rivers	18.5
Forks of Nicolai and Thompson Rivers	30.5
Nicoamen Reserve, left bank Fraser River, sixty-eight miles on Yale and Lytton Road	61
Deadman's Creek	575
Nicolai River	918
Buonaparte Creek	471
Nicolai Lake, east bank	670
Nicolai Lake Lagoon	60
Shuswap Lake	3,112
Shuswap Lake	1,900
Adam's Lake, east side	1,000
Kamloops River, at the forks of North and South Thompson Rivers	6,000

(Adapted from: "Return of Indian Reserves," B.C., *Journals,* 1st Parl., 2d sess., 1872-73, appendix, *Sessional Papers.*)

Item 2

Lieutenant-Governor Trutch to Prime Minister Sir John A. Macdonald, October 14, 1872

Govt. House, Victoria, B.C.,
Oct. 14th, 1872.

My Dear Sir John,

I received your letter of the 25th ult. the day before yesterday on my return home from a visit of inspection to the interior of B.C. where — at Ashcroft — Senator Cornwall's place — I met Mr. Fleming on his arrival from the other side of the Rocky Mountains. As you will of course hear from himself a full account of his trip and of his impressions as to the country, the line of proposed railway and the competing advantages of the rival Fraser River and Bute Inlet routes, I will only say on this subject that he and his party have made the quickest journey of which we have record between Fort Garry and Victoria — and yet appear as fresh and hearty as if they had not travelled one hundred miles.

I am very glad to find that you are pleased at the result of the steps I took to secure Sir Francis's selection for Vancouver Dist. and I trust the latter has written to Mr. Bunster through whose withdrawal his return by acclamation was effected, and that you may think fit to take some notice of Bunster should an opportunity occur. Had I received the news of Sir George's defeat for Montreal two days sooner he would have been returned for Yale District, as well as for Provencher, but the nomination for the last remaining election in B.C. had already taken place ere the result of the Montreal election was reported here. I cannot tell you how deeply all here regret the serious indisposition which withdraws him for a time from public life, and to me specially who have had the privilege of his friendship, his illness, so unexpectedly announced, occasions heartfelt sorrow. I trust he may soon be so restored in health as to be able to resume his duties, for I am sure that to you particularly and to the country at large his loss would be a great calamity.

At the same time with your letter under reply in which you ask me to write you my private opinion as to Dr. Powell's fitness for the situation of Indian Agent in this Province I received your telegram of 2nd inst. acquainting me of his having been appointed to that office, which would have seemed to render superfluous any further allusion to the subject but that it appears to me a matter of such paramount importance to all interests in this country that I think it my duty to convey to you my ideas thereon, and have also taken the opportunity to express the same views more fully to Mr. Fleming who on his arrival at Ottawa will place you in possession thereof, and will also give you the benefit of his own impression as to the Indians of B.C. and their management. . . .

Dr. Powell has a very good standing here. He has been in good practice in his profession and is reputed to possess business ability, but he is entirely without any special knowledge of Indian matters, has had no experience in managing Indian affairs, has hardly ever been out of Victoria during his residence in this Province, and cannot therefore know much of or concerning our Indians and is certainly unknown by them. Now whether he is at all fit for the post of Indian Agent in B.C. depends on the scope of duties and the extent of authority to be attached to the office; in fact on the manner in which the Indian Department is to be organized here and the system to be adopted towards the Indians. Dr. Powell might perform the duties of the office well enough if acting under the immediate direction and advice of some one of more experience here, but I should not certainly consider it otherwise than most likely to result in all sorts of complications and dissatisfactions if the management of our Indians were left in his hands altogether.

We have in B.C. a population of Indians numbering from 40,000 to 50,000, by far the larger portion of whom are utter savages living along the coast, frequently committing murder and robbery among themselves, one tribe upon another, and on white people who go amongst them for purposes of trade, and only restrained from more outrageous crime by being always treated with firmness, and by the consistent enforcement of the law amongst them to which end we have often to call in aid the services of H.M. ships on the station. I cannot see how the charge of these Indians can be entrusted to one having no experience among them, nor do I think it likely that the assistance of the Navy would be willingly and effectively given to any subordinate officer of the Government. Without further descanting on the matter however, I may tell you that I am of opinion, and that very strongly, that for some time to come at least the general charge and direction of all Indian affairs in B.C. should be vested in the Lt. Governor, if there is no constitutional objection to such arrangement, and that instead of one there should be three Indian Agents, one for Vancouver Island, one for the Northwest Coast and the third for the interior of the mainland of the Province, which latter gentleman might very properly be a Roman Catholic, as the Indians in this section are for the most part under the influence of missionaries of that persuasion. Then as to Indian policy I am fully satisfied that for the present the wisest course would be to continue the system which has prevailed hitherto, only providing increased means for educating the Indians, and generally improving their condition moral and physical. The Canadian system, as I understand it will hardly work here. We have never bought out any Indian claims to lands, nor do they expect we should, but we reserve for their use and benefit from time to time tracts of sufficient extent to fulfil all their reasonable requirements for cultivation or grazing. If you now commence to buy out Indian title to the lands of B.C. you would go back of all that has been done here for 30 years past and would be equitably bound to compensate the tribes who inhabited the districts now settled farmed by white people equally with those in the more remote and uncultivated portions. Our Indians are sufficiently satisfied and had better be left alone as far as a new system towards them is concerned, only give us the means of educating them by teachers employed directly by Govt. as well as by aiding the efforts of the missionaries now working among them.

To be rid of all concern with our Indian affairs would of course free me of a very considerable part of the trouble and anxiety I have had for the past year, but, however glad I might be at such a release, I have thought it my duty to express to you my conviction that you had better for some time to come continue the general charge of all Indian matters in B.C. in the Lt. Governor, divide the Province into three districts and appoint an Agent in each subject to direction from the Lt. Governor. By such a course you would secure through the Lt. Governor the benefit of the experience of those who during the past 13 or 14 years have managed the Indian affairs of the country, I mean the County Court Judges, who would be likely to feel diminished inclination to become the assistants of any official of a grade below their own.

I believe I have written all I need to on this matter and I fear at such lengths as to be tedious, but it is one of much importance to this Province, the care of the Indians here being, as I regard it, and have intimated to you in former letters the most delicate and presently momentous responsibility of the Dominion Government within the Province.

Faithfully yours,
Joseph W. Trutch.

The Rt. Honorable
Sir John A. Macdonald, K.C.B.

(Source: Sir Joseph Pope, *Correspondence of Sir John Macdonald: Selections from the Correspondence of the Right Honourable Sir John Alexander Macdonald, G.C.B., First Prime Minister of the Dominion of Canada.* (Toronto: Oxford University Press, 1921, pp. 183-85.)

Item 3

Indian Petition to Dr. I. W. Powell, July 14, 1874

The Petition of the undersigned, Chiefs of Douglas Portage, of Lower Fraser, and of the other tribes on the seashore of the mainland to Bute Inlet, humbly sheweth:-

1. That your petitioners view with a great anxiety the standing question of the quantity of land to be reserved for the use of each Indian family.

2. That we are fully aware that the Government of Canada has always taken good care of the Indians, and treated them liberally, allowing more than 100 hundred acres per family; and we have been at a loss to understand the views of the Local Government of British Columbia, in curtailing our land so much as to leave in many instances but few acres of land per family.

3. Our hearts have been wounded by the arbitrary way the Local Government of British Columbia have dealt with us in locating and dividing our Reserves. Chamiel, ten miles below Hope, is allowed 488 acres of good land for the use of twenty families; at the rate of 24 acres per family; Popkum, eighteen miles below Hope, is allowed 369 acres of good land for the use of four families; at the rate of 90 acres per family; Cheam, twenty miles below Hope, is allowed 375 acres of bad, dry, and mountainous land for the use of twenty-seven families: at the rate of 13 acres per family; Yuk-yuk-y-yoose on Chilliwhack River, with a population of seven families, is allowed 42 acres, 5 acres per family; Sumass (at the junction of Sumass River and Fraser) with a population of seventeen families, is allowed 43 acres of meadow for their hay, and 32 acres of dry land; Keatsy, numbering more than one hundred inhabitants, is allowed 108 acres of land. Langley and Hope have not yet got land secured to them, and white men are encroaching on them on all sides.

4. For many years we have been complaining of the land left us being too small. We have laid our complaints before Government officials nearest to us: they sent us to some others; so we had no redress up to the present; and we have felt like men trampled on, and

are commencing to believe that the aim of the white men is to exterminate us as soon as they can, although we have been always quiet, obedient, kind, and friendly to the whites.

5. Discouragement and depression have come upon our people. Many of them have given up the cultivation of land, because our gardens have not been protected against the encroachments of the whites. Some of our best men have been deprived of the land they have broken and cultivated with long and hard labour, a white man enclosing it in his claim, and no compensation given. Some of our most enterprising men have lost a part of their cattle, because white men had taken the place where those cattle were grazing, and no other place left but the thickly timbered land, where they die fast. Some of our people now are obliged to cut rushes along the bank of the river with their knives during the Winter, to feed their cattle.

6. We are now obliged to clear heavy timbered land, all prairies having been taken from us by white men. We see our white neighbors cultivate wheat, peas, &c., and raise large stocks of cattle on our pasture lands, and we are giving them our money to buy the flour manufactured from the wheat they have grown on same prairies.

7. We are not lazy and roaming-about people as we used to be. We have worked hard and a long time to spare money to buy agricultural implements, cattle, horses, &c., as nobody has given us assistance. We could point out many of our people who have those past years bought with their own money ploughs, harrows, yokes of oxen, and horses; and now, with your kind assistance, we have a bright hope to enter into the path of civilization.

8. We consider that 80 acres per family is absolutely necessary for our support, and for the future welfare of our children. We declare that 20 or 30 acres of land per family will not give satisfaction, but will create ill feelings, irritation amongst our people, and we cannot say what will be the consequence.

9. That, in case you cannot obtain from the Local Government the object of our petition, we humbly pray that this our petition be forwarded to the Secretary of State for the Provinces, Ottawa.

Therefore your petitioners humbly pray that you may take this our petition into consideration, and see that justice be done us, and allow each family the quantity of land we ask for.

And your petitioners, as in duty bound, will ever pray.

Signed by Peter Ayessik, Chief of Hope, and Alexis, Chief of Cheam, and by 54 other chiefs of Douglas Portage, Lower Fraser, and Coast.

July 14, 1874.

("Return ... for ... all correspondence relating to Indian affairs ... since the beginning of 1874," B.C., *Journals*, 1st Parl., 4th sess., 1875, appendix, *Sessional Papers*, pp. 674-75.)

Item 4

Sir James Douglas to Dr. I. W. Powell, Indian Commissioner, re Colonial Indian Lands. October 14, 1874.

Sir:

The question presented in your letter of the 9th. Oct., being limited to one specific point, hardly affords breadth of scope enough to admit of an explicit reply without going more largely into the matter. You ask if during the period of my Governorship of British Columbia there was any particular basis of acreage used in setting apart Indian Reserves?

To this enquiry I may briefly rejoin, that in laying out Indian Reserves no specific number of acres was insisted on. The principle followed in all cases, was to leave the extent & selection of the land entirely optional with the Indians who were immediately in the Reserve; the surveying officers having instructions to meet their wishes in every particular & to include in each reserve the permanent Village sites, the fishing stations, & Burial grounds, cultivated land & all the favorite resorts of the Tribes, & in short to include every piece of ground to which they had acquired an equitable title through continuous occupation, tillage or other investment of their labour. This was done with the object of securing to each community their natural or acquired rights; of removing all cause for complaint on the ground of unjust deprivation of the land indispensable for their convenience or support, & to provide against the occurrence of Agrarian disputes with the white settlers.

Before my retirement from office several of the Reserves, chiefly in the lower district of Frasers River & Vancouvers Island, were regularly surveyed and marked out with the sanction & approval of the several communities concerned, & it was found on a comparison of acreages with population that the land reserved, in none of these cases exceded the proportion of 10 acres per family, so moderate were the demands of the Natives.

It was however never intended that they should be restricted or limited to the possession of 10 acres of land, on the contrary, we were prepared, if such had been their wish to have made for their use much more extensive grants.

The Indian Reserves in the Pastoral country east of the Cascades, especially in Lytton & Thompson's River districts where the natives are wealthy, having in many instances, large numbers of horses & cattle were, on my retirement from office, only roughly traced out upon the ground by the gold commissioners of the day. These latter Reserves were necessarily laid out on a large scale, commensurate with the wants of these tribes; to allow sufficient space & range for their cattle at all seasons.

Such is an outline of the policy & motives which influenced my Government when determining the principle on which these grants of land should be made. Moreover, as a safeguard & protection to these Indian Communities who might, in their primal state of ignorance & natural improvidence, have made away with the land, it was provided that these Reserves should be the common property of the Tribes, & that the title should remain vested in the Crown, so as to be unalienable by any of their own acts. The policy of the Government was carried even a step beyond this point, in providing for the future. Contemplating the probable advance of the Aboriginies in knowledge & intelligence & assuming that a time would certainly arrive when they might aspire to a higher rank in the social scale, & feel the essential wants of & claims of a better condition, it was determined to remove every obstacle from their path, by placing them in a most favourable circumstances for acquiring land in their private & individual capacity, apart from the Tribal Reserves. They were, therefore, legally authorized to acquire property in lands, either by direct purchase at the Government offices, or through the operation of the preemption laws of the Colony, on precisely the same terms & considerations in all respects, as other classes of Her Majesty's subjects.

These measures gave universal satisfaction when they were officially announced to the Native Tribes & still satisfy their highest aspirations.

A departure from the practice then adopted with respect to this class of native rights will give rise to unbounded disaffection, & may imperil the vital interests of the province.

This letter may be regarded & treated as an official communication.

I remain
Dear Sir
Yours Sincerely
(Signed) JAMES DOUGLAS

Lieut.-Col Powell,
Indian Commissioner.

(Courtesy Mr. B. A. McKelvie, Victoria.)

Item 5, Part I

McKenna-McBride Agreement, September 24, 1912

Memorandum of an Agreement arrived at between J. A. J. McKenna, Special Commissioner appointed by the Dominion Government to Investigate the Condition of Indian Affairs in British Columbia, and the Honourable Sir Richard McBride, as Premier of the Province of British Columbia.

Whereas it is desirable to settle all differences between the Governments of the Dominion and the Province respecting Indian lands and Indian Affairs generally in the Province of British Columbia, therefore the parties above named, have, subject to the approval of the Governments of the Dominion and of the Province, agreed upon the following proposals as a final adjustment of all matters relating to Indian Affairs in the Province of British Columbia:-

1. A Commission shall be appointed as follows: Two Commissioners shall be named by the Dominion and two by the Province. The four Commissioners so named shall select a fifth Commissioner, who shall be the Chairman of the Board.

2. The Commission so appointed shall have power to adjust the acreage of Indian Reserves in British Columbia in the following manner:

(a) At such places as the Commissioners are satisfied that more land is included in any particular Reserve as now defined than is reasonably required for the use of the Indians of that tribe or locality, the Reserve shall, with the consent of the Indians, as required by the Indian Act, be reduced to such acreage as the Commissioners think reasonably sufficient for the purpose of such Indians.

(b) At any place at which the Commissioners shall determine that an insufficient quantity of land has been set aside for the use of the Indians of that locality, the Commissioners shall fix the quantity that ought to be added for the use of such Indians. And they may set aside land for any Band of Indians for whom land has not already been reserved.

3. The Province shall take all such steps as are necessary to legally

reserve the additional lands which the Commissioners shall apportion to any body of Indians in pursuance of the powers above set out.

4. The lands which the Commissioners shall determine are not necessary for the use of the Indians shall be subdivided and sold by the Province at public auction.

5. The net proceeds of all such sales shall be divided equally between the Province and the Dominion, and all moneys received by the Dominion under this Clause shall be held or used by the Dominion for the benefit of the Indians of British Columbia.

6. All expenses in connection with the Commission shall be shared by the Province and Dominion in equal proportions.

7. The lands comprised in the Reserves as finally fixed by the Commissioners aforesaid shall be conveyed by the Province to the Dominion to deal with the said lands in such manner as they may deem best suited for the purposes of the Indians, including a right to sell the said lands and fund or use the proceeds for the benefit of the Indians, subject only to a condition that in the even of any Indian tribe or band in British Columbia at some future time becoming extinct, then any lands within the territorial boundaries or the Province which have been conveyed to the Dominion as aforesaid for such tribe or band, and not sold or disposed of as hereinbefore mentioned, or any unexpended funds being the proceeds of any Indian Reserve in the Province of British Columbia, shall be conveyed or repaid to the Province.

8. Until the final report of the Commission is made, the Province shall withhold from pre-emption or sale any lands over which they have a disposing power and which have been heretofore applied for by the Dominion as additional Indian Reserves or which may during the sitting of the Commission, be specified by the Commissioners as lands which should be reserved for Indians. If during the period prior to the Commissioners making their final report it shall be ascertained by either Government that any lands being part of an Indian Reserve are required for right-of-way or other railway purposes, or for any Dominion or Provincial or Municipal Public Work or purpose, the matter shall be referred to the Commissioners who shall thereupon dispose of the question by an Interim Report, and each Government shall thereupon do everything necessary to carry the recommendations of the Commissioners into effect.

Signed in duplicate at Victoria, British Columbia, this 24th day of September, 1912.

(Signed) J. A. J. McKenna,
(Signed) Richard McBride.

Witness:
(Signed) E. V. Bodwell.

([Canada] [Royal Commission on Indian Affairs], *Report of the Royal Commission on Indian Affairs for the Province of British Columbia* [Victoria: Acme Press, 1916], I:10-11.)

Item 5, Part II

Order-in-Council of 27th November, 1912

Certified Copy of a Report of the Committee of the Privy Council Approved by His Royal Highness the Governor-General, on the 27th November, 1912.

The Committee of the Privy Council have had under consideration a Report, dated the 26th October, 1912, from the Superintendent-General of Indian Affairs, submitting an Agreement entered into by Your Royal Highness' Special Commissioner and the Honourable the Prime Minister of British Columbia respecting Indian Reserves in that Province, together with a report of the Commissioner.

The Minister of Justice, to whom the said report was referred, observes that the Agreement contemplates the constitution of a Commission with certain powers, and confirmation of the proceedings of the Commission by the two Governments;

That the statutory authority of your Royal Highness-in-Council to constitute this Commission is to be found in Part 1 of the Enquiries Act, Revised Statutes of Canada, 1906, Chapter 104, and it appears to the Minister that in view of the Statutory provisions the proceedings of the Commission must be subject to approval.

The Minister of Justice, therefore, advises that the approval of the Agreement should be subject to a further provision which should be accepted by the Government of British Columbia before the Agreement can become effective providing that notwithstanding anything in the Agreement contained, the acts and proceedings of the Commission shall be subject to the approval of the two Governments, and that the Governments agree to consider favourably the Reports, whether final or interim, of the Commission, with a view to give effect, as far as reasonably may be, to the acts, proceedings and recommendations of the Commission, and to take all such steps and proceedings as may be reasonably necessary with the object of carrying into execution the settlement provided for by the Agreement in accordance with its true intent and purpose.

The Committee, concurring, advise that a copy hereof approving of the Agreement, subject to the aforesaid modification, be transmitted to the Lieutenant-Governor of British Columbia for the information and approval of his Government.

The Committee further advise that, as the British Columbia Indian question has been the subject of communications from the Colonial Office, Your Royal Highness may be pleased to forward a copy of this Minute to the Right Honourable the Secretary of State for the Colonies.

All of which is respectfully submitted for approval.

(Signed) Rodolphe Boudreau,
Clerk of the Privy Council.

([Canada] [Royal Commission on Indian Affairs], *Report of the Royal Commission on Indian Affairs for the Province of British Columbia* [Victoria: Acme Press, 1916], I:17.)

Item 6

Extracts from the Introduction to Report of the Royal Commission on Indian Affairs for the Province of British Columbia

By Orders-in-Council dated the 27th day of November, 1912, P.C. 3277, and the 23rd day of April, 1913, Your Royal Highness was pleased to appoint a Royal Commission to investigate and make recommendations regarding the lands reserved for Indians in the Province of British Columbia and regarding such additional lands as might appear to be required for the necessary use of the Indians of the Province, subject to the terms of the Agreement entered into between the Governments of Canada and of the Province of British Columbia, executed on the 24th day of September, 1912, and signed, on behalf of the Dominion Government, by its Commissioner, Mr. J. A. J. McKenna, and on behalf of the Province by Sir Richard McBride, K.C.M.G., Prime Minister of the Province.

In the performance of its duties Your Commission endeavoured to inform itself as to the history of the administration of Indian Affairs in the Province, and the causes leading to the appointment of your Commission.

In the years 1850, 1851 and 1852, Sir James Douglas made certain agreements with some three or four hundred Indians under which they surrendered their rights to comparatively small portions of Vancouver Island in consideration of a cash payment and the reservation to them of their village sites and enclosed fields, "to be kept for" their "own use, for the use of" their "children" and "for those who may follow after."

When the first Legislative Assembly of the Colony of Vancouver Island met in the summer of 1856, the Indian question was at once given prominence. In his inaugural address, Governor Douglas, after referring to the feeling of insecurity engendered by "the presence of large bodies of armed savages" who had visited the Colony from the North, said: "I shall, nevertheless, continue to conciliate the good will of the native Indian tribes by treating them with justice and forbearance and by rigidly protecting their civil and agrarian rights."

The Secretary of State for the Colonies in his despatches to

Governor Douglas constantly expressed the solicitude of the Imperial Government for the welfare of the Indians and the safeguarding of their rights.

In the despatch of the 11th April, 1859, Lord Carnarvon wrote Governor Douglas:

"I am glad to perceive that you have directed the attention of the House to that interesting and important subject, the relations of Her Majesty's Government and of the Colony to the Indian race. Proofs are unhappily still too frequent of the neglect which Indians experience when the white man obtains possession of their country, and their claims to consideration are forgotten at the moment when equity most demands that the hand of the protector should be extended to help them. In the case of the Indians of Vancouver Island and British Columbia, Her Majesty's Government earnestly wish that when the advancing requirements of colonization press upon lands occupied by members of that race, measures of liberality and justice may be adopted for compensating them for the surrender of the territory which they have been taught to regard as their own."

And on the 20th May, 1859, in acknowledging Governor Douglas' despatch of the 14th of that month on the subject of the policy to be observed towards the Indian tribes and conveying the Governor's "opinion as to the feasibility of locating the Indians in native villages, with a view to their protection and civilization," His Lordship wrote:

"I am glad to find that your sentiments respecting the treatment of the native races are so much in accordance with my own, and I trust your endeavors to conciliate and promote the welfare of the Indians will be followed by all persons whom circumstances may bring into contact with them. But whilst making ample provision under the arrangements proposed for the future sustenance and improvement of the native tribes, you will, I am persuaded, bear in mind the importance of exercising due care in laying out and defining the several Reserves, so as to avoid checking at a future day the progress of the white colonists."

On the 5th March, 1861, the Governor officially directed the Chief Commissioner of Lands and Works to "take measures so soon as practicable, for making out distinctly the Indian Reserves throughout the Colony." He added that "the extent of the Indian Reserves to be defined" was to be "as they may severally be pointed out by the natives themselves." And the Chief Commissioner gave directions accordingly to the officers in charge of the several districts.

According to Governor Trutch's despatch of the 3rd November, 1871: "The authority of the Governor for creating such reservations was based, up to 1865, on the mainland portion of British Columbia, and up to 1870, in Vancouver Island, on the power conferred upon him to this effect by his Commission and the Royal instructions, and since those dates on the provisions of the Land Ordinances, 1865 and 1870, respectively."

In the report made on the 17th August, 1875, by the late Mr. Justice Walkem, when Attorney-General, he described the tracts set aside before the Union for Indians "as the joint and common property of the several tribes, being intended for their exclusive use and benefit, and especially as a provision for the aged, the helpless, and the infirm."

By the Thirteenth Article of the Terms of Union it is provided:— That (1) "the charge of the Indians, and the trusteeship and management of the lands reserved for their use and benefit, shall be assumed by the Dominion Government";

That (2) "a policy as liberal as that hitherto pursued by the British Columbia Government shall be continued by the Dominion Government after the Union,"

and

That (3) "to carry out such policy, tracts of land of such extent as it has hitherto been the practice of the British Columbia Government to appropriate for that purpose shall from time to time be conveyed by the local Government to the Dominion Government, in trust for the use and benefit of the Indians."

The Terms of Union were sanctioned by the Imperial Government, and were given force and effect by an order of Her Majesty in Council under the British North America Act and thereby became as much a part of the Act as if they had been embodied in it.

The first legislation of the Dominion respecting Indians was enacted by Chapter 42 of the Statutes of 1868. It provided that "all lands reserved for Indians — or held in trust for their benefit, shall be deemed to be reserved and held for the same purposes as before this Act."

At the time of the entry of British Columbia into the Dominion, the Federal Act of 1868 continued in force; and a further enactment, Chapter 6, of the Statutes of 1869, had been made for the gradual enfranchisement of the Indians. It provided (and the law remains with variations) for the subdivision of Reserves into lots, and the holding thereof by individual Indians under location tickets, with a view to the subsequent issue of "Letters Patent" to the holders of such tickets as enfranchised Indians.

At the time of the Union there was no definition of Indian Reserves in the British Columbia Ordinances. In the Ordinance of 1870 respecting Crown Lands there is a provision exempting from pre-emption reserved lands and Indian settlements. But the policy of British Columbia as to allotting and holding lands for the use and benefit of the Indians was clearly defined in practice. And a schedule of Indian Reserves existing at the Union was furnished the Dominion.

By the Land Act of 1875 legislative authority was given for setting apart lands for the purpose of meeting the obligations of the Province under the Thirteenth Article of the Terms of Union. Section 60 of that Act sets forth, as one of the purposes for which land shall be reserved, that "of conveying the same to the Dominion Government in trust for the use and benefit of the Indians."

In the meantime a difference arose between the two Governments as to the basis of acreage of Reserves. The Dominion Government proposed that "each family be assigned a location of eighty acres of land of average quality, which shall remain permanently the property of the family for whose benefit it is allotted."

Correspondence followed, and on the 25th July, 1873, the Provincial Government formally decided that the Dominion requirement of eighty acres per family "was greatly in excess of the grants considered sufficient by the previous Governments of British Columbia," and proposed that "Indian Reserves should not exceed a quantity of twenty acres for each head of a family of five persons."

The Superintendent-General of Indian Affairs, Hon. David Laird, in a memorandum of 1st March, 1874, suggested the allotting of "twenty acres to every Indian being the head of a family, without reference to the number in the family." The suggestion was concurred in by the Province, as per Minute of the Executive Council of the 15th June, 1874, and steps were taken to proceed on that understanding.

Then the Reverend Mr. Duncan intervened and suggested inter alia (1) that no basis of acreage be fixed for Reserves; (2) that each nation of Indians be dealt with separately on their respective claims; (3) that for a proper adjustment of such claims the Dominion and Provincial Governments each provide an agent to visit the Indians, investigate conditions and report; and (4) that, in case of any Reserve being abandoned, or the Indians on it decreasing so that its extent is disproportionate to the number of occupants, such Reserve or part of a Reserve might revert to the Provincial Government.

The Provincial Government adopted Mr. Duncan's view in so far as it dispensed with a basis of acreage and provided for reversion. The Dominion Government expressed its readiness to adopt his proposal in full, barring his suggested agency of allotment.

The Province concurred, and the two Governments then entered into the agreement of 1875-6, under which a joint Commission was constituted to allot Reserves.

The agreement set forth that the Commission was "to fix and determine for each nation separately, the number, extent, and locality of the Reserve or Reserves to be allotted to it"; that "no basis of acreage be fixed — but that each nation of Indians of the same language be dealt with separately"; that "each Reserve shall be held in trust for the use and benefit of the nation of Indians to which it has been allotted"; that, "in the event of any material increase or decrease hereafter of the numbers of a nation occupying a Reserve, such Reserve shall be enlarged or diminished, as the case may be, so that it shall bear a fair proportion to the members of the Band occupying it"; and that "the extra land required for any Reserve shall be allotted from Crown lands, and any land taken off a Reserve shall revert to the Province."

The reversionary interest thus created proved a stumbling block to administration. A sort of dual ownership was set up which made it practically impossible for the Dominion Government to dispose, for the benefit of the Indians, as in other parts of the Dominion, of any of the reserved land or the timber or other valuables thereon or therein.

The Land Act of 1875 provided for the conveyance of lands to the Dominion Government "in trust for the use and benefit of the Indians." By Section 9, of Chapter 38 of the Statutes of 1899, an amendment was made by adding to the provision in the Land Act these words, "and in trust to reconvey the same to the Provincial Government in case such lands at any time ceased to be used by such Indians." In 1911 this enactment was made:

"Provided always that it shall be lawful for the Lieutenant-Governor in Council to at any time grant, convey, quit claim, sell or dispose of, on such terms as may be deemed advisable, the interest of the Province, reversionary or otherwise, in any Indian Reserve or any portion thereof." (vide Section 127, Chapter 129, R.S., B.C., 1911).

In the previous year the following had been enacted:

"There shall not be registered in any Land Registry Office any title derived from His Majesty the King in the right of Canada ... land forming part, or that at any time formed part, of an Indian Reserve, without the sanction of the Lieutenant-Governor in Council." (Vide Section 2, Chapter 27, Statutes 1910, and Section 59, Chapter 127, R.S., B.C., 1911).

To remove the administrative entanglement thus occasioned, and to provide for the final and complete allotment of lands for Indians in British Columbia, the Agreement hereinbefore quoted in full was entered into by the Governments of the Dominion and the Province, and this Commission was appointed thereunder....

Your Commission was accompanied, when travelling over the various Agencies, by the District Inspectors of the Department of Indian Affairs and the Indian Agents, to all of whom they are much indebted for useful local knowledge of persons and places, for which this deserved acknowledgment is made.

In fulfilment of the duties of the Commission it was necessary to visit the Indians of all the various tribes and bands and their Reserves, to explain the object of the Commission and the restrictions imposed, to hear the views of the Indians on all matters connected with the work of the Commission, and to examine the Indians under oath on matters connected with the work of the Commission; also to hear the representations of Public bodies — Municipal Councils, Boards of Trade, etc. — where friction appeared to exist, or a request for a hearing was made.

Your Commission found that the 25,000 Indians to be visited were scattered all over the Province and along the Coastline, and the amount of travelling, both by sea and land, would consume a very considerable length of time. In this connection it may be mentioned that the area of the Province is some 395,000 square miles — equal to one-tenth of the Canadian total area, larger than the States of California, Washington and Oregon combined, or than Italy, Switzerland and France, and three times the size of the United Kingdom, and with a Coastline of 7,000 miles, all of which had to be covered.

Another obstacle to expediting work arose from the occupations of the Coast Indians, whose Reserves could only be visited at stated times of the year. All of the Coast Indians are fishermen and leave their Reserves when the salmon run occurs, and your Commission had numerous letters from these Indians requesting that meetings should be so arranged as to avoid interruption of their work. The managers of the salmon canneries also made similar requests. With Indian villages dotted all along the 7,000 miles of Coastline, a considerable portion of three Summers was occupied in this work.

Some 5,655 folios of typewritten evidence and 253 exhibits have been taken and your Commission, desiring to keep expense of printing within bounds, and with the consent of the Governments concerned, arranged a system of tabulation, giving the material of the evidence, which will appear with maps and conclusions reached, as embodied in the Commission's Minutes of Decision, in a separate chapter for each of the fifteen Agencies. Thus it is hoped that a clear and concise Report is presented at a minimum of cost. At the same time, the extended evidence is sent to both Governments in twenty-seven volumes for future reference....

In the course of enquiries, when visiting the various Tribes and Bands of Indians, it was impressed on your Commission that there existed a very strong feeling regarding proper protection for their graveyards, and steps have been taken in most cases to recommend the reservation of small areas for such purposes. In some instances, however, the plots required would be so small that it was not deemed wise to recommend that reserves should be created involving a large outlay for surveys. It is, therefore, recommended that, where such cases arise, the Governments of the Dominion and the Province should, mutually, arrange for the protection of these graves.

On every occasion where meetings were held with the Indians, they expressed their views freely on questions of administration, which are dealt with in another Report submitted by Your Commission under authority of an Order of Your Royal Highness-in-Council dated the 10th day of June 1913....

([Canada], [Royal Commission on Indian Affairs], *Report of the Royal Commission on Indian Affairs for the Province of British Columbia* [Victoria: Acme Press, 1916], I: 14-20.)

Item 7

Statement of the Allied Indian Tribes of British Columbia for the Government of British Columbia

Part II — Report of the Royal Commission

Grounds of Refusal to Accept

In addition to the grounds shown by our general introductory remarks, we mention the following as the principal grounds upon which we refuse to accept as a settlement the findings of the Royal Commission:—

1. We think it clear that fundamental matters such as tribal ownership of our territories require to be dealt with, either by concession of the governments, or by decision of the Judicial Committee, before subsidiary matters such as the finding of the Royal Commission can be equitably dealt with.

2. We are unwilling to be bound by the McKenna-McBride Agreement, under which the findings of the Royal Commission have been made.

3. The whole work of the Royal Commission has been based upon the assumption that Article 13 of the Terms of Union contains all obligations of the two governments towards the Indian Tribes of British Columbia, which assumption we cannot admit to be correct.

4. The McKenna-McBride Agreement, and the report of the Royal Commission ignore not only our land rights, but also the power conferred by Article 13 upon the Secretary of State for the Colonies.

5. The additional reserved lands recommended by the report of the Royal Commission, we consider to be utterly inadequate for meeting the present and future requirements of the Tribes.

6. The Commissioners have wholly failed to adjust the inequalities between Tribes, in respect of both area and value of reserved lands, which Special Commissioner McKenna, in his report, pointed out and which the report of the Royal Commission has proved to exist.

7. Notwithstanding the assurance contained in the report of Special Commissioner McKenna, that "such further lands as are required will be provided by the Province, in so far as Crown lands are available."

The Province, by Act passed in the spring of the year 1916, took back two million acres of land, no part of which, as we understand, was set aside for the Indians by the Commissioners, whose report was soon thereafter presented to the government.

8. The Commissioners have failed to make any adjustment of water-rights, which in the case of lands situated within the Dry Belt, is indispensable.

9. We regard as manifestly unfair and wholly unsatisfactory the provisions of the McKenna-McBride Agreement relating to the cutting off and reduction of reserved lands, under which one-half of the proceeds of sale of any such lands would go to the Province, and the other half of such proceeds, instead of going into the hands or being held for the benefit of the Tribe, would be held by the Government of Canada for the benefit of all the Indians of British Columbia.

Part III — Necessary Conditions of Equitable Settlement
Conditions Proposed as Basis of Settlement

We beg to present for consideration of the two Governments the following which we regard as necessary conditions of equitable settlement:

1. That the Proclamation issued by King George III in the year 1763 and the Report presented by the Minister of Justice in the year 1875 be accepted by the two Governments and established as the main basis of all dealings and all adjustments of Indian land rights and other rights which shall be made.

2. That it be conceded that each Tribe for whose use and benefit land is set aside (under Article 13 of the "Terms of Union") acquires thereby a full, permanent and beneficial title to the land so set aside together with all natural resources pertaining thereto; and that Section 127 of the Land Act of British Columbia be amended accordingly.

3. That all existing reserves not now as parts of the Railway Belt or otherwise held by Canada be conveyed to Canada for the use and benefit of the various Tribes.

4. That all foreshores whether tidal or inland be included in the reserves with which they are connected, so that the various Tribes shall have full permanent and beneficial title to such foreshores.

5. That adequate additional lands be set aside and that to this end a per capita standard of 160 acres of average agricultural land having in case of lands situated within the dry belt a supply of water sufficient for irrigation be established. By the word "standard" we mean not a hard and fast rule, but a general estimate to be used as a guide, and to be applied in a reasonable way to the actual requirements of each tribe.

6. That in sections of the Province in case of which the character of available land and the conditions prevailing make it impossible or undesirable to carry out fully or at all that standard the Indian Tribes concerned be compensated for such deficiency by grazing lands, by

timber lands, by hunting lands or otherwise, as the particular character and conditions of each such section may require.

7. That all existing inequalities in respect of both acreage and value between lands set aside for the various Tribes be adjusted.

8. That for the purpose of enabling the two Governments to set aside adequate additional lands and adjust all inequalities there be established a system of obtaining lands including compulsory purchase, similar to that which is being carried out by the Land Settlement Board of British Columbia.

9. That if the Governments and the Allied Tribes should not be able to agree upon a standard of lands to be reserved that matter and all other matters relating to lands to be reserved which cannot be adjusted in pursuance of the preceding conditions and by conference between the two governments and the Allied Tribes be referred to the Secretary of State for the Colonies to be finally decided by that Minister in view of our land rights conceded by the two Governments in accordance with our first conditions and in pursuance of the provisions of Article 13 of the "Terms of Union" by such method of procedure as shall be decided by the Parliament of Canada.

10. That the beneficial ownership of all reserves shall belong to the Tribe for whose use and benefit they are set aside.

11. That a system of individual title to occupation of particular parts of reserved lands be established and brought into operation and administered by each Tribe.

12. That all sales, leases and other dispositions of land or timber or other natural resources be made by the Government of Canada as trustee for the Tribe with the consent of the Tribe and that all who may have rights of occupation affected, and that the proceeds be disposed of in such way and used from time to time for such particular purposes as shall be agreed upon between the Government of Canada and the Tribe together with all those having rights of occupation.

13. That the fishing rights, hunting rights, and water rights of the Indian Tribes be fully adjusted. Our land rights having first been established by concession or decision we are willing that our general rights shall after full conference between the two Governments and the Tribes be adjusted by enactment of the Parliament of Canada.

14. That in the connection with the adjustment of our fishing rights the mater of the international treaty recently entered into which very seriously conflicts with those rights be adjusted. We do not at present discuss the matter of fishing for commercial purposes. However, that matter may stand. We claim that we have a clear aboriginal right to take salmon for food. That right the Indian Tribes have continuously exercised from time immemorial. Long before the Dominion of Canada came into existence that right was guaranteed by Imperial enactment, the Royal Proclamation issued in the year 1763. We claim that under that Proclamation and another Imperial enactment, Section 109 of the British North America Act, the meaning and effect of which were

explained by the Minister of Justice in the words set out above, all power held by the Parliament of Canada for regulating the fisheries of British Columbia is subject to our right of fishing. We therefore claim that the regulations contained in the treaty cannot be made applicable to the Indian Tribes, and that any attempt to enforce those regulations against the Indian Tribes is unlawful, being a breach of the two Imperial enactments mentioned.

15. That compensation be made in respect of the following particular matters:

(1) Inequalities of acreage or value or both that may be agreed to by any Tribe.

(2) Inferior quality of reserved lands that may be agreed to by any Tribe.

(3) Location of reserved lands other than that required agreed to by any Tribe.

(4) Damages caused to the timber or other natural resources of any reserved lands as for example by mining or smelting operations.

(5) All moneys expended by any Tribe in any way in connection with the Indian land controversy and the adjustment of all matters outstanding.

16. That general compensation for lands to be surrendered be made.

(1) By establishing and maintaining an adequate system of education, including both day schools and residential industrial schools, etc.

(2) By establishing and maintaining an adequate system of medical aid and hospitals.

17. That all compensation provided for by the two preceding paragraphs and all other compensation claimed by any Tribe so far as may be found necessary be dealt with by enactment of the Parliament of Canada and be determined and administered in accordance with such enactment.

18. That all restrictions contained in the Land Act and other Statutes of the Province be removed.

19. That the Indian Act be revised and that all amendments of that Act required for carrying into full effect these conditions of settlement, dealing with the matter of citizenship, and adjusting all outstanding matters relating to the administration of Indian Affairs in British Columbia be made.

20. That all moneys already expended and to be expended by the Allied Tribes in connection with the Indian land controversy and the adjustment of all matters outstanding be provided by the Governments.

(Canada, Senate, *Journals*, 16th Parl., 1st sess., 1926-27, appendix, Special Joint Committee on Claims of Allied Indian Tribes of British Columbia. *Report and Evidence*, 1927, pp. 33 and 35-36. Extracts from the larger Statement made on November 12, 1919, pp. 31-38.)

Selected Bibliography

"Administration of Mineral Lands in the Railway Belt." British Columbia. Legislative Assembly. *Sessional Papers,* 5th Parl., 4th sess., 1890.

Anderson, Alexander C. "Report." Canada. Parliament. *Sessional Papers,* 3d Parl., 5th sess., 1878, no. 10, special appendix D.

Bancroft, H. H. *History of British Columbia, 1792-1887.* Works of Hubert Howe Bancroft, vol. 32. San Francisco: History Company, 1887.

Borthwick, D. "Settlement in British Columbia." *Transactions of the Eighth British Columbia Natural Resources Conference ... 1955.* British Columbia Natural Resources Conference, 1955.

Brebner, J. B. *North Atlantic Triangle.* Toronto: Ryerson, 1945.

British Columbia. *The Consolidated Statutes of British Columbia, Consisting of the Acts, Ordinances & Proclamations of the Formerly Separate Colonies of Vancouver Island and British Columbia, and of the Provinces since the Union with Canada, with Table of Acts and Alphabetical Index.* Published by authority. Revised and consolidated by the Commission appointed under the "Consolidated Statutes Act, 1877." Victoria: Printed by R. Wolfenden, Gov't. Printer, James Bay, 1877.

———. *Land Laws of British Columbia: Together with Land Office Forms and Regulations.* Victoria: R. Wolfenden, 1873.

———. *The Laws ... Consisting of the Acts, Ordinances & Proclamations of the Formerly Separated Colonies, Vancouver Island and British Columbia, and of the United Colony of British Columbia.* By authority compiled and published under the "Revised Statutes Act, 1871." Victoria, Printed at the Government Printing Office, 1871.

———. [*Proclamations and Ordinances, 1858-1864.* Victoria, New Westminster, 1858-64.]

———. *Revised Statutes,* 1911, 1924, 1936.

———. *Revised Statutes, Appendix ... 1871, Containing Certain Repealed Colonial Laws Useful for Reference, Imperial Statutes Affecting British Columbia. Proclamations, Etc.* Victoria, Printed by Richard Wolfenden ... at the Government Printing Office, n.d.

———. *Statutes*, 1873-78, 1880, 1882-92, 1894-1901, 1903-1904, 1904, 1906, 1908, 1912-13, 1919-20, 1926-27.

British Columbia. Commission on Condition of Indians of the North-West Coast. *Papers Relating to the Commission Appointed to Enquire into the Condition of the Indians of the North-West Coast*. Victoria: Richard Wolfenden, Government Printer, 1888.

British Columbia. Department of Lands. Annual reports of officials of the department, 1873, 1875, 1876, 1885-1913. British Columbia. Legislative Assembly. *Sessional Papers*, 1873-74, 1876, 1877, 1886-1914.

British Columbia. Department of Mines. Annual reports of the Minister of Mines, 1874, 1879, 1912, 1913. British Columbia. Legislative Assembly. *Sessional Papers*, 1875, 1880, 1913, 1914.

British Columbia. Legislative Assembly. *Journals*, 1872, 1872-73, 1878, 1884, 1887, 1889, 1898, 1900.

———. ———, 1872, 1872-73, 1873-74, 1875. Appendixes. *Sessional Papers*.

———. *Sessional Papers*, 1876, 1877, 1878, 1879, 1881, 1883, 1885, 1886, 1887, 1888, 1889, 1890, 1892, 1894, 1900, 1901, 1902, 1903, 1905, 1906, 1907, 1908, 1909, 1910, 1911, 1912.

British Columbia. Legislative Assembly. Select Committee ... in Respect to Legalizing Sales of Land in the Province since 1870. "Report." British Columbia. Legislative Assembly. *Journals*, 1st Parl., 2d sess., 1872-73. Appendix. *Sessional Papers*.

British Columbia. Legislative Assembly. Select Committee on Land Ordinance, 1870. "Report." British Columbia. Legislative Assembly. *Journals*, 1st Parl., 2d sess., 1872-73. Appendix. *Sessional Papers*.

British Columbia. Legislative Assembly. Select Committee upon the Method of Granting Leases. "Report." British Columbia. Legislative Assembly. *Sessional Papers*, 2d Parl., 1st sess., 1876.

British Columbia. Legislative Council. *Journals*, 1864.

———. *Ordinances Passed by the Legislative Council of British Columbia During the Session from January to April, 1865*. New Westminster: Government Printing Office, n.d.

———. *Ordinances Passed by the Legislative Council of British Columbia ... 1867*. New Westminster: Government Printing Office, n.d.

———. *Ordinances Passed by the Legislative Council of British Columbia ... 1868-69*. Victoria: Government Printing Office, n.d.

British Columbia. Office of the Agent General for British Columbia, London, Eng. "First and Second Reports ... 1902-03." British Columbia. Legislative Assembly. *Sessional Papers*, 10th Parl., 1st sess., 1903-1904.

British Columbia, Provincial Archives Department. "Report ... 1913." British Columbia. Legislative Assembly. *Sessional Papers*, 13th Parl., 2d sess., 1914.

British Columbia. Royal Commission of Inquiry on Timber and Forestry. "Final Report ... 1909-1910." British Columbia. Legislative Assembly. *Sessional Papers*, 12th Parl., 2d. sess., 1911.

British Columbia Gazette, January 3, 1887.

Canada. Commission of Conservation. Committee on Forests. *Forests of British Columbia*, by H. N. Whitford and R. D. Craig, under the direction of Clyde Leavitt. Ottawa: 1918.

Canada. Department of Indian Affairs. Annual reports, 1884, 1886, 1887, 1890, 1922, 1924. Canada. Parliament. *Sessional Papers*, 1885, 1887, 1888, 1891, 1923, 1925.

Canada. Department of Railways and Canals. *Railway Statistics of the Dominion of Canada, for the Year Ended June 30, 1917*. Ottawa: J. de Labroquerie Taché, King's Printer, 1918.

Canada. Geographic Board. *Handbook of Indians of Canada*. Published as an appendix to the tenth report of the Geographic Board of Canada. Reprinted from *Handbook of American Indians North of Mexico*, published as *Bulletin* 30, Bureau of American Ethnology.... Ottawa: Printed by C. H. Parmelee, Printer to the [King] ..., 1913.

Canada. Indian Reserve Commission. ["Report."] Canada. Parliament. *Sessional Papers*, 6th Parl., 2d sess., 1888, no. 15, special appendix, no. 1.

Canada. Parliament. *Parliamentary Debates*. 3 vols. Ottawa, 1870-72. Vol. 2. 1871.

———. *Sessional Papers*, 1878, 1880, 1886, 1899, 1909, 1921.

Canada. Parliament. House of Commons. *Debates*, 1867.

———. *Journals*, 1871.

———. *Official Report of the Debates*, 1884, 1886, 1925.

[Canada.] [Royal Commission on Indian Affairs.] *Report of the Royal Commission on Indian Affairs for the Province of British Columbia*. 4 vols. Victoria: Acme Press, 1916.

Canada. Parliament. Senate. *Journals*, 16th Parl., 1st sess., 1926-27. Appendix to the Journals of the Senate.... Special Joint Committee of the Senate and House of Commons Appointed to Inquire into the Claims of the Allied Indian Tribes of British Columbia, as Set Forth in Their Petition Submitted to Parliament in June 1926. *Report and Evidence*. Printed by order of Parliament. Ottawa: F. A. Acland, Printer to the [King] ..., 1927.

Canada Gazette, October 4, 1879; July 29, 1881; February 11, 1890.

Carson, P. A. *Railway Belt Hydrographic Survey for 1911-12*. Canada, Department of the Interior, Water Power Branch, Water Resources Paper, no. 1. Ottawa: Government Printing Bureau, 1914.

Farwell, A.S. "Report on the Kootenay Indians." British Columbia. Legislative Assembly. *Sessional Papers,* 4th Parl., 3d sess., 1884.

Fisher, Robin. "Joseph Trutch and Indian Land Policy." *B.C. Studies,* 12 (Winter 1971-72), pp. 3-33.

Flumerfelt, A. C. "Forest Resources." In *Canada and Its Provinces,* Adam Shortt and Arthur Doughty, general eds. 23 vols. Toronto: Brook, 1914-17. Vol. 22.

Gosnell, R. E. "Colonial History, 1849-1871." In *Canada and Its Provinces,* Adam Shortt and Arthur Doughty, general eds. 23 vols. Toronto: Brook, 1914-17. Vol. 21.

———. "History of Farming." In *Canada and Its Provinces,* Adam Shortt and Arthur Doughty, general eds. 23 vols. Toronto: Brook, 1914-17. Vol. 22.

———. *Memorandum for the Hon. Mr. Justice Martin, Commissioner in Re Railway Lands of British Columbia, Re Conveyance of Railway Belt and Peace River Lands to British Columbia.* Ottawa: 1927.

Great Britain. Colonial Office. "CO 60, British Columbia Original Correspondence, 1858-1871: Despatches from the Governors of British Columbia, Draft Replies, Interdepartmental and Miscellaneous." Microfilmed. London: microfilm made on behalf of the Public Archives of Canada from the Public Record Office, London, n.d.

[———.] *Copies of Extracts of Correspondence Relative to the Discovery of Gold in the Fraser's River District in British North America.* Presented to both Houses of Parliament by command of Her Majesty, July 2, 1858. London: Printed by George Edward Eyre and William Spottiswoode ... for Her Majesty's Stationery Office, 1858.

[———.] *Miscellaneous Papers Relating to British Columbia, 1859-1869.* 5 papers in 1 vol. [London: 1859-69.]

———. *Papers Relative to the Affairs of British Columbia.* Presented to both Houses of Parliament by command of Her Majesty, 1859-1862. 4 pts. London: Printed by George Edward Eyre and William Spottiswoode ... for Her Majesty's Stationery Office, 1859-62.

Grunsky, H. W. "Water Legislation and Administration in British Columbia." In British Columbia, Department of Lands, "Report of the Minister of Lands." British Columbia. Legislative Assembly. *Sessional Papers,* 13th Parl., 1st sess., 1913.

———. "Water Rights in the British Columbia Railway Belt." In Canada, Department of the Interior, Dominion Water Power Branch, *Annual Report 1915-1916.* Ottawa, 1917.

Hodgins, William Egerton, comp. *Correspondence, Reports of the Ministers of Justice and Orders in Council upon the Subject of Dominion and Provincial Legislation, 1867-[1920.]* Compiled under the direction of the ... Minister of Justice. 2 vols. Ottawa: Government Printing Bureau, 1896-1922.

Howay, F. W. "Political History, 1871-1913." In *Canada and Its Provinces*, Adam Shortt and Arthur Doughty, general eds. 23 vols. Toronto: Brook, 1914-17. Vol. 21.

———. "The Raison d'Etre of Forts Yale and Hope." *Proceedings and Transactions of the Royal Society of Canada*, 3d ser., 16 (1922), sec. 2, pp. 49-64.

———, Sage, W. N., and Angus, II. F. *British Columbia and the United States*, edited by H. F. Angus. Toronto: Ryerson, 1942.

"Indian Lands, Mining Regulations." In *The Consolidated Orders in Council of Canada under the Authority and Direction of His Excellency the Governor-General in Council*, compiled by H. H. Bligh. Ottawa: Printed by Brown Chamberlain, Printer to the Queen . . . , 1889.

Kennedy, W. P. M. *Statutes, Treaties and Documents of the Canadian Constitution*, Toronto: Oxford University Press, 1930.

LaViolette, Forrest E. *The Struggle for Survival*. Toronto: University of Toronto Press, 1961.

McKelvie, B. A. "Lieutenant-Colonel Israel Wood Powell, M.D., C.M." *British Columbia Historical Quarterly*, 9 (1947), 33-54.

McLean, S. J. "National Highways Overland." In *Canada and Its Provinces*, Adam Shortt and Arthur Doughty, general eds. 23 vols. Toronto: Brook, 1914-17. Vol. 10.

"Memorandum Re British Columbia's Claims for Special Consideration." In "Report on Mission to Ottawa." British Columbia. Legislative Assembly. *Sessional Papers*, 12th Parl., 3d sess., 1912.

"A Memorial from the British Columbian Convention to the Imperial Government." *British Columbian* (New Westminster), February 28, 1861.

Ormsby, Margaret A. "The Relations between British Columbia and the Dominion of Canada, 1871-1885." Ph.D. dissertation, Bryn Mawr, 1937.

"Papers Connected with the Indian Land Question," British Columbia. Legislative Assembly. *Sessional Papers*, 2d Parl., 1st sess., 1876.

Papers on the Union of British Columbia with the Dominion of Canada . . . ordered by the House of Commons to be printed, 3 August 1869. N.p., n.d. In [Great Britain. Colonial Office], *Miscellaneous Papers Relating to British Columbia, 1859-1869*. 5 papers in 1 vol. [London, 1859-69.]

"Papers Relating to Dominion Lands within the Province." British Columbia. Legislative Assembly. *Sessional Papers*, 4th Parl., 4th sess., 1886.

"Papers Relating to the Island Railway, the Graving Dock, and the Railway Lands." British Columbia. Legislative Assembly. *Sessional Papers*, 4th Parl., 1st sess., 1883.

"Papers Relating to the Ownership of the Precious Metals within the Railway Belt." British Columbia. Legislative Assembly. *Sessional Papers*, 4th Parl., 4th sess., 1886.

Pope, John, ed. *Correspondence of Sir John Macdonald: Selections from the Correspondence of the Right Honourable Sir John Alexander Macdonald, G.C.B., First Prime Minister of the Dominion of Canada.* Toronto: Oxford University Press, 1921.

"Regulations Governing the Disposal of Dominion Lands Containing Minerals." In *The Consolidated Orders in Council of Canada under the Authority and Direction of His Excellency the Governor-General in Council*, compiled by H. H. Bligh. Ottawa: Printed by Brown Chamberlain, Printer to the Queen . . . , 1889.

"Report of the Government of British Columbia on the Subject of Indian Reserves." British Columbia. Legislative Assembly. *Sessional Papers*, 2d Parl., 1st sess., 1876.

Sanders, Douglas. "The Nishga Case." *B.C. Studies*, 19 (Autumn 1973), 3-20.

Scholefield, E. O. S., and Gosnell, R. E. *A History of British Columbia.* 2 pts. in 1 vol. Vancouver: British Columbia Historical Association, 1913.

———, and Howay, F. W. *British Columbia from the Earliest Times to the Present.* 4 vols. Vancouver: S. J. Clarke Publishing Co., 1914-21.

Shankel, George Edgar. "The Development of Indian Policy in British Columbia." Ph.D. dissertation, University of Washington, 1945.

Skelton, O. D. "General Economic History." In *Canada and Its Provinces*, Adam Shortt and Arthur Doughty, general eds. 23 vols. Toronto: Brook, 1914-17. Vol. 21.

Sproat, G. M. "Report on the Kootenay Country." British Columbia. Legislative Assembly. *Sessional Papers*, 4th Parl., 3d sess., 1884.

Vancouver Island. Governor. *Despatches: Governor Blanshard to the Secretary of State, 26th December 1849, to 30th August, 1851.* New Westminster: Printed at the Government Printing Office, n.d.

Vancouver Island. House of Assembly. Committee on Crown Lands, Vancouver Island. *Report, June 14th, 1864.* 3rd Parl., 1st sess., 1863-64. [Committee print.] N.p.: n.d.

Index

BISHOP'S UNIVERSITY
LIBRARY
LENNOXVILLE